Words Their Way™ for Parents, Tutors, and School Volunteers

Michelle Picard
Arlington Public Schools

Alison Meadows
Alexandria City Public Schools

Marcia Invernizzi
University of Virginia

Donald R. Bear
Iowa State University

Francine Johnston
University of North Carolina at Greensboro

Pearson

330 Hudson Street, NY, NY 10013

Editorial Director: Kevin M. Davis
Portfolio Manager: Drew Bennett
Portfolio Management Assistant: Maria Feliberty
Executive Field Marketing Manager: Krista Clark
Executive Product Marketing Manager: Christopher Barry
Content Producer: Yagnesh Jani
Procurement Specialist: Deidra Smith
Cover Photo: Rob Marmion/Shutterstock, Monkey Business Images/Shutterstock, Amble Design/Shutterstock
Cover Designer: Cenveo
Full-Service Project Management: iEnergizer Aptara®, Ltd.
Composition: iEnergizer Aptara®, Ltd.
Printer/Binder: LSC Communications
Cover Printer: Phoenix Color
Text Font: Janson Text LT Pro 9.75/12

Library of Congress Cataloging-in-Publication Data

Names: Picard, Michelle (Educator), author.
Title: Words their way for parents, tutors, and school volunteers / Michelle Picard, Arlington Public Schools, Alison Meadows, Alexandria City Public Schools, Marcia Invernizzi, University of Virginia, Donald R. Bear, Iowa State University, Francine Johnston, University of North Carolina at Greensboro.
Description: New York, NY : Pearson, [2018] | Includes bibliographical references and index.
Identifiers: LCCN 2016058658| ISBN 9780132882637 (pbk.) | ISBN 0132882639 (pbk.)
Subjects: LCSH: English language—Orthography and spelling—Study and teaching. | Vocabulary—Study and teaching.
Classification: LCC LB1574 .P47 2018 | DDC 372.63/2—dc23 LC record available at https://lccn.loc.gov/2016058658

1 17

Pearson

ISBN-10: 0-13-288263-9
ISBN-13: 978-0-13-288263-7

This book is dedicated to
the parents, teachers, tutors, and school volunteers
who work with children and adolescents
to promote literacy and word knowledge
in reading, writing, spelling and vocabulary.
It is also dedicated to
our own teachers and family members
who instilled the love of words and learning
in our own lives.

Michelle Picard
Alison Meadows
Marcia Invernizzi
Donald R. Bear
Francine Johnston

Letter from the Authors

Dear Reader,

The word study approach has helped students become better readers and spellers for several decades through hands-on activities learning how spelling works in words. This book is designed for parents, tutors, and school volunteers seeking to use this approach in working with children in schools or at home. Parents and volunteers are important partners for schools, and this book is designed to cultivate that partnership.

Words Their Way for Parents, Tutors, and School Volunteers provides readers with a description of five developmental stages of spelling as well as how reading, writing, and spelling are integrated. We share a collection of purposeful and hands-on activities, along with the explicit knowledge you need to talk about spelling and vocabulary confidently across all stages of development.

Although we recommend that everyone read the first two chapters to gain a broad understanding of spelling development (Chapter 1) and the word study basics (Chapter 2), we provide a literacy checklist to help you determine your child's current stage of spelling development. With this knowledge, you may choose to read the stage chapter most applicable to your child (Chapters 3–7) or to read the book from cover to cover to gain a wide understanding of word study across the five stages. We also recommend that all readers read the "Frequently Asked Questions" (Chapter 8), as these address many of the questions we have heard over the years from parents, tutors, and school volunteers. We refer to "your child" throughout the text, meaning either your child as a parent or a child that you work with as a tutor or school volunteer.

As you may note in the "About the Author" section, we each bring a unique perspective to this book. As professors, school leaders, teachers, and parents ourselves, we have seen the powerful difference that the word study approach can make in a child's reading, writing, spelling and vocabulary development. This book is designed to connect research-based practice, schools, and homes across the country.

We wish you happy reading!

Michelle Picard Alison Meadows Marcia Invernizzi
Donald R. Bear Francine Johnston

About the Authors

Michelle Picard is the K–12 supervisor of English Language Arts in Arlington Public Schools in Virginia. She holds both a Masters and a Doctoral degrees from the University of Virginia, focused on literacy education, research, and leadership. She spent over a decade teaching elementary and middle school, followed by positions as a K–12 reading and literacy specialist, Director of Early Childhood and Elementary Education, adjunct professor, and director of a summer graduate reading clinic. She authored the 2011 CODiE award-winning professional learning course *Words Their Way Online*.

Alison Meadows is the assistant principal of Lyles–Crouch Traditional Academy in Alexandria City Public Schools in Virginia. Alison is a former classroom teacher, special education teacher, reading specialist, and literacy coach. She has also served as an adjunct professor for the Curry School of Education at the University of Virginia, and continues to work with schools as a literacy consultant. Her background and interests focus on literacy development, developmental spelling, reading intervention, and professional learning for educators.

Marcia Invernizzi is the Henderson Professor of Reading Education at the Curry School of Education at the University of Virginia, and executive director of the McGuffey Reading Center there. She and her multilingual doctoral students enjoy exploring developmental universals in English and non-English orthographies. A former English and reading teacher, Marcia extends her experience working with children who experience difficulties learning to read and write in numerous intervention programs, such as Virginia's Early Intervention Reading Initiative and Book Buddies.

Donald R. Bear is professor emeritus in literacy education at Iowa State University and University of Nevada, Reno, where he taught at all levels and directed reading centers. He is an author and co-author of numerous articles, chapters, and 16 books, including *Words Their Way*, (6th ed.), *Words Their Way for PreK–K Learners*, *Words Their Way with English Learners* (2nd ed.), *Vocabulary Their Way* (2nd ed.), and *Words Their Way with Struggling Readers, 4–12*. Donald has been a classroom teacher and is involved in innovative professional development activities, and his work in assessment and word study is used widely. He has received several awards for teaching and service, and is currently a board member of the International Literacy Association.

Francine Johnston is retired from the School of Education at the University of North Carolina at Greensboro, where she coordinated the reading master's program and directed a reading clinic for struggling readers. Francine is a former first-grade teacher and reading specialist, and she continues to work with schools as a consultant.

Companion Volumes

Additional stage-specific companion volumes provide you with a complete curriculum of reproducible sorts and detailed directions, including:

- *Words Their Way®: Letter and Picture Sorts for Emergent Spellers* (2nd ed.), by Donald R. Bear, Marcia Invernizzi, Francine Johnston, and Shane Templeton
- *Words Their Way®: Word Sorts for Letter Name–Alphabetic Spellers* (3rd ed.), by Francine Johnston, Donald R. Bear, Marcia Invernizzi, and Shane Templeton
- *Words Their Way®: Word Sorts for Within Word Pattern Spellers* (3rd ed.), by Marcia Invernizzi, Francine Johnston, Donald R. Bear, and Shane Templeton
- *Words Their Way®: Word Sorts for Syllables and Affixes Spellers* (2nd ed.), by Francine Johnston, Marcia Invernizzi, Donald R. Bear, and Shane Templeton
- *Words Their Way®: Word Sorts for Derivational Relations Spellers* (2nd ed.), by Shane Templeton, Francine Johnston, Donald R. Bear, and Marcia Invernizzi

Other related volumes are designed to meet the needs of students in specific age groups:

- *Words Their Way® for PreK–K*, by Francine Johnston, Marcia Invernizzi, Lori Helman, Donald R. Bear, and Shane Templeton
- *Vocabulary Their Way®: Word Study with Middle and Secondary Students* (2nd ed.), by Shane Templeton, Donald R. Bear, Marcia Invernizzi, Francine Johnston, Kevin Flanigan, Lori Helman, Diana Townsend, and Tisha Hayes
- *Words Their Way® with Struggling Readers: Word Study for Reading, Vocabulary, and Spelling Instruction, Grades 4–12*, by Kevin Flanigan, Latisha Hayes, Shane Templeton, Donald R. Bear, Marcia Invernizzi, and Francine Johnston

Additional volumes are specifically designed to meet the needs of English learners:

- *Words Their Way® with English Learners: Word Study for Phonics, Vocabulary, and Spelling* (2nd ed.), by Lori Helman, Donald R. Bear, Shane Templeton, Marcia Invernizzi, and Francine Johnston
- *Words Their Way®: Emergent Sorts for Spanish-Speaking English Learners*, by Lori Helman, Donald R. Bear, Marcia Invernizzi, Shane Templeton, and Francine Johnston
- *Words Their Way®: Letter Name–Alphabetic Sorts for Spanish-Speaking English Learners*, by Lori Helman, Donald R. Bear, Marcia Invernizzi, Shane Templeton, and Francine Johnston
- *Words Their Way®: Within Word Pattern Sorts for Spanish-Speaking English Learners*, by Lori Helman, Donald R. Bear, Marcia Invernizzi, Shane Templeton, and Francine Johnston

Acknowledgments

We are proud to bring *Words Their Way* to a broader parent and school community, and are thankful for the support of our colleagues. We thank the many teachers, students, and families we have worked with over many years who have helped deepen our own understanding of literacy development and partnerships with parents. We also thank the reviewers of our manuscript for their careful consideration and comments: Kristen McAuliffe, Caitlin Miller, Jessica L. Owens, Lisa Roddy-Burns, and Elizabeth Serene. Many thanks to Miryam Chandler, Michelle Hacker, and all the staff at Pearson for their expertise and support.

Brief Contents

CHAPTER 1 What Is Word Study and Why Is It Important? 2

CHAPTER 2 Word Study Basics 26

CHAPTER 3 Emergent Learners 46

CHAPTER 4 Beginning Readers in the Letter Name-Alphabetic Stage of Spelling 82

CHAPTER 5 Transitional Readers in the Within Word Pattern Stage of Spelling 110

CHAPTER 6 Intermediate Readers and Writers in the Syllables and Affixes Stage of Spelling Development 134

CHAPTER 7 Advanced Readers and Writers in the Derivational Relations Stage of Spelling Development 158

CHAPTER 8 Frequently Asked Questions 180

Appendices 196

Glossary 218

Index 222

Detailed Contents

CHAPTER 1 What Is Word Study and Why Is It Important? 2

Word Study Overview 3

What Is Word Study and Why Is It Important? 3

How Is Word Study Different from Traditional Spelling? 4

Purpose and Principles 4

Assessment 4

Instructional Methods and Routines 4

Grading and Monitoring Progress 7

The Three Layers of the English Language 7

Sound 7

Pattern 8

Meaning 8

Stages of Literacy Development 8

How Can Parents Determine Their Child's Stage of Development? 8

Emergent Learners 9

Beginning Readers in the Letter Name–Alphabetic Stage of Spelling 13

Transitional Readers in the Within Word Pattern Stage of Spelling 15

Intermediate Readers in the Syllables and Affixes Stage of Spelling 16

Advanced Readers in the Derivational Relations Stage of Spelling 19

A Brief Summary 23

CHAPTER 2 Word Study Basics 26

Word Study in the Classroom 27

The Role of Word Sorting 28

A Sorting Example: *-ible* and *-able* 30

Ten Principles of Word Study Instruction 32

Look for What Students Use but Confuse 32

A Step Backward Is a Step Forward 32

Use Words Your Child Can Read 32

Compare Words That "Do" with Words That "Don't" 32

Sort by Sound and Sight 32

Begin with Obvious Contrasts 33

Avoid Rules 33

Work for Automaticity 33

Return to Meaningful Texts 34

Effective Practices in Word Study 34

Essential Techniques 34

Sort Introduction 35

Daily Student Sorting 37

Writing Sort 37

Word Hunt 38

Reflecting On the Big Ideas or Underlying Generalizations 40

Word Study Notebooks 40

Vocabulary Notebooks 41

Word Study Games 41

Memory 41

Taboo 41

Speed Sort 41

Blind or No Peeking Sort 43

Commercial Games 43

A Brief Summary 44

CHAPTER 3 Emergent Learners 46

Stage Overview: Emergent Learners 47
- Reading 47
- Writing 49
- Spelling 51
- Early Literacy Skills 51
  - *Oral Language, Concepts and Vocabulary 52*
  - *Phonological Awareness 52*
  - *Phonemic Awareness 53*
  - *Phonics 54*
  - *Alphabet Recognition 54*
  - *Concepts About Print 55*
  - *Concept of Word 55*

Understanding Picture Sorts 56
- Sort Support: What You and Your Child Need to Know at the Emergent Stage 56
  - *Concept Sorts 56*
  - *Phonological Awareness 56*
  - *Alphabet Recognition 57*
  - *Letter Sounds 57*
- Let's Talk About It! 57
  - *How Are the Pictures Alike in Each Category? How Are They Different? 59*
  - *Are There Any Pictures That Do Not Fit? Why? 59*
  - *What Do You Learn from This Sort? 59*

Early Literacy Skills With Parents, Tutors, and School Volunteers 60
- Oral Language, Concepts, and Vocabulary 60
  - *Talk 60*
  - *View and Discuss Educational Television 60*
  - *Narrate Everyday Experiences with Your Young Child 62*
  - *Read and Talk about Books 62*
  - *Reread Books 63*
  - *Share Wordless Books 64*
  - *Retell Stories and Tell Your Own 64*
  - *Share Concept Books 65*
  - *Play with Concept Sorts 65*
- Phonological Awareness 66
  - *Read Books That Include Rhyme and Language Play 66*
  - *Share Rhymes, Jingles and Songs 67*
  - *Rhyming Sorts 67*
  - *Rhyming Story Extensions 68*
  - *Play a Game: Whose Name Has More Syllables? Let's Clap to Find Out! 68*
  - *Play Rhyming Games 68*
- Phonics (Letter Sounds) 68
  - *Sort Beginning Pictures or Objects 69*
  - *Create Sound Bags 69*
  - *Play a Game: Sound I Spy 69*
  - *Play a Game: The Name Game 69*
  - *Play Commercial Alphabet Games 69*
- Alphabet Knowledge (Letter Recognition) 69
  - *Begin with Your Child's Name 70*
  - *Sing the Alphabet Song and Track the Letters 70*
  - *Read Alphabet Books 70*
  - *Make Your Own Alphabet Book 71*
  - *Play Alphabet Games 71*
  - *Play with Magnetic Alphabet Letters 71*
  - *Font Sorts 72*
  - *Go on a Letter Hunt 72*
  - *Play a Game: Alphabet Puzzles 72*
- Concepts about Print (CAP) 72
  - *Draw Attention to Print in the Environment 72*
  - *Read to Your Child and Provide Books for Your Child to Handle 73*
  - *Use Language That Refers to Literacy Vocabulary 74*
  - *Play a Game: Can You Find …? 74*
- Concept of Word 74
  - *Practice Fingerpointing to the Words in Familiar Text 75*
  - *Build and Read Simple Words 75*
  - *Read Predictable Pattern Books, Point to Words, and Encourage Memory Reading 75*
  - *Play a Game: Stand Up and Be Counted 75*
  - *Create Cut-Up Sentences 75*
- Writing 76
  - *Supply a Wide Variety of Writing Materials 76*
  - *Model and Discuss Practical Writing 76*
  - *Create Dictated Captions Together 77*
  - *Encourage Your Child to Write for a Variety of Purposes 77*
  - *Write for Sounds 77*

A Brief Summary 77

CHAPTER 4 Beginning Readers in the Letter Name–Alphabetic Stage of Spelling 82

Stage Overview: Beginning Readers in the Letter Name–Alphabetic Stage of Spelling 83

Reading 83

Writing 86

Spelling 87

What Do Children Do or Spell Correctly at This Stage? 88

What Do Children "Use But Confuse" at This Stage? 88

What Is Absent at This Stage? 89

Understanding Picture and Word Sorts 89

Let's Talk About It! 89

How are the pictures or words alike in each category? 90

Are there any pictures or words that do not fit? Why? 90

What did you learn from this sort? What are the big ideas or the underlying generalization you can learn from this sort? 90

Sort Support: What You and Your Child Need to Know at the Letter Name–Alphabetic Stage 91

Beginning Consonant Sounds 91

Blends and Digraphs 92

Same Vowel Word Families 92

Mixed Vowel Word Families 93

Short Vowels 94

Oddballs 94

Affricates 94

Preconsonantal Nasals 95

Spelling Strategies 95

Use invented spelling 96

Sound-it-out 96

Know it in a snap 96

Chunk known word parts 96

Use analogy 96

Word Study with Parents, Tutors, and School Volunteers 96

Follow the Path Games 97

Bingo 97

Memory 98

Match! 98

Build, Blend, and Extend 98

Word Family Wheels and Flip Books 98

Show Me 99

Making Words with Cubes 99

Roll the Dice 100

Go Fish! 100

Guess My Word 100

Commercial Products 100

Supporting Reading and Writing 101

Reading 101

Reading Aloud to Your Child 101

Beginning Reader Texts 102

Predictable Readers 103

Decodable Readers 103

Beginning Readers 103

Personal Readers 103

Guiding Your Child's Reading 104

Book introductions 104

Choral and echo reading 104

Partner or buddy reading 104

Talking about reading 104

What to say when your child doesn't know a word 105

Increasing sight vocabulary 105

Writing 107

Sound Boards 107

Dictations or Silly Sentences 107

Practical Writing 108

A Brief Summary 108

CHAPTER 5 Transitional Readers in the Within Word Pattern Stage of Spelling 110

Stage Overview: Transitional Readers and Writers in the Within Word Pattern Stage of Spelling 111

Reading 111

Writing 114

Vocabulary 114

Spelling 115

What Do Students Spell Correctly? 115

What Do Students "Use But Confuse"? 115

What Is Absent? 116

Understanding Picture and Word Sorts 116

Let's Talk About It! 116

How Are the Pictures or Words Alike in Each Category? How Are They Different? 117

Are There Any Pictures or Words That Do Not Fit? Why? 117

Which Spelling Patterns Are More Frequent? Less Frequent? 118

Is Each Spelling Pattern More Commonly Found at the Beginning, Middle, or End of the Word? 118

Does Meaning Influence the Spelling of These Words? 119

What Do You Learn from This Sort? What Are the Big Ideas or the Underlying Generalizations of This Sort? 119

Sort Support: What You and Your Child Need to Know at the Within Word Pattern Stage 119

Common and Less Common Long Vowel Patterns 120

R-Influenced Vowels 120

Diphthongs and Other Ambiguous Vowels 121

Complex Consonants 122

Homophones 123

Spelling Strategies 123

Use Analogy 123

Use the "Best Bet" Strategy 124

Encourage Students to Try a Word Several Ways: Have-a-Go 124

Word Study With Parents, Tutors, and School Volunteers 124

Word Study Notebooks 124

Word Study Uno 125

Guess My Category 125

Word Operations (or Change a Word Part) 125

Vowel Concentration 126

Vowel Rummy 126

Declare Your Category! 126

Homophone Dictionaries 127

Homophone Rummy 127

Homophone Win, Lose, or Draw 127

Books That Feature Homophones and Homographs 127

Follow-the-Path Games 128

The Spelling Game 129

Supporting Reading and Writing 129

Reading 129

Select Books with Your Child 129

Monitor the Time Your Child Reads at Home 130

Read Aloud to Your Child 130

Talk about Reading 131

Build Fluency through Poetry and Repeated Readings 131

Writing 131

Encourage Your Child to Write for a Variety of Purposes and Share Their Writing 131

Provide Interesting Writing Materials 131

Explore Writing Assignments from School 132

A Brief Summary 132

CHAPTER 6 Intermediate Readers and Writers in the Syllables and Affixes Stage of Spelling Development 134

Stage Overview: Intermediate Readers and Writers in the Syllables and Affixes Stage of Spelling 135

Reading 135

Writing 137

Spelling 138

What Do Children Do or Spell Correctly at This Stage? 138

What Do Children "Use But Confuse" at This Stage? 138

What Is Absent at This Stage? 139

Vocabulary 139

Understanding Polysyllabic Word Sorts 140

Let's Talk About It 141

How Are the Words Alike in Each Category? How Are They Different? 141

Are There Any Words That Do Not Fit? Why? 142

What Do You Learn from This Sort? What Are the Big Ideas or Underlying Generalizations You Can Learn from This Sort? 142

Sort Support: What You and Your Child Need to Know at the Syllables and Affixes Stage 142

Exploring Polysyllabic Words 143

Compound words 143

Homophones 143
Homographs 143
Inflected Endings 143
Plurals 143
Adding –ed and –ing 144
Comparatives and superlatives (-er/-est) 144
Open and Closed Syllables 144
Vowel Patterns in Accented Syllables 145
Long vowel patterns in accented syllables 146
R-influenced vowels in accented syllables 146
Ambiguous vowels in accented syllables 146
Vowel Patterns in Unaccented Syllables 146
Exploring Consonants 146
Hard and Soft Consonants 146
Silent Consonants 146
Sounds of /k/ spelled ck, ic, and x 147
Other Unique Consonant Patterns 147
Affixes: Prefixes and Suffixes 147
Spelling Strategies 148
Use the "Best Bet" Strategy 148
Spell by Syllable 148
Use Prefixes, Suffixes, and Roots (Word Parts) 148
Check for a Spelling–Meaning Connection 148
Encourage Students to Try a Word Several Ways: Have-a-Go 148
Use Spelling Dictionaries and Digital Resources 149
Use Spell Check 149
Word Study With Parents, Tutors, and School Volunteers 149
Word Study Notebooks 149
Strategies and Activities to Develop Academic Vocabulary 149
Concept and Semantic Maps 150
Frayer Model 151
List-Group-Label 151
Strategies and Activities to Develop Spelling 151
Card Games 151
Board Games 152
Prefix Spin 153
Supporting Reading and Writing 153
Reading 153
Read Aloud to Your Child 153
Listen to Audiobooks 154
Keep It Social 154
Discuss Vocabulary 154
Support Academic Reading in School 154
Writing 154
Ask Your Child to Share Writing from School 155
Provide Feedback for Revision on Organization and Composition 155
A Brief Summary 155

CHAPTER 7 Advanced Readers and Writers in the Derivational Relations Stage of Spelling Development 158

Stage Overview: Advanced Readers and Writers in the Derivational Relations Stage of Spelling 159
Reading 159
Writing 162
Vocabulary 163
Spelling 163
What Do Children Do or Spell Correctly at This Stage? 163
What Do Children "Use But Confuse" at This Stage? 164
Understanding Polysyllabic Word Sorts 164
Let's Talk About It! 164
Sort Support: What You and Your Child Need to Know at This Stage 165
Affixes: Prefixes and Suffixes 165
Consonant and Vowel Alternations 167
Consonant Alternations 167
Vowel Alternations 168
Predictable Spelling Changes in Consonants and Vowels 168
Greek and Latin Roots 169
Advanced Suffixes 170
Assimilated or Absorbed Prefixes 170
Spelling Strategies 171
Word Study With Parents, Tutors, and School Volunteers 171
Word Study Notebooks 171
Strategies and Activities to Develop Vocabulary and Spelling 172
Word Collection Routine 172
Examine Word Origins 172
Online Resources for Word Study 173
Word Trees 174
Brainburst 174
Word Part Shuffle 175
Vocabulary Notecards 175
Shades of Meaning 175

Supporting Reading and Writing 175
Reading 175
Read Aloud and Share Audiobooks 175
Promote Literacy through Digital Devices 176
Share Your Own Reading and Engage in Theirs 176
Explore Academic Reading and Vocabulary 176
Writing 176
Celebrate and Share Writing 176
Write for Authentic Audiences 177
Explore Academic Writing across Disciplines 177
A Brief Summary 177

CHAPTER 8 Frequently Asked Questions 180

Frequently Asked Questions 181
Question 1: Why Is Word Study Important? 181
Question 2: Why Do Some People Say That You Shouldn't Teach the Names of the Letters? 182
Question 3: What Order Should We Teach the Alphabet Letters and Their Sounds? 182
Question 4: If I Allow My Child to Use Invented or Phonetic Spelling, Will He or She Learn to Spell Incorrectly? 182
Question 5: What If My Child Can Sort the Words Correctly and Gets Them Correct on the Spelling Test, But Doesn't Spell Them Correctly in His or Her Daily Writing? 183
Question 6: How Do I Know If My Child Is Making Progress in Spelling? 183
Question 7: Should Children Progress through a Stage in a Single Year? 185
Question 8: In Which Stage Should My Child Be Performing to Reach Grade Level Expectations? 185
Question 9: Why Don't We Encourage Children to Just Memorize the Words? 185
Question 10: Why Don't We Teach the "Rules" of Spelling? 185
Question 11: Does Word Study Work for English Learners? 186
Question 12: Does Word Study Work for Students Identified with Learning Disabilities? 186
Question 13: Does Word Study Work for Gifted and Other High-Achieving Students? 186
Question 14: Will My Child Get Tired of Sorting? 186
Question 15: What Do I Do If My Child Continues to Get the Same Sorts? 186
Question 16: When My Child Asks How to Spell a Word, Should I Tell How to Spell It? Should I Correct My Child's Spelling? 187
Question 17: How Can I Help My Child When They Do Not Know How to Spell a Word? 187
Use Invented Spelling 188
Sound-It-Out 188
Know It in a Snap 188
Chunk Known Word Parts 188
Use Analogy 188
Use the Best Bet Strategy 188
Encourage Students to Try a Word Several Ways: Have-a-Go 188
Spell by Syllable 189
Use Prefixes, Suffixes, and Roots (Word Parts) 189
Check for a Spelling–Meaning Connection 189
Use Spelling Dictionaries and Digital Resources 189
Use Spell Check 189
Question 18: What If My Child's School Is Not Practicing Developmental Spelling? 190
Question 19: What If My Child Mispronounces Words? Will It Affect Reading and Writing? 190
Question 20: What Do I Do When My Child Cannot Read a Word? 190
Question 21: How Do I Know If My Child Is Reading on Grade Level? 190
Question 22: How Are Reading Levels Described? What Are the Letters and Numbers Used to Describe Reading Levels? 190
Question 23: What Affects My Child's Comprehension? 192
Question 24: What Can I Do If My Child Is Not Reading on Grade Level? 192
Question 25: Should We Allow Our Child to Be Retained If He or She Is Not Reading or Writing on Grade Level? 192
Question 26: How Do I Know If My Child Is Dyslexic? 193

APPENDICES

Appendix A Sort Support for Spellers 196
Appendix B Sound Board for Beginning Consonants and Digraphs 207
Appendix C Games and Templates for Sorts 209

Glossary 218

Index 222

Words Their Way™ for Parents, Tutors, and School Volunteers

chapter 1

What Is Word Study and Why Is It Important?

Source: Monkey Business Images/Shutterstock

In our age of modern technology, people sometimes suggest that spelling is not that important. Parents may comment that they were not good spellers themselves, or question if spelling is important given the use of computers and spellcheck.

Studies confirm that when children learn how spelling patterns work, improvements are observed not only in spelling, but also in word recognition, writing skill, and reading comprehension (Carlisle, 2004; Ehri & Wilce, 1987; Henderson, 1990; McCandliss, Beck, Sendak, & Perfetti, 2003). In other words, when you study word parts, it is easier to read, write, and spell those parts and to put them together into words. To illustrate this phenomenon, consider the musical *Mary Poppins*. Julie Andrews made the word *supercalifragilisticexpialidocious* accessible to young viewers. The popular song rhymed the word *supercalifragilisticexpialidocious* with *atrocious* and *precocious*.

Despite being a nonsense word, children are able to sing, read, and make a solid attempt at spelling the word because it is made up of a number of identifiable syllables or units of meaning.

Word Study Overview

Do you remember how you were taught to spell? Take a moment and think about how you learned spelling and vocabulary in the classroom. How were words selected? What activities did you use to learn the words? Did it change from grade to grade? In our experience as educators, we have worked with hundreds of teachers and parents who have answered this question and two common responses are given. First, participants tell us that the teacher provided a single list for the entire classroom. They were asked to write sentences and definitions, copy misspelled words 5 to 10 times each, and complete worksheets, crossword puzzles, and word searches. Quizzes were given weekly.

The second common response is similar. People tell us that they were taught a spelling rule such as "*i* before *e* except after *c*, and when sounding like *a* as in *neighbor* and *weigh*." The teaching activities used to reinforce the rule were the same as those described in the first example. Both of these approaches to spelling and vocabulary learning are typical of a traditional approach. Spelling was an exercise in memory, an exercise in retaining the spelling of specific words.

What Is Word Study and Why Is It Important?

Instead of the traditional approach, many schools now use a developmental approach also known as **word study**. Word study is a developmental, student-centered approach to teaching phonics, spelling, and vocabulary that is integrated with reading and writing instruction. Based on several decades of research (Henderson, 1990; Henderson & Beers, 1980; Templeton, 2011; Templeton & Bear, 1992), word study engages students in hands-on, active categorization and study of how words work—how sound, pattern, or meaning are represented in their daily reading and writing. The goal of word study extends beyond the retention of specific words by teaching students to transfer those spellings to other words that share similar pronunciations or meanings.

A typical first-grade student, for example, may learn words in a short vowel rhyming family, such as those in the *-at* family: *bat*, *cat*, *fat*, *hat*, *mat*, *pat*, *rat*, and *sat*. In a word study approach, students compare these words to those in another related family, such as the *-ot* family: *hot*, *cot*, *rot*, *dot*, *got*, and *not*. Students learn the difference between two short vowel sounds. They also learn that by changing the initial consonant or blend, you can accurately spell a number of words that do not appear on the spelling list, such as *chat*, *flat*, *spot*, and *plot*. An upper-grade student may learn that when they understand how to spell *courage*, they also have gained insight to the accurate spellings of *courageous*, *encourage*, *encourages*, *encouraging*, *encouragement*, *discourage*, *discourages*, *discouraging*, and *discouragement*.

Word study benefits students of all ages and stages (Morris, Blanton, Blanton, Nowacek, & Perney, 1995; Morris, Nelson, & Perney, 1986; Helman & Bear, 2007; Invernizzi & Worthy, 1989) in regular educational settings as well as those receiving special education and gifted education services. It is beneficial to students who are learning English as a second, third, or fourth language, as well as to students who speak standard or nonstandard dialects.

How Is Word Study Different from Traditional Spelling?

Historically, traditional approaches to spelling instruction were based on repetition and memory. In contrast, the developmental approach focuses on analysis, reflection, and then transfer of what is learned about spelling features to new and unfamiliar words. Table 1.1 shows the differences between the traditional and developmental approaches.

PURPOSE AND PRINCIPLES Both traditional and developmental approaches seek to develop phonics, spelling, and vocabulary knowledge in students, but there are key differences. Although the traditional approach assumes that students learn best from a common grade-level curriculum with an approach focused on repetition and rote memorization, word study emphasizes the development of word knowledge through analysis. The goal is not only to spell individual words, but also to understand common spelling principles or big ideas that can be applied to new words. If a child can spell the long *a* patterns *ai* as in *rain* and *a-consonant-e* as in *cake*, they can learn to spell *train*, *pain*, *distain*, *refrain*, and *shake*, *lake*, *take*, *bake*, and *mistake*.

ASSESSMENT In a traditional approach, the goal of assessment is to determine if students can spell a discrete set of words correctly at a single point in time—the spelling test. Each item is scored as either right or wrong, with no interpretation of errors. Word study instruction *begins* with an assessment of spelling knowledge known as a **qualitative spelling inventory** that is a series of spelling tests that increase in difficulty and are designed to assess a child's understanding of specific spelling patterns rather than knowledge of individual words. Student responses are analyzed to assess which spelling features a student may demonstrate consistently, frequently, or not at all. Unlike a traditional spelling test, students are afforded credit or points for specific spelling features that are produced correctly. There are several of these tools available to assess children's developmental spelling stages (Bear, Invernizzi, Templeton, & Johnston, 2011; Ganske, 2013; Invernizzi, Juel, Swank, & Meier, 2006; Schlagal, 1992). In a developmental approach, teachers use a qualitative spelling assessment several times per year and routinely monitor student reading and writing to ensure that students are using what they have learned in all aspects of literacy.

Inventories are used to determine each child's **instructional level** by learning what a child knows, uses but confuses, and has absent. To use a baseball metaphor, the instructional level is the strike zone, and the area between a batter's shoulders and knees where a ball crossing home plate is called a *strike*. It is the perfect "sweet spot" for instruction that is neither too challenging nor too easy, and allows children to hit it out of the park with their learning!

INSTRUCTIONAL METHODS AND ROUTINES In a traditional approach to spelling, whole-group lessons are delivered with a common spelling list, organized by theme, spelling feature, or spelling rule. For example, a grade-level spelling list might focus on words with the spelling feature *ea* as in *treat* and be accompanied by a rule such as, "When two vowels go walking, the first one does the talking." Single-feature spelling lists, however, do not explore the conditions under which a pattern is represented or not represented in a word because a point of comparison is absent. For example, the *ea* word list may include

TABLE 1.1 Comparison of Traditional and Developmental Spelling

	Traditional Spelling	Developmental Spelling
Purpose and Principles	• Emphasizes rote memorization of individual words, rules, and exceptions • Assumes that pre-existing knowledge is consistent across age and/or grade level	• Focuses not only on individual words, but also on the big ideas and how knowledge can be generalized to other words • Assumes that students have varied pre-existing word knowledge based on experience and development, not age
Assessment	• Considers spelling as all or nothing; words are right or wrong • Used to determine grade-level spelling proficiency exclusively • Used in comparison to grade-level spelling	• Considers partial credit for correct spelling features (qualitative) • Used to — determine a developmental stage or instructional level — analyze spelling features (what students know, use but confuse, and what is absent in spelling) — form small groups — determine a starting point for instruction — monitor progress
Instructional Methods and Routines	• Uses rote-memory exercises and drills to memorize words; activities encourage visual memory and repetition to learn individual words • Taught as a separate spelling program with no connection to reading, writing, or vocabulary • Taught in whole group based on grade-level curriculum • Uses a common spelling list based on grade level by theme, grade level, or single spelling features	• Emphasizes the examination of groups of words and spelling features for similarities and differences • Uses word sorting and related activities such as word hunts, speed sorts, and writing sorts • Emphasizes the active manipulation and examination of words in order to form generalizations • Integrates into a literacy program; connections are made across reading, writing, and spelling • Taught in small groups based on assessment and common instructional needs • Uses different sets of words according to students' pre-existing knowledge
Grading and Monitoring Progress	• Assigns grades based on weekly assessments • Emphasizes correct spelling through memorization, grading, and correction	• Assigns grades based on completion of word study work and ongoing development • Uses progress monitoring as demonstrated on nongraded qualitative spelling inventories given 2–4 times per year

beat, cheat, wheat, treat, read, mean, team, lead, but avoid words with *ea* that represent a short *e* sound such as *bread, dead, breath, tread,* and *spread,* or additional long-*e* words such as *street, three, me,* or *field.*

Another common traditional approach is to provide spelling lists customized by the teacher to reflect a content or vocabulary perspective. For example, a teacher may have selected words based on geography terms (Figure 1.1). Although these words are related in meaning, which is helpful in learning vocabulary, the words do not share similar spelling features, and in some situations children are asked to spell words that they cannot read. Rote memorization is required to be successful on the eventual spelling assessment because meaning is the only underlying principle connecting the words.

FIGURE 1.1 Theme-Based Spelling List: Geography Terms

island	delta	prairie	desert	river	basin
ocean	mountain	valley	stream	peninsula	rainforest
tundra	lake	pond	isthmus	watershed	field
meadow	plateau	mesa	gorge	canyon	continent

In contrast to the traditional whole-class model, word study instruction occurs in small groups according to the child's instructional spelling level. Word study lessons are tailored to the specific needs of the group members. By participating in different lessons, group members do not waste time learning spelling features that they have already mastered or those that are beyond their current level of understanding. Instruction focuses on spelling features in the strike zone that contribute to students' phonics, spelling, and vocabulary knowledge. All students, whether performing on, above, or below grade-level norms, benefit from instruction that builds on what they already understand.

For example, one group may focus on a sort comparing the long and short *i* sounds and patterns, such as short *i* in *bib* versus long i in *bike* (*i-consonant-e*), *knight* (*-igh*), and sky (*y*) (Figure 1.2). Given the deliberate focus not only on individual words but also on the underlying generalizations, children engage in reflection on how the spelling features work in words, considering questions such as these:

Which spelling patterns and/or sounds are the same in each category?
Are there any oddballs or words that do not appear to follow the pattern? Why?
What are the big ideas (or the underlying principles) to be learned in this sort?
Which features are most common and least common?
What position in words makes the most sense for specific features?

Using the sort in Figure 1.2, for example, students may determine that there are at least four spelling patterns with *i*, such as *i-consonant-e* as in *bike*, *-igh* as in *knight*, and *-y* as in *fly*. Once students collect as many words as they can in these patterns, also known as a **word hunt**, they will realize that the pattern *-igh* as in *knight* and *i-consonant-e* as in *bike* are very common and are usually captured between a beginning and ending sound. The pattern *y* as in *sky* is less common and has a smaller collection of words that follow this pattern. Also, when the letter *y* represents a long *i* sound, it is usually found at the end of a word. Position is helpful in determining which vowel pattern to use in an unfamiliar word. Students may also discover that *y* also represents the long *e* sound as in *baby* and *happy*. Reflecting on the similarities and

FIGURE 1.2 Typical Long and Short *i* Sort

short *i* *bib*	***iCe* *bike***	***igh* *knight***	***y* *fly***
lit	strike	fight	sky
spill	kite	night	try
split	white	light	cry
rip	smile	right	why
knit	time	might	shy

differences among groups of words is the foundation of word study. Many other activities described in Chapter 2 also contribute to a systematic, hands-on, multisensory approach to automating word knowledge in reading and writing.

GRADING AND MONITORING PROGRESS In a traditional spelling program, spelling assignments and a weekly quiz are graded with each word as either correct or incorrect. In a word study program, weekly or biweekly quizzes may also be used; however, they are often graded by awarding credit for spelling the specific feature correct as well as the word. Grades in both approaches are also often provided on weekly assignments.

Progress may be monitored through weekly quizzes and the review and observation of the student's daily spelling and writing in either approach. In the word study approach, progress is also monitored through the periodic use of a qualitative spelling inventory several times per year.

The Three Layers of the English Language

Before we review the stages of development, it is essential to understand that the foundation for developmental word study is based on the three layers of the English language as seen in Figure 1.3: sound, pattern, and meaning. Over time, your child acquires an understanding of how sound (phonics), pattern (orthography), and meaning (morphology) affect spelling, reading, and writing. In the early stages of development, children progress from an overreliance on sound, in which they associate one sound with one letter, to the realization that the patterns in English must also be considered (*mad*, *made*, *maid*), and finally to meaning units (*un* as in *unlikely*). At the later stages of development, mature readers and writers integrate all three layers of the language. Following is a brief review of the three layers of the English language. Once you know your child's stage of development, you are able to recognize how sound, pattern, and meaning affect their literacy development.

SOUND Our spelling system is **alphabetic**, meaning that it represents the relationship between letters and sounds. In the word *sat*, each sound is represented by a single letter; we

FIGURE 1.3 Stages of Reading and Writing Associated with Sound, Pattern, and Meaning

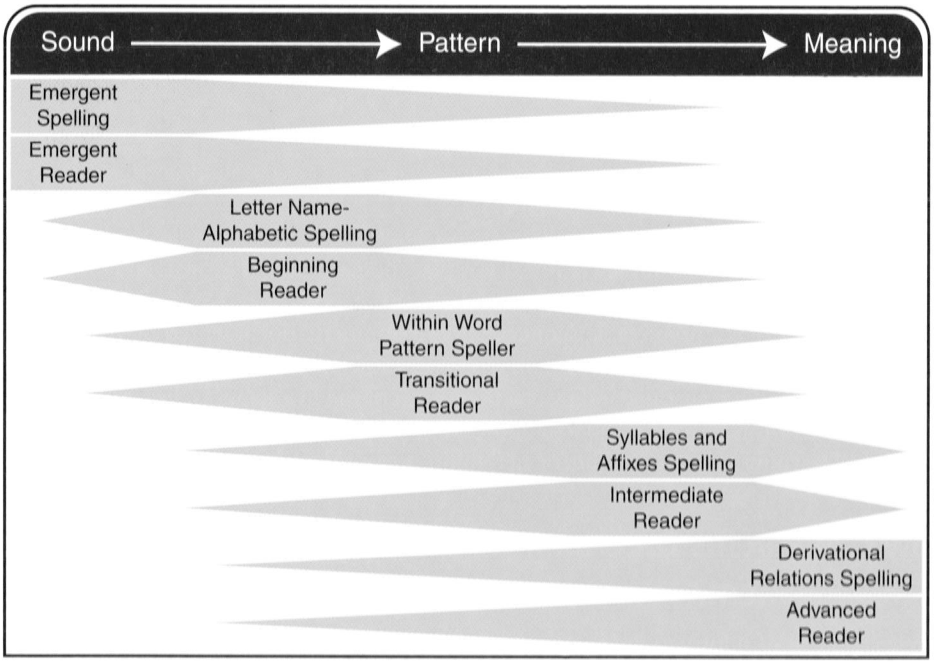

Source: From *"Words Their Way Online Workshop"* by Michelle Picard. Copyright © by Pearson Education, Inc. Reprinted with permission of David Picard.

blend the sounds /s/, /a/, and /t/ to read and write the word *sat*. In the word *chin*, we still hear three sounds even though there are four letters, because the first two letters, *ch*, represent a single sound. So we can match letters (or pairs of letters) to sounds from left to right to create words. This **alphabetic layer** in English spelling is dependent on sound, and you will discover that our youngest readers and writers rely heavily on this layer in both the emergent and letter name–alphabetic stages of development.

PATTERN As we gain experience with the sounds and letters in English, we begin to notice that all words are not completely phonetic. You may ask, "Why don't we spell all words the way they sound?" If we did, words like *cape*, *bead*, and *light* would look like *cap*, *bed*, and *lit*, but these spellings, of course, already represent other words. The **pattern layer** therefore overlies the alphabetic or sound layer. There are 44 sounds in English, but only 26 letters in the alphabet. Different combinations of letters, also known as *spelling features*, represent similar sounds. For example, the single sound of long *a* has multiple patterns: *ai* as in *rain*, *a-consonant-e* as in *cake*, *ay* as in *play*, *ea* as in *steak*, *eigh* as in *eight*, *ei* as in *veil*, and *au* as in *gauge*. The pattern of spelling features is the second layer of English spelling and is a central focus of the within word pattern stage.

MEANING The third layer of English orthography is the **meaning layer**. Groups of letters can represent meaning directly. Examples of these units or groups of letters are prefixes, suffixes, and Greek and Latin roots. As one example of how meaning functions in the spelling system, think of the prefix *re-*, whether we hear it pronounced "ree" as in *rethink* or "ruh" as in *remove*. In both of these words its spelling stays the same, despite their differences in pronunciation, because *re-* directly represents meaning. Why is *composition* not spelled COMPUSITION? The answer? Spelling is related to meaning. The spelling of the second vowel in the related words *compose* and *composition* stays the same, even though the pronunciation of the second syllable is different. Likewise, the word part *photo* in *photograph*, *photographer*, and *photographic* signals **spelling–meaning connections** among these words, despite the changes in sound that the letter *o* represents. Spelling–meaning connections have important implications not only for spelling, but also for vocabulary development.

The three layers of English—sound, pattern, and meaning—play a central role in learning to read, write, and spell. As you explore the stages of spelling development, note how all three layers of the language influence your child's reading, writing, and spelling.

Stages of Literacy Development

How is spelling connected to reading and writing? What does it mean to be in a specific stage of development? In this section, we discuss the characteristics of children in each of these stages in terms of reading, writing, and spelling.

There are five developmental spelling stages associated with particular reading, writing, and spelling characteristics. Table 1.2 illustrates that these periods of growth and development are not solely dependent on chronological age or grade.

Although there is a predictable sequence of development, documented by research, individual children move along the continuum based on a variety of factors, including experiences with language, reading, writing, and instruction. Each of the five stages is discussed in detail in the remainder of this chapter. Understanding stage development provides insight to support your child's learning and increase his or her abilities to read, write, or spell.

How Can Parents Determine Their Child's Stage of Development?

The best source of information for parents about their children's stage of development is the classroom teacher. Teachers who use a developmental approach for literacy understand that reading, writing, and spelling behaviors are interrelated. We strongly recommend that you

TABLE 1.2 Stages of Development

Typical Grade Level	Grades PreK–mid 1	Grades K–early 3	Grades 1–mid 4	Grades 3–8	Grades 5–12
Typical Ages	1–7	4–9	6–12	8–14	10+
Reading & Writing Stage	Emergent	Beginning	Transitional	Intermediate	Advanced
Spelling Stage	Emergent	Letter Name-Alphabetic	Within Word Pattern	Syllables and Affixes	Derivational Relations

meet with the teacher and ask for information regarding your child's reading, writing, and spelling characteristics. Ask to see what your child's unedited writing looks like. Ask how your child is assessed in reading, writing, and spelling, and how progress is monitored. Ask what you can do to support your child. Your child's teacher is an important partner in your child's education.

To help you determine which stage most likely represents your child's development, we have included the Qualitative Literacy Checklist in Table 1.3 This checklist was designed to examine a child's spelling in unedited writing. Similar to a qualitative spelling inventory, the checklist is used to determine what types of features are known, which features are used but confused, and the degree to which students are applying spelling knowledge in actual writing. This checklist offers examples of spelling errors students make, and matches these errors to stages of spelling. In addition, it offers observable characteristics of reading and writing. The checklist can be used with a formal qualitative spelling inventory to identify stage of development and monitor progress over time.

This Qualitative Literacy Checklist gives broad descriptions of the developmental progression and can be used to guide you in identifying your child's stage of development. First, carefully read each item in the checklist and consider whether your child has mastered the specific skills or demonstrates the specific characteristics outlined in each section. Remember that in word study instruction, we are trying to identify the level at which children benefit most from instruction, neither too easy nor too difficult. The stage with all of the boxes checked is in the too-easy range. The stages with no or very few checks are likely in the too-difficult range. The stage at which some—but not all—of the boxes are checked is most likely your child's instructional spelling level.

Next, read the description in this chapter of the stage you have identified. As you read, consider whether this stage of development closely describes the reading, writing, and spelling behaviors of your child or children. Also, consider reading the stage before and/or after to develop an understanding of the differences between stages. Finally, consult Table 1.4 Stages of Literacy Development: Characteristics of Readers, Writers, and Spellers, which briefly outlines the reading, writing, and spelling characteristics of each stage and provides common spelling errors. Once you feel confident that you have determined the appropriate stage for your child, proceed to Chapter 2, which explains the essential routines, strategies, and games to promote effective reading, writing, and spelling development both inside and outside the classroom. Chapter 2 serves as a resource to which you can return repeatedly to learn and use essential strategies and activities to support your child's development.

Emergent Learners

Emergent learners are typically preschool to mid first grade-age students. Children at this age pretend to read and write often with support from a parent or teacher. Children who have been exposed to stories often recite or retell familiar stories, such as the story of *The Gingerbread Man* (Schmidt, 1985). They may sit on their parent's lap, look at the pictures and the room

TABLE 1.3 Qualitative Literacy Checklist

Level		Spelling Behaviors		Reading and Writing Behaviors
Emergent Learners (Chapter 3)		Does your child know a few letters and/or sounds, but not all?		Does your child pretend to read or recite stories from memory?
		Does your child use random strings of letters or shapes that resemble letters in his or her writing?		Does your child draw or scribble when writing?
Beginning Readers and Writers at the Letter Name–Alphabetic Stage (Chapter 4)		Does your child represent the strongest sounds? (For example, *BD* for *bed, SKR* for *housekeeper*)		Does your child know the names of most letters of the alphabet and many of the letter sounds?
		Does your child partially represent blends and digraphs? (For example, *SP* for *ship*)		Does your child understand that print goes from left to right and top to bottom?
		Does your child use logical vowel substitutions with a letter–name strategy? (For example, *FLOT* for *float*, *BAD* for *bed*)		Does your child know and use some high-frequency words (for example, *mom, I, love*) in reading and writing?
		Does your child spell some consonant digraphs and blends correctly? (For example, ***sh****ip*, ***wh****en*, ***fl****oat*)		Does your child understand the difference between pictures and text in both reading and writing?
		Does your child spell some short vowels correctly?		Does your child have a basic concept of the word (able to point correctly to words in a memorized text)?
		Does your child include the *m* or *n* in front of other consonants? (*lu****m****p*, *sta****n****d*)		Does your child read predictable, decodable, or early readers on his or her own?
Transitional Readers and Writers at the Within Word Pattern Stage (Chapter 5)		Does your child spell most one-syllable short vowel words correctly? (For example, *cap*, *slip*, *jump*)		Does your child know and use many high-frequency words in reading and writing correctly?
		Does your child spell all beginning and ending consonants, blends, digraphs, and short vowels correctly?		Does your child read silently?
		Does your child experiment with long vowel patterns? (For example, silent *E* at the end of words, extra vowels in the middle of words)		Does your child read without using a finger to point during reading?
		Does your child use but confuse long vowels in single syllable words? (*FLOTE* for *float*, *TRAYN* for *train*, *DRIEV* for *drive*)		Does your child read and understand short chapter books?
		Does your child spell common consonant digraphs and blends correctly? (For example, ***sl****ed*, ***dr****eam*, ***fr****ight*)		Does your child write multipage pieces?

TABLE 1.3 (*Continued*)

Level	Spelling Behaviors	Reading and Writing Behaviors
	Does your child spell complex consonant clusters correctly? (For example, *spe**ck***, *swi**tch***, *smu**dge***)	Does your child use correct punctuation at the end of sentences and correct capitalization?
	Does your child spell most other vowel patterns correctly? (For example, *sp**oi**l*, *ch**ew**ed*, *s**er**ving*)	
Intermediate Readers and Writers at the Syllables and Affixes Stage (Chapter 6)	Does your child spell most single-syllable words correctly?	Does your child read aloud with fluency and expression?
	Does your child spell most high-frequency words correctly?	Does your child write for a variety of purposes (For example, essays, journals, reports, stories)?
	Does your child struggle with spelling multisyllabic words?	Does your child include supporting information and detail in writing?
	Does your child add inflectional endings correctly? (For example, *rain**ing***, *walk**ed***, *chew**ed***, *hopp**ing***, *beach**es***, *show**er***)	Does your child use specialized vocabulary in writing?
	Does your child spell junctures between syllables correctly? (For example, *ca**tt**le*, *ce**ll**ar*, *ca**rr**ies*, *bo**tt**le*)	Does your child read for a variety of purposes in fiction and nonfiction?
	Does your child spell unaccented final syllables correctly? (For example, *bott**le***, *fortun**ate***, *civil**ize***)	Does your child revise and edit his or her own work?
	Does your child spell prefixes and suffixes correctly? (For example, ***mis**behave*, ***pre**pare*, *cell**ar***, *color**ful***)	Does your child use the spelling of word parts to understand word meaning?
Advanced Readers and Writers at the Derivational Relations Stage (Chapter 7)	Does your child spell most polysyllabic words correctly? (For example, *fortunate*, *confident*)	Does your child read a wide range of materials for a variety of purposes?
	Does your child struggle primarily with multisyllabic words derived from Latin and Greek?	Does your child write sophisticated and critical responses?
	Does your child spell assimilated prefixes correctly? (For example, *illiterate*, *correspond*, *succeed*)	Does your child have well-developed study skills, including textbook reading, note taking, adjusting reading rates, test taking, report writing, and reference work?
	Does your child use related words to spell unaccented vowels correctly? (For example, *conf**i**dent/conf**i**de*, *cust**o**dy/cust**o**dian*, *acad**e**mic/acad**e**my*)	

around them, and chime in, "Run, run, as fast as you can. You can't catch me. I'm the Gingerbread Man." Or they may tell you that the Gingerbread Man ran away from a little old man, a little old woman, and a cow. Although emergent learners are able to recite or retell familiar phrases or events of the story, they do not match their retellings to the actual print. They depend on picture cues and are unable to point to individual words or to distinguish among letters, words, and pictures. This is because emergent learners do not yet understand the connection between the spoken and written words. They simply mimic the reading and language of parents, caretakers, and teachers.

Emergent writers and spellers also use pretend writing and spelling at this stage. They mimic adult writing behavior. To illustrate this idea, consider the thoughts of one of our emergent writers. Anna, at age 4, drew rows of long, wavy patterns across the page and said to her mom, "Look, I'm writing like a grown-up." She then read the contents of her story about the time she and her friend Lynnie had gone to the park to collect leaves, pinecones, and small stones. Once emergent children understand that their ideas can be recorded, they scribble, draw, or create random strings of letters to communicate; however, parents and caretakers are unable to read the message, as an emergent writer has an incomplete or nonexistent knowledge of the alphabet. Children in the emergent stage do not use conventional letter–sound matches, a hallmark of the stage. Note in Figure 1.4 four examples of early emergent writing. In time, emergent learners learn that their spoken words can be written using a consistent correspondence between letters and sounds.

In Figure 1.5, Christopher, a kindergarten student, writes about his trip to the aquarium. His picture depicts a rich oral story in which he tells his listeners all about the sea creatures he sees at the aquarium, and he is able to form and recognize some letters. His writing also reveals another story. Christopher understands that his ideas can be communicated in writing, and that he must use letters to do so. He has used 14 different upper-case letters and two figures that appear to be the number 1 in his writing. Interestingly, seven of these letters are in his name. It is actually common for children to learn and use the letters in their name first because they have personal significance. Still, Christopher has not made a connection between letters and sounds. There is no phonetic match between the letters and sounds. Christopher's

FIGURE 1.4 Early Emergent Writing

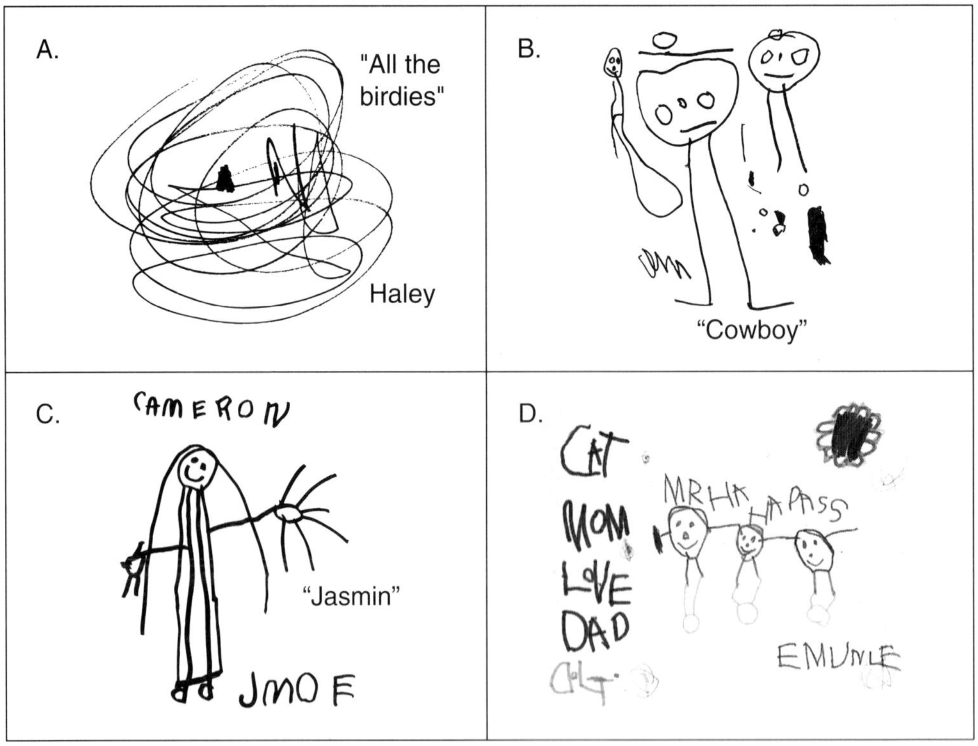

Source: From dissertation by Janet Bloodgood (1996). Adapted with permission.

piece is indecipherable to a reader because the letters lack a correspondence to sounds, and thus, his spoken words do not match his written ones.

You may also notice that he has used very few spaces between words. Although Christopher is learning that his thoughts may be recorded and read, he has not developed a **concept of word** in text, or the critical match between spoken words and written words. Letter sounds and plenty of practice fingerpoint reading memorized text are necessary to make that match.

In Figure 1.6, another kindergarten student, Mandy, has written about her day in the snow building a snowman. Her drawing provides a clear picture of the story she is trying to communicate and she has used a variety of letters. Most of the letters are capitalized and she uses four of the five letters in her name: *M, A, N,* and *Y.* She also uses the letters *I, T, U, O, C,* and *P,* with a few illegible forms. Mandy is most certainly working to learn the alphabet and will eventually match letters to sounds.

Chapter 3 contains detailed information on children's emergent reading, writing, and spelling, and extensive strategies to support development throughout this stage.

FIGURE 1.5 Christopher's Writing Sample in the Emergent Stage of Spelling

Source: From "*Words Their Way for Parents: How to Support Your Childs Phonics, Spelling, and Vocabulary Development*, 1st Ed." by Christopher. Copyright © 2018, by Alison Meadows.

FIGURE 1.6 Mandy's Writing Sample in the Emergent Stage of Spelling

Source: From "*Words Their Way for Parents: How to Support Your Childs Phonics, Spelling, and Vocabulary Development*, 1st Ed." by Mandy. Copyright © 2018, by Caitlin Miller.

Beginning Readers in the Letter Name–Alphabetic Stage of Spelling

Beginning readers in the **letter name-alphabetic stage of spelling** are typically kindergarten to early third grade. One of our first-grade students, Heather, shared her immense disappointment with her parents that she had not "learned to read" on the first day of school! This enthusiasm and high expectations are typical of beginning readers. Children at this stage are able to point to individual words. This allows them to remember words that they've seen repeatedly during their fingerpoint reading and they begin to recognize a limited selection of words such as *mom, dad, dog,* and *I.* Through phonics instruction, they learn to decode or identify other words. Beginning readers appear to read fluently, when they are reading short, **predictable books** with plenty of picture support, such as Bill Martin and Eric Carle's *Brown Bear, Brown Bear, What Do You See?* Children read, "Brown Bear, Brown Bear, what do you see? I see a red bird looking at me. Red bird, red bird, what do you see? I see a yellow duck looking at me." In this example, children rely on their memory for the repeated pattern and the first letter of each word to read the story.

As children learn beginning consonant sounds and have repeated experienced fingerpoint reading in predictable texts, they begin to recognize simple words, often referred to as **sight words.** Teachers also introduce students to decodable and leveled readers that control the text for limited new words and patterns. Readers still rely on pictures, but they also use the beginning-letter sounds to determine what the words say. If there is a picture of a muffin on the page, the first letter *M* prompts the child to call out "muffin" regardless of the remaining letters. Children learn to examine all of the letters and parts of a word through the phonics instruction they receive in word study.

Beginning readers are letter name–alphabetic spellers. Initially, they use their knowledge of alphabet letter names in a very literal fashion. When they see a letter and say the name, the pronunciation of the name cues the letter sound. Most letter names contain the associated letter sound in the name; for example, children spell the word *I* with the letter *I* because there is a perfect match between the name and sound. They use the letter *R* for the word *are* or the letter *U* for the word *you.* This strategy is used to spell; children consider the letter to identify the letter sound. This is true for many—but not all—consonant letters, and is only partially true for vowels, which have at least two sounds. Beginning readers' letter name–alphabetic strategy is most apparent in their invented spellings of words that start with consonants that *don't* have the associated letter sound in its name, such as W ("double-yoo"). In searching for the letter associated with the /w/ sound at the beginning of *when*, early beginning readers often choose the letter name *Y* because the letter name *Y* contains the /w/ sound in its name. So the spelling of *YN* for *when* is phonetically accurate using letter–name logic.

Children at this stage write short pieces of writing requiring great concentration. To write a sentence, a child must consider their original thought, segment the sounds that make up the first word, choose the letters to match those sounds, then form the letters. This is a labor-intensive process because their phonics knowledge is quite limited and little is automatic. Teachers and parents can often read these pieces if they understand the letter–name logic behind the invented spellings.

Typical letter name–alphabetic writing and spelling are illustrated in Figures 1.7 and 1.8. Wendy, a first-grade student, writes a two-sentence story about a recent field trip to the Washington Monument: "The Washington Monument is big. I went to it with school," using invented spelling and a few **high-frequency words**. She correctly spells the words *the*, *is*, *big*, and *it*. She also uses her phonetic knowledge to spell the following words: WASHN for *Washington*, MANIUMIN for *monument*, WEN for *went*, WIT for *with*, and SCOOL for *school*. She supplies enough of a letter–sound match that readers are able to read the words. Also of interest is

FIGURE 1.7 Wendy's Writing Sample in the Letter Name–Alphabetic Stage of Spelling

Source: From "*Words Their Way for Parents: How to Support Your Childs Phonics, Spelling, and Vocabulary Development*, 1st Ed." by Wendy. Copyright © 2018, by Alison Meadows.

FIGURE 1.8 Tarik's Writing Sample in the Letter Name–Alphabetic Stage of Spelling

Source: From *"Words Their Way Online Workshop"* by Tarik. Used with permission of Alison Meadows.

Wendy's use of dashes between words. This is an early indication that Wendy is conscious of individual words. She is providing the reader with an additional cue for where her words begin and end. Soon she will understand that spaces are sufficient to indicate an individual word.

Similar to Wendy, Tarik in Figure 1.8 composes a single sentence with a detailed drawing of a print-rich classroom. He is writing a chapter book, and this page is about the classroom. He writes, "The classroom is for everyone." Common in letter name–alphabetic spellers, we note a heavy reliance on sound in the spelling of the word EZ for *is*, OL for *all*, and OV for *of*. Tarik is focused on identifying the match between sounds and letters.

Finally, Sumaya in Figure 1.9 also demonstrates writing and spelling in letter name–alphabetic stage of spelling in her poem "Being Myself." She writes:

Being Myself

Sometimes I'm a princess
Sometimes I'm a pirate
Sometimes I'm a mother
Sometimes I'm a ballerina
Sometimes I'm a teacher
Sometimes I'm a nurse
Sometimes I work for my sister, but
I like just being me.

FIGURE 1.9 Sumaya's Writing Sample in the Letter Name-Alphabetic Stage of Spelling

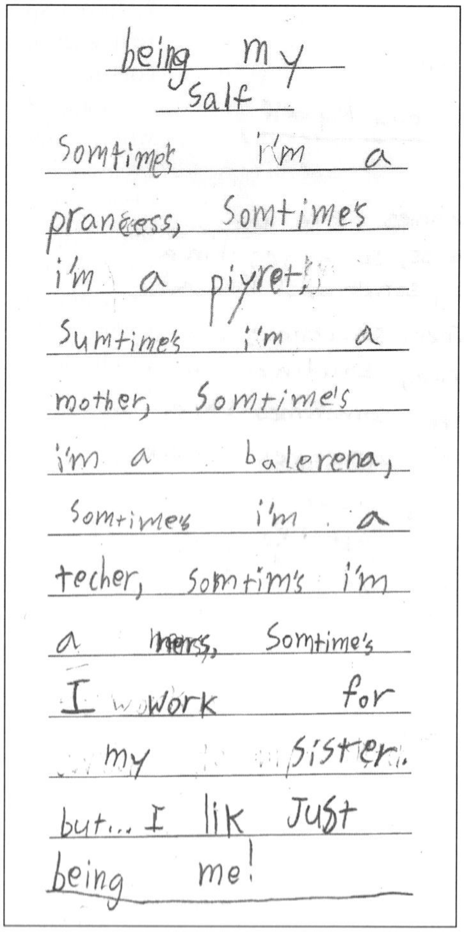

Source: From "*Words Their Way for Parents: How to Support Your Childs Phonics, Spelling, and Vocabulary Development*, 1st Ed." by Sumaya. Copyright © 2018, by Alison Meadows.

Sumaya demonstrates a clear concept of word, the understanding that words are separated by space, and she conveys her message clearly. She has spelled several words correctly, including *a, I, my, I'm, mother, for, but, sister* and *just*. She uses invented spelling and her additional spellings are largely dependent on sound letter correspondence as in PRANCES for *princess*, SOMTIMES and SUMTIMES for *sometimes*, BALERINA for *ballerina*, TECHER for *teacher*, PIYRET for *pirate*, and *LIK* for like. Although she understands that letters represent sounds and is skillful about their match, she does not yet recognize the need for additional letters to indicate long vowel sounds as in *teacher* and *like*. She is late in the letter name–aphabetic stage of spelling.

Chapter 4 contains detailed information on children's reading, writing, and spelling in this stage, as well as extensive strategies to support their development throughout the stage.

Transitional Readers in the Within Word Pattern Stage of Spelling

Transitional readers in the **within word pattern stage of spelling** are typically in first to mid fourth grade and have begun to read short chapter books ranging from series such as *Henry and Mudge* (Rylant), *Ivy and Bean* (Barrows), and *The Time Warp Trio* (Scieszka), to chapter books such as *The Chocolate Touch* by Patrick Catling. Transitional readers typically enjoy books written in series. These series provide the reader with familiar characters, style, and story structure. Children at this stage become more confident in their reading and take pride in counting and recording the number of books they have completed.

Transitional readers are able to recognize a large number of words automatically and have begun to develop other word recognition skills, such as using a familiar word like *lake* to decode an unfamiliar word like *mistake*. The actual rate or speed at which a child can read increases dramatically, and they are now able to read silently; consequently, the amount of reading also tends to increase from the previous stage.

In writing and spelling, there is also an increase in fluency, the ease with which children generate and write their ideas, and in the sheer amount of writing produced. Children are able to write and spell a large number of words automatically, without having to think consciously about letter formation or sounds. Narratives and reports reflect more detail and organization. Children spell single syllable, short vowel words correctly as well as a number of high-frequency words. Confusions in spelling primarily focus on long vowel patterns, complex consonant clusters (such as *dge* vs. *ge*, or *ck* vs. *k*) and *r*-influenced patterns (*ir*, *ar*, *er*, *or*, *ur*).

Each of these characterisics is showcased in Figure 1.10. Henry, a fourth-grade student, writes a multipage story about a day when his sister came home from college. He describes the events of his day: ordering a cheeseburger at Burger King, talking on the phone, excercising, and playing video games. His writing is organized around a single topic, and he has spelled many high-frequency words correctly, such as *one*, *came*, *I*, *and*, *we*, *for*, *after*, and *then*. Henry also spells most of the short vowel words correctly, including *win*, *put*, *his*, *back*, and *sister*. When we examine the common long vowel words, we notice that some are correct, as in *play*, and others are used but confused, as in CHESE for *cheese*, SWETING for *sweating*, and SPRAYE for *spray*. Henry knows that he needs an additional vowel to mark or indicate the long vowel sound and provides an extra letter in *cheese* and *spray*. During this stage, he learns that some patterns are more common than others. For example, the *ee* combination is far more common than *e-consonant-e*. He also learns that the vowel combination *ea* can be both long, as in *meat* and *feat*, and short, as in *bread* and *dead*.

In Figure 1.11, Caleb, a fourth-grade student, writes to his teacher about the book *Sammy Keyes and the Search for Snake Eyes* by Wendelin Van Draanen. The spelling in his journal response shows that he is using but confusing common long vowel patterns. He spells WEARD for *weird*, MOAST for *most*. The spellings of WITCH for *which*, WRIGHT for *right*, and CARCTERS for *characters* indicates his confusion with the silent letters so common in this stage. Even though these two samples are quite different, both are examples at the within word pattern stage of spelling development based on their spelling patterns.

Chapter 5 contains detailed information on children's reading, writing, and spelling in this stage and extensive strategies to support their development throughout the stage.

Intermediate Readers in the Syllables and Affixes Stage of Spelling

Intermediate readers in the **syllables and affixes stage of spelling** are typically in third through eighth grades. During this stage, children read and write with fluency. At this stage in the upper elementary and middle grades, reading and writing increasingly focus on content-area subjects. Background knowledge, experience, vocabulary, and the level at which a text is written all affect comprehension.

Intermediate readers read a variety of fictional texts representing a range of difficulty levels, such as *The One and Only Ivan* by Katherine Applegate (grade 3), *Hatchet* by Gary Paulsen (grade 4), *Star Girl* by Jerry Spinelli (grade 6), *Monster* by Walter Dean Myers (grade 8), or *Esperanza Rising* by Pam Munoz Ryan (grade 5). In addition to fiction or narrative texts, children read more expository (or informational) text, including high-interest topics such as *Blizzard! The Storm That Changed America* by Jim Murphy (grade 6), *We Are the Ship: The Story of Negro League Baseball* by Kadir Nelson (grade 7), or *Chasing Lincoln's Killer* by James Swanson (grade 8). Reading interests tend to specialize at this intermediate stage. They may become especially interested in specific authors, subjects, or types of books. Intermediate readers in the upper grades are expected to read, evaluate, and synthesize a variety of non-fiction texts including essays, photo-essays, textbooks, and Internet sources for a specific purpose. In school, students are asked to write research papers, lab reports, essays, blogs, and multimedia presentations. Content-area reading challenges intermediate readers with increasingly complex and unfamiliar vocabulary. To progress in their literacy development, intermediate readers benefit from large blocks of time devoted to reading and writing and discussion of word meanings. Word study instruction explores word parts and meanings.

Intermediate readers and writers are also expected to write and spell with increasing sophistication. As their reading becomes more varied, so does their writing. Students are

FIGURE 1.10 Henry's Writing Sample in the Within Word Pattern Stage of Spelling

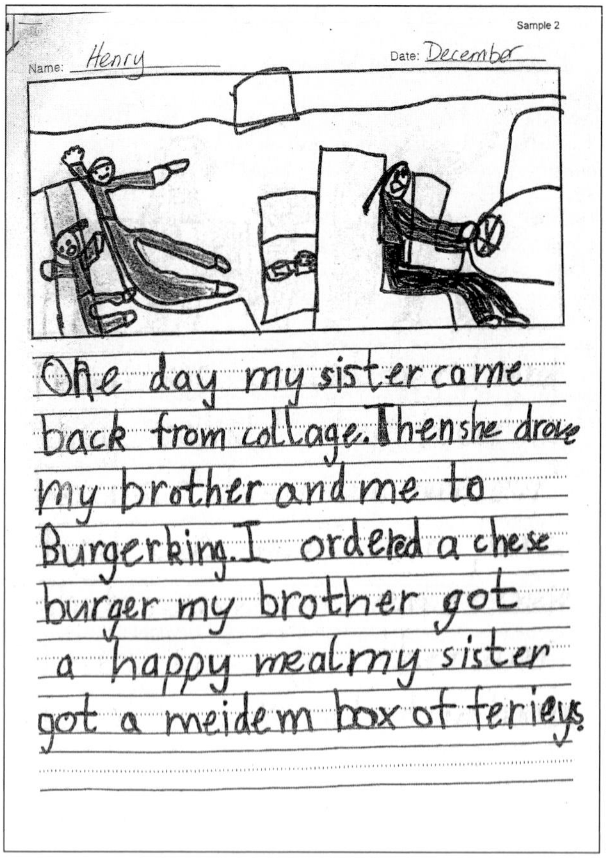
Sample 2

Name: Henry Date: December

One day my sister come back from collage. Then she drove my brother and me to Burgerking. I orderd a chese burger my brother got a happy meal my sister got a meidem box of ferieys.

Source: From *"Words Their Way Online Workshop"* by Henry. Copyright © by Pearson Education, Inc. Used with permission of Michele Picard.

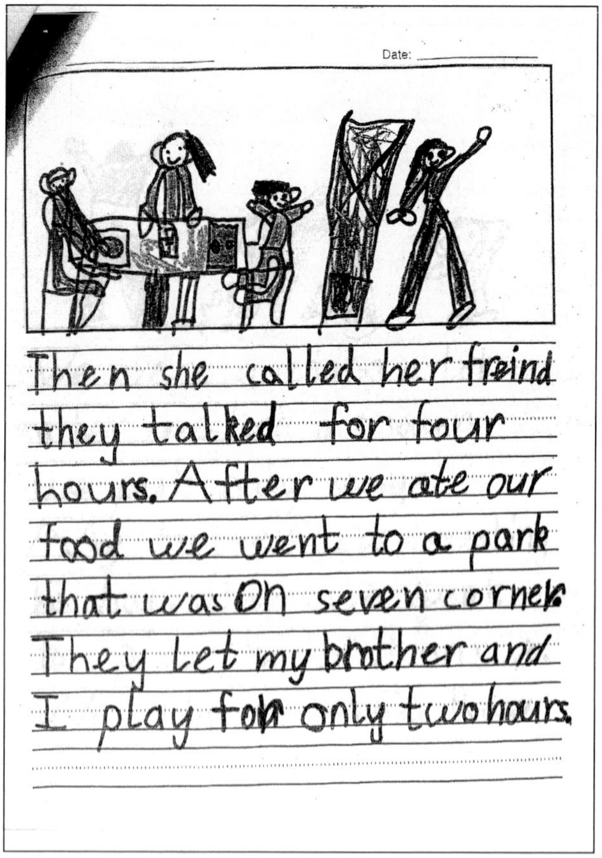
Date:

Then she called her freind they talked for four hours. After we ate our food we went to a park that was on seven corners They let my brother and I play for only two hours.

Source: From *"Words Their Way Online Workshop"* by Henry. Copyright © by Pearson Education, Inc. Used with permission of Michele Picard.

Name: Date:

We were sweting a lot after we took a shower we put body spraye. My brother was brushing his hair. Then we went to play play station two. We played Raw.

Source: From *"Words Their Way Online Workshop"* by Henry. Copyright © by Pearson Education, Inc. Used with permission of Michele Picard.

Name: Date:

My losing then I let him win. Then we were tiped then we went to sleep.

Source: From *"Words Their Way Online Workshop"* by Henry. Copyright © by Pearson Education, Inc. Used with permission of Michele Picard.

FIGURE 1.11 Caleb's Writing Sample in the Within Word Pattern Stage of Spelling

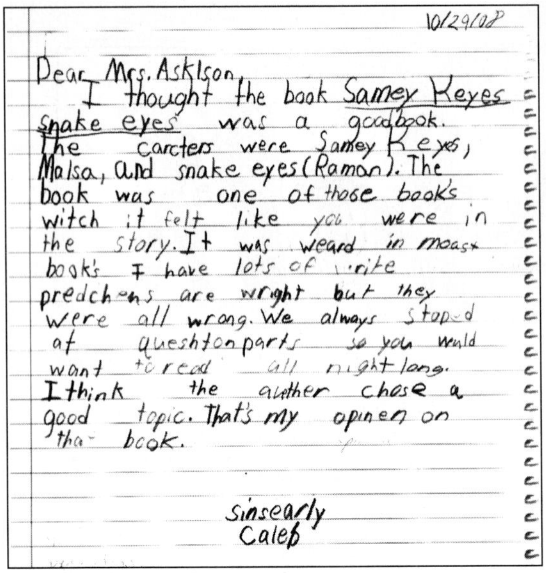
10/29/08
Dear Mrs. Asklson,
I thought the book Samey Keyes
snake eyes was a goodbook.
The carcters were Samey Keyes,
Malsa, and snake eyes (Ramon). The
book was one of those book's
witch it felt like you were in
the story. It was weard in moast
book's I have lots of write
predchens are wright but they
were all wrong. We always stoped
at queshtonparts so you wuld
want to read all night long.
I think the auther chose a
good topic. That's my opinen on
tha book.

sinsearly
Caleb

Source: From "*Words Their Way for Parents: How to Support Your Childs Phonics, Spelling, and Vocabulary Development*, 1st Ed." by Caleb. Copyright © 2018, by Michelle Picard.

FIGURE 1.12 Rudy's Writing Sample in the Syllables and Affixes Stage of Spelling

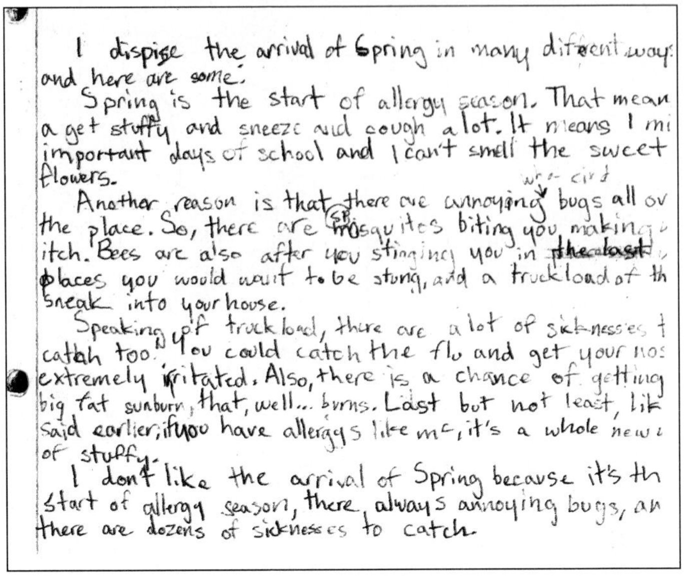
I dispise the arrival of Spring in many diffrent ways
and here are some.
Spring is the start of allergy season. That mean
a get stuffy and sneeze and cough a lot. It means I mi
important days of school and I can't smell the sweet
flowers.
Another reason is that there are annoying bugs all ov
the place. So, there are mosquites biting you makin
itch. Bees are also after you stinging you in the last
places you would want to be stung, and a truckload of th
sneak into your house.
Speaking of truckload, there are a lot of sicknesses t
catch too. You could catch the flu and get your nos
extremely irritated. Also, there is a chance of getting
big fat sunburn, that, well... burns. Last but not least, lik
said earlier, if you have allergys like me, it's a whole new
of stuffy.
I don't like the arrival of Spring because it's th
start of allergy season, there always annoying bugs, an
there are dozens of sicknesses to catch.

Source: From "*Words Their Way for Parents: How to Support Your Childs Phonics, Spelling, and Vocabulary Development*, 1st Ed." by Rudy. Copyright © 2018, by Alison Meadows.

asked to write essays, stories, journals, reports, observations, persuasive arguments, speeches, and general explanations. Upper elementary and middle-school teachers expect students to write pieces that are several pages in length, are organized, and provide supporting examples and evidence for each argument or explanation. Children are taught and expected to use clear organization, conventional punctuation, capitalization, and grammar. Also, teachers begin to consider tone, word choice, imagery, clarity, and overall composition.

In spelling, intermediate children have mastered single-syllable words with short and long vowel sounds and many high-frequency words. Intermediate children use but confuse spelling features in multisyllabic words. A large part of the stage focuses on what happens to spelling when syllables and affixes join. For example, a learner at this stage might study whether to double a final consonant when adding an inflected ending, such as the *p* in the word *shopping*, or whether to drop the final *e* before adding an inflected ending in words like *making*. Intermediate children may spell SHOPING for *shopping* and MAKEING for *making*. They are unclear as to when to drop the final *e* and when to double the final consonant when adding *-ing* and *-ed* endings.

In Figure 1.12, Rudy, a fourth-grade student, writes a witty description of the downside to spring. He despises spring because of allergies, bugs, and illness. This one-page essay is clearly organized, provides supporting examples, and includes the strong voice and sense of humor indicative of intermediate writers. His spelling is conventional and includes very few mistakes. Note that he spells single-syllable short and long vowel words correctly. He also represents multisyllabic words such as *sickness*, *annoying*, *irritated*, *getting*, and *arrival* correctly. Rudy's errors relate to more sophisticated prefixes and suffixes and the spelling changes associated with adding them on (DISPISES for *despises*, ALLERGYS for *allergies*). Rudy is late in the syllables and affixes stage.

In Figure 1.13 Megan, a fifth-grade student, has written a fiction story about finding a treaure chest, acting like pirates, finding gold, and having the luxury of wealth. Her piece is written in a series of clearly defined paragraphs. She uses dialog, increasingly sophisticated vocabulary such as *amazing*, *observed*, and *engraving*, and a creative title, "Yo, Yo, Yo, Ho, Ho." She spells most high-frequency short- and long-single syllable words correctly. Several spellings in the piece indicate that she is using but confusing spelling where syllables join together. For example, Megan spells STOPED for *stopped* and PAPPER for *paper*. These misspellings indicate that she is unsure when to double a consonant before adding an inflected ending such as *-ed* or *-er*. She confuses WRIGHT for *write* and misspells PIRETS

FIGURE 1.13 Megan's Writing Sample in the Syllable and Affixes Stage of Spelling

Yo, Yo, Yo, Ho, Ho

Megan January 3, 2008

"Thump, thump, thump, crash"
the door slames open. We all look
at Ms. Haus our teacher. We see her
holding a chest in her hands. We stoped
what we were doing and listend to Ms. Haus.

"Good morning class" she said.
"Good morning Ms. Haus" we all said.
"Today we are going to be like pirets. She
called us to the carpet to ubsury the chest.
We all started to search for the key.

I came across a papper. It kind of looked like
a note. I unfolded the papper and insid was the key.
I started to read the note. It sard "Dear new
owner, I hope you take care of this chest with care.
I'v left all the gold in there for you. I don't
want another fight whith other pirets.

If you want to wright back, then send it
to me by tomarow. I'm leaving for a treasure
hunt the nextday. Good luck Sinceearly Jack Sparow.

Source: From *"Words Their Way Online Workshop"* by Megan. Copyright © by Pearson Education, Inc. Used with permission of Michele Picard.

I was amosed. I told Ms. Haus.
"I found the key!" We opend the chest
carfaly and slowly. The letter was write all the
gold was insid. We found ingraving that said
("To Megan Oliver"). I took it home. I got to
keep all of the loote.

The next day she told us the story. "It was
a blue box and it was heavy as she caried it to
her house. She bought it at the dock.

In my house everyone was happy that we
were rich. Now I can have enything I wan't like
chocolat. That would be good. I hope that
I can tell someone els my story soon.

Source: From *"Words Their Way Online Workshop"* by Megan. Copyright © by Pearson Education, Inc. Used with permission of Michele Picard.

for *pirates*, CARFULY for *carefully*, and SINCEARLY for *sincerely*, among others. All errors indicate that she is in the syllables and affixes stage of development.

Chapter 6 contains detailed information on children's reading, writing, and spelling in this stage and extensive strategies to support their development throughout the stage.

Advanced Readers in the Derivational Relations Stage of Spelling

Advanced readers in the **derivational relations stage of spelling** are typically in grades 5 to 12. Characteristics of children in this stage mirror those in the previous intermediate stage who are negotiating syllables and affixes. Children in both the intermediate and advanced stages have increasingly varied and complex reading and writing assignments. They are asked to use multiple sources, read critically, and synthesize their own ideas with newly acquired knowledge. Nonfiction selections such as essays, textbooks, newspaper or Internet sources, and expository pieces become staples in their reading. Advanced readers are able to read and understand a wide variety of reading material. There is considerable overlap between reading levels in the intermediate and advanced stages. Fiction examples at this stage include *Wonder* by R. J. Palacio, *The Secret Sky: A Novel of Forbidden Love in Afghanistan* by Atiya Abawi, *Whale Talk* by Christopher Crutcher, *Between Shades of Gray* by Ruta Sepetys, *I Know Why the Caged Bird Sings* by Maya Angelou, and *To Kill a Mockingbird* by Harper Lee. Nonfiction examples include *The Port Chicago 50: Disaster, Mutiny and the Fight for Civil Rights* by Steve Sheinkin, *Bomb: The Race to Build and Steal the World's Most Dangerous Weapon* by Steve Sheinkin, *The President's Been Shot* by James L. Swanson, and *How They Croaked: The Awful Ends of the Awfully Famous* by Georgia Bragg.

Derivational relations spellers are able to spell most words with simple prefixes and suffixes correctly. The few errors they make revolve around derivationally related words. Derivationally related words are words that have related meanings but a different part of speech as indicated by a derivational suffix. For example, although the words *reside* and *resident* are related in meaning, *reside* is a verb whereas *resident* is a noun, as indicated by the derivational suffix *-ent*. Although the vowel sound changes in the second syllable from a long-*i* sound in *reside* to an *uh* sound in *resident*, the spelling of the vowel remains the same to signal their relationship in meaning. The focus of this stage is learning about the spelling–meaning connections in derivationally related words. For this reason, word study is also is inextricably intertwined with vocabulary.

In Figure 1.14, Laura, a seventh-grade student, creates a fictitious journal entry for a social studies class. She describes her life as a married schoolteacher in Oklahoma during the Great Depression. Her writing is organized, incorporates historical facts, is expressive, and conveys a strong voice. The assignment reflects the expectation for synthesis of reading multiple sources and learning about this period in time. She does not appear to have any spelling errors. Writers at this stage commonly avoid words that they cannot spell, and use alternate words or spellcheck.

Chapter 7 contains detailed information on supporting children's reading, writing, and spelling in the derivational relations stage, and extensive strategies to support their development throughout this stage. Table 1.4 provides an overview of the stages of literacy discussed in this chapter and in the subsequent chapters.

FIGURE 1.14 Laura's Writing Sample in the Derivational Relations Stage of Spelling

Social Studies Fictitious Journal Entry

Depression is in the air everywhere. I have not had the money to pay for something to write with for such a long time. The 1920's were such a wonderful time. I was dancing and singing in clubs a few years ago, and now I am just struggling to keep my home.

I married ten years ago, (wow, was it really that long ago?) when I was twenty-nine years old to a man named Henry Johnson. We moved out to Oklahoma, and had two children. My oldest daughter is named Chloe after my mother, and my youngest son is named Micheal.

Henry is a farmer, and I am working as a schoolteacher, but these past few years, neither of us have made much money. No one has. Farmers goods are not worth as much as they used to be. Many people have lost their jobs, and banks have closed down. People bought things on credit and invested in the stock market during the twenties, and when the stock market crashed in 1929, many people lost thousands of dollars. Henry and I had bought some stocks, and we have some debt from credit, but not so much that we were devastated by the loss. My brother Liam and his wife lost so much money that they had to sell their house. Luckily, they do not have any children and were able to move in with my brother Aidan and his family.

We did not have to sell anything of ours at first, but with business down, we are losing money quickly. I felt upset that my children will not get to experience a better childhood financial situation than I did, but there is nothing we can do. Henry made Micheal a small model train and I sewed him a teddy bear out of some old feed sacks, knowing that we would not be able to buy him real toys.

On top of everything, in Oklahoma, we have to deal with dust. Because the land was over cultivated to produce more crops during the war, the dirt is very loose, and dust storms come, making the sky pitch black and your mouth with a gritty feel all of the time. The dust storms are enough to kill someone, and we have to take many precautions at any sign of a storm.

Times are hard, but I have much more faith in our new president than I did in our last one. Our last president, Herbert Hoover was popular because of his work during the Great War, but I never agreed with his views on the economy. Franklin Delano Roosevelt (FDR) seems like his presidency will help the country more than Hoover's did. Roosevelt gives me much more faith in the banks and the government. His inaugural speech was broadcast on the radio yesterday, and he said that "The only thing we have to fear is fear itself." I think that this was very wise of him. He is going to start something called "Fireside Chats" where he will be on the radio to talk about what the government is doing to help the economy out of this financial crisis. "The New Deal" is what he calls his plan. A new deal is definitely what everyone needs these days.

Source: From "*Words Their Way for Parents: How to Support Your Childs Phonics, Spelling, and Vocabulary Development, 1st Ed.*" by Laura. Copyright © 2018, by Michelle Picard.

TABLE 1.4 Stages of Literacy Development: Characteristics of Readers, Writers, and Spellers

	Emergent Readers in the Emergent Stage of Spelling	Beginning Readers and Writers in the Letter–Name Alphabetic Stage of Spelling	Transitional Readers and Writers in the Within Word Pattern Stage of Spelling	Intermediate Readers and Writers in the Syllables and Affixes Stage of Spelling	Advanced Readers and Writers in the Derivational Relations Stage of Spelling
Reading Characteristics	*Emergent Readers* Typically preschool to mid first-grade students Engage in retelling of stories; pretend reading Unable to match speech to print or identify individual words Lack the understanding that English text is read from left to right (directionality) Pretend reading: fluent recitation or retelling as reading	*Beginning Readers* Typically kindergarten to early third-grade students Read predictable, decodable, and/or leveled text Developing a concept of word and the ability to identify word on the written page Beginning to recognize some words by sight Able to sound out or decode words Often point to the words on the page as he or she reads Read at a slow, labored pace Use picture clues to support comprehension	*Transitional Readers* Typically first- to early fourth-grade students Read short chapter books; an increasing number of words Shift to silent reading (faster than oral) Read with increased fluency and expression Read texts with less picture support and more text Recognize a larger number of words automatically	*Intermediate Readers* Typically third- to eighth-grade students Read fiction and nonfiction texts ranging from third- to eighth-grade level Focus on nonfiction texts Read with fluency and expression Background knowledge, experience, and vocabulary affect comprehension significantly Word knowledge closely tied to vocabulary growth Word recognition (and spelling) focused on polysyllabic words	*Advanced Readers* Typically fifth- to twelfth-grade students Read fiction and nonfiction texts for a variety of purposes ranging from fifth- to twelfth-grade level Focus on nonfiction texts Background knowledge, experience, and vocabulary significantly affect comprehension Word knowledge closely tied to vocabulary growth Read with fluency and expression
Writing Characteristics	*Emergent Writers* Pretend writing Scribble letters and numbers and symbols to represent ideas Unable to match letters and sounds Use drawing to represent ideas Neglect to space "words"; sometimes use lines and dots to separate ideas	*Beginning Writers* Use invented spelling Demonstrate an overreliance on sound Use limited number of high-frequency words Write short pieces of text Express an egocentric perspective	*Transitional Writers* Use a number of high-frequency words correctly Write multiple paragraphs and pages Use short vowel words correctly Write with increasing fluency, voice, expression, and organization Can elaborate their ideas by adding information	*Intermediate Writers* Write for a variety of purposes (reports, essays, journals, stories) Write with increased organization, fluency, and expression Provide supporting information and detail Use sophisticated and specialized vocabulary	*Proficient Writers* All of the preceding characteristics Write responses that are sophisticated and critical

(Continued)

TABLE 1.4 Stages of Literacy Development: Characteristics of Readers, Writers, and Spellers (*continued*)

	Emergent Readers in the Emergent Stage of Spelling	Beginning Readers and Writers in the Letter–Name Alphabetic Stage of Spelling	Transitional Readers and Writers in the Within Word Pattern Stage of Spelling	Intermediate Readers and Writers in the Syllables and Affixes Stage of Spelling	Advanced Readers and Writers in the Derivational Relations Stage of Spelling
Spelling Characteristics	*Emergent Spellers* Incomplete knowledge of alphabet Spelling lacks letter–sound correspondence	*Letter–Name Alphabetic Spellers* Applies the alphabet literally, using the letter names to spell letter sounds Spells phonetically, representing one sound for one letter Uses invented spelling Overreliance on sound Spells few words from memory or sight Spells name correctly	*Within Word Pattern Spellers* Spells most single-syllable short vowel words correctly Spells most beginning consonant digraphs (*th, sh, ch, wh*) and two-letter consonant blends correctly Attempts to use silent long vowel markers (NALE for *nail*) Spells many high-frequency words correctly and automatically (e.g., *the, they, and, I, like, from*)	*Syllables and Affixes Spellers* Spells most single-syllable short and long vowel words correctly Makes errors in polysyllabic words at the point of syllable juncture Spells most high-frequency words correctly	*Derivational Relations Spellers* Spells most words correctly Makes errors on low-frequency multisyllabic words derived from Latin and Greek combining forms Have mastered high-frequency words
Common Spelling Errors	Random strings of letters Drawings Scribbling	B, BD, BAD for *bed* S, SHP, SEP, SHP for *ship* S, SD, SAD, SED for *send* L, LP, LOP for *lump* B, BK, BAK for *back* DADT for *Daddy*	SNAIK for *snake* FELE for *feel* FLOTE for *float* BRIET for *bright* SPOLE for *spoil* CHUED for *chewed* CRAUL for *crawl*	SHOPING for *shopping* KEPER for *keeper* SELLER for *cellar* CONFUSSHUN for *confusion* PLESHURE for *pleasure* CAPCHUR for *capture* DISPOSUL for *disposal*	OPPISITION for *opposition* TERADACTIL for *pterodactyl* PROHABITION for *prohibition* EXHILERATE for *exhilarate* SOLEM for *solemn* CRITASIZE for *criticize* AMMUSEMENT for *amusement*

A BRIEF SUMMARY

In this chapter, we described the developmental model of spelling instruction known as *word study*, why word study is important, and how word study is different from traditional spelling. We also described the reading, writing, and spelling characteristics of learners in each of the five developmental stages, as well as how you as a parent can determine the spelling stage of your own child.

Understanding a developmental approach to literacy, and specifically the stage in which your child is performing, will inform you as to how you can support your child's development. Chapter 2 is a must-read for parents, tutors, and school volunteers because it outlines many of the techniques, strategies, and games that are used in a word study approach, both in schools and at home. Chapters 3 through Chapters 7 provide a comprehensive look at the five developmental stages of development: emergent, letter name–alphabetic, within word pattern, syllables and affixes, and derivational relations. Each chapter describes the stages of the child's reading, writing, and spelling characteristics; showcases writing examples; and explains useful activities and spelling strategies. In addition, each chapter contains a section on what you and your child need to know about sound, pattern, and meaning at each specific stage of development. All suggestions for parents, tutors, and school volunteers are designed to promote your child's literacy development and to support instruction at school. The final chapter, Chapter 8, is devoted to frequently asked questions and answers related to developmental spelling and overall literacy development.

REFERENCES

Bear, D. R., Invernizzi, M., Templeton, S., & Johnston, F. (2011). *Words their way: Word study for phonics, vocabulary, and spelling instruction* (5th ed.). Boston, MA: Pearson.

Carlisle, J. F. (2004). Morphological processes that influence learning to read. In C. A. Stone, E. R. Silliman, B. J. Ehren, & K. Apel (Eds.), *Handbook of langauge and literacy: Development and disorders (pp.* 318–339*)*. New York, NY: Guilford Press.

Ehri, L. C., & Wilce, L. (1987). Does learning to spell help beginners learn to read real words? *Reading Research Quarterly, 18*, 47–65.

Ganske, K. (2013). Word journeys: Assessment-guided phonics, spelling, and vocabulary instruction (2nd ed.). New York, NY: Guilford.

Helman, L. A., & Bear, D. R. (2007). Does an established model of orthographic development hold true for English learners? In D. W. Rowe, R. Jimenez, D. L. Compton, D. K. Dickinson, Y. Kim, K. M. Leander, & V. J. Risko (Eds.), *56th Yearbook of the National Reading Conference* (pp. 266–280).

Henderson, E. H. (1990). *Teaching spelling*. (2nd ed.). Boston, MA: Houghton Mifflin.

Henderson, E. H., & Beers, J. (Eds.). (1980). *Developmental and cognitive aspects of learning to spell.* Newark, NJ: International Reading Association.

Invernizzi, M., Juel, C., Swank, L., & Meier, J. (2006). *Phonological Awareness Literacy Screening for Kindergarteners (PALS-K).* Charlottesville, VA: University Printing Services.

Invernizzi, M., & Worthy, J. W. (1989). An orthographic-specific comparison of the spelling errors of LD and normal children across four levels of spelling achievement. *Reading Psychology, 10*, 173–188.

McCandliss, B., Beck, I. L., Sendak, R., & Perfetti, C. (2003). Focusing attention on decoding for children with poor reading skills: Design and preliminary tests of word building intervention. *Scientific Studies of Reading*, 7(1), 75–104.

Morris, D., Blanton, L., Blanton, W. E., Nowacek, J., & Perney, J. (1995). Teaching low achieving spellers at their "instructional level." *Elementary School Journal, 92*, 163–177.

Morris, D., Nelson, L., & Perney, J. (1986). Exploring the concept of "spelling instructional level" through the analysis of error-types. *Elementary School Journal, 87*, 181–200.

Schlagal, R. (1992). Patterns of orthographic development into the intermediate grades. In S. Templeton & D. Bear (Eds.), *Development of orthographic knowledge and the foundations of literacy: A memorial Festschrift for Edmund H. Henderson* (pp. 31–52). Hillsdale, NJ: Lawrence Erlbaum.
Templeton, S. (2011). Teaching spelling in the English/language arts classroom. In D. Lapp & D. Fisher (Eds.), *The handbook of research on teaching the English language arts* (3rd ed.). New York, NY: Routledge.
Templeton, S., & Bear, D. (Eds.). (1992). *Development of orthographic knowledge and the foundation of literacy: A memorial Festschrift for Edmund H. Henderson.* Hillsdale, NJ: Lawrence Erlbaum.

CHILDREN'S LITERATURE REFERENCES

Abawi, A. (2014). *The secret sky: A novel of forbidden love in Afghanistan.* New York, NY: Philomel Books.
Angelou, M. (2010). *I know why the caged bird sings.* New York, NY: Random House.
Applegate, K. (2015). *The one and only Ivan.* New York, NY: Harper Collins.
Barrows, A., & Blackall, S. (2006). *Ivy and Bean.* San Francisco, CA: Chronicle Books.
Bragg, G. (2011). *How they croaked: The awful ends of the awfully famous.* New York, NY: Bloomsbury Publishing.
Catling, P. S. (1952). *The chocolate touch.* New York, NY: Harper Collins.
Crutcher, C. (2009). *Whale talk.* New York, NY: Harper Collins.
Lee, H. (2014). *To kill a mockingbird.* New York, NY: Harper Collins.
Martin, B., & Carle, E. (1996). *Brown bear, brown bear, what do you see?* New York, NY: Henry Holt and Company.
Murphy, J. (2000). *Blizzard! The storm that changed America.* New York, NY: Scholastic.
Myers, W. D. (1999). *Monster.* New York, NY: HarperCollins.
Nelson, K. (2006). *We are the ship: The story of Negro League baseball.* New York, NY: Hyperion.
Palacio, R. J. (2012). *Wonder.* New York, NY: Alfred A. Knopf.
Paulsen, G. (1987). *Hatchet.* New York, NY: Aladdin Paperbooks.
Ryan, P. M. (2000). *Esperanza rising.* New York, NY: Scholastic.
Rylant, C. (1987). *Henry and Mudge in puddle trouble.* New York, NY: Aladdin Paperbacks.
Schmidt, K. (1985). *The gingerbread man.* New York, NY: Scholastic.
Scieszka, J. (1991). *The time warp trio: Knights of the kitchen table.* New York, NY: Puffin Books.
Sepetys, R. (2011). *Between shades of gray.* New York, NY: Philomel Books.
Sheinkin, S. (2014). *The Port Chicago 50: Disaster, mutiny and the fight for civil rights.* New York, NY: Roaring Brook Press.
Sheinkin, S. (2012). *Bomb: The race to build and steal the world's most dangerous weapon.* New York, NY: Roaring Brook Press.
Spinelli, J. (2000). *Star girl.* New York, NY: Alfred A. Knopf.
Swanson, J. L. (2013). *The president's been shot: The assassination of John Fitzgerald Kennedy.* New York, NY: Scholastic.
Swanson, J. L. (2009). *Chasing Lincoln's killer.* New York, NY: Scholastic.
Swanson, J. L. (2013). *The president's been shot: The assassination of John Fitzgerald Kennedy.* New York, NY: Scholastic.
Van Draanen, W. (2003). *Sammy Keyes and the search for snake eyes.* New York, NY: Yearling.

chapter 2

Word Study Basics

Source: Rob Marmion/Shutterstock

In this chapter, we provide an overview of what a high-quality word study program looks like in schools and describe the 10 guiding principles of word study instruction. We describe typical word study routines and provide step-by-step guidance for instructional activities you can use to support your child's development of spelling, word recognition, reading, writing, and vocabulary. If your child is not participating in a school that uses word study, you will still find this chapter useful as the activities and techniques described may serve as an engaging set of family games designed to support spelling and reading development.

In either case, we recommend that you talk to your child's teacher about what instruction looks like in the classroom during reading, writing, and spelling, and how you can assist your child. Table 2.1 outlines a few questions that may facilitate a productive conversation. Also, consider purchasing a set of picture and word sorts commensurate with your child's stage of development and use the guidance throughout this text to support your child's literacy development. Table 2.2 provides a list of the supplemental texts for *Words Their Way: Word Study for Phonics, Spelling, and Vocabulary*.

TABLE 2.1 Questions to Ask Your Child's Teacher

1. Describe my child's stage of development: Reading? Writing? Spelling?
   Is he or she below, meeting, or exceeding typical grade-level expectations?
2. Share any assessments of reading, writing, and spelling you have used with my child. How can they help us to support him or her?
3. Do you have a weekly routine for spelling, reading, and writing? What is it and how can we support you and our child with the routines? Are there homework routines?

Word Study in the Classroom

Although developmental spelling is common in many school systems, it is not in all of them, and the implementation varies based on the training opportunities provided to teachers, resources allocated to instruction, and time. Following are some of the key characteristics you are likely to see in a school implementing developmental spelling instruction:

- ✓ **Assessment:** Students are assessed using a qualitative spelling inventory three times a year, and teachers use short, quick checks of progress with spelling features.
- ✓ **Small Group Instruction:** Teachers explicitly teach small-group word study lessons at least three times per week based on assessment. Instruction is differentiated for each group's needs.
- ✓ **Integrated:** Word study lessons are integrated with reading and writing instruction. Students have multiple opportunities to manipulate/sort words and write and read those words in a variety of ways until they become automatic. Teachers prompt students to connect word knowledge when they are reading or writing unfamiliar words.
- ✓ **Routines:** Classrooms have a weekly word study routine including a variety of word study activities designed to promote thinking and fluency in categorizing words (sorts, speed sorts, writing sorts, hunts, dictations, games, and reflections).

TABLE 2.2 Sorts for Spellers of All Stages

Stages of Spelling Development	Books with Sorts and Explanations
Emergent	*Words Their Way Letter and Picture Sorts for Emergent Readers* by Johnston, Templeton, Invernizzi, and Bear
Letter Name–Alphabetic	*Words Their Way Sorts for Letter Name Alphabetic Spellers* by Bear, Invernizzi, Johnston, and Templeton
Within Word Pattern	*Words Their Way Sorts for Within Word Pattern Spellers* by Templeton, Johnston, Invernizzi, and Bear
Syllables and Affixes	*Words Their Way Sorts for Syllables and Affixes Spellers* by Templeton, Johnston, Invernizzi, and Bear
Derivational Relations	*Words Their Way Sorts for Derivational Relations Spellers* by Templeton, Bear, Invernizzi, and Johnston

✓ **Word Study Notebooks:** Students maintain word study notebooks in which they keep their word study assignments and reflections of the underlying spelling principles.
✓ **Rich Discussions:** Students and teachers routinely discuss the underlying spelling principles or the big ideas—how understanding sound, patterns, and meanings within words helps them to be better readers, writers, and spellers.

Although your child's school may not yet be implementing all the components of developmental spelling listed, you can integrate these core characteristics at home in your own study of words and discussion of their patterns.

The Role of Word Sorting

Sorting is at the heart of word study. It is the core activity which guides children toward understanding spelling patterns and applying them in reading and writing. Categorizing is a fundamental way that humans make sense of their world. We naturally seek order by finding similarities among various objects, events, ideas, and concepts. Word study builds on this natural way of looking at the world by guiding children to find commonalities in how words are spelled.

Sorting allows students to construct their own knowledge as they discover, on their own, the similarities and differences among words. The teacher has supported this learning by carefully providing sorts with contrasting sounds and associated patterns. The basic process of sorting remains consistent across the five stages and is described in detail later in this chapter as we review the essential word study routines and techniques. Within this process are many sorting variations that can be done independently, or with a teacher or a partner.

There are three basic types of sorts that reflect the three layers of English language described in Chapter 1: **sound sorts**, **pattern sorts**, and **meaning sorts**. Sound sorts are primarily conducted using pictures at the emergent and letter name–alphabetic stages. Children are asked to name each picture, listen carefully for a specific sound, and then sort the pictures accordingly under **headers** with **key pictures** or letters. In Figure 2.1, children sort pictures by beginning sound under headers with the upper- and lower-case letters and a picture key. In Figure 2.2, children at the letter-name stage conduct a sound sort with long and short *i* pictures.

FIGURE 2.1 Sound Sort for Beginning Sounds

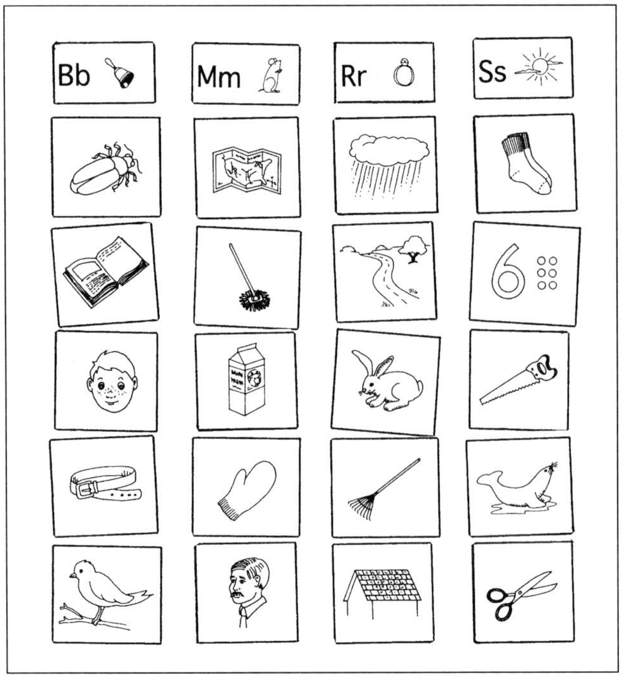

Source: Donald R., *Words Their Way*, 6th Ed., © 2016. Reprinted and Electronically reproduced by permission of Pearson Education, Inc., New York, NY.

FIGURE 2.2 Sound Sort for Long and Short *i*

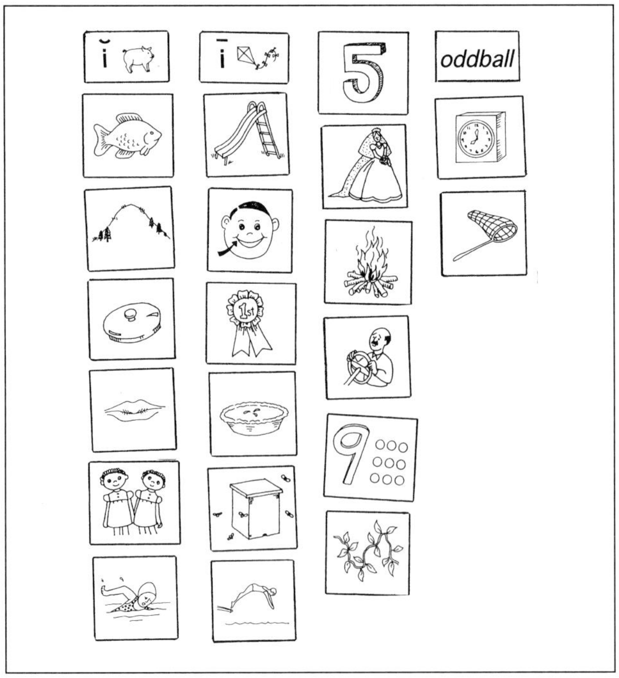

Source: Invernizzi, Marcia R.; Johnston, Francine; Bear, Donald R.; Templeton, Shane R., *Words Their Way: Word sorts for within word pattern spellers*, 1st Ed., ©2004. Reprinted and Electronically reproduced by permission of Pearson Education, Inc., New York, NY.

Although sorting pictures by sound is common at the early stages, sound sorts can also be done with printed words. For example, a group of words with *a* may be sorted by sound into short *a* and long *a* words without regard to the spelling patterns; *rain*, *gate*, and *stay* would all be sorted together because they have the same long *a* sound, as would *hat*, *stag*, and *have*, which all have the short *a* sound.

In pattern sorts, children attend to the patterns made by specific groups of letters or letter sequences in words. For example, letter-name spellers sort by rhyming word families (*hat*, *rat*, *fat* versus *map*, *cap*, *sap*) looking at the letter patterns that represent each rhyming family (*-at*/*-ap*) as seen in Figure 2.3. Within word pattern spellers may sort by long vowel patterns (*cone*, *hope*, *stone* versus *road*, *soap*, *float* versus *show*, *blow*, *know*) as they examine the different ways to spell the long *o* sound. Many pattern sorts are also used in a complementary way with sound sorts. In the example seen in Figure 2.4, children first sort by sound to discriminate between the sounds of short *o* and long *o*. They then sort by pattern to discover that the single sound of long *o* can actually be spelled multiple ways (Figure 2.5). Later, more advanced spellers sort to discover the more complicated consonant and vowel patterns.

Meaning sorts can be used to either expand understanding of vocabulary through concept sorts or to discover how meaning influences spelling through spelling–meaning sorts. **Concept sorts** can be used across all stages by sorting objects, pictures, or words into common categories based on meaning. With the youngest learners, children may sort buttons, dolls, toy animals, or other objects by common characteristics (Figure 2.6). Older students may sort science vocabulary words or terms from a reading selection (Figure 2.7). These types of sorts are highly useful for deepening understanding of concepts in content areas as well as expanding vocabulary.

Meaning sorts are also used to demonstrate the impact of meaning on spelling. Students quickly understand this core concept as they begin to learn about homophones; *maid* and *made* are spelled differently to indicate their different meanings. Conversely, words that are related

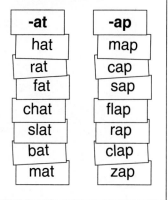

FIGURE 2.3 Sorting by Word Families *-at* and *-ap*

-at	**-ap**
hat	map
rat	cap
fat	sap
chat	flap
slat	rap
bat	clap
mat	zap

FIGURE 2.4 Sorting by Sound with Long *O* Patterns

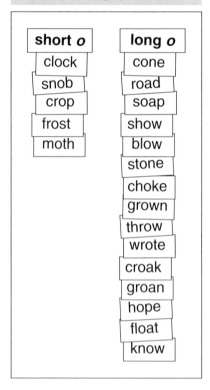

short *o*	**long *o***
clock	cone
snob	road
crop	soap
frost	show
moth	blow
	stone
	choke
	grown
	throw
	wrote
	croak
	groan
	hope
	float
	know

FIGURE 2.5 Sorting by Pattern with Long *O* Patterns

CVC short ŏ	**CVVC $\overline{\textbf{oa}}$**	**CVCe oCe**	**CVV $\overline{\textbf{ow}}$**
stop	boat	bone	snow
clock	road	cone	show
snob	soap	hope	blow
crop	float	stone	know
frost	groan	wrote	throw
moth	croak	choke	grown

FIGURE 2.6 Meaning Concept Sorts with Objects

Source: Michelle Picard

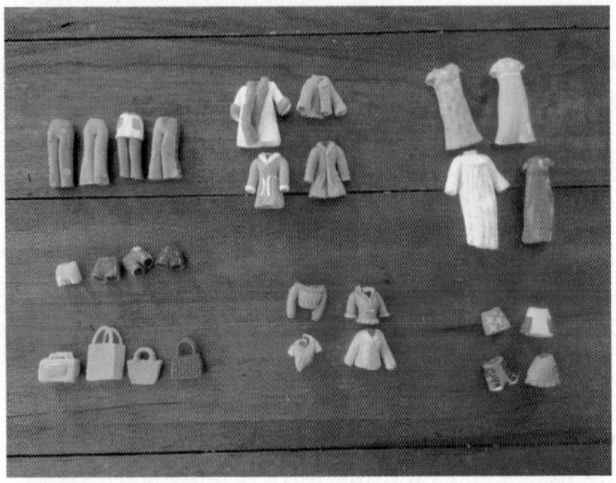

Source: Michelle Picard

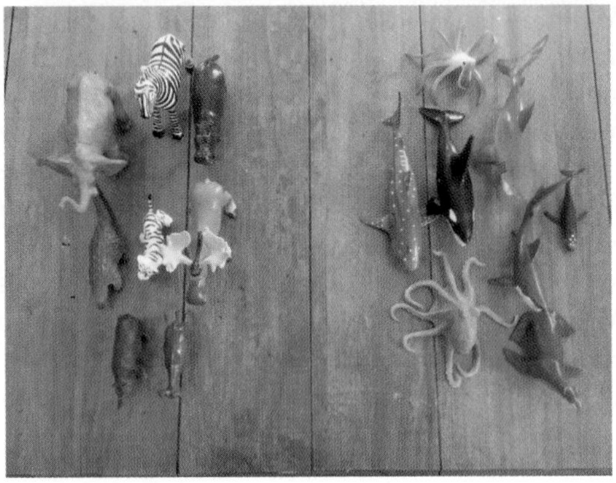

Source: Michelle Picard

in spelling often share similar spellings. In the late stages, students sort words by common roots and stems such as the *-spect* in *spectator*, *inspect*, and *spectacular* versus the *-port* in *transport*, *import*, and *portable* (Figure 2.8). Overall, sorting or categorizing words is at the heart of all word study learning.

FIGURE 2.7 Meaning Concept Sort with Reading Vocabulary

Weather	Boat Terms	Birds
squall	rigging	henbird
mist	bow	vireo
breeze	stern	wren
brisk	schooner	beak
ominous	helm	breast
cloudy	mainmast	
sunshiny	capsize	

A Sorting Example: *-ible* and *-able*

The best way to understand the power of word study is to do a sort together. Let's work through a sample sort for more advanced spellers. We next examine words with the spelling features *-able* as found in *dependable* and *-ible* as found in *edible*. Both *-able* and *-ible* are **suffixes**, that is, combinations of letters that can be added to the end of a word or a word **root**. Here are the words we will examine:

> *affordable, allowable, audible, breakable, comfortable, compatible, credible, dependable, edible, eligible, favorable, feasible, gullible, horrible, invincible, legible, preferable, predictable, punishable, reasonable, remarkable, visible*

The simple task of sorting these words by common features makes the *-ible* and *-able* patterns immediately apparent (Figure 2.9). It is not difficult to see that some words are spelled with *-able* and others with *-ible*. The real question is, when? When should we use the suffix *-ible* and when should we use *-able*? To figure this out, underline the **base word** or word stem, without the *-able* or *-ible* ending. Now, look to see any commonalities in each category. What do you notice? Do you see that the words with the suffix *-able* are added to a *base word*, a whole word, which can stand alone? For instance, if you take the *-able* off of *affordable*, you still have a whole word left in the base word, *afford*. What about the group with the suffix *-ible*? Is there a base word that can stand alone if you remove the *-ible*? Do you notice that the words with the suffix *-ible* are added to word roots or word stems that cannot stand alone? If you take the *-ible* off of *visible*, you have *vis*, a Latin stem meaning *to see*. The next step is to *reflect* on how *-able* and *-ible* appear to work, and to hypothesize when each is used.

FIGURE 2.8 Meaning Sort with Latin Roots

spect	***port***	***form***
inspection	export	conform
deformed	perspective	porable
retrospect	import	format
formation	spectator	transport
inspector	reporter	reform
transform	prospect	inportant
spectacle	spectacular	support
aspect	prospector	portfolio

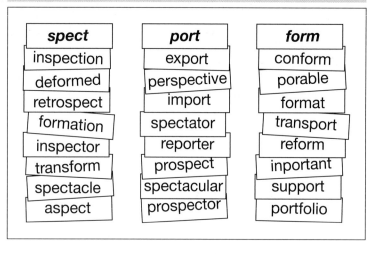

FIGURE 2.9 Suffix Sort with *-ible* and *-able*

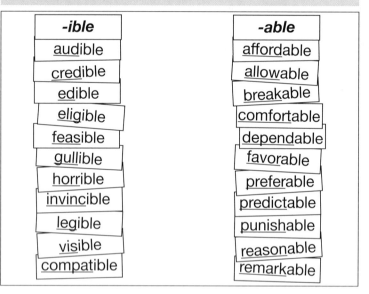

-ible	***-able***
audible	affordable
credible	allowable
edible	breakable
eligible	comfortable
feasible	dependable
gullible	favorable
horrible	preferable
invincible	predictable
legible	punishable
visible	reasonable
compatible	remarkable

The underlying concept for this sort, often referred to as the *big idea*, may be stated as follows:

> *The suffix -able is usually affixed (joined or added) to base words, whole words that have meaning independent of the prefixes or suffixes. The suffix -ible is usually affixed to word parts of Latin or Greek origin.*

Further discussion of this word sort may lead you to discover that adding these *-able* and *-ible* suffixes creates descriptive words (adjectives) that describe or tell what something is like. *Afford*, a verb, becomes *affordable*, the act of being able to purchase something. *Visible* describes something that can be seen. As you notice and categorize more words ending in *-able* and *-ible*, you may come to the generalization about these spellings: The suffixes *-ible* and *-able* indicate that a word is an adjective.

An important aspect of word study involves testing hypotheses and evaluating their consistency. In the case of *-able* and *-ible*, your hypothesis might be, "Add *-able* to base words that can stand alone; add *-ible* to word parts that cannot stand alone." To test this hypothesis, you would have to examine other words that end in *-able* and *-ible* to see if this generalization holds. As you read and write new words, you might encounter *combustible*, a word that does not support your hypothesis. Exceptions do exist in English, although by their very exceptionality, they are memorable.

Reflection within word study leads to gains not only in spelling but also in reading and writing. Once it is understood how *-ible* and *-able* affect the meaning of words, a student encountering an unfamiliar word, such as *deplorable*, can divide the word into parts. *Deplore* means to *disapprove*, *regret*, or *lament*, and *-able* means having "a quality of." A student who is able to read and write words with these known parts can also figure out the meaning of similar words.

As the *-able* and *-ible* sort has illustrated, word study engenders not only an understanding of how individual words can be spelled, but also an understanding of how specific spelling features work in other words. You may be familiar with the following proverb: "If you give a man a fish, you feed him for a day. If you teach a man to fish, you feed him for a lifetime." Word study is like teaching students to fish. Examining words and spelling features

FIGURE 2.10 Ten Principles of Word Study

Ten Principles of Word Study

1. Look for what students use but confuse.
2. A step backward is a step forward.
3. Use words students can read.
4. Compare words that "do" with words that "don't."
5. Sort by sound and sight.
6. Begin with obvious contrasts.
7. Don't hide exceptions.
8. Avoid rules.
9. Work for automaticity.
10. Return to meaningful texts.

leads not only to correct spelling, but to an understanding of how sound, pattern, and meaning work in other unfamiliar words. In the next section, we discuss the 10 principles of word study. As you read this section, consider how each of these principles are reflected in the sort with *-ible* and *-able*.

Ten Principles of Word Study Instruction

The 10 principles of word study instruction (Figure 2.10) guide word study and set the approach apart from other approaches to the teaching of phonics, spelling, and vocabulary.

LOOK FOR WHAT STUDENTS USE BUT CONFUSE Children and adults cannot learn things they do not already know something about. This is the underlying principle of **instructional level**. In Chapter 1, we refer to the instructional level as the "strike zone." The concepts are neither too difficult (above the shoulders) nor too simple (below the knees). By using a qualitative spelling inventory, instruction can be planned deliberately based on the spelling features that our children are using but confusing, instead of those that have been mastered or are completely absent.

A STEP BACKWARD IS A STEP FORWARD Once we identify a child's stage of developmental word knowledge and the spelling features under negotiation (using but confusing), take a step backward and build a firm foundation. Then, in setting up categories, contrast something new with something that is already known. It is important to begin word study activities where students will experience success. For example, children in the within word pattern stage of development who are ready to examine long vowel patterns begin by contrasting the known short vowel patterns with long vowel sounds that are being introduced for the first time. For example, words with the known short *o*, such as *cop*, *hop*, *stop*, *hot*, *got*, and *chop*, are compared to words with the new long *o* pattern (CVCe), as in *cone*, *hope*, *mope*, and *tone*. Children move quickly to sorting pattern. A step backward is the first step forward in word study instruction, which allows children to build on what they already know.

USE WORDS YOUR CHILD CAN READ Because learning to spell involves a match between the spoken language and the orthography, your child should analyze words that he or she can readily pronounce. It is easier to look across words for consistency of pattern when the words are easy to pronounce. Known words come from any and all sources that children can read. If your child continues to get stuck on a word, you can set that word aside for later study.

COMPARE WORDS THAT "DO" WITH WORDS THAT "DON'T" To learn what something *is*, you must also know what it is *not*. Contrasts are essential to building our own understanding of categories. For example, a very young child may refer to all men as "daddies" before they understand that a "daddy" is a man who has a child. Young children may initially refer to four-legged animals as dogs, until they discern the differences among animals. The same is true for learning how to spell with letters and sounds. Children learn that the letter–sound matches between *B* and *M* are distinct. They also learn that some letters have two sounds, such as the letter *C*, which is hard in words such as *cup*, *cap*, and *cot* and soft in words such as *circle*, *cent*, and *cycle*. Single sounds can also be represented with more than one spelling feature. For example, the sound /k/ as in *kite* can be spelled with a *C* as in *coach*, a *K* as in *keep*, the letters *CH* as in *chorus*. Contrasts allow children to reflect on how letters, sounds, and spelling features do and do not work in words.

SORT BY SOUND AND SIGHT We examine words by how they sound and how they are spelled. Both sound and visual pattern are integrated into our understanding of the layers of the English language. Too often, teachers, parents, and students focus on visual patterns at the expense of how words are alike in sound. The sorts in Figures 2.11 and 2.12

illustrate the way students move from a sound sort to a visual pattern sort. First, students sort by differences in sound between hard and soft *G*; then students subdivide the sound sort by orthographic patterns. See what you can discover from this sort.

You may notice that the sound of the letter *G* can be either soft as in *page* or hard as in *leg*. If you look closely, you will also discover that *G* is soft when followed by the letter *e*, and hard when in the final position in a single-syllable word. You may also notice in the second sort that *-dge* and *-ge* are both soft, whereas the final *-g* is hard. Sorting by sound and sight leads you to the understanding that the cluster *-dge* is used with short vowel, single-syllable words and *-ge* is used in words with long vowels. Sorting by sound and sight or pattern is critical to understanding the underlying generalizations in decoding and spelling.

FIGURE 2.11 Sort by Sound: Soft and Hard *G*

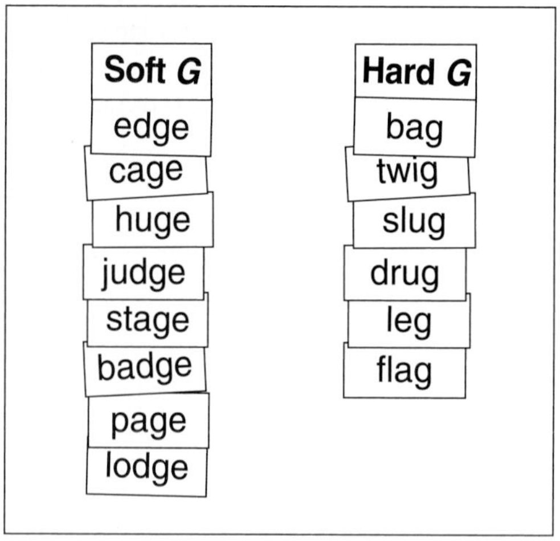

FIGURE 2.12 Sort by Pattern: Soft and Hard *G*

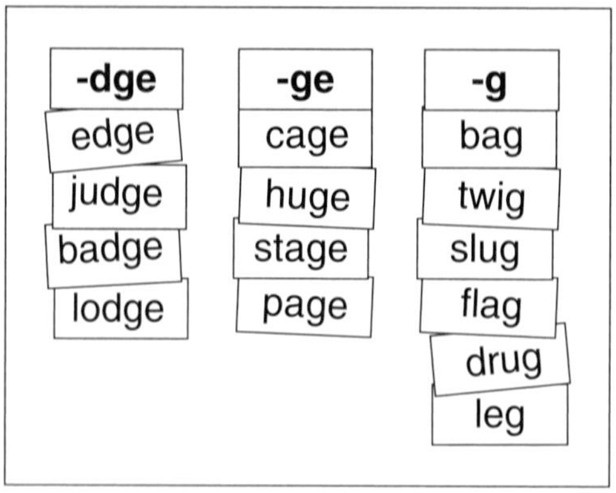

BEGIN WITH OBVIOUS CONTRASTS Teachers using a developmental spelling approach are sure to begin with obvious contrasts. For example, when children first examine initial consonants, teachers begin to contrast letters that are visually and phonetically different, such as *B* and *M*. These letters are completely different in the way they look and sound. It is better to begin by contrasting *M* with something totally different at first, such as *S*. It is important to begin with dissimilar letters and sounds before working toward finer distinctions as these categories become quite automatic. Move from general, gross differences to more specific discriminations.

DON'T HIDE EXCEPTIONS Exceptions arise when students make generalizations. Do not hide these exceptions. For example, in looking at long vowels, students find exceptions. In a long *a* sort, for example, words such as *said* and *have* appear to have common long patterns (*ai* and *aCe*). They do not, however, have the long vowel sounds; therefore they are considered **oddballs**.

AVOID RULES Teaching spelling rules suggests that there is a guarantee of accuracy, a 100% consistency. Although the English language is predictable and based on sound, pattern, meaning, and history, there are few—if any—rules that work 100% of the time. It is disingenuous to suggest such consistency, and disheartening to children to discover so many rule breakers. For example, one of the most common rules is, "When two vowels go walking, the first one does the talking," but this rule is frequently violated in words like *head*, *boot*, or *soil*. Some research reviews of the most common words have found that this rule is accurate less than 50% of the time.

Learning about English spelling requires students to consider sound and pattern simultaneously to discover consistencies in spelling. This requires both reflection and continued practices. We can support the development of generalizations by ensuring that the word or picture sorts make the consistencies (and inconsistencies) explicit, and to instill in children the habit of looking at words, asking questions, and searching for order. Rules are useful if you already understand the underlying concepts at work, but memorizing rules is not the way children make sense of how words work. Rules are no substitute for experience.

WORK FOR AUTOMATICITY Accuracy in sorting is not enough; accuracy and speed in spelling and reading are the sure sign of mastery. Acquiring **automaticity** in sorting and recognizing orthographic patterns leads to the fluency necessary for proficient reading and writing. Your child will begin each new sort by sorting with some hesitancy and deliberate thought, much like when we learn anything for the first time, like riding a bike or driving a car. With experience, your child will move toward accurate and automatic identification of sound, pattern, and meaning units in words. Keep sorting until they do. Ultimately, your child will recognize and write the spelling features automatically!

RETURN TO MEANINGFUL TEXTS After sorting, children should return to meaningful texts to hunt for other examples to add to their categories. These hunts allow students to include more difficult vocabulary. For example, after sorting one-syllable words into categories labeled *cat*, *drain*, and *snake*, a student added *tadpole*, *complain*, and *relate*. Through this simple **word hunt**, this child extended the pattern-to-sound consistency in one-syllable words to stressed syllables in two-syllable words.

The 10 principles of word study in Figure 2.10 can be boiled down to one golden rule of word study instruction: *Teaching is not telling* (James, 1958). In word study, children sort and analyze words in order to develop understanding about how sound, pattern, and meaning function in the English language.

Effective Practices in Word Study

Effective classroom word study instruction consists of clear weekly routines for word study. Most teachers choose to follow a 5-day cycle, with the new set of contrasting spelling features introduced on Monday and assessed on Friday. Although this is the most common schedule, teachers make adjustments to best fit their needs. Consistent routines provide instructional support for the students both at school and home. When students are familiar with the routines and procedures of word study, they are able to fully focus their attention on the new patterns and words to be studied.

In schools, the *sort* is the key to word study instruction. Students are given a sheet of paper with 15–24 pictures or words as seen in previous figures, which represent at least two different spelling features. Depending on the stage, these sorts may include all pictures, all words, or a combination of both. Students cut apart the cards so that they may sort or categorize them by sound and/or pattern. Focusing on this weekly sort, a wide variety of word study instructional strategies are used by the teacher in small group instruction throughout the week and complemented by related activities in independent and sometimes homework activities. Small word study groups are formed based on the student's assessment information. Teachers meet with each small group 3–5 times per week. The teacher leads a lesson or observes students as they work with partners, provides feedback, and prompts students to look and listen for similarities and differences among the words and spelling features. Teachers also assess their students' progress. Weekly instructional routines center around six word study essentials: sort introduction, daily sorting, writing sort, word hunt, reflecting on the underlying principle or the big ideas, and the use of word study notebooks. Ideally, all of these techniques are a part of the weekly routine and can be repeated at home. You may choose to briefly review these techniques now, and then revisit the steps in more detail when you have read the stage most appropriate for your child and are ready to try out some of these activities. This section is intended to give you step-by-step guidance while you are implementing the described techniques.

Essential Techniques

Although there are many different activities that can be used in word study, we have found that there are six essential techniques that should be included within each word study cycle (Table 2.3). These essential techniques ensure that children learn not only the words in the sort, but also the underlying principles of the patterns in order to be able to apply them to any word. Students learn how to apply this knowledge in reading, writing, and spelling. It is helpful for parents and tutors to understand these techniques that are used regularly in word study classrooms. In order to support the classroom instruction at home, step-by-step guidelines are provided for each of the essential techniques. These are the steps used by teachers in the classroom and could easily be used at home as well.

TABLE 2.3 Essential Word Study Techniques

Six Essential Instructional Techniques in a Developmental Spelling Program	
1. Sort Introduction	Begin by modeling or directing the student sort. The sort is designed to explicitly teach spelling features in a child's instructional level.
2. Daily Sorting	Children and young adults engage in sorting several times in a day to develop fluency, automaticity, and understanding. Speed and accuracy matter as much as the underlying principles.
3. Writing Sort	Similar to sorting, a writing sort allows learners to hear a word and write it into the appropriate spelling feature category. Ultimately, writing sorts bridge our understanding from recognition to actually spelling the word in context.
4. Word Hunt	In a word hunt, parents, teachers, and children have the opportunity to identify words from familiar text that follow and do not follow the spelling features under study. This increases the vocabulary words in the sort and also explicitly connects reading and writing in text.
5. Reflection	Each week, conversation and inquiry leads to a new understanding about sound, pattern, and meaning. Guidance for leading the discussion and reflection is in the "Let's Talk About It" sections.
6. Word Study Notebooks	In schools, each student keeps a record of all of his or her work in a single notebook. This may include copied sorts, word pictures, sentences, collections of words, word hunts, timed speed sort, vocabulary collections, dictations, writing sorts and more. This notebook demonstrates growth over time, and also serves as a reference for your child.

SORT INTRODUCTION The beginning of a word study cycle always begins with a *sort introduction*. If your child is in a school using word study, the teacher completes this sort introduction with a small group. If not, you can follow the same steps to introduce sorts at home. An adult with one set of sort cards conducts the sort introduction. It is important, because children generally need our guidance in order to discover how sound, pattern, and meaning work in words. Effective word study instruction requires directed explicit teaching that also allows for student-centered discoveries.

1. ***Introduce words.*** Begin by reviewing each of the words in the sort to make sure the child can read all of the words and understand each word's meaning, discussing new vocabulary as needed. During the introduction, it is important to note that words often have multiple meanings. For example, the simple word *stand* can refer to the following contexts or definitions: a music *stand*, a lemonade *stand*, to physically *stand*, to make a political *stand*, and so on. In addition, for picture sorts, it is important that children know the correct label for each picture in this sort. Students learning English as a new language spend significantly more time learning new vocabulary. Although this is important, remember that the lesson is focused on spelling and word recognition.
2. ***Display headers.*** Display the headers in the sort. Headers are key words or pictures that go at the top of each group and identify the category. Some headers may have a picture and a word example on the same card. Display and discuss these headers and the sounds, patterns, or meanings they represent.
3. ***Model sorting.*** After introducing the words and headers, model the "compare and contrast" process of sorting. At this point, you are usually still the only one with the sort in hand. The child observes and listens as you think aloud while modeling sorting individual words. For example, in a sort comparing pictures that begin with *sh-* and *th-*, you might say, "Ship, shhhip, shhhip. I hear the */sh/* sound like in *sheep*, so I will put *ship* under the

header that says *sh-* under the picture of the sheep." Continue modeling several words in this fashion, alternating examples from each category.

4. ***Ask children to help with sorting.*** Once students are beginning to grasp the concept of the sort, the teacher asks them to help place the words into categories. Students take turns following the same procedure, analyzing and placing words by comparing them to the headers. The teacher may give each student a few words to place so that the entire sort is complete.
5. ***Check and reflect.*** Whenever children sort, they are asked to follow three steps: sort, check and reflect. This procedure begins in the sort introduction. To check, the child reads down each column of words to make sure they all belong in that category. Any words that may not belong are discussed and changed to the correct category. To reflect, the child discusses how the words have been sorted and why they have been sorted in this fashion. Teachers ask children to compare and declare what is the same and what is different about words within and across categories. This portion of the procedure is necessary to solidify understanding of not just the specific words, but also the reason the words have been grouped together by sound, pattern, or meaning. It is necessary to model how to reflect on the sort as children become accustomed to this process. Children can be prompted to reflect using these starters:

   - These words all …
   - All the words in this group …
   - I noticed that …
   - This word is an oddball because …

   The reflection conversation revolves around three key questions designed to focus on the general principles to be learned from the specific sort (Figure 2.13). Each stage chapter includes a section titled "Let's Talk About It," which describes in detail the process of reflecting and identifying the big ideas for each specific stage. Questions and prompts are provided for parents and teachers to support students as they explore phonics (sound), orthography (spelling patterns), and morphology (meaning). Additional guidance about specific features is also included in each chapter's *Sort Support* section.
6. ***Discuss oddballs.*** In many sorts, there are words or pictures that do not fit into the designated categories. These words are often referred to as *oddballs.* For example, in a sort that compares short *o* words, such as *hop*, with long *o* words with a silent *e*, such as *hope*, the word *come* would be considered an oddball. Although it has the same pattern as *hope*, it does not have the long *o* sound. Children enjoy identifying these oddballs; their differences are best remembered in contrast to the patterns they break. Although there are exceptions to spelling in English, they often form patterns of their own. For example, the words *have*, *love*, *dove*, and *give* are exceptions to the "silent *e* at the end of a word makes the vowel long" generalization or rule; however, these words all share the letter *v*.
7. ***Children sort, check, and reflect.*** After the initial sort introduction, the child completes the sort, check, and reflect routine with their weekly set of words with your support or on their own. Either way, check to make sure your child has correctly completed the sort.

FIGURE 2.13 Reflection Discussion Questions

Let's Talk About It!

- How are the words or pictures the same in each category?
- Are there any oddballs, words that do not appear to follow the pattern? Why?
- What can we learn from this sort? What are the underlying principles or the big ideas to be learned in this sort?

With the exception of the later stages, children are asked to "Say It and Lay It" when they sort; they should be saying each word out loud as they sort words under the appropriate headers. This ensures that the children are reading each word, rather than just looking for just a visual pattern. Learning to read and spell requires associating visual patterns with categories of sound and meaning.

DAILY STUDENT SORTING One of the goals of word study is to help students recognize and be able to spell specific spelling patterns accurately and automatically and to generalize these patterns to new words with similar sounds or meaning. Neither automaticity nor the ability to generalize the pattern to other words occurs without practice and opportunity. Consider when you learned to drive a car. As a novice, you had to deliberately think about how to start the car, the steps to back up, the amount of pressure on the gas and brake pedals, how to merge into traffic and change lanes, and following the speed limits. Over time, these and other considerations became less deliberate and more automatic. The same is true with reading, writing, and spelling. To support the accurate and automatic recognition and eventually the production of spelling features, daily sorting is an essential part of the word study routine. Students sort their words at least once a day, but likely multiple times as they may be sorting with the teacher, independently, and at home (Figure 2.14). Daily student sorting is important, because it builds an automatic recognition of spelling patterns as they relate to categories of sound or meaning.

FIGURE 2.14 Daily Student Sorting in Action

Source: Michelle Picard

During each sort, children are expected to continue the sort, check, and reflect routine. The last step in the routine, reflection, is the first step toward generalizing. By reflecting on how words in a given category are the same and how they are different from the words in the other category, children begin to understand the underlying principles that govern English spelling, principles that can be generalized to other words not yet studied.

1. ***Sort.*** After putting out the headers, children sort the pictures or words into columns.
2. ***Check.*** After sorting, children read down each column to make sure that all words have been placed correctly and make any adjustments as needed.
3. ***Reflect.*** Children explain in their own words how the cards have been sorted and describe the commonalities among them. They also explain any oddballs.

WRITING SORT A writing sort is a valuable instructional technique in which one person calls out the words from the weekly sort. The child is then able to spell the word correctly from memory according to one of the assigned spelling feature categories. **Blind writing sorts** should be distinguished from writing or copying a sort. Also, this technique is not used until students have had ample time to practice sorting. Step-by-step guidelines are as follows:

1. ***Establish format.*** The writing sort can be done in a variety of ways using the word study notebook, loose writing paper, or a whiteboard. To prepare for the writing sort, guide your child to divide the paper into columns and write a header for each one. These headers match the headers from the sorts. Briefly review the patterns under study by pointing out the spelling features identified in each category.
2. ***Provide examples.*** Provide an example word for each category. This is generally a very familiar word, or likely the example on the actual header in the sort.
3. ***Dictate, discuss, and write words from the sort.*** Next, dictate or call out words from the sort and ask your child to write them under the appropriate header. Guide your child to discuss where they wrote the words and why. It is important to note that this is not an assessment or test; rather, it is an opportunity for your child to receive

FIGURE 2.15 Writing Sort in Action

Source: Used with permission of Alison Meadows.

FIGURE 2.16 Completed Writing Sort

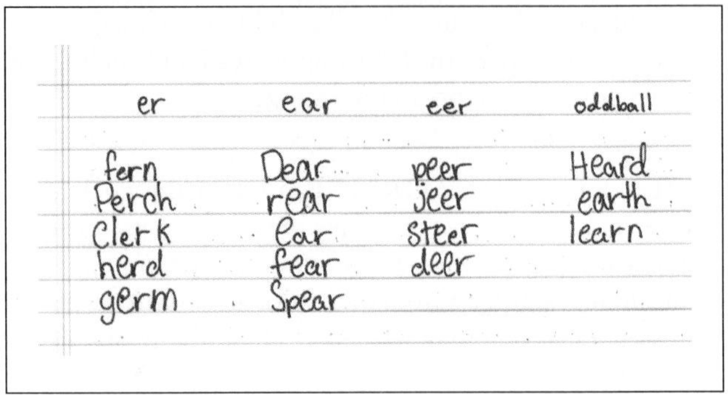
er
ear
eer
oddball
fern
Dear
peer
Heard
Perch
rear
jeer
earth
Clerk
Ear
Steer
learn
herd
fear
deer
germ
Spear

Source: From "*Words Their Way for Parents: How to Support Your Childs Phonics, Spelling, and Vocabulary Development*, 1st Ed.". Copyright © 2018, by Michelle Picard.

immediate feedback and to practice distinguishing words with different spelling features, and to discuss the underlying principles that differentiate them.

4. ***Dictate, discuss, and write new words.*** Following the same procedure, now include words that were not in the original sort but contain the same spelling patterns. Remember the goal of word study is not only to learn the specific words in the sort each week, but also to generalize those spelling patterns to new words. When children are successful applying feature knowledge to new words, they progress along the developmental continuum.
5. ***Check and reflect.*** Finish the writing sort by following the same process used in any sort. Your child checks by reading down the words in each column to make sure they all belong and then reflect by explaining how the words have been sorted and written. Blind writing sorts require children to use their knowledge of phonics (sound), orthography (pattern), and morphology (meaning) without seeing the words. Writing sorts connect word study to writing and reading.

Figure 2.15 displays a young learner using a dry-erase board to complete a writing sort comparing short I and long I words with the CVCe pattern. Figure 2.10 shows a complete writing sort from a child studying *r*-controlled vowels in the within word pattern stage. Another version of the writing sort for children in beginning stages is known as *writing for sounds*, in which emergent and letter name-alphabetic children use invented spelling to write words with the sounds being studied. In this version, children may not spell the entire word correctly, but we guide them to use the features they have studied. Their words often just include the beginning and ending consonants.

WORD HUNT The word hunt is another key tool to helping children solidify understanding of sounds, patterns, and meaning units so that they can extend each to their spelling and writing. During a word hunt, your child browses through familiar text, text that has been read previously, looking for words with similar sounds, patterns, or units of meaning. Examples of hunts can be seen in Figures 2.17 and 2.18. This technique helps your child learn about position, frequency, and related words. Children are introduced to new vocabulary, and examine which patterns are the most and least frequent. They also find oddballs, or words that do not follow the general spelling principles. This knowledge helps them spell unfamiliar words. Word hunts are a powerful connection between reading and word study lessons. Making the link between word study and reading strengthens the connections between spelling and word recognition and between writing and reading. Step-by-step guidelines are below.

1. ***Establish format.*** The word hunt is usually recorded in a word study notebook or on a chart. To prepare for a word hunt, guide your child to divide the paper into columns and write a header for each one. These headers match the headers from the sort. An oddball column is also included, as children are likely to find words that could be considered oddballs within their sort.
2. ***Provide examples.*** Provide an example for each header, usually a very familiar word, or the example on the actual header in the sort. Ask your child to record the example words.
3. ***Guide your child to hunt for words.*** Provide or guide your child to select text for the word hunt. Guide your child to search through familiar books for words that have the same sounds, patterns or meaning units currently being studied. You should provide guidance on the number of words to collect and/or the amount of time to spend collecting. In the early stages and in the final stages, you should provide text that is filled with the spelling features under study. Your child records the words into the appropriate categories. Guide a discussion to focus on vocabulary, sound, pattern, and meaning, and how this knowledge affects reading and writing. It is also an opportunity to correct any misconceptions. During the word hunt, students frequently want to write down every word that has the same visual spelling pattern without making sure it also has the same sound being studied. For example, if children are asked to search for long and short *a* words, they often write every word they find that has the letter *a* in it, without consideration of the sound. For example, the word *said* may be selected. Despite the presence of the letter *a* or the long spelling pattern *ai*, there is neither a short nor long *a* sound within the word. The word *said* is a perfect oddball for this sort. For this reason, it is important that the words gathered are reviewed by an adult and their categorical placement in the word study notebook is discussed in terms of sound, pattern, and meaning.
4. ***Check and reflect.*** Finish the word hunt by following the same process used in sorting. Guide your child to check by reading the words in each column to make sure they all belong. Then reflect on the meaning, the spelling feature, and the number of words found

FIGURE 2.17 Completed Word Hunt: Unaccented Syllables *-or, -ar, -er*

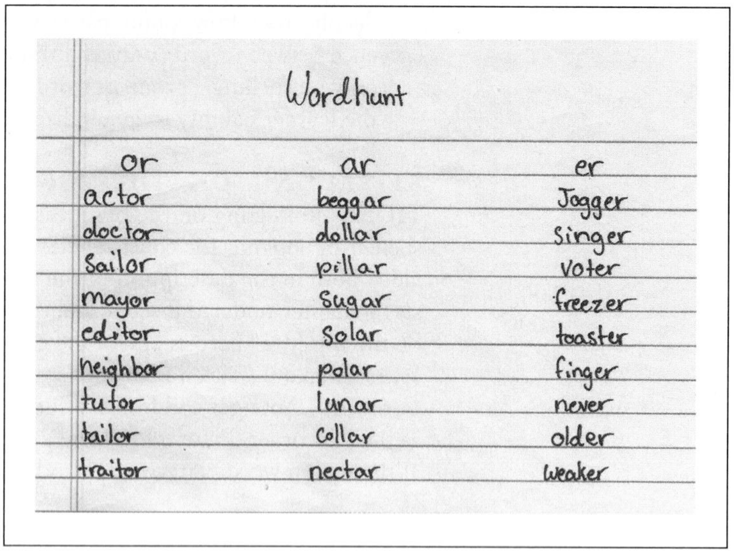
Wordhunt

or	ar	er
actor	beggar	Jogger
doctor	dollar	Singer
Sailor	pillar	Voter
mayor	Sugar	freezer
editor	Solar	toaster
neighbor	polar	finger
tutor	lunar	never
tailor	Collar	older
traitor	nectar	weaker

Source: From "*Words Their Way for Parents: How to Support Your Childs Phonics, Spelling, and Vocabulary Development*, 1st Ed.". Copyright © 2018, by Michelle Picard.

FIGURE 2.18 Completed Word Hunt: Word Roots *dic-, aud-, vis-*

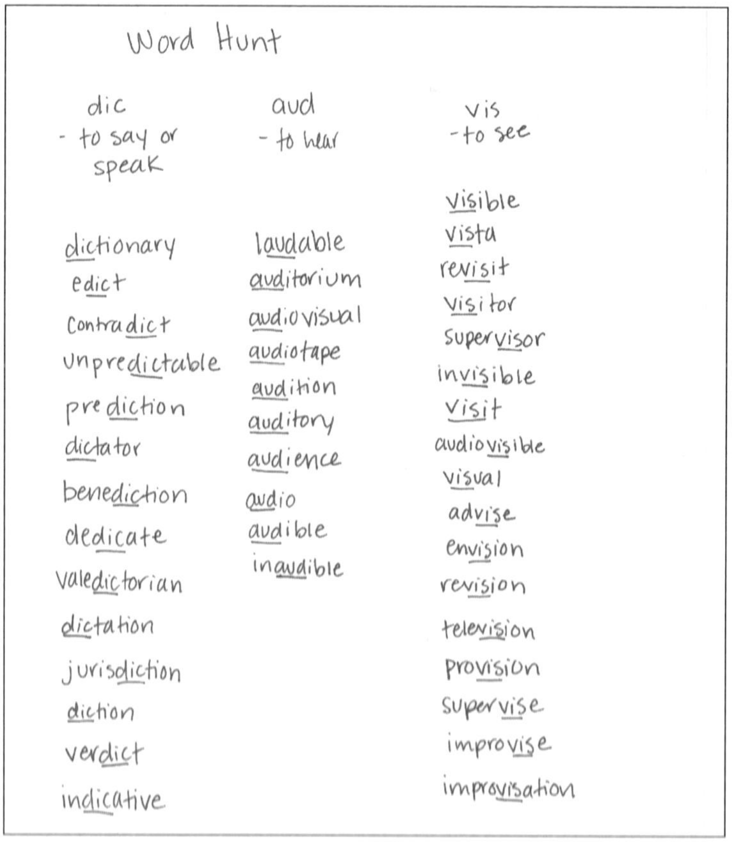
Word Hunt

dic - to say or speak	aud - to hear	vis - to see
dictionary	laudable	visible
edict	auditorium	vista
Contradict	audiovisual	revisit
unpredictable	audiotape	visitor
prediction	audition	supervisor
dictator	auditory	invisible
benediction	audience	visit
dedicate	audio	audiovisible
valedictorian	audible	visual
dictation	inaudible	advise
jurisdiction		envision
diction		revision
verdict		television
indicative		provision
		supervise
		improvise
		improvisation

Source: From "*Words Their Way for Parents: How to Support Your Childs Phonics, Spelling, and Vocabulary Development*, 1st Ed.". Copyright © 2018, by Michelle Picard.

for each category. Parents and teachers encourage children to *reflect*, to consider what they have learned about the spelling of words and how their understanding of why words are spelled the way they are supports them as a reader and a writer. Reflection, thinking deeply about how sound, pattern, and meaning are used in words, is a fundamental difference between word study and traditional spelling approaches. Word study is focused not only on spelling a group of words with similar and dissimilar spelling features, but also on the learner's ability to generalize this knowledge to unknown words.

REFLECTING ON THE BIG IDEAS OR UNDERLYING GENERALIZATIONS Reflecting on the big ideas teaches children that they can figure out how a word is spelled by looking for consistencies among related words. Step-by-step guidelines are provided both in the description of the essential technique "Sort Introduction," and also in each stage chapter under the section entitled "Let's Talk About It." We also include "Reflecting on the Big Idea" here as one of the essentials given its great importance. Children can also be asked to create written reflections of their learning describing the big ideas learned in their own words. Younger children can summarize their learning orally and then have an adult serve as their recorder. Figures 2.19 and 2.20 display examples of written reflections from students at the within word pattern stage and the syllables and affixes stage.

WORD STUDY NOTEBOOKS Word study notebooks are commonly used in classrooms that use a developmental spelling approach. They are a place in which students

FIGURE 2.19 Written Reflection on Ambiguous Vowels (*-ou, -ow*)

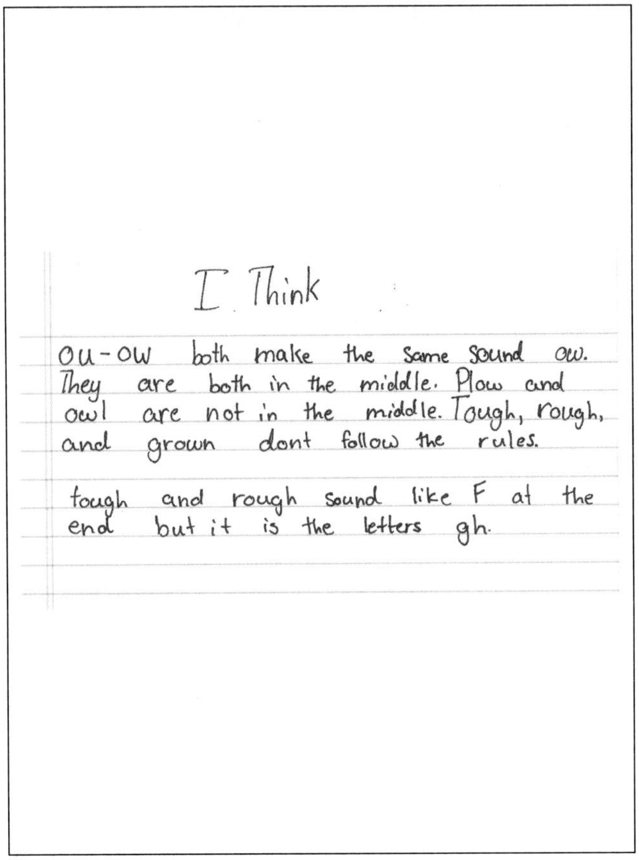

I Think

ou-ow both make the same sound ow. They are both in the middle. Plow and owl are not in the middle. Tough, rough, and grown dont follow the rules.

tough and rough sound like F at the end but it is the letters gh.

Source: From "*Words Their Way for Parents: How to Support Your Childs Phonics, Spelling, and Vocabulary Development*, 1st Ed.". Copyright © 2018, by Michelle Picard.

FIGURE 2.20 Written Reflection on Unaccented Syllables (*-le, -el, -il,* and *-al*)

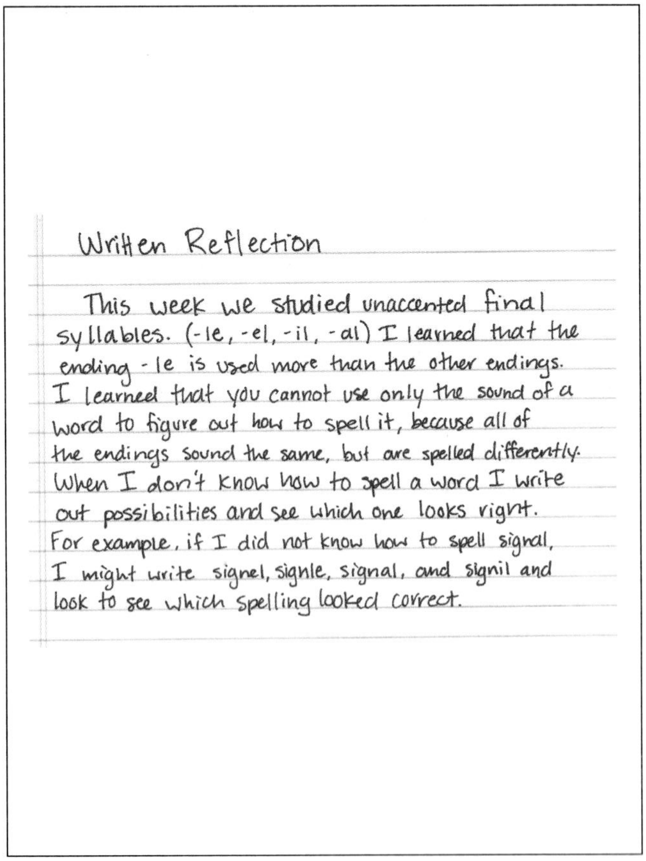

Written Reflection

This week we studied unaccented final syllables. (-le, -el, -il, -al) I learned that the ending -le is used more than the other endings. I learned that you cannot use only the sound of a word to figure out how to spell it, because all of the endings sound the same, but are spelled differently. When I don't know how to spell a word I write out possibilities and see which one looks right. For example, if I did not know how to spell signal, I might write signel, signle, signal, and signil and look to see which spelling looked correct.

Source: From "*Words Their Way for Parents: How to Support Your Childs Phonics, Spelling, and Vocabulary Development*, 1st Ed.". Copyright © 2018, by Michelle Picard.

write their word sorts and complete other related activities, including writing sorts, word hunts, word pictures, speed-sort times, and vocabulary collections. The notebooks can be folders, spiral notebooks, composition notebooks, or three-ring binders. Generally, there is also a storage system for the word study cards, such as an envelope or a baggie attached to the notebook. The notebook travels back and forth between home and school so that students can practice their sorts and extend learning through additional activities.

The word study notebook serves a few important purposes. First, it is an effective management system for collecting word study assignments. It provides documentation of what has been studied throughout the year and serves as a resource for children and parents to consult. It demonstrates a child's progress and is a useful tool for parents, tutors and teachers to discuss what a student is working on in spelling, which we know is related to reading and writing. It is also a place in which students can collect vocabulary from their reading and oral discussions, and analyze these words for their spelling–meaning connections. A word study notebook at home is an effective tool to support word knowledge development. Word study notebooks may also have a section for vocabulary. (Vocabulary notebooks are described next.) Figure 2.21 displays a word study notebook example and several pages of work from different student notebooks including a written reflection about a sort, a glued short and long e sort, a sort in which the child has highlighted the key vowel sounds, and lists of words with the Greek root *photo* the prefix *un-*.

VOCABULARY NOTEBOOKS Create a notebook dedicated to vocabulary. Make this a fun family project by using a notebook that all family members can share, and give it an exciting name (e.g., "The Rowe Family Book of Amazing Words"). Use the notebook to collect all different kinds of words. The categories are truly limited only by your imagination. Each page in the notebook can be dedicated to a specific category of words, or for some categories you may even need several pages. The vocabulary notebook can serve as a great tool to extend word knowledge in sound, pattern, and meaning within words. Examples of word categories to collect are outlined in Table 2.4.

Word Study Games

Word study is designed to be student-centered, hands-on learning, so it is natural that games would be an integral part of instruction. The word study and vocabulary games included here can be used with children across most of the five stages. There are many other stage-specific word study activities to support your child's learning included in each individual stage chapter.

MEMORY In the same style of the picture-card games, children use the picture or word cards from their sort to play Memory or Concentration. Using the sort cards, place all the cards face down, spread out. Partners take turns flipping over two cards at a time, trying to find a matching pair. Matches are made using spelling patterns or vowel sounds, not the exact same word. For example, if your child is using a long *o* sort, the words *toast* and *float* would match because they each have a long *o* vowel, which is represented through the spelling pattern *-oa*. Memory can be played in pairs, small groups, or even independently.

TABOO Children use their picture or word cards from their sort to play Taboo. All the cards are placed face down in one pile. Children take turns pulling a card without letting their partner see the word. The child provides clues regarding meaning and spelling patterns to try to get their partner to guess the word. For example, for the word *gray*, the clues might include "rhymes with *play*, a color, a mixture of black and white, has the long *a* sound."

SPEED SORT Children sort their words as fast as they can while being timed. Then they sort again and try to beat their original times. Children are racing against themselves rather than someone else, although exceptions are sometimes made to race the teacher or race a

FIGURE 2.21 Word Study Notebook Examples

Source: Michelle Picard

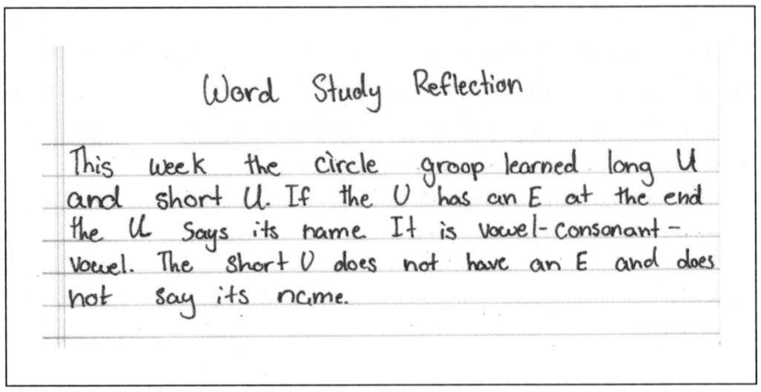
Word Study Reflection

This week the circle groop learned long U and short U. If the U has an E at the end the U Says its name. It is vowel-consonant-Vowel. The short U does not have an E and does not say its name.

Source: From "*Words Their Way for Parents: How to Support Your Childs Phonics, Spelling, and Vocabulary Development*, 1st Ed.". Copyright © 2018, by Michelle Picard.

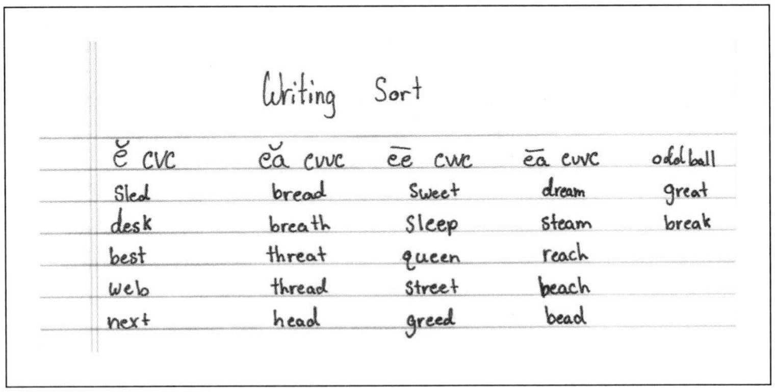
Writing Sort

ĕ cvc	ĕa cvvc	ē e cvvc	ē a cvvc	oddball
Sled	bread	Sweet	dream	great
desk	breath	Sleep	steam	break
best	threat	queen	reach	
web	thread	Street	beach	
next	head	greed	bead	

Source: From "*Words Their Way for Parents: How to Support Your Childs Phonics, Spelling, and Vocabulary Development*, 1st Ed.". Copyright © 2018, by Michelle Picard.

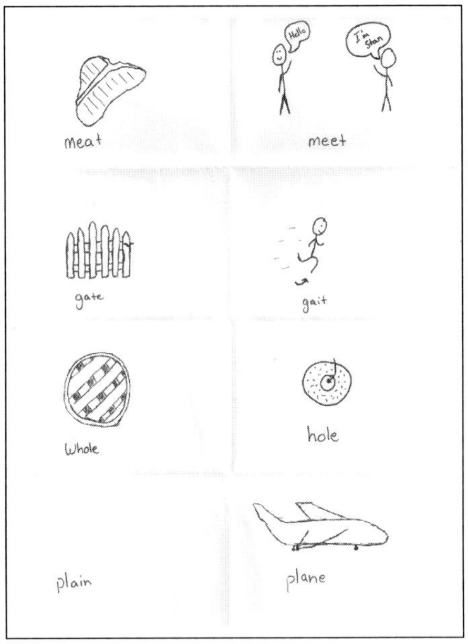

Source: Michelle Picard

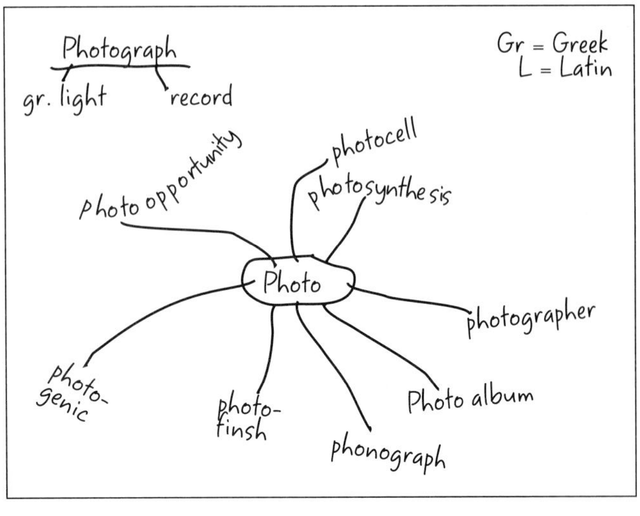

Source: DONALD R., WORDS THEIR WAY, 6th Ed., © 2016. Reprinted and Electronically reproduced by permission of Pearson Education, Inc., New York, NY.

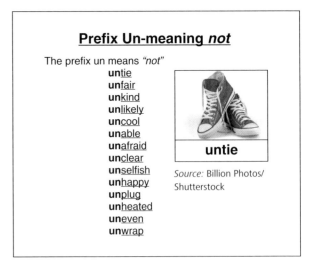

Prefix Un-meaning *not*

The prefix un means *"not"*

untie
unfair
unkind
unlikely
uncool
unable
unafraid
unclear
unselfish
unhappy
unplug
unheated
uneven
unwrap

untie

Source: Billion Photos/ Shutterstock

Source: Michelle Picard

TABLE 2.4 Word Categories for the Vocabulary Notebook

Types of Words, Word Parts, and Phrases	Definitions	Examples
Homophones	Words that sound the same but are spelled differently and have different meanings	*made/maid, pear/pare/pair*
Homographs	Words that are spelled the same but are pronounced differently and have different meanings	*record:* "I have heard that record" or "We need to record your voice"
Compound Words	Words created when two smaller words are joined to make a new word	*blacktop, bookshelf, shellfish*
Prefixes	A word part attached to the beginning of a base word or root; prefixes change the meaning of a word	*pre-, mis-, dis-, un-*
Suffixes	A word part attached to the ending of a base word or root; suffixes indicate the part of speech	*-ness, -ment, -ly, -ic*
Word Parts/Roots	A Greek or Latin root that forms the base of a word	*graph,* as in *graphic, photograph* *spect* as in *spectacles, spectacular,* and *inspection*
Onomatopoeia	Words that represent sounds	*buzz, splat, bam, zoom*
Palindromes	Words or phrases that read the same backwards and forwards	*race car, never odd or even*
Idioms	Phrases or expressions that mean something other than a literal meaning	*It's raining cats and dogs,* or *She has butterflies in her stomach*
Puns	A play on words or a joke based on multiple-meaning words	*The weatherman who forecast snow in July is a bit of a flake*
Oxymorons	Phrase with contradictory terms	*jumbo shrimp, plastic silverware*
Collective Nouns	A noun that appears singular in form, but denotes a group	*Gaggle of geese, cluster of grapes*
Extra Long Words	Words with multiple syllables	*Floccinaucinihilipilification* – meaning "of little to no value"
Sensational Science Words	Words from science that are interesting.	*meteorology, photosynthesis, precipitation*
New Words I Have Learned	Words that are interesting	*tintinnabulation, onomatopoeia*

beloved adult. You are welcome to race against your child, but be prepared, it is not as simple as you might expect!

BLIND OR NO PEEKING SORT Guide your child to sort the words without actually seeing the cards. The headers are displayed, then all the other cards are placed face down in a pile. Select a card and read it to your child. Ask him or her to sort without seeing the word. Children must be able to visualize the word or be able to recall the overall sound, pattern, or meaning represented in each category. Children can also be asked to explain why they are placing each word in a column.

COMMERCIAL GAMES There are a number of commercially produced games that are fun and develop word knowledge, including *Scrabble, Boggle, Scattergories, Quiddler, Bananagrams, Up Words, Crossword Puzzles, Charades, Taboo, Mad Libs,* and *Password.* There are also online games such as *Words with Friends* for mobile devices. All of these will quickly become fun family favorites, focused on expanding word knowledge and vocabulary.

A BRIEF SUMMARY

In this chapter, we described what word study looks like in schools and the 10 principles on which word study is based. We shared how parents can use word study routines, strategies, and games to support your child's developing word knowledge. Step-by-step guidelines for six essential techniques were described, including introducing a sort, daily sorting, writing sorts, word hunts, identifying the big idea, and the use of word study notebooks. In addition, we described a number of hands-on activities, games, and extensions that can be played at home. In Chapters 3 through 7, we discuss each stage of spelling development in detail and how parents, tutors, and school volunteers can help their children. Each stage chapter includes the following sections:

- *Stage Overview:* This section describes the common characteristics of students in reading, writing, and spelling at each stage.
- *Understanding Picture and Word Sorts:* This section includes two parts. First, *Let's Talk About It!* provides guidance in how to discuss the common spelling sounds and patterns studied at this stage with your child. Second, *Sort Support* explains each specific common spelling feature to be studied and how word knowledge can be generalized to other words by exploring the underlying principles of spelling features at this stage. This section is intended to guide your own understanding of phonics (sound), orthography (pattern), and morphology (meaning).
- *Word Study with Parents, Tutors, and School Volunteers:* This section provides tips for games and activities that parents, tutors, and school volunteers may use at home and outside the classroom to support the development of word knowledge.
- *Supporting Reading and Writing:* The final section provides tips and strategies to promote all aspects of your child's literacy development, specifically reading and writing that complement growth in spelling knowledge.

REFERENCE

James, W. (1958). *Talks to teachers on psychology and to students on some of life's ideas.* New York, NY: Norton. (Original work published 1899.)

chapter 3

Emergent Learners

Source: Courtesy of Matthew Hubbard

Source: Amble Design/Shutterstock

One afternoon 5-year-old Abby and her mom were playing with magnetic alphabet letters on the refrigerator. Abby was hunting for the letters to make her name, saying "My name starts with A, B, nudda [another] B, and Y!" After making her name, Abby's mom helped her choose and name other letters. Abby's mom held out the letter M and asked, "What letter is this?" Abby confidently replied, "Mom! It's the letter W. You are holding it upside down."

At 5 years old, Abby had already begun to acquire two fundamental concepts for emergent learners—the ability to identify letters and the understanding that print carries meaning. As adults, we tend to think that children in preschool or kindergarten "learn the alphabet." However, learning the alphabet is not a one-step process, and it is embedded in a larger landscape of language and literacy. Learning the alphabet actually involves a number of skills children must learn to do:

- Recite the letters of the alphabet in order and/or sing the alphabet song
- Identify and name both lower- and upper-case letters
- Form or print the letters
- Associate sounds with letters

In Abby's case, her knowledge of literacy and alphabet-letter sounds was emerging and continued to develop with the support of her family and teachers. These growing skills were built on a foundation of thousands of home experiences singing songs, talking to friends and family, repeating rhymes, listening to stories, watching musicals, retelling stories, and looking at letters on blocks and in books.

The word *emerge* comes from the Latin origin *emergere*, meaning "to come forth into view or notice, to come into existence." In their first year of life, emergent learners experience the world through sights and sounds and begin to acquire language and literacy. An emergent learner undergoes changes much like the metamorphosis from caterpillar to butterfly. A skilled observer can spot many small changes that lead to a remarkable transformation.

This chapter is devoted to emergent learners like Abby, typically found in preschool and kindergarten. The word study approach, founded on research, is built around the idea that children make the greatest progress possible if we teach lessons based on their individual strengths and target areas of challenge. In this chapter, you will read about the common characteristics of children's reading, writing, and spelling at the emergent stage (Table 3.1), learn about spelling features appropriate for this stage and how to talk about them with your child, review a series of games and activities to support emerging literacy and word study at home, and understand how to make connections among spelling, reading, and writing.

Stage Overview: Emergent Learners

Reading

Have you ever read aloud to a young child nestled on your lap while small hands obscure the page and prevent you from seeing the text? When it happened, did the child turn around, look at you quizzically, and wonder why you had stopped reading? The fact is that young children do not realize that you are dependent on the text—and specifically on the written words—in order to tell the story! One of the early concepts learned by emergent readers is that the spoken word, our ideas, songs, rhymes, stories, and facts, can be written and later read aloud or silently. This is an abstract concept, and one that we are not likely to explain to our children. It is nevertheless an important understanding for children to acquire through experience with print.

Although emergent learners cannot yet read in the traditional sense, they can often retell a favorite story, such as *The Very Hungry Caterpillar* by Eric Carle. They "read" the story from

TABLE 3.1 Characteristics of Emergent Learners

	Emergent Readers in the Emergent Stage of Spelling
Reading Characteristics	Emergent Readers • Typically preschool to kindergarten students • Engage in retelling of stories—pretend reading • Unable to match speech to print or identify individual words • Lack the understanding that English text is read from left to right (directionality) • Pretend reading; fluent recitation or retelling as reading
Writing Characteristics	Emergent Writers • Pretend writing • Scribble letters and numbers and symbols to represent ideas • Unable to match letters and sounds • Use drawing to represent ideas • Neglect to space "words"—sometimes use lines and dots to separate ideas
Spelling Characteristics	Emergent Spellers • Incomplete knowledge of alphabet • Spelling lacks letter–sound correspondence
Common Spelling Errors	• Random strings of letters • Drawings • Scribbling
Instructional Focus	• Oral language, concepts and vocabulary • Concepts about Print (CAP) • Concept of Word (COW) • Phonological awareness • Phonemic awareness • Alphabet recognition • Phonics

the pictures by retelling what the caterpillar ate each day (one apple, two pears, three plums, etc.), followed by the patterned refrain, "But he was *still* hungry." Children at this stage are able to use the pictures to make up a story or retell a story from memory. They have not yet learned to attend to the actual print on the page. The literacy of these children is emerging, or "coming into existence."

The reading of an emergent child is best described as **pretend reading** or **memory reading**. Although neither meets the criteria for the conventional definition of reading, both are essential practices to progress. Pretend reading is basically a paraphrase or spontaneous retelling that children produce while turning the pages of a familiar book. Young children mimic adult reading of a well-known story, such as the previous example of *The Hungry Caterpillar*, or perhaps the well-known fairytale *Jack and the Beanstalk*. The emergent child makes up a story cued by the sequence of pictures. They might include phrases such as "Fe fi fo fum!" or other snippets of text. Often, they imitate the voice and cadence of written language (Sulzby, 1986) so that they "sound" as though they are reading.

Memory reading is more exacting than pretend reading. It involves an accurate recitation of the exact text accompanied by pointing to the print in some fashion. Reading from memory helps children coordinate spoken language with print at the level of words, sounds, and letters. Children may chant from the book *Crocodile Beat*, "Down by the jungle in the heat of the day, the crocodile sits and awaits his prey" (Jorgenson, 1995: pp. 1–2), and attempt to point to print on the pages. Most likely, they have memorized the text from repeated readings, and they begin to understand that the print plays a critical role in the "telling" of the story.

Emergent children's attempts to touch individual words while reading from memory are initially quite inconsistent and vague. Children gradually acquire **directionality**, realizing that they should move left to right, top to bottom, and end up on the last word on the page. However, the units that come in between are a blur until the systematic relationship between letters and sounds is understood. The ability to fingerpoint or accurately track words in print while reciting text from memory is a phenomenon called **concept of word** (COW). It is a watershed event that separates the emergent reader from the beginning reader in the letter name–alphabetic stage (Henderson, 1981; Morris, 1992).

Emergent learners are also described as being in the *pre-alphabetic stage* because they don't understand the form and function of the alphabet (Ehri, 1997). Nevertheless, they still learn to identify a few words, such as their names, the names of friends and family, and signs in their environment, but they learn to do so by using non-alphabetic cues, such as the shape of a stop sign. They may identify a large retail store because it starts with the big red K, but they are not systematic in their selection of any particular cue. Emergent learners lack an understanding of the alphabetic principle or show only the beginning of this understanding.

Writing

Like emergent reading, early emergent writing is largely pretend and follows a typical progression as children learn about letters, sounds, and conventions of print (Figure 3.1). Regardless of most children's cultural backgrounds or where they live, this pretend writing occurs spontaneously wherever writing is encouraged, modeled, and incorporated into play (Ferreiro

FIGURE 3.1 The Evolution of Emergent Writing

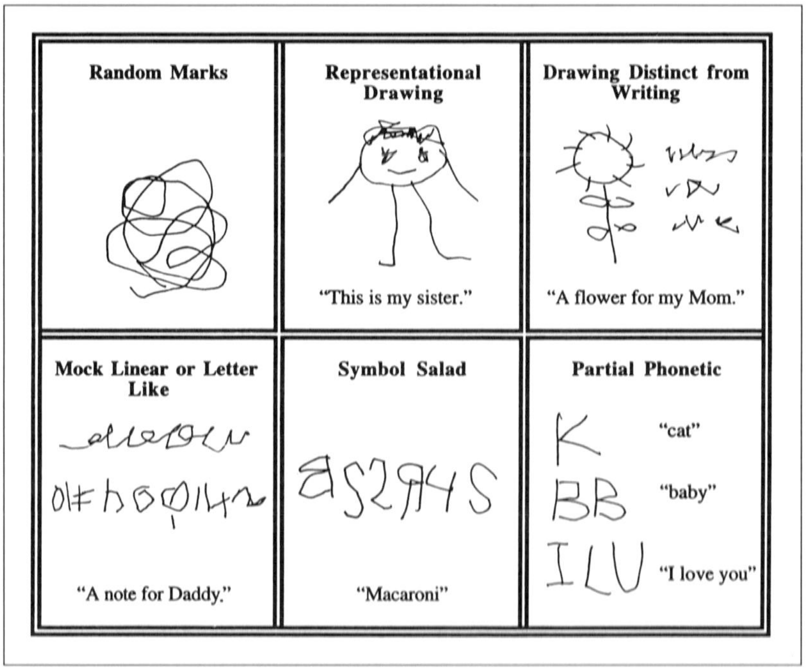

FIGURE 3.2 Edward's Writing Sample from Kindergarten

Source: From "*Words Their Way for Parents: How to Support Your Childs Phonics, Spelling, and Vocabulary Development*, 1st Ed.". Copyright © 2018, by Alison Meadows.

& Teberosky, 1982). The first task as an emergent writer is to discover that scribbling can represent something and thereafter, to differentiate drawing from writing and representation from communication. Children must come to realize that a drawing of a flower does not actually say "flower." Writing is necessary to communicate the complete message. When asked to write a story in preschool, it is not uncommon to observe children draw or scribble images. At this request, our friend William, 4 years old, drew three circles with what appeared to be long stick legs and feet. He said, "My story is my family." This is similar to the image in the top row, second panel of Figure 3.1 labeled, "This is my sister."

The top row of the same figure presents a progression of drawings and their accompanying labels and phrases that show a clear differentiation between picture and writing. The bottom row of the same figure shows the movement from mock linear writing to real writing that uses letters to represent speech sounds. It is helpful to understand that children become aware of words and sounds as a consequence of learning to read and write.

As emergent learners learn some letters, they may begin to include them in their writing. Often, the first letters they use are the same as the ones in their name. However, the letters may have no relationship to speech sounds. Writing is usually impossible to read at the emergent stage, unless your child already told you what you were supposed to say. Emergent writing may also include numbers or random marks. This type of writing is sometimes referred to as a "symbol salad," also shown in Figure 3.1.

In Figure 3.2, Edward, a kindergarten child, has created a picture of his home and family members using a random string of letters. He has used what appear to be arbitrary capital letters to tell the story: L, B, P, E, J, I, L, T, E, W, M. When asked to read it, he says, "This is my family in the kitchen." We know that Edward is an emergent learner because there is no evidence of **phonics**, a match between letters and sounds, nor is there evidence of individual words. Still, he has demonstrated several important understandings: he knows letters, in addition to drawings, are used to communicate meaning. He knows where to position the picture and the print on the page, how to form and identify letters, and maybe even spell his name correctly. When children lack a *concept of word*, the understanding that words are made of letters and represent meaning, word boundaries and spaces are also obscured or nonexistent in their writing. Note how all of the letters run together. However, words gradually begin to evolve as distinct entities with their boundaries defined by beginning and ending sounds.

These typical characteristics of emergent writing can be seen in additional writing samples. In Figure 3.3, note that the first image depicts a late emergent writer representing letters and sounds in the sentence "I like housekeeping," without including any spaces. In the next image (Figure 3.4), another child in the next stage of development has written the same sentence with additional sounds and letters and has included spaces between words.

FIGURE 3.3 Late Emergent Writing without Word Boundaries

FIGURE 3.4 Early Letter Name–Alphabetic Writing with Word Boundaries

Emergent writers are pretend writers, striving to be like mom, dad, sister, and brother. Many of us have stories in which very young children have written a sign, a joke, a grocery list, or a story. We skillfully ask the child to read the text, because although we applaud the effort, it is indecipherable. This is the case for preschool and primary teachers as well. We celebrate the act of writing and the desire to express oneself, and we foster the knowledge required to communicate through writing.

Spelling

Spelling and writing are essentially the same skills at the emergent stage. In the early emergent stage, children learn to hold a pencil, marker, or crayon and to make marks on paper. These marks are best described as scribbles that lack directionality and may not serve to communicate meaning. At some point during the emergent stage these scribbles evolve to be more representational drawings, and children learn that print is distinct from drawings, as can be seen in the top right of Figure 3.1. This frame shows the drawing as distinct from the writing, which is assigned a specific message: "A flower for my Mom."

Eventually, children begin to include letter-like forms and letters, as seen in the last box of Figure 3.1. Children begin to spell at the end of the emergent stage when they use specific letters to represent sounds as in the last box of this same figure. These efforts are only partial at first—spelling *cat* with *K* because the *cuh* sound is the first and most dominant sound they can detect in the word and matches the beginning sound of the letter name *K*. In some cases they might use a letter for each syllable in a word, such as spelling *baby* with *BB*. By the end of the emergent stage, children are beginning to use letters to represent speech sounds in a systematic way. In order to truly begin spelling, children must do the following:

- Know some letters—not all, but enough to get started
- Know how to form or write some of the letters they know
- Know that letters represent speech sounds
- Attend to the sounds within spoken words and match those sounds to letters

TABLE 3.2 Early Literacy Skills for Emergent Learners

Oral Language, Concepts, and Vocabulary	The understanding that words represent ideas and concepts that can be used to share thoughts and experiences with others
Phonological Awareness (PA)	The ability to identify and reflect on sounds within spoken words including syllables, rhyme, and single sounds
Phonemic Awareness	The recognition of the smallest units of speech sounds within words (e.g., the words *cat* and *ship* both have three phonemes or units of sound: /c/ - /a/ - /t/ and /sh/ - /i/ - /p/)
Phonics	The systematic relationship between letters and sounds
Alphabet Recognition	The ability to identify and name upper- and lower-case letters
Concepts about Print (CAP)	A set of understandings about how books are organized (e.g., front to back page turning, titles, illustrations), how print is oriented on the page (i.e., top to bottom and left to right), and how other features of print relate to how print is read (e.g., bold, italics, punctuation)
Concept of Word (COW)	The ability to match spoken words with printed words, as demonstrated by the ability to accurately point to each word of a memorized text

Early Literacy Skills

Now that we have provided an overview of emergent reading, writing, and spelling, we would also like to share some more in depth discussion of specific early literacy skills that contribute to both reading and writing. Table 3.2, *Early Literacy Skills for Emergent Learners*, describes essential understandings that children must acquire to become literate. These are not, however, linear skills. Young children do not have to acquire one skill before another; rather, they are connected, overlap, and build on one another, like stackable plastic building bricks or Russian nesting dolls. A discussion of each is provided in this section.

ORAL LANGUAGE, CONCEPTS AND VOCABULARY Children come to school with widely varying language experiences (Biemiller & Slonim, 2001). In one classic study, researchers estimated that by 3 years of age, some children had heard 3 million more words than other children, and by the time they enter school, some children have heard 30 million more words than others (Hart & Risley, 1995). A well-developed vocabulary is an essential part of reading and school success (Cunningham & Stanovich, 2003), and vocabulary growth is important for children of all ages (Biemiller, 2001, 2004).

Initially, children develop oral language, concepts, and vocabulary by listening to and interacting with parents, caretakers, family, and friends. When a child is an infant or toddler, the adult is often responsible for the entire conversation. For example, a mother may ask her child, "Do you want some juice?" and proceed to answer the question and extend the conversation, "Yes, you want some apple juice. You like apple juice." A father pulls his 14-month-old daughter's highchair up to the kitchen table while making pancakes. As he prepares the batter, he asks, "What's next? Flour? That's right, we add two cups of flour and mix it up. Can you help me mix it up?" With each step, he is introducing his daughter to vocabulary and to concepts such as *flour*, *vanilla*, *eggs*, *bowl*, *spoon*, *beat*, *hot*, *mix*, *pour*, *flip*, *butter*, and *syrup*. Experiences like making pancakes create a rich environment for learning language, which is, in part, the basis for literacy development. Adults should engage children in conversation at every opportunity, and should consciously use language that includes new vocabulary and complex sentences.

In addition to conversation around our day-to-day experiences, parents are encouraged to read aloud and talk about the words and ideas represented in both stories and informational texts. Studies have shown that there are more new words introduced in a children's book than in a typical adult conversation (Cunningham & Stanovich, 1997). For example, in the award-winning children's picture book *Tops and Bottoms* by Janet Stevens, children are introduced to the concept that vegetables grow both above the ground ("tops," like lettuce and corn) and beneath the ground ("bottoms," like carrots and potatoes). In addition to the overall concept of how and where vegetables grow, other interesting vocabulary is introduced in this story. Examples include *trickster*, *energetic*, *harvesting*, *profit*, and *grunted*. Children love hearing the story of how the clever hare outsmarts the lazy bear in order to get food for his family. As parents narrate experiences and read aloud books with their children, they are developing their child's oral language, vocabulary, and conceptual knowledge.

PHONOLOGICAL AWARENESS The word *phonological* includes two Greek roots—*phono*, meaning "sound," and *logo*, meaning "the study of." **Phonological awareness** is the ability to pay attention to, isolate, identify, and manipulate or exchange segments of speech or sounds *without* letters and text. It is an oral language skill that develops gradually over time. In Table 3.3, we outline the phonological awareness skills that young children acquire during this stage.

Children notice larger sound segments like rhyme and syllables more easily than smaller sound segments such as individual speech sounds (Justice & Pullen, 2003; Pufpaff, 2009). Phonological awareness is developed through playing with language (Yopp, 1992). Books, songs, and games help children learn to recognize and later create their own rhymes. They learn that *take*, *lake*, and *make* rhyme, but *cap* does not. They learn to divide words into syllables and that their own names are a good place to start. For example, *Jason* is two syllables (Ja/son), *Katherine* is three syllables (Kath/er/ine), and *Ray* is one syllable. Children also learn to blend syllables: given two chunks, such as *hot* and *dog*, they blend the chunks into *hotdog*. They delete or ignore syllables when asked to say *hotdog* without *hot (dog)*. Finally, children learn to notice individual speech sounds, also known as **phonemes**, and they develop **phonemic awareness**.

TABLE 3.3 Phonological Awareness Skills

Category	Skills	Informal Questions Used to Determine a Child's Phonological Awareness
Rhyme	Recognizing rhymes Producing rhymes	Does *hat* rhyme with *cat*? What rhymes with *blue*?
Syllables	Breaking words into syllables Blending syllables together to make words Segmenting words into syllables	How many parts are in the word *pancake*? What are the two parts of *pancake*? Can you clap the syllables that are in your name? If we put *pan* and *cake* together, what do we get? What are the two parts of *hotdog*?
Individual Sounds	Identify beginning, middle and ending sounds Blend sounds together to make words Segment words into sounds Change sounds in words	What is the beginning sound of *cup*? What do you hear at the end of *fast*? What am I saying: *j – ump*? What am I saying: *b – u – g*? What sounds are in *cat*? (c – a – t) Can you change the /m/ in *meat* to /s/?

FIGURE 3.5 The Relationships among Phonological Awareness, Phonemic Awareness, and Phonics

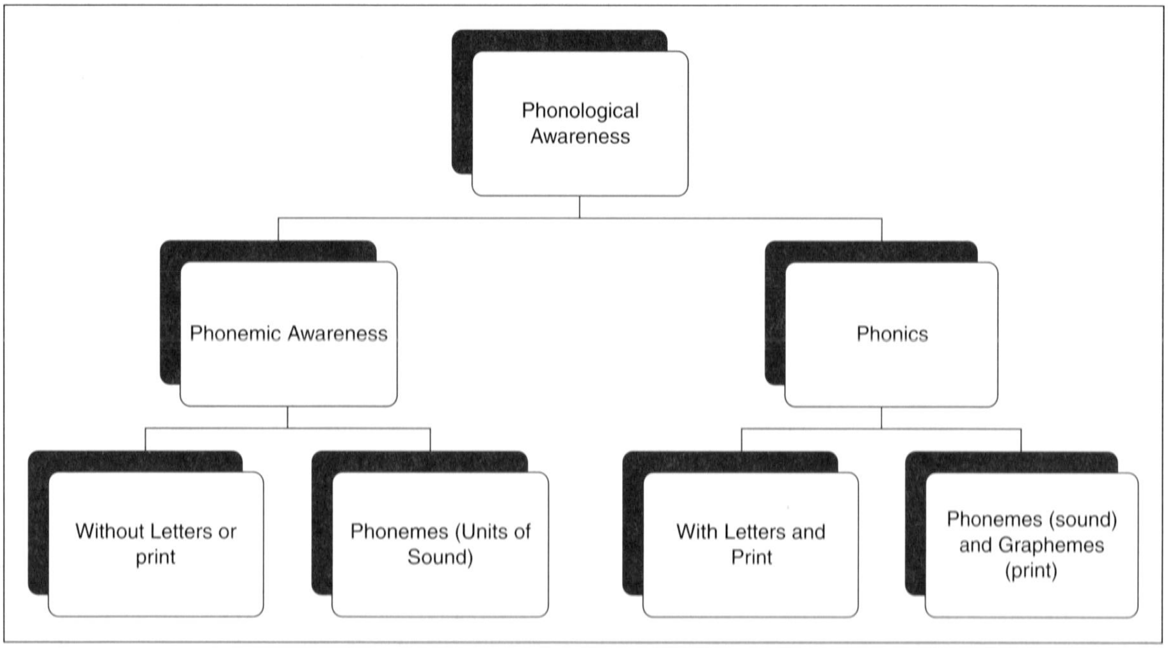

PHONEMIC AWARENESS In Figure 3.5, notice that *phonemic awareness* is a subcategory of *phonological awareness* and refers to the ability to identify and reflect on the smallest units of speech sounds—individual phonemes, such as the initial sound /b/ in *bear* or /ch/ in *child*. The ability to divide spoken words into individual sounds or phonemes illustrates a person's use of phonemic awareness, such as breaking *sit* or *thick* into three phonemes each (/s/-/i/-/t/ and

FIGURE 3.6 Pig Latin: An Example of Sophisticated Phonological Awareness

Have you ever spoken Pig Latin as a child? Pig Latin is a language game in which the speaker creates words by removing the first consonant (or consonant cluster) and attaching it to the end of the word followed by the final sound *-ay*. So the word *pig* becomes *igpay*. Words that begin with a vowel, such as *each,* do not require a manipulation other than the attachment of *-ay* to the end of the word. The word *each* becomes *eachay*. Now it's your turn. Try to read and understand the following sentence: "Igpay atinlay isay unfay!" or "Pig Latin is fun!" Pig Latin is an example of highly skilled ability to identify and manipulate sound without text. Emergent readers are more than a stone's throw from this level of mastery, but our point here is that phonological awareness generally precedes *phonics,* when letters and sounds are matched. Phonological awareness must be developed before or simultaneously while learning to read.

/th/-/i/-/ck). Note that although the word *thick* has five letters, it only has three phonemes, so when we are talking about phonemic awareness, we are talking about individual speech sounds within words. Over time, children also learn to manipulate phonemes to create new words. For example, when a child can "take away" the sound /m/ from *meat* and state the word is *eat*, she or he is manipulating the individual sounds or phonemes within the word. Ideas for helping your child develop phonological awareness and phonemic awareness are described later in this chapter. For a sophisticated example of phoneme manipulation, see Figure 3.6. Note that in order to speak Pig Latin, a child's game, you must have a facility and automaticity with sound to reposition sounds to create new words to speak fluently. Speaking the sentence, "Have a good day," or "Avehay a oodgay ayday," takes some real thought and phonological awareness.

A certain amount of phonological and phonemic awareness is critical to future spelling and reading success, and participation in phonological awareness activities has a positive influence on beginning reading (Ball & Blachman, 1988). Phonological awareness, however, does not precede or follow other components of emergent literacy development. Research suggests that phonological awareness and phonemic awareness develop concurrently, or at the same time, with other proficiencies. Growth in one area stimulates growth in another (Ehri, 2006; Morris, Bloodgood, Lomax, & Perney, 2003; Perfetti, Beck, Bell, & Hughes, 1987). Phonological and phonemic awareness are critical skills for learning to read (Cunningham, James, Cunningham, Hoffman, & Yopp, 1998).

PHONICS *Phonics* is the systematic relationship between letters and sounds. Unlike phonological and phonemic awareness, which are purely language-based skills, phonics introduces print, specifically letters, sounds, and spelling features. During the emergent stage, children learn their letters, attend to speech sounds, and begin to make these systematic connections. In the emergent stage, children learn that individual letters can "stand for" individual speech sounds, as *b* is /b/ in *button* and *burger*. Later on, in subsequent stages, children learn that a letter may represent two sounds, as with the letter *c*, which can have a hard sound (*cookie*) or a soft sound (*cycle*). For now, the goal is to associate specific speech sounds with specific letters. This insight is essential to learning to read, write, and spell.

ALPHABET RECOGNITION Among the early literacy skills that are traditionally studied, the one that appears to be the strongest predictor of reading success on its own is letter naming (Griffin, Burns, & Snow, 1998; Lonigan, Schatschneider, & Westberg; The National Early Literacy Panel [NELP], 2008). Children who are able to name letters accurately and automatically demonstrate reading readiness. There is a great deal to learn about the 26 letters of the alphabet. Letters have names, a set sequence, sounds, and upper- and lower-case forms. They must be written in particular ways, and orientation is critical. In the three-dimensional world, a chair is a chair, whether you approach it from the front or the back, or from the left or the right. Not so with letters. You may remember that earlier in the chapter, Abby identified the letter *M* as the letter *W*. Orientation is the critical difference. Print is one of the few things in life in which direction makes a difference, so it is not surprising that many children confuse *b* and *d* or *p* and *q* for some time. Young children also confuse letters that share visual features: *S* may be mistaken for *Z*, *E* for *F*, *h* for *n*, and so forth (Ehri & Roberts, 2006).

Learning the names of the letters is an important first step toward learning the sounds associated with the letters. Most letter names have sounds that are associated with their names. For example, the letter *B* sounds like the word *bee* and it begins with /b/, and the letter *Z* sounds like the letter name (*zee*) and begins with /z/. Other letters, however, do not have a sound clue embedded in the letter name, as with *H* ("aitch"), *W* ("double you") and *Y* ("wie"). Not surprisingly, these letters are often the most difficult to learn.

CONCEPTS ABOUT PRINT Children are surrounded by print on signs, package labels, magazines, television, and even on the clothes they wear; however, children need adults to talk about the purposes print serves and the special ways in which the visual forms or print are organized. With regard to books, **Concepts about Print** (CAP) refers to a set of understandings about how text is organized. As children watch you turn the pages, they learn that books are organized from the front to the back as they watch you turn the pages, but unless you point to words as you read, they are not likely to realize how print is organized from the top of the page to the bottom, or from the left to the right. Typically, children attend to the illustrations and have little interest in features of print. However, in order to learn to read, they need extensive concepts about print. When you read aloud to your children, point out the title and the author's name and begin to use terms that apply to literacy, such as letter, word, sentence, picture, and illustration.

CONCEPT OF WORD Emergent children have not yet developed a concept of word (COW). This fundamental skill is defined as the ability to match the spoken and written word, as evidenced by accurately pointing to or **tracking** a memorized text. As adults, we recognize that there are five distinct words in the first line of the rhyme "Sam, Sam, the baker man." Emergent children, however, cannot yet distinguish one word from another, and may be completely unaware that there are spaces between words. As children become aware that print has something to do with sound units, such as syllables, their fingerpointing may become more precise and change from a gross rhythm to a closer match. This rudimentary COW works well for one-syllable words, but not so well for words of two or more syllables. When they track "*Sam, Sam, the baker man*," they may now point six times: Sam/Sam/the/ba/ker/man. When they pronounce *-ker*, the second syllable of *baker*, they may point to the next word, *man*. Figure 3.7 illustrates the phenomenon of getting off track on two-syllable words.

FIGURE 3.7 Trying to Match Voice to Print (Concept of Word)

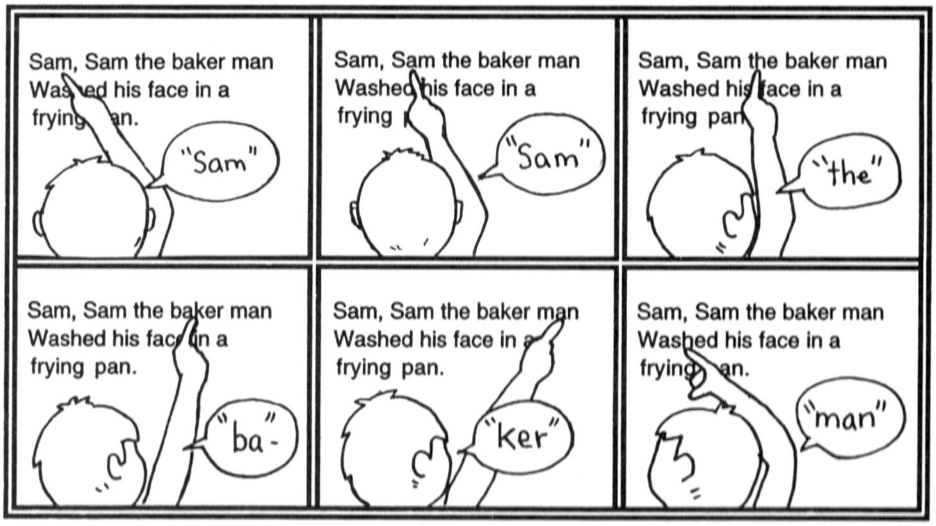

As children learn the alphabet and the sounds associated with the letters, beginning sounds anchor the children's fingerpointing more directly to the memorized recitation. They realize that when they say the word *man*, they need to have their finger on a word beginning with an *m*. If they do not, then they must start again and try to better coordinate beginning sounds with beginning-word boundaries. A concept of word develops over time with experience tracking words, learning phonics, and applying letter-sound matches to beginning-word boundaries in text.

Understanding Picture Sorts

This section focuses on the use of sorting as a way to develop literacy skills in emergent learners. Your child may bring home sorts from school, or you may choose to engage in sorting on your own. Ready-to-print sorts and directions for how to use them can also be found in *Words Their Way: Letter and Picture Sorts for Emergent Spellers* by Bear, Invernizzi, Johnston, and Templeton (2010).

In the *Sort Support* section, we describe what you and your children need to know about specific spelling features and briefly describe the types of sorts used by emergent learners. In the *Let's Talk About It* section, we describe how to guide your child through a beginning sound sort, and provide key questions to guide purposeful conversations with your child.

FIGURE 3.8 Concept Sort for Vehicles

Sort Support: What You and Your Child Need to Know at the Emergent Stage

At the emergent stage, students are introduced to a number of concepts and four types of sorts—concept (vocabulary), rhyming (phonological awareness), alphabet recognition, and beginning-sound sorts (phonics). A brief description of each follows and provides some of the specific underlying principles to be learned at this stage of development. These activities and sorts are described in more detail in the following *Early Literacy Skills at Home* section of this chapter.

CONCEPT SORTS Emergent learners are constantly acquiring new language and ideas. With every experience, book, video, or trip, children are learning to put labels to new objects and less tangible concepts such *birthday*, *holiday*, or *country*. Parents have a profound influence on the words that children acquire through discussion, experience, and reading books together. **Concept sorts** are another fun way to develop vocabulary and thinking with your child. You and your child collect and categorize objects or pictures by characteristics, such as animals/plants, fruit/vegetables, or farm/city. Figure 3.8 illustrates one possible concept sort based on vehicles.

PHONOLOGICAL AWARENESS As previously discussed, **phonological awareness** is the ability to identify and reflect on sounds, apart from meaning, in spoken language. It is purely language based. Parents can be tremendously helpful in developing a child's sensitivity to sounds through books, songs, rhyming games, and other activities outlined in the next section. Rhyme sorts can also help your child develop phonological awareness. Figure 3.9 illustrates three rhyming families. The word *clock* rhymes with *block*, *rock*, *sock* and *lock*, while *fly* rhymes with *pie*, *cry*, *eye* and *tie*, and finally *pan* rhymes with *van*, *can*, *man* and *fan*. Children use images to develop a sensitivity to rhyme.

ALPHABET RECOGNITION At this stage, your child learns to recognize each of the lower-case and upper-case letters of the alphabet. Related sorts include upper-case/lower-case matching sorts (Figure 3.10) and font sorts (Figure 3.11).

LETTER SOUNDS Through a variety of sorts, books, and activities, children learn that each consonant and vowel is associated with at least one sound and, in several cases, with more than one sound (Figure 3.12). We discuss one example in detail in the *Let's Talk About It* section. The big ideas to be learned by emergent spellers by the end of the stage are summarized in Table 3.4.

Let's Talk About It!

A fundamental difference between traditional approaches to phonics and spelling and the developmental approach is the way teachers, parents, and students talk about letters, sounds, and spelling features. Sorting is central to the word study methodology, because it requires students to compare and contrast features. Understanding gained through this process is enhanced by a wide variety of other instructional activities described later in this chapter.

Let's talk about an example at the emergent stage of spelling development. This example is a beginning sound sort contrasting *M* and *R*, and is designed to teach the sounds of these two letters (Figure 3.13). As we discuss in Chapter 2, you begin by making sure your child can name each of the pictures. Talk about a few of the pictures and their meanings.

FIGURE 3.9 Sample Sort: Rhyming Sort

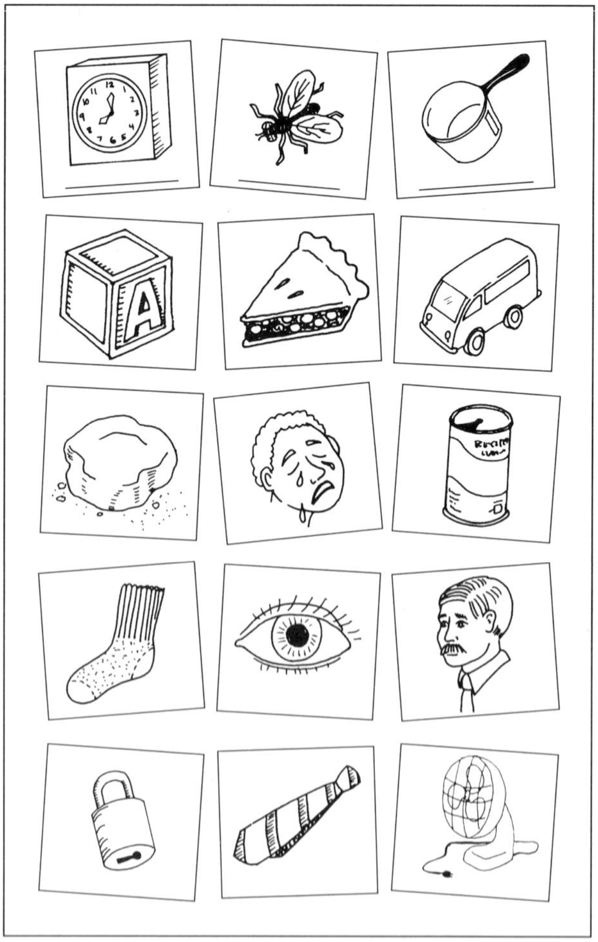

FIGURE 3.10 Alphabet Matching

Source: Used with the permission of Alison Meadows.

FIGURE 3.11 Font Sort with *C* and *D*

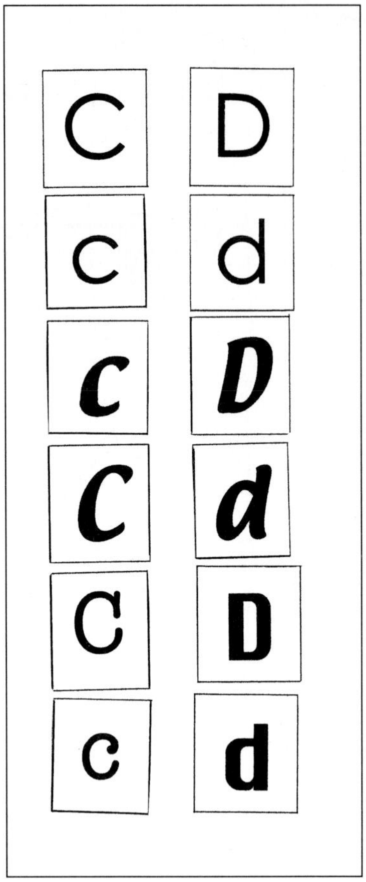

FIGURE 3.12 Beginning Sound Sort: For *S* and *M*

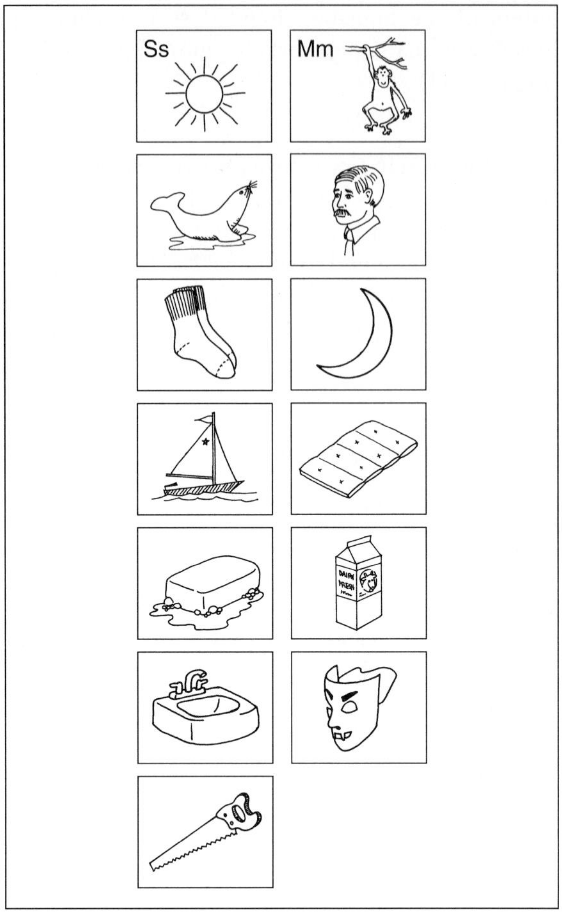

TABLE 3.4 Big Ideas for Emergent Learners

Sort Types Spelling Features	Big Ideas
Concept Sorts	✓ We can organize items by what is the same or different. ✓ We use different words to describe characteristics.
Rhyming Sorts	✓ Words that rhyme have the same sounds at the end.
Alphabet Recognition	✓ There are 26 upper-case letter forms. ✓ There are 26 lower-case letter forms. ✓ Letters can be printed with different fonts.
Beginning Consonants	✓ Letters represent speech sounds. ✓ Some letters represent more than one sound, such as *c* or *g*. ✓ Words that start with the same sound usually start with the same letter. ✓ We can emphasize the beginnings of words out to listen for the beginning sound.

Create two categories by displaying the headers (cards with the letters *Mm* and *Rr* to represent /m/ and /r/). Next, model for your child how to sort. Select the picture card *man* and say, "This is a picture of a *man*, mmmmman. I hear /mmmm/ at the beginning of the word *man*. *Man* starts with the letter *M*." Place the card under the letter *M*. Select the picture card *run* and say, "This is a picture of *run*, rrrun. I hear /rrrr/ at the beginning of the word *run*. *Run* starts with the letter *R*. Place the card under the letter *R*." Pick up another picture such as *milk*. Say something like, "Mmmmilk. *Milk* starts like mmmman, so I will put it under the *M*." Repeat with one or two more pictures, modeling how you say the name of the picture and compare it to *man* and *run*. At some point, say, "Now it is your turn to sort. Pick a picture and say the word and decide if it goes with the letter *M* or if it goes with the letter *R*." Encourage your child to "say it and lay it" as they place each picture in a category. Together, sort the remaining picture cards. Offer support as needed to name the pictures and stretch out the first sounds. Make sure to also name the letters for each sound.

Once the pictures are sorted, ask your child to name all of the pictures in a single column to be sure they all start with the same sound. Say, "Let's read the pictures under the letter *M: man, milk, monkey, mop, moon, match, mitten*." Repeat with the picture cards under the letter *R*. This allows the child an opportunity to hear the initial sounds and correct any misplaced cards. If your child needs assistance, help him or her identify the incorrect card by suggesting, "There is one picture that doesn't sound right in this column." If this is not enough, name three pictures, including two that are correct and the one that is incorrect. The goal is to increase your child's word knowledge and sensitivity to the letter sound association. Then use the three guiding questions outlined in Figure 3.14 to reflect on the sort.

HOW ARE THE PICTURES ALIKE IN EACH CATEGORY? HOW ARE THEY DIFFERENT? Using the sort shown in Figure 3.13, you and your child consider and discuss the similarities and differences across and within the sort. All of the pictures under the letter *M* have the same beginning sound. Likewise, all of the pictures under the letter *R* have the same beginning sound.

ARE THERE ANY PICTURES THAT DO NOT FIT? WHY? Sometimes a sort may include pictures that do not fit in the sort. If so, help your child identify these pictures and discuss why they do not fit in the sort. For example, if this sort included a picture of *ball*, this picture does not fit in either category. Sometimes children also call a picture by a different name, such as *bunny* for *rabbit*. These pictures start with different beginning sounds and do not fall in the same categories. They may be placed aside and discussed later.

WHAT DO YOU LEARN FROM THIS SORT? In this case, children learn that *M* and *R* are each associated with particular sounds. The letter *M* is associated with the sound /m/ and is heard at the beginning of the words *mouse*, *moon*, and *man*. The letter *R* is associated with the sound /r/ as is

FIGURE 3.13 Beginning Sound Sort for *M/R*

Source: Bear, Donald R.; Invernizzi, Marcia R.; Johnston, Francine; Templeton, Shane, *Words Their Way Letter and Picture Sorts for Emergent Spellers*, 2nd Ed., ©2010. Reprinted and Electronically reproduced by permission of Pearson Education, Inc., New York, NY.

FIGURE 3.14 Let's Talk About It! Guiding Questions

Let's Talk About It!

1. How are the pictures alike in each category? How are they different?
2. Are there any pictures that do not fit? Why?
3. What do you learn from this sort?

heard at the beginning of *rabbit*, *rake*, and *run*. In addition, students gain the following understandings as they work through a variety of beginning sound sorts:

- Sorting is putting similar words, objects, or pictures together.
- We can stretch words out to listen for just the beginning sounds.
- Letters represent sounds.
- Words that start with the same sound usually start with the same letter.
- Some letters represent more than one sound, such as *G* in *giraffe* and *gold*, or *C* in *call* and *cent*.

Early Literacy Skills With Parents, Tutors, and School Volunteers

In this section, we share specific examples of how you can support the development of early literacy skills and word knowledge outlined in Table 3.2 for children at the emergent stage. Through reading and writing activities, word study instruction for the emergent readers aims toward the development of six main components of the learning to read process:

1. Oral language, concepts and vocabulary
2. Phonological awareness (PA) (including phonemic awareness)
3. Phonics (letter sounds)
4. Alphabet recognition
5. Concepts about Print (CAP)
6. Concept of Word (COW)

These six components constitute a comprehensive instruction "diet" for early literacy learning and instruction (Invernizzi, 2002). If all components are addressed on a daily basis, no matter how far along the emergent continuum a child may be, conventional reading and writing should inevitably follow.

Oral Language, Concepts, and Vocabulary

Young children at the age of 4 or 5 have already acquired a working oral vocabulary of more than 5,000 words (Justice, 2006). By the time they enter kindergarten, most children have learned an average of 13,000 words. Children at this age often confuse concepts and related words as they try to make sense of the world around them. After learning about animals at preschool, Clara shared with her mother how animals are different by saying, "Some animals are *males* and some animals are *meat eaters*." Although her information was technically correct, she has clearly not developed understanding of how these terms relate. An adult may understand that animals are either male or female, and meat eaters or plant eaters. To refine understanding of their growing vocabulary, children must have language experiences, such as conversations and being read to, that allow them to hear both new vocabulary as well as complex sentences. In the following section, we offer a number of suggestions to develop oral language, concepts, and vocabulary.

TALK You can make a profound difference in your child's language development by engaging your child in conversation every day about a variety of topics—school, friends, books, television programs, and shared experiences. Tips for extending language are described in Table 3.5.

VIEW AND DISCUSS EDUCATIONAL TELEVISION It may seem counterintuitive in a book about literacy to encourage television viewing, but there are a number of high-quality children's programs that support literacy and language. *Sesame Street* was groundbreaking

TABLE 3.5 Tips for Extending Language and Developing Vocabulary

Recommendations	Descriptions
Get close and listen	It is important that your child understands that you are listening and are interested in what he or she is saying. Get close and make sure that you are making eye contact. If you are standing, consider kneeling or sitting so that you can be level with your child and face him or her directly.
Provide encouragement	As your child speaks, provide support and acknowledgment by small interjections, such as, "Really?" or "Hmmm," or by nodding your head. Use phrases such as, "Tell me more."
Respond and expand	Acknowledge what your child has said by repeating or paraphrasing the content of their comments and expand on it. Add more information. For example, after visiting the zoo, you may say, "What did you see at the zoo?" If child says "A lion!" you may provide an expanded version of the same idea by saying, "You saw a brown lion. I saw a black and white zebra!"
Ask open-ended questions	You may also ask probing questions or provide extended vocabulary by asking questions such as, "What color was the lion?" or "What did the lion do?" Consider using open-ended questions such as, "What did you think about ______? How did you feel about that?" "What did you do at ______ (school, pool, park, friend's house)?"
Explain new words and encourage your child to use them	As you share stories, experiences, and conversations, be sure to provide child-friendly explanations of new words that are encountered: "A zebra looks sort of like a horse but has stripes," or "What color were the zebra's stripes?"

television which has, for over 50 years, used the educational power of media to help children with language development, literacy, and mathematics. This program and others like it promote knowledge of the alphabet, letter sounds, language, and diverse experiences. Today, there are many educational programs worth exploring, including those listed in Table 3.6. In addition to educational television, there are many similar programs available for purchase, download, or library checkout.

TABLE 3.6 Educational Television Programs for Young Children

Sesame Street	Dragon Tales	Reading Rainbow
Bill Nye the Science Guy	Bubble Guppies	Clifford the Big Red Dog
Zoboomafoo	The Wiggles	Thomas the Tank Engine
Between the Lions	Go, Diego, Go!	The Magic School Bus
Dora the Explorer	Daniel Tiger's Neighborhood	Word Girl
Super Why!	Curious George	Sid the Science Kid
The Cat in the Hat	Martha Speaks	Caillou

One caveat is that it is better to watch these shows *with* your child as opposed to leaving your child to watch them independently. The shared experience of watching these educational programs provides many opportunities for further talk and learning. Follow up by asking your child to tell you something they liked or learned. Ask them to tell you what happened, and encourage elaboration by asking what happened next or why things may have happened. Parents are also encouraged to make thoughtful choices and limit the amount of television viewing for young children.

NARRATE EVERYDAY EXPERIENCES WITH YOUR YOUNG CHILD Every experience we have has the possibility of contributing to our child's knowledge of the world, and specifically how they are able to use language to describe the experience. Going to the grocery store, doing laundry, making dinner, watching children's television, playing games, and many other everyday activities are rich opportunities to develop language. Although shopping may be mundane to you, imagine the experience for the little growing person sitting in your cart: colors, smells, words, sounds, textures, people, and so many questions like, "Is that a fruit and what does it taste like?" When you bring a young child to the grocery store, provide the written list to the child and talk about looking for the apples, bananas, and mangoes (and count them too!). Narrate the trip by talking about the food going into your cart and ask questions. Create a dialogue with your child while deliberately introducing new words. When you pick up a pineapple ask, "Can you feel the outside of the pineapple? It's very rough." Allow your child to touch the fruit. Realize that the dialogue is important, even if it is one-sided. Don't expect an answer to every question, and don't worry if your child doesn't join in. Supermarkets can be exciting and overwhelming places! Your conversation helps your child make sense of the experience as they develop concepts and vocabulary.

Connect a visit to the bookstore or library with your everyday experiences. Consider looking for books with subjects that follow your experiences, such as those listed in Figure 3.15. For example, Lois Ehlert's alphabet book, *Eating the Alphabet: Fruits and Vegetables from A to Z*, is a great read following (or before!) a trip to the grocery store. Simple field trips to the park, a pond, the beach, a pool, a car wash, the library, the zoo, or a relative's home can create rich opportunities to learn language because they provide unique experiences.

FIGURE 3.15 Books about Everyday Experiences

Books about Everyday Experiences

Aliki (1996). *Hello! Goodbye!* Greenwillow.
Alda, Arlene. (2009). *Hello, Goodbye*. Tundra Books.
Brown, Margaret Wise. (1995). *A Child's Goodnight Book*. HarperFestival.
Brown, Margaret Wise. (1995). *Goodnight Moon*. HarperFestival.
Brown, Margaret Wise. (1995). *Big Red Barn*. HarperFestival.
Cousins, Lucy. (1999). *Maisy's Bedtime*. Candlewick.
Cousins, Lucy. (1999). *Maisy Dresses Up*. Candlewick.
Cousins, Lucy. (1999). *Maisy's Pool*. Candlewick.
Cousins, Lucy. (2001). *Maisy Goes Shopping*. Candlewick.
Cousins, Lucy. (2010). *Maisy Goes to Preschool*. Candlewick.
Cousins, Lucy. (2010). *Maisy Takes a Bath*. Candlewick.
Crews, Donald. (1993). *School Bus*. Greenwillow.
Ehlert, Lois (1998). *Planting a Rainbow*. Harcourt.
Ehlert, Lois. (1989). *Eating the Alphabet: Fruits and Vegetables from A to Z*. Harcourt Brace.
Fox, Mem. (1997). *Time for Bed*. Harcourt Brace.
London, Jonathan. (1998). *Froggy Goes to School*. Puffin.
London, Jonathan. (2008). *Froggy Learns to Swim*. Puffin.
London, Jonathan. (1998). *Froggy Rides a Bike*. Puffin.
London, Jonathan. (2004). *Froggy Goes to the Doctor*. Puffin.
London, Jonathan. (2007). *Froggy's Sleepover*. Puffin.
London, Jonathan. (2003). *Froggy Eats Out*. Puffin.
London, Jonathan. (2010). *Froggy Goes to Camp*. Puffin.
Ziefert, Harriet. (2012). *ABC Dentist*. Blue Apple Books.

READ AND TALK ABOUT BOOKS Children's books, both fiction and nonfiction, provide rich opportunities for children to be exposed to new vocabulary. Even picture books designed for very young children introduce interesting words that might not otherwise enter conversation. For example, in the picture book *Goodnight, Goodnight Construction Site* by Sheri Duskey Rinker and Tom Lichtenheld, the story describes what happens on a construction site using rhyme.

TABLE 3.7 Tips for Reading Aloud with Your Child

Recommendations	Descriptions
Select a book	Select a book with rich language that is age appropriate.
Introduce the book	Introduce the book by reading the title and naming the author and illustrator. Look at the cover and the first few pages to set a purpose for reading. Ask your child, "What do you think this book is about?" Browse through the pages and discuss what you and your child see before reading.
Connect to experiences	Connect the concepts in the book to your child's background. For example, if the story involves a pet and your child has a pet, say, "Look, the little boy has a pet dog just like you," or "This little girl loves her grandma too."
Develop vocabulary	Identify words that you suspect are new to your child. Point to the word and/or a picture and supply a brief, child-friendly definition. "This is a papaya. It's a fruit."
Expand language	Encourage your child to talk and expand on your child's comments and phrases to provide more complex sentences and vocabulary. For example, if your child says she likes the dog in the story, you may restate and expand her comments by saying, "You like the dog playing in the park with the ball."
Invite your child to participate	Invite your child to chime in if the read aloud includes a common phrase such as "*Run, run, run as fast as you can. You can't catch me, I'm the gingerbread man!*" from *The Gingerbread Man*, or "*But he was still hungry*," from *The Very Hungry Caterpillar.*
Retell the story	Encourage your child to go back through the book and use the pictures to retell what happened.
Reread favorites	Reread favorite stories. It is very common for children to want to hear the same stories, jingles, and rhymes. Rereading to your child allows him or her to learn more about language, rhyme, and vocabulary.

The book includes many interesting vocabulary words, such as *construction*, *site*, *load*, *beam*, *might*, *rough*, *crane*, *stretching*, *reaching*, *bulldozer*, and *excavator*. In *Slowly, Slowly, Slowly Said the Sloth*, Eric Carle uses pictures to introduce readers to a unique mix of animals, including *armadillo*, *anaconda*, *poison dart frog*, *bat*, *hoatzin*, *tapir*, *peccary*, *puma*, *anteater*, *postman butterfly*, *toucan*, and of course, the *sloth*. Parents can create opportunities to grow their child's vocabulary and concepts by reading and engaging in conversation about words. Refer to Table 3.7 for tips on reading aloud with your child and Figure 3.16 for a list of *Let's Read and Find Out* books.

REREAD BOOKS Young children who have had the experience of being read to routinely ask to have the same book read over and over and over. This is, in fact, an excellent practice, and provides the opportunity for children to question the meaning of new words when they hear them repeatedly. Children are likely to focus on the concepts, illustrations, and language play in the first several readings of a book. Over time, children notice specific words,

FIGURE 3.16 Let's Read and Find Out Readers

Aliki. (2000). *Let's Read and Find Out: My Five Senses*. HarperCollins.

Branley, Franklyn M. (2000). *Snow Is Falling*. HarperCollins.

Branley, Franklyn M. (2006). *Air Is All Around You*. HarperCollins.

Jenkins, Priscilla Belz. (1991). *Let's Read and Find Out: A Nest Full of Eggs*. HarperCollins.

Jordan, Helene. (2000). *Let's Read and Find Out: How to Grow a Seed*. Harper Collins.

Pfeffer, Wendy. (1994). *Let's Read and Find Out: From Tadpole to Frog*. HarperCollins.

Pfeffer, Wendy. (1996). *Let's Read and Find Out: What's It Like to Be a Fish*. HarperCollins.

Rockwell, Ann. (2008). *Let's Read and Find Out: Clouds*. HarperCollins.

Showers, Paul. (1991). *Let's Read and Find Out: How Many Teeth*. HarperCollins.

Showers, Paul. (1997). *Let's Read and Find Out: Sleep Is for Everyone*. HarperCollins.

such as *excavator*, from *Goodnight Construction Site*, which may spark a conversation. Rereading books allows children multiple exposures to words and ideas.

As you reread, your child may learn to recite the text. For example, twins Clara and Libby, age 3, routinely asked their mom to read *Too Purply* by Jean Reidy (2013). The girls often joined their mother by reciting,

> *Not these clothes!*
>
> *Too itchy,*
> *Too scratchy,*
> *Too stitchy,*
> *Too matchy.*

Clara and Libby learned the meaning of words that represent unique ideas such as *stitch-y* and *match-y* and enjoyed their own participation. As a side note, Clara often told her mom that it was not her turn: "Mommy, not you." She was proud of her skill as a reader, although clearly the reading is recitation at this stage. Young children who have been read to frequently in their home or school may also take the opportunity to pretend read to their stuffed animals, dolls, pets, or, in this case, to a sibling. The family dog might be serenaded with a song and a book such as *Down by the Bay* by Raffi.

> *Down by the bay*
> *Where the watermelons grow*
> *Back to my home*
> *I dare not go*
> *For if I do*
> *My mother will say*
>
> *"Have you ever seen a goose*
> *Kissing a moose?"*
> *Down by the bay*

The recitation may not be perfect, but the experience emphasizes early literacy skills such as concepts about print, phonological awareness, and vocabulary development.

SHARE WORDLESS BOOKS Wordless books require that the reader pay close attention to the details of the illustrations in order to discover the story. As you share a wordless book with your child, point to specific parts of the illustrations and narrate what is occurring. Invite your child to tell you what is happening. In Mercer Mayer's *A Boy, A Dog, a Frog, and a Friend*, readers encounter a mischievous turtle that interrupts the fishing adventures of a young boy and his trustworthy dog and frog. There are several books in the series by Mercer Mayer about a boy, a dog, and a frog, all of which endear the reader, provide humor, and create an opportunity to talk about story. Other wordless books for young children are included in Figure 3.17.

FIGURE 3.17 Wordless Books for Young Children

Briggs, Raymond. (1978). *The Snowman*. Random House.
Day, Alexandra. (1991). *Good Dog, Carl*. Simon & Schuster Books for Young Readers.
Day, Alexandra. (1997). *Carl's Birthday*. Farrar, Straus and Giroux.
Day, Alexandra. (1991). *Carl's Summer Vacation*. Simon & Schuster Books for Young Readers.
Mayer, Mercer. (1993). *A Boy, a Dog, a Frog and a Friend*. Dial.
Mayer, Mercer. (2003). *A Boy, a Dog, and a Frog*. Dial.
Mayer, Mercer. (2003). *Frog Goes to Dinner*. Dial.
Mayer, Mercer. (2003). *One Frog Too Many*. Dial.
Mayer, Mercer (2003). *Frog Where Are You*? Dial.
Mayer, Mercer (2003). *Frog on His Own*. Dial.
Lee, Suzy. (2008). *The Wave*. Chronicle Books.
Lehman, Barbara. (2004). *The Red Book*. Houghton Mifflin.
Lehman, Barbara. (2006). *Museum Trip*. Houghton Mifflin.
Pinkney, Jerry. (2009). *The Lion and the Mouse*. Little, Brown Books for Young Readers.
Pinkney, Jerry. (2013). *The Tortoise and the Hare*. Little, Brown Books for Young Readers.
Raschka, Chris. (2011). *A Ball for Daisy*. Schwartz & Wade.
Rohmann, Eric. (1997). *Time Flies*. Dragonfly Books.
Thompson, Bill. (2010). *Chalk*. Marshall Cavendish Children's Books.
Wiesner, David. (1991). *Freefall*. HarperCollins.
Wiesner, David. (2011). *Tuesday*. Houghton Mifflin.

RETELL STORIES AND TELL YOUR OWN Encourage your child to retell the stories you have shared. After reading familiar or new stories, ask your child to retell the story using the pictures. This practice promotes the development of oral language and vocabulary, while also enhancing concepts about print. Also, tell or retell family stories. Our children love to hear the story of when they were born, family trips, or adventures of when their mom and dad were young. Stories can be simple. One of our families fondly retells the story of how the family

TABLE 3.8 Tips for Talking about Concept Books

Recommendations	Descriptions
Introduce the book	Introduce the book by reading the title and discussing the cover. If you are reading *Mouse Paint* by Ellen Stoll Walsh, for example, you may suggest that the book is going to be about mice painting different colors. You may point to the mice and the splashes of color. Ask your child to describe what he or she sees on the cover and throughout the book.
Read the book aloud	Read the concept book aloud using your voice to emphasize the concepts in the book.
Label objects and concepts	Label concepts on the page by pointing and saying, "Look! That is a _____.
Ask questions	Ask your child questions about the book and allow him or her to talk about what is seen.
Connect to experiences	Make connections between the book and your child's experiences. To use the example of *Mouse Paint*, you might ask for the child's favorite color or recognize colors in the room around you. "Your shirt is blue, just like in the book."
Encourage retelling	Encourage your child to tell you what he or she sees and thinks about on each page. Once the book is finished, ask your child to flip through the pages and talks about what he or she sees.
Reread frequently	Reread favorite concept books. It is very common for children to want to hear the same book over and over. Rereading to your child allows him or her to learn more about language, rhyme, vocabulary, and concepts.

visited Washington D.C. during a spring break and all of the Easter candy melted in the car.

SHARE CONCEPT BOOKS Concept books are designed for young children to introduce simple ideas such as colors, shapes, animals, opposites, and types of clothing. Typically, the books have very little text with a focus on the pictures, such as Tana Hoban's *Is It Red? Is It Yellow? Is It Blue?* and Eric Carle's *My Very First Book of Shapes*. Concept books allow parents to introduce language and appropriate labels or questions about objects and ideas: "This book is about colors all around us. What color is the sky?" Concept books categories include the alphabet, counting, color, shape, vegetables, animals, trucks, time, and size. Table 3.8 presents some tips on discussing concept books with your child, and Figure 3.18 provides a list of concept books to explore.

PLAY WITH CONCEPT SORTS Concept sorts, discussed earlier in the chapter, are great ways to develop a child's vocabulary, oral language, and background knowledge. Just as concept books are used to generate conversation, parents can create concept sorts using everyday objects. Select a group of objects or pictures that have similarities and differences. For example, toys such as building blocks, dolls, miniature cars, and stuffed animals can be used for sorting. Household objects can also be sorted, such as keys, buttons, photographs, toys, clothing, shoes, nuts and

FIGURE 3.18 Concept Books

Crews, Donald. (1995). *Ten Black Dots*. Greenwillow.
Crews, Donald. (1995). *Freight Train*. Scholastic.
Ehlert, Lois. (1990). *Color Farm*. Harper Collins.
Ehlert, Lois. (1990). *Growing Vegetable Soup*. Voyager Books.
Ehlert, Lois. (1992). *Planting a Rainbow*. HMH Books for Young Readers.
Fleming, Denise. (1996). *Lunch*. Square Fish.
Fox, Mem. (2010). *Ten Little Fingers. Ten Little Toes*. HMH Books for Young Readers.
Hoban, Tana. (1978). *26 Letters and 99 Cents?* Greenwillow Books.
Hoban, Tana. (1978). *Is It Red? Is It Yellow? Is It Blue?* Greenwillow Books.
Hoban, Tana. (1986). *Red, Blue, Yellow Shoe.* Greenwillow Books.
Hoban, Tana. (1992). *Fish Eyes: A Book You Can Count on.* Greenwillow Books.
Hoban, Tana. (1997). *Is It Larger? Is It Smaller?* Greenwillow Books.
Hoban, Tana. (1997). *Exactly the Opposite.* Greenwillow Books.
Hoban, Tana. (1996). *Shapes, Shapes, Shapes.* Greenwillow Books.
Hoban, Tana. (2000). *Cubes, Cylinders, Cones, and Spheres.* Greenwillow Books.
Intriago, Patricia. (2011). *Dot.* Margaret Ferguson Books.
Tullet, Herve. (2011). *Press Here.* Chronicle Books.
Walsh, Ellen Stoll. (1995). *Mouse Paint.* HMH for Young Readers.
Walsh, Ellen Stoll. (1995). *Mouse Count.* HMH for Young Readers.

FIGURE 3.19 Concept Sort with Hot- and Cold-Weather Items

bolts, dried beans, and pasta. The objects should have different characteristics such as shape, color, texture, material, or size. For example, toy animal figures can be sorted into many categories:

- Habitat: animals that live on land, animals that live in water, animals that live in both
- Movement: animals that can fly, run, slither
- Number of legs: zero, two, four
- Animals with fur, fins, or feathers

In addition to developing a child's conceptual understanding, many new vocabulary terms are introduced during sorting. With the previous example, a child may be introduced to concepts of color, texture, number, and movement. They learn the names of animals and describing words, such as *fast*, *rough*, *large*, and *feathered*. Concept sorts can be very simple (sorting objects by color) or complex (sorting vertebrate animals into mammals, reptiles, birds, fishes, and amphibians). Figure 3.19 shows a concept sort with hot and cold weather items.

Phonological Awareness

Phonological awareness (PA) consists of an array of understanding about speech sounds that includes sensitivity to syllables, rhyme, alliteration (beginning sounds), and phonemes. Syllables, rhyme, and alliteration are the best places to start with emergent learners, and several activities for developing these are included here. In addition, in Figure 3.20 we provide a few questions that support conversation with young children around phonological awareness.

READ BOOKS THAT INCLUDE RHYME AND LANGUAGE PLAY Reading books with rhyme and language play offers a rich opportunity to teach phonological awareness with young children. For example, Jane Yolen and Mark Teague wrote and illustrated the popular picture book series including *How Do Dinosaurs Say Goodnight?*, *How Do Dinosaurs Go To School?*, and *How Do Dinosaurs Say I Love You?* Each book includes rich language and rhyme as human parents deal with their challenging dinosaur children.

As emergent learners hear the rhyme over and over, they may memorize and recite their favorite stories. Many books written for young children include rhyming words. Take the time to bring attention to some of the words that rhyme. For example, you might say, "Listen to the rhyming words, *mood/food*." Sometimes you can also pause and let the child supply the rhyming word. From *How Do Dinosaurs Say I Love You?*, you could say to your child, "*You woke in the morning in such a bad mood. Then sat at the table and fussed with your . . .*" and ask the child to fill in the missing rhyming word. Books such as *Is Your Mama a Lama?* or *I Can't, Said the Ant* work especially well for leaving the rhyming

FIGURE 3.20 Prompts to Develop Phonological Awareness

- I heard two words that rhyme. Can you find them?
- Can you find a word that begins with the sound ____?
- Can you find a word that ends with the ___ sound?
- Can you find a word that begins like ____'s name?
- What sound does the word ______ begin with?

FIGURE 3.21 Books with Rhyme and Language Play

Alborough, Jez. (2000). *Duck in a Truck.* HarperCollins.
Ahlberg, Janet and Allan. (1999). *Each Peach Pear Plum.* Viking.
Bryan, Sean. (2007). *A Boy and His Bear.* Arcade Publishing.
Cameron, Polly. (1961). *I Can't Said the Ant.* Scholastic.
Christelow, Eileen. (1989). *Five Little Monkeys Jumping on the Bed*. Boston: Clarion Books.
Cole, Joanna & Calmenson, Stephanie. (1991). *The Eensty, Weentsy Spider.* HarperCollins.
Cowley, Joy. (1998). *Nicketty-Nacketty Noo-Noo-Noo*. Mondo Publishing.
Dewdney, Anna. (2005). *Llama, Llama Red Pajama.* Viking.
DePaola, Tomie. (1988). *Hey Diddle Diddle.* Puffin.
Guarino, Deborah. (1989). *Is Your Mama a Llama?* Scholastic.
Hoberman, Mary Ann. (1998). *Miss Mary Mack.* HMH Books for Young Readers.
Hoberman, Mary Ann. (2000). *The Seven Silly Eaters*. HMH Books for Young Readers.
Jorgenson, Gail. (1995). *The Crocodile Beat*. Scholastic.
Lies, Brian. (2008). *Bats at the Library*. Houghton Mifflin.
Martin, Jr., Bill. (2006). *"Fire! Fire!" Said Mrs. McGuire.* Harcourt.
Martin, Jerome. (1992). *Carrot, Parrot.* The Trumpet Club.
Peet. Bill. (2008). *The Caboose Got Loose*. HMH Books for Young Readers.
Slate, Joseph. (2001). *Miss Bindergarten Gets Ready for Kindergarten*. Puffin.
Sendak, Maurice. (1991). *Chicken Soup with Rice: A Book of Months*. HarperCollins.
Yolen, Jane. (2009). *How Do Dinosaurs Say I Love You?* Blue Sky Press.
Weeks, Sarah. (2002). *Mrs. McNosh Hangs Up Her Wash.* HarperCollins.
Westcott, Nadine. (1993). *There's a Hole in the Bucket.* Lippincott.
Wilson, Karma. (2009). *Bear Snores On*. Harcourt.
Ziefert, Harriet & Ehrlich, Fred. (2008). *A Bunny Is Funny*. Blue Apple Books.

word up to the listener. In *Is Your Mama a Llama?*, the book is structured to encourage readers and listeners to guess the rhyming word.

You and your child will enjoy reading and rereading books that feature rhyme and language play, including those highlighted in Figure 3.21.

SHARE RHYMES, JINGLES AND SONGS In addition to reading aloud, share music and rhymes filled with language play. There are many artists who write and perform for children, including The Wiggles, Raffi, Jack Johnson, Yo Gabba Gabba, The Laurie Berkner Band, Dan Zanes, Bill Harley, The Fresh Beat Band, and Jessica Harper. Listen to their recordings at bedtime or in the car and learn the songs along with your child to sing together. Some songs lend themselves to inventive fun with rhymes and sounds. Figure 3.22 contains a list of songs that have also been made into children's picture books.

RHYMING SORTS Teachers, parents, and volunteers can support the development of phonological awareness in young children through the use of rhyming sorts. At first, children may not understand what you mean by the term *rhyme*, so be sure to model and talk about how the words are alike: "Listen, *bed/red*. *Bed* and *red* are rhyming words because they sound alike at the end." Sorts can be created with pictures or objects and must include at least two rhyming families or patterns. Often the rhyming sort is connected to a familiar rhyme or story. After reading a story about body parts, such as *Here Are My Hands* by Bill Martin and John

FIGURE 3.22 Books with Rhymes, Jingles, and Songs

Glazer, Tom. (1995). *On Top of Spaghetti.* Harcourt Brace.
Hoberman, MaryAnn. (2002). *The Eensy, Weensy Spider.* LB Kids.
Jones, Carol. (1998). *This Old Man.* HMH Books for Young Readers.
Norwith, Jack. (1999). *Take Me Out to the Ball Game*. Aladdin.
Peek, Merle. (1988). *Mary Wore Her Red Dress*. HMH Books for Young Readers.
Peek, Merle. (1981). *Rollover! A Counting Song.* HMH Books for Young Readers.
Raffi. (1988). *Down by the Bay*. Crown Books.
Raffi. (1989). *Five Little Ducks.* Crown Books.
Schwartz, Amy. (1999). *Old MacDonald.* Scholastic.
Trapani, Iza. (2004). *How Much Is That Doggie in the Window?* Charlesbridge.
Trapani, Iza. (2001). *Baa, Baa, Black Sheep.* Charlesbridge.
Trapani, Iza. (1996). *I'm a Little Teapot.* Charlesbridge.
Trapani, Iza. (1998). *Mary Had a Little Lamb. Charlesbridge.*
Trapani, Iza. (1999). *Row, Row, Row Your Boat.* Charlesbridge.
Trapani, Iza. (1994). *Twinkle, Twinkle, Little Star.* Charlesbridge.
Westcott, Nadine. (1992). *Peanut Butter and Jelly: A Play Rhyme.* Harcourt.
Westcott, Nadine. (1990). *The Lady with the Alligator Purse.* Little, Brown Books for Young Readers.
Zelinsky, P.O. (1990). *The Wheels on the Bus.* Dutton Publishing.

FIGURE 3.23 Body Part Rhyming Sort

FIGURE 3.24 Odd-One-Out

Archambault, you can engage your child in a rhyming picture sort with body parts, as in Figure 3.23.

Begin by asking your child to name all the parts of a body shown in the pictures. Explain that two of the body parts rhyme (*toes* and *nose*) and name the pictures to find them. Put *toes* under *nose*. Continue by saying, "What else rhymes with *nose*? Let's name the other pictures and listen for words that rhyme with *nose*." Find the *hose* and the *rose* and place them under *nose*. Explain that the words *hose* and *rose* rhyme with nose, but are not body parts. Repeat with the other body part picture cards as a starting point, engaging your child as much as possible. After sorting, name the picture in each column, emphasizing the common sound. The big idea here is that rhyming pictures have the same sound at the end of the word. Rhyming sorts can be created with pictures or small objects purchased in children's toy stores.

RHYMING STORY EXTENSIONS Rhyming read-alouds can be followed by picture sorts for rhymes. For example, a rhyming sort extension to *Oh, A-Hunting We Will Go* might match up pictures of animals and the places they will go (*fox/box*, *mouse/house*, *goat/boat*, etc.). To make it easier for beginners, lay out just two pictures that rhyme along with one that does not. This odd-one-out setup, shown in Figure 3.24, enables children to identify more readily the two rhyming pictures. They only have to pick up the first card, in this example a *cat* or a *duck*, and match the rhyming object, *bat* or *truck (cat, bat* and *duck, truck)*. Alternatively, you and your child may name the three pictures in a row, such as *cat*, *ball*, and *bat*, and your child identifies which picture does not belong. In this example, *ball* does not belong because it does not have the same rhyming sound as *cat* and *bat*. Be sure to focus on sounds, not meaning. A *ball* and a *bat* are related through sport and beginning sound; however, building phonological awareness in children requires that they consider the sound of words apart from their meaning, and in this case we are focused on rhyme.

PLAY A GAME: WHOSE NAME HAS MORE SYLLABLES? LET'S CLAP TO FIND OUT! Choose two names that differ in the number of syllables. Say each name and clap to each syllable. Ask which name has more syllables. For example, *Mo-ham-mad* is three syllables and *An-na* is two; therefore Mohammed has more syllables. Repeat with names of family and friends. Please note that this game is purely oral; we are not referencing print.

PLAY RHYMING GAMES There are a number of games that can be played which emphasize rhyme that may be purchased commercially, or you may create your own rhyming sorts, rhyming bingo, and rhyming concentration. Many electronic rhyming games are also available to play on tablets or other devices.

Phonics (Letter Sounds)

Many of the activities discussed here apply to both alphabet recognition and letter sounds. Each can be used to support a growing understanding of the alphabet and its function in words. The key concept you want your child to know is that each letter of the alphabet is associated with at least one sound. They eventually also learn that some letters are associated with more than one sound. The letters *G* and *C*, for example, can be soft or hard, as in *gentle* (soft) or *goat* (hard) and or *cycle* (soft) or *cup* (hard). Some letters share a letter sound with another letter name or sound; the /k/ sound can be spelled with *C* as in *cat* or *K* as in *kite*. These letters require more attention, and at this stage it is best to stick to one sound.

SORT BEGINNING PICTURES OR OBJECTS Children first learn to identify the beginning sounds, usually consonants, in words. As children are just beginning to understand letter–sound correspondence, sorts can be created that include the letters they have learned. This often begins with the letters in their own names. Obvious contrasts are usually taught first, such as *B* compared to *M* and *R* compared to *S*. Letters that are similar in formation (b/d/p) are generally taught separately, as are letters with similar sounds, such as *P* and *B*. Beginning consonant picture sorts include all pictures to sort with a header that includes the upper- and lower-case letter with a key picture. The sorting process for beginning sound sorts was detailed earlier in the chapter in the *Let's Talk About It* example with *M* and *R*.

FIGURE 3.25 Sample Sort: Beginning Consonants

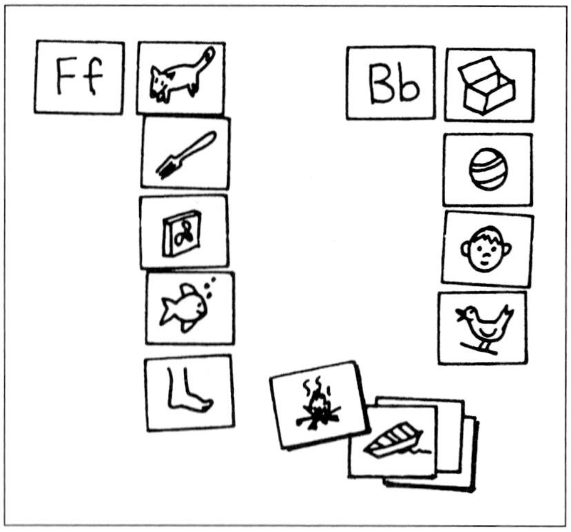

Games that explicitly connect the letters of the alphabet with their sounds are very useful for emergent learners. You can purchase or create beginning picture or object sorts in the same style of the sort shown in Figure 3.25. Begin with only two letters and sounds, such as *F* and *B*, and objects or pictures that begin with these initial sounds. Have your child sort into two categories while reciting the names aloud. For example, your child may sort pictures of *fox*, *fork*, *fan*, *fish*, and *foot* into one category, and *box*, *ball*, *boy*, and *bird* into another. In order to sort the objects or pictures, the child must say each word aloud and identify the beginning sound. Classrooms and schools using a developmental word study approach engage preschool and kindergarten children in beginning sound sorts on a weekly basis.

CREATE SOUND BAGS Create sounds bags with your child. Label the outside of a paper sack with an upper-case and lower-case letter of the alphabet. Help your child to search through your house looking for items that start with that sound. These sound bags can later be used for object sorts when you mix the objects from two bags together.

PLAY A GAME: SOUND I SPY I Spy is a time-tested game in which children and parents examine their surroundings (or pages in a book) and locate something. In this case, the parent might say, "I spy something that begins with /t/." The child's job is to use the beginning sound to guess the mystery object. In this example the child might refer to *table* which begins with the letter T.

PLAY A GAME: THE NAME GAME In this game, the parent or tutor chooses an initial consonant, sound such as /b/. Each person playing the game substitutes the first letter in his or her own name with the beginning consonant. So, a child named Libby might say *Libby-Bibby*. Josh might say *Josh-Bosh*, and Mommy might say *Mommy-Bommy*. The game continues with additional players, and then the initial letter sound can be changed.

PLAY COMMERCIAL ALPHABET GAMES There are many commercially produced games for parents and educators that address alphabet knowledge. These games can be used at home to support your child in learning the names of the letters and the sounds they make.

Alphabet Knowledge (Letter Recognition)

Learning the alphabet involves a series of steps, including identifying and forming letters and to match letters with beginning sounds in words. This section describes ways in which you can develop a child's ability to recognize and name letters. There are 26 upper-case and 26 lower-case letters in the English language. Your child must be able to recognize the shape and orientation of each letter. Some letters appear to be the same, with the exception of their orientation. For example, the lower-case letters *b*, *d*, and *p* all have the same shape, but it is their orientation that defines which letter is represented. Many of the following ideas can also be used to begin teaching children to associate letters with sounds.

BEGIN WITH YOUR CHILD'S NAME There is great power in a child's name. Emergent children tend to learn the letters in their own name before others because there is a personal significance to the letters. Also, parents tend to encourage their child to spell their names on the refrigerator with magnetic letters or with alphabet puzzle pieces. Build your child's name with letter cards, tiles, foam, or plastic letters, using both upper-case and lower-case letters. Mix them up and spell the name again. Identify the letters as you spell. Spell your child's name with upper-case letters in the first row and ask your child to match lower-case letters in the row below, as shown in Figure 3.26. Ask your child to touch and name each letter. Scramble the top row and repeat. Ask your child to match letter cards to spell his or her name, and then practice writing the letters, as shown in Figure 3.27.

FIGURE 3.26 Brandon's Name Puzzle

FIGURE 3.27 Name Grid for Beth

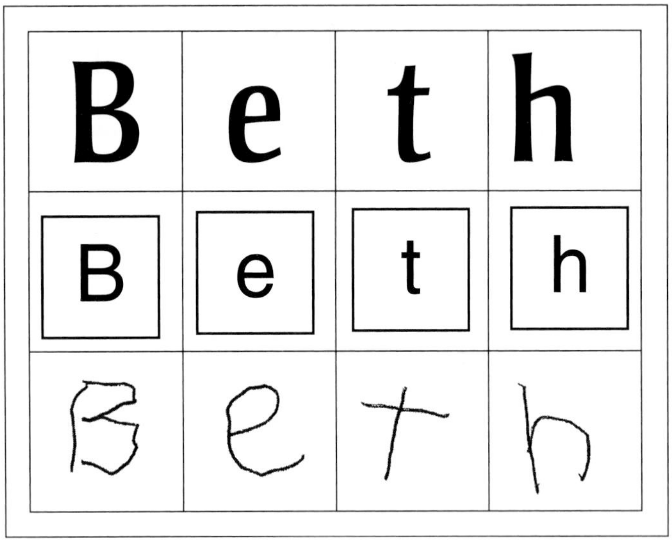

Play Concentration with the set of upper-case and lower-case letters needed to spell a child's name. You may remember that Abby could spell her name "A – B – nudda B – Y" as a result of practice with magnetic letters. Although capitals are typically easier to learn than lower-case letters, names are a good place to introduce the concept of two kinds of letters, and we advise introducing both.

SING THE ALPHABET SONG AND TRACK THE LETTERS Sing the traditional alphabet song, but also look for versions online with accompanying videos. As you sing with your child, provide an alphabet book, puzzle, or magnetic letters that can be matched to the song. Versions of the alphabet song include several by Dr. Jean, such as *Who Let the Letters Out?*, *Alphardy*, *Sing and Sign*, and *Phonercise*.

READ ALPHABET BOOKS Thousands of engaging alphabet books exist, from the very simple *Chicka Chicka Boom Boom* by Martin and Archambault to the more content-rich series by author Jerry Palotta, including *A: The Airplane Alphabet Book* through *Y: The Yucky Reptile Alphabet Book*. Palotta's books are based on a theme or an area of interest, such as animals, dinosaurs, insects, or fruits. These books create opportunities not only to develop knowledge of the alphabet, but also to increase vocabulary and conceptual knowledge—a goal discussed at the beginning of the chapter. We offer a list of some alphabet books, but there are many more that you can find in your local library and bookstore. Take the time to point to the letters, name them, and encourage your child to do the same. Many alphabet books feature pictures of objects spelled with the featured letter, and these offer the opportunity to focus attention on beginning sounds as well. Alphabet books are prolific.

FIGURE 3.28 Alphabet Books

Alphabet Books

Aylesworth, Jim. (1992). *Old Black Fly.* Henry Holt & Company.
Baker, Keith. (2010). *LMNO Peas*. Beach Lane Books.
Base, Graeme. (1986). *Animalia*. Harry Abrams.
Carle, Eric. (2007). *Eric Carle's ABCs*. Grossett & Dunlap.
Ehlert, Lois. (1989). *Eating the Alphabet: Fruits and Vegetables from A to Z.* Harcourt Brace.
Ernst, Lisa. (1996). *The Letters Are Lost.* Puffin.
Gaiman, Neil. (2008). *The Dangerous Alphabet Book*. Harper Collins.
Isadora, Rachel. (1992). *City Seen from A to Z.* Greenwillow Books.
Johnston, Stephen T. (1999). *Alphabet City*. Puffin (Caldecott Honor Book).
Kontis, Alethea. (2006). *AlphaOops: The Day Z Went First.* Candlewick.
Lear, Edward. (2005). *A Was Once an Apple Pie.* Orchard Books.
Lobel, Anita. (1981). *On Market Street*. Greenwillow Books.
Martin, Bill, & Archambault, John. (1989). *Chick Chicka Boom Boom*. Simon & Schuster.
McLimans, David. (2006). *Gone Wild: An Endangered Animal Alphabet*. Walker Childrens (Caldecott Honor Book).
McPhail, David. (1989). *Animals A to Z*. Scholastic.
Musgrove, Margaret. (1992). *Ashanti to Zulu: African Traditions*. Puffin Books (Caldecott Honor Book).
Palotta, Jerry. (1999). *The Airplane Alphabet Book*. Charlesbridge.
Palotta, Jerry. (1989). *The Yucky Reptile Alphabet Book*. Charlesbridge.
Palotta, Jerry., and Thomason, B. (1992). *The Vegetable Alphabet Book*. Charlesbridge.
Pelletier, David. (1996). *The Graphic Alphabet Book*. Scholastic (Caldecott Honor Book).
Seuss, Dr. (1963). *Dr. Seuss' Alphabet Book.* Random House.
Sobel. June. (2006). *Shiver Me Letters: A Pirate ABC*. HMH Books for Young Readers.
Van Allsburg, Chris. (1987). *The Z Was Zapped: A Play in Twenty-Six Acts*. HMH Books for Young Readers.
Wood, Audrey, and Wood, Bruce. (2003). *Alphabet Mystery*. Blue Sky Press.

Although we highlight titles in Figure 3.28, be advised to talk to a librarian, as there are hundreds of quality titles.

MAKE YOUR OWN ALPHABET BOOK The best alphabet book of all is a child's personal alphabet scrapbook. Create a page for each letter in a notebook, binder, or staple a pack of paper. Draw or paste pictures from coloring books, photographs, or magazines onto each lettered page and label them. You might start with photos of family members and pets. Be sure to give your child a key image with a strong letter–sound match. For example, you do not want to use the word/picture *elephant* for the letter *E* because many children hear the letter *L* at the beginning of the word. Select transparent sounds (*E* as in *eagle* has the long *e* sound).

PLAY ALPHABET GAMES A number of commercial alphabet puzzles and games are available in stores. There are also many games and applications to download to your computer or handheld devices. Look for games that provide the upper- and lower-case letters and a picture with which to associate that letter and sound.

PLAY WITH MAGNETIC ALPHABET LETTERS Magnetic alphabet letters are a wonderful way to spend a few minutes each day learning the names and shapes of letters. You might ask your child to

- find the letters in his or her name
- put the letters in order

FIGURE 3.29 Font Sort

- sort letters he or she knows and those he or she does not know
- match upper- and lower-case letters
- sort letters with straight lines versus letters with curvy lines
- sort upper- and lower-case letters
- spell (with your help) the first names of family members

FONT SORTS Children need to see a variety of print styles before they are readily able to identify their ABCs in different contexts. Draw your child's attention to different letter forms wherever you encounter them. Environmental print is especially rich in creative lettering styles. At home, create a font sort (Figure 3.29) and encourage your child to collect all the versions of a single letter; repeat for other letters.

GO ON A LETTER HUNT Give your child a highlighter or a crayon and a page of print, such as the ads from a newspaper, and challenge them to find a particular letter wherever they can find it. Start with the letters in their name: "Sam, can you find all the *S*s on this page and mark them?" When Sam looks for the letter *A*, he not only needs to look for a letter that differs in its upper- and lower-case forms, but the different form that lower-case *A* takes in most print.

PLAY A GAME: ALPHABET PUZZLES Create a simple set of puzzles designed to practice the pairing of upper-case and lower-case letters. Select a shape that interests your child (soccer balls, mittens, flowers, etc.) and is easy to replicate. Cut enough shapes for each letter in the alphabet using any shape easy to replicate. Write an upper-case letter on one half and the matching lower-case letter on the other half. Cut the shapes in half using a zigzag line. Make each zigzag slightly different so the activity is self-checking. Your child can practice saying the names of the letters and match the upper-case and lower-case forms. There are many commercial and electronic products readily available that follow the style of alphabet puzzles described here.

Concepts about Print (CAP)

Concepts of print are best learned in the context of reading and writing. Songs that you sing, poems and jingles that you learn, and portions of longer books with catchy memorable refrains (such as, "I'll huff and I'll puff and I'll blow your house down!") can be great starting points for developing these early literacy skills. In addition to the activities provided here, please take a moment to review Table 3.9 for ways to discuss concepts about print when reading and writing with your child. The left column illustrates the skills we want to develop in our young children, and the right column provides helpful comments to reference print during reading and writing.

DRAW ATTENTION TO PRINT IN THE ENVIRONMENT The world is full of print, but children are not likely to pay much attention unless adults take the time to point it out and explain what purpose it serves. Point to stop signs, exit signs, and restroom signs and explain what they say. We want to share the understanding that print carries meaning and is made up of letters and sounds. Point to and name the labels on cereal boxes, canned food, and drink cartons. Draw their attention to the signs for places you visit frequently, such as Target, Home Depot, or Giant. Ask, "What is the beginning letter or sound?" and "How do you know that is the sign for Target?" It may be the logo, so be prepared to point out the beginning sound and letter T.

Whenever you use print (reading a recipe, writing a "to do" list, looking at advertisements in the newspaper), there is an opportunity to help your child learn why print is important and how it works. Children learn from their parent's comments. We have

TABLE 3.9 CAP and Print Referencing Examples

Functions of Print	Print Referencing during Reading and Writing
Print is speech written down, and once written down it does not change	I'm going to write down what you say and then we can read it back.
Print is different from illustrations	You look at the picture while I read what it says over here.
Print carries a message	Here are the words to "Humpty Dumpty."
Print serves many purposes	Here is the recipe for cookies. Let's read and find out what ingredients we need.
Forms of Print	**Print Referencing during Reading and Writing**
Book-handling skills—Start with the cover and turn from front to back	Let's look at the cover of the book to see what it is about.
Directionality—Print is oriented left to right, with a return sweep, and top to bottom	This is the top of the page where I will start reading. Then I will go to the next line. Show me where to go next.
Language related to units of print—Letters (upper- and lower-case), numbers, words, sentences, lines	There are four letters in this word. Let's name them. The first letter is a capital because it is a person's name.
Language related to books—Title, author, illustrator, title page, dedication, poem, song, beginning, end	We have read another book by this author. Where do we look for the author's name?
Language related to phonological awareness—Syllable, sound, beginning and ending	This is a long word. Let's clap the syllables in *caterpillar*. Can this word be *rug*? What is the first sound in *rug*?
Punctuation and special print—Periods, question marks, exclamation marks, quotation marks, bold print, italics	Listen to how I read this sentence. It ends with an exclamation point, so I want to make it sound exciting.
Concept of word—Words are composed of a string of letters; words are separated by spaces	Watch while I point to the words in this sentence. We need to leave a space here before we write the next word.
Word identification—Words can be identified in different contexts	Here is the word *cat*. Can you find the word again on this page? What should you look for? What is the beginning sound?

Source: Michelle Picard, Alison Meadows, Marcia Invernizzi, Francine Johnston, Donald R. Bear, *Words Their Way for Parents: How to Support Your Childs Phonics, Spelling, and Vocabulary Development*, 1st Ed., © 2018, p. 065–066. Pearson Education, Inc., New York, NY.

the opportunity to focus your our child's attention on the forms and functions of print as described in Table 3.9.

READ TO YOUR CHILD AND PROVIDE BOOKS FOR YOUR CHILD TO HANDLE As you read, you are modeling how to handle a book, reading the title and turning pages. Provide sturdy board books so children can imitate your behavior. Children in literacy-rich homes have access to books in the living room, the bedroom, the car, and even at times in the bathroom. In order for children to learn about books, they must have access to durable pages and friendly texts.

Children need to learn book-handling skills, such as which side is the front, and how print is oriented. In English, the print is oriented from left to right, which is not the case for Hebrew or Chinese. As your child plays with durable board books, you have the opportunity to develop language around the print, words, books, phonology, and letter sounds.

TABLE 3.10 Tips for Prompting Concept of Word

Prompts to Develop COW through Reading	Prompts to Develop COW through Writing
• Point to each word as you read the line with me.	• We need to leave a space here before we write the next word
• Let's count the words in the first line.	• What are the sounds in the next word?
• Where is the first word in this line/page? Find the last word on this page.	• How many sounds are in the word (insert short vowel word)? Let's write them. Alternatively, you can build the words with magnetic letters.
• How many words are in this line?	
• Where does the first word begin?	
• Where does the word end?	
• How do you know where one word ends and another begins? (Encourage your child to notice the spaces between words and the initial consonant sound.)	
• Can you find the word ___ on this page? How do you know it's the word___? (Encourage your child to identify the first letter sound in the word.)	
• What letters are in this word?	
• Can you find a word that you know?	
• Find a small word. Find a long word.	

USE LANGUAGE THAT REFERS TO LITERACY VOCABULARY As you read with your child, take the time to point out the cover of the book and name the author and illustrator. As you read the title, point to each word to model fingerpointing or tracking the text. When the print is large or simple, you might also point to the words as you read. For example, Mo Willems's *Don't Let the Pigeon Drive the Bus* and Susan Meddaught's *Martha Speaks* both feature speech bubbles with a few words in each. Point to the words as you read their comments. Occasionally point out the difference between a sentence, word, letter, or punctuation mark to familiarize your child with those literacy terms, but keep such discussions conversational and informal. For example, you might say something like, "This sentence starts with a capital *A*, just like in your name!" or "Look at this long word [pointing to *hippopotamus*]!" Invite your child to point to words if the book is simple and familiar.

PLAY A GAME: CAN YOU FIND . . .? Once your child begins to learn letters of the alphabet, such as the letters in his or her name, you might ask him or her to locate a letter on the page or a word that begins with a particular letter. Other ideas include asking children to find a capital letter, the title, specific words, or words that rhyme with something. Your questions depend on what concepts you have introduced by modeling and labeling as well as the needs of your child. If he or she is working on the alphabet, ask about letters. If he or she is working on directionality, ask for the first and last words.

Concept of Word

When children are learning about letters and sounds at the same time they are fingerpoint reading from memory, there is a complementary process at work. Learning the letters and sounds provides an anchor to the words in a text and begins to shape a child's understanding of where one word begins and ends. Similarly, in order to fingerpoint to individual words with spaces between, a child begins to look for letter sounds that match their memorized text. Fingerpoint reading to familiar rhymes and pattern books help your child achieve a concept of word and solidify the development of letters and sounds. As parents and teachers, we can support this development by engaging in conversation with your child with a few well-placed questions, as outlined in Table 3.10. Remember to read and enjoy the text and limit the number of prompts to maintain a natural conversation.

PRACTICE FINGERPOINTING TO THE WORDS IN FAMILIAR TEXT Help your child memorize a brief selection of text through lots of practice. This likely comes naturally with a favorite read-aloud book or nursery rhyme. Then guide your child to practice accurately fingerpointing to the words as he or she recites the poem or jingle. The goal is not for your child to decode (sound out or identify) the words, but to practice synchronizing awareness of the beginning sounds of the memorized words, her knowledge of letter–sound correspondences, and beginning-word boundaries. Eventually, your child will use the first letter of each word to anchor fingerpointing accuracy.

BUILD AND READ SIMPLE WORDS You can support the development of concept of word by building words with wooden or magnetic letters. Shop for letters in the local toy or craft stores. Letters come in all kinds of sizes and styles (foam, magnetic, block) but pick out those that have a simple font. Begin with the child's name, arranging the letters in order and then mixing them up for your child to put back in order. Then move on to simple words such as *mom*, *dad*, *cat*, and *dog*. Say the word slowly to model how to listen for sounds in the word. For example, you might say, "Let's make the word *mom*. Listen to the first sound *mmmmmmmmom*. What letter do we need for that sound? As a child listens to the sounds and finds the letters need to spell *mom* or *dad*, they are learning how words are created and the beginnings of phonics.

READ PREDICTABLE PATTERN BOOKS, POINT TO WORDS, AND ENCOURAGE MEMORY READING Predictable books are typically written for young children with a repeating pattern. Bill Martin Jr. made these books very popular with his award-winning title *Brown Bear, Brown Bear* (1970):

> *Brown Bear, Brown Bear, What do you see?*
> *I see a red bird looking at me.*
> *Red Bird, Red Bird, What do you see?*
> *I see a yellow duck looking at me.*

The pattern repeats, and young children are able to participate in the reading of the text. After listening to the text several times, the child remembers which animal is next and repeats the rhyme. You can encourage your child to begin pointing to the familiar refrains. Figure 3.30 lists some of our favorite predictable books.

PLAY A GAME: STAND UP AND BE COUNTED The development of concept of word is greatly enhanced as children build a repertoire of known songs and nursery rhymes. Read or recite one of these familiar rhymes, such as "Little Bo Peep has lost her sheep, and doesn't know where to find them." Take turns standing up for each word and reciting the poem. You may stand for *Little*, your child for *Bo*, and back to you for *Peep*, and repeat until the rhyme is complete. You may also discuss how many words are in the jingle. A variation is to have your child recite the rhyme and add a block for each word, then count the cubes (words).

CREATE CUT-UP SENTENCES Using favorite lines from children's books is a great way to build concept of word through working with familiar a piece of text. Write favorite sentences or phrases on a strip of paper. The best sentences to choose are those that come from a book read so often that your child can recite them by heart. For example, if you and your child have been reading the preschool and kindergarten favorite *Pete the Cat: I Love My White Shoes* by Eric Litwin, you might write, "I

FIGURE 3.30 Predictable Books

Carle, Eric. (1997). *Have You Seen my Cat?* Aladdin.
Carle, Eric. (1999). *From Head to Toe.* Harper Festival.
Carle, Eric. (2005). *Does a Kangaroo Have a Mother Too?* HarperCollins.
Guarino, Deborah. (1997). *Is Your Mama a Llama?* Scholastic.
Litwin, Eric. (2011). *Pete the Cat: I Love My White Shoes*. Harper Collins.
Litwin, Eric. (2013). *Pete the Cat and His Four Groovy Buttons*. Harper Collins.
Martin, Bill. (1970). *Brown Bear, Brown Bear, What Do You See?* Henry Holt & Company.
Martin, Bill. (1997). *Polar Bear, Polar Bear, What Do You Hear?* Henry Holt & Company.
Martin, Bill. (1998). *Here Are My Hands.* Henry Holt & Company.
Neitzel, Shirley. (1994). *The Jacket I Wear in the Snow.* Greenwillow.
Tafuri, Nancy. (1991). *Have You Seen My Duckling?* Greenwillow.
Williams, Sue. (1989). *I Went Walking.* HMH for Young Readers.
Williams, Sue. (1989). *Let's Go Visiting.* HMH for Young Readers.

FIGURE 3.31 Cut-Up Sentences: He swam in the water.

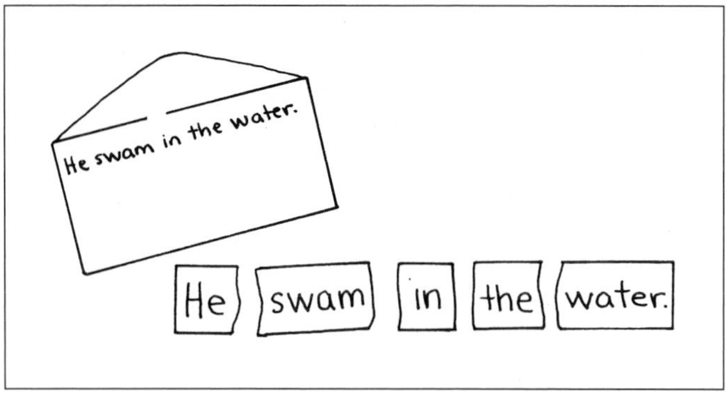

FIGURE 3.32 Cut-Up Sentences: Five little ducks went out one day.

love my white shoes." Point to each of the words and read the sentence with your child several times. Count the words with your child. Then have your child help you cut up the sentence and mix up the word cards. The spaces between words are not obvious to emergent children, so be prepared to model how to cut them. Together, reassemble the sentence and read it aloud. Demonstrate how to find the words in order to rebuild the sentence: "I'm looking for the word *love*. *Love* starts with *lllll* . . . can you help me find the word *love*?" or "What letter would you expect to see at the beginning of *my*?" You can also encourage your child to use the capital letter and end punctuation to help sequence the words in order to reinforce concepts about print. You may want to write the complete sentence on an envelope as a model, and then store the cut-up sentence in the envelope to be used again (Figure 3.31). Your child can create illustrations to go with the sentences (Figure 3.32). Eventually, your child will be able to recreate the sentence without looking at the model. With *Pete the Cat*, you could even begin to offer other color words so that your child can also create "I love my blue shoes" or "I love my red shoes."

Writing

Writing with your child offers many opportunities to stimulate language and to model the use of the alphabet, concepts about print, concept of word, phonological awareness, and letter–sound matches. Young children write, or pretend to write, well before they learn to read, provided they are encouraged to do so. The trick in emergent literacy instruction is to give that encouragement. As a parent, you can provide immediate and ready access to writing materials and model how to use writing. Children need to observe literate behaviors long before they are expected to master them for their own independent use.

SUPPLY A WIDE VARIETY OF WRITING MATERIALS Children enjoy mimicking the behavior of their parents, other adults, and older children. Keep a ready supply of writing instruments and paper for children to choose to use whenever they like, including colored pencils, markers, highlighters, alphabet stamps, sticky notes, stationary, postcards, and colored paper.

MODEL AND DISCUSS PRACTICAL WRITING Tell your child about what you are doing when you are writing for practical tasks. Show how and why you write notes, letters, emails, recipes, and so on. You can also invite your child to help you with these practical writing tasks. For example, keep a shopping list and have your child help you add items and then check them off as you find them, or ask your child to add to greeting cards or letters that you write to friends or relatives, even if the writing is scribbles. Your child will quickly learn to enjoy creating practical writing, as can be seen in young Sam's reminder for his mom that their dog Henry had an appointment; he used his developing knowledge of letter sounds to attempt writing "Henry appointment" (Figure 3.33).

FIGURE 3.33 Sam's Practical Writing

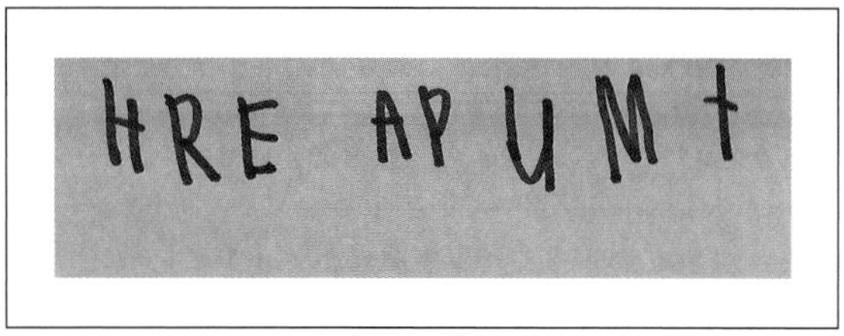

Source: Michelle Picard

Although the message is difficult to read, Sam was demonstrating his understanding that writing is purposeful and carries meaning to others.

FIGURE 3.34 Drawing with a Dictated Caption

CREATE DICTATED CAPTIONS TOGETHER When your child completes a drawing, ask him or her to tell you about it and write what they say as a caption, as seen in the example in Figure 3.34. Read the sentence back as you point to the words, and then invite your child to read along with you. These captioned drawings can be displayed and reread. You can also use family photos to stimulate conversation and early writing. For example, you might print out a picture from a trip and ask your child to tell you something about it. After seeing you write down their words, children can be encouraged to do their own writing to go along with their drawing.

ENCOURAGE YOUR CHILD TO WRITE FOR A VARIETY OF PURPOSES Create opportunities for your child to use markers, pencils, crayons, and paper and to share their pieces. Children begin with scribbles and drawings, and we should applaud these early attempts at writing. A good way to get children started with their own writing is to encourage them to label a picture. For example, Figure 3.35 shows a drawing of a tree in the fall with the child's label "*FL*." Kaitlyn has labeled her picture *fall* with the beginning and final consonant. It was proudly displayed on the refrigerator, often the first gallery for children to showcase their work. Although in this example the label is fairly straightforward and predictable, this is not always the case. You may wonder how to react if your child brings a page of undecipherable scribbles, random letters, or even a few that match conventional sound–letter correspondences. Your child may say, "Look at this, Mommy!" In such cases, say, "This is wonderful! Would you read it to me?" This also provides a chance to talk about the first letter sounds.

FIGURE 3.35 Kaitlyn's Labeled Drawing

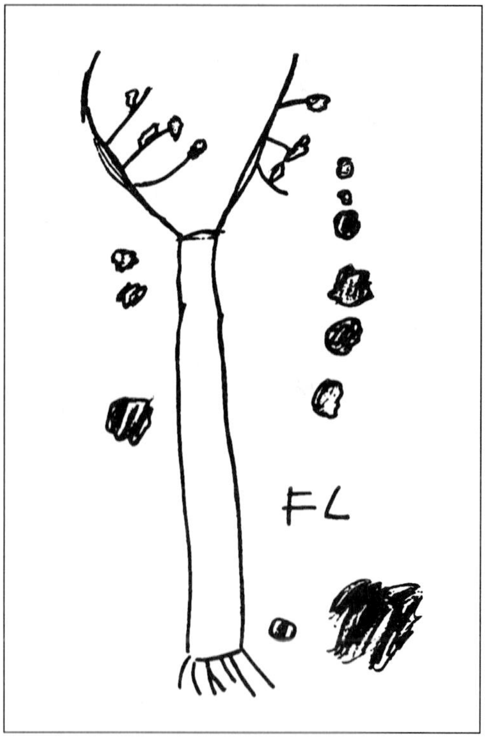

WRITE FOR SOUNDS Children learning letter sounds can be encouraged to write, and specifically to write the sounds that they hear. If you and your child complete a picture sort of beginning sounds, you can ask your child to try to spell the words. The goal is not to have conventional spelling at this time, but rather to make an association between the initial sound and the first letter in the word, such as *M* for *moon* or *B* for *baby*.

A BRIEF SUMMARY

In this chapter, we described characteristics typical of emergent learners; provided guidance on understanding rhyming, concept, and picture sorts; and described a wide variety of games and activities to promote early literacy development at home. In Chapter 4, we focus on children described as beginning readers and writers in the letter name-alphabetic stage of spelling development.

REFERENCES

Ball, E, W., & Blachman, B. A.. (1988). Phoneme segmentation training: Effect on reading readiness. *Annals of Dyslexia, 38*, 208–225.

Bear, D. R., Invernizzi, M. R., Johnston, F. R., & Templeton, S. (2010). *Words their way: Letter and picture sorts for emergent spellers* (2nd ed.). Boston, MA: Allyn & Bacon.

Biemiller, A., & Slonim, N. (2001). Estimating root word vocabulary growth in normative and advantaged populations: Evidence for a common sequence of vocabulary acquisition. *Journal of Educational Psychology*, 93(3): 498.

Biemiller, A. (2001). Teaching vocabulary: Early, direct, sequential. *American Educator*, 25(1), 24–28.

Biemiller, A. (2004). Teaching vocabulary in the primary grades: Vocabulary instruction needed. In J. F. Baumann & E. J. Kame'enui (Eds.), *Vocabulary instruction: Research to practice* (pp. 28–40). New York, NY: Guilford Press.

Cunningham, A. E., & Stanovich, K. E. (1997). What reading does for the mind. Journal of Direct Instruction, Vol. 1, No. 2, pp. 137–149.

Cunningham, A. E. & Stanovich, K. E. (2003). Reading matters: How reading engagement influences cognition. In J. Flood, D. Lapp, J. Squire, & J. Jenson (Eds.), *Handbook of research on teaching in the English language arts* (vol. 2, pp. 857–867). Nahwah, NJ: Lawrence Erlbaum.

Cunningham, James W., Cunningham, P. M., Hoffman, J. V., & Yopp, H. K. (1998). Phonemic Awareness and the Teaching of Reading: A Position Statement from the Board of Directors of the International Reading Association. International Reading Association. www.reading.org.

Ehri, L. C. (1997). Learning to read and learning to spell are one and the same, almost. In C. A. Perfetti, L. Rieben, & M. Fayol (Eds.), *Learning to spell: Research, theory, and practice across languages* (pp. 237–269). Mahwah, NJ: Lawrence Erlbaum Associates.

Ehri, L. (2006). Alphabetics instruction helps students learn to read. *Handbook of orthography and literacy*, 649–677.

Ehri, L. C., & Roberts, T. (2006). The roots of learning to read and write: Acquisition of letters and phonemic awareness. *Handbook of early literacy research*, 2, 113–131.

Ferreiro, E. & Teberosky, A. (1982). *Literacy before schooling*. Portsmouth, NH: Heinemann.

Griffin, P., Burns, M. S., & Snow, C. E. (Eds.). (1998). *Preventing reading difficulties in young children*. Washington, D.C.: National Academies Press.

Hart, B., & Risley, T. R. (1995). *Meaningful differences in the everyday experiences of American children*. Baltimore. Paul C. Brookes.

Henderson, E. H. (1981). *Learning to read and spell: The child's knowledge of words*. DeKalb, IL: Northern Illinois Press.

Invernizzi, M. (2002). Concepts, sounds, and the ABCs: A diet for a very young reader. In D. M. Barone & L. M. Morrow (Eds.), *Literacy and young children* (pp. 140–157). New York, NY: Guilford Press.

Justice, L. M.. (2006). *Communication sciences and disorders: An introduction*. Upper Saddle River, NJ: Person/Merrill/Prentice Hall.

Justice, L. M., Kaderavek, J. N., Fan, X., Sofka, A., & Hunt, A. (2009). Accelerating preschoolers' early literacy development through classroom-based teacher child storybook reading and explicit print referencing. *Language, Speech, & Hearing Services in Schools, 40*, 67–85.

Justice, L. M., & Pullen, P. C. (2003). Promising interventions for promoting emergent literacy skills: Three evidence-based approaches. *Topics in Early Childhood Special Education, 23*(3): 99–113.

Lonigan, C. J., Schatschneider, C., & Westberg, L., & The National Early Literacy Panel (NELP). (2008). Identification of children's skills and abilities linked to later outcomes in reading, writing, and spelling. National Institute for Literacy (Ed.), *Developing early literacy: Report of the national early literacy panel* (pp. 55–106). Washington, D.C.: National Institute for Literacy.

Morris, D. (1981). Concept about word: A developmental phenomenon in the beginning reading and writing process. *Language Arts, 58*(6), 659–668.

Morris, D. (1992). Concept of word: A pivotal understanding in the learning-to-read process. In S. Templeton & D. Bear (Eds.), *Development of orthographic knowledge and the foundations of literacy* (pp. 53–77). Hillsdale, NJ: Erlbaum.

Morris, D., Bloodgood, J. W., Lomax, R. G., & Perney, J. (2003). Developmental steps in learning to read: A longitudinal study in kindergarten and first grade. *Reading research quarterly, 38*(3): 302–328.

Perfetti, C. A., Beck, I., Bell, L. C., & Hughes, C. (1987). Phonemic knowledge and learning to read are reciprocal: A longitudinal study of first grade children. Merrill-Palmer Quarterly

Pufpaff, L. A. (2009). A developmental continuum of phonological sensitivity skills. *Psychology in the Schools*, 46(7), 679-691.
Risley, T. & Hart, B. (1995). Meaningful differences in the everyday experiences of young American children. Baltimore, MD: Paul H. Brookes Publishing Co., Inc.
Sulzby, E. (1986). Writing and reading: Signs of oral and written language organization in the young child. *Emergent Literacy: Writing and Reading*, 50–89.
Yopp, Hallie K. (1992). Developing phonemic awareness in young children. *The Reading Teacher 45.9*: 696–703.

CHILDREN'S LITERATURE REFERENCES

Alborough, J. (2000). *Duck in a truck.* HarperCollins.
Ahlberg, J. & Allan. (1999). *Each peach pear plum.* Viking.
Allsburg, C. (1987*). The Z was zapped: A play in 26 acts.* Houghton Mifflin Books for Children.
Aliki. (2000). *Let's read and find out: My five senses.* HarperCollins.
Aliki. (1996). *Hello! Goodbye!* Greenwillow.
Alda, A. (2009). *Hello, goodbye.* Tundra Books.
Aylesworth, J. (1992). *Old black fly.* Henry Holt & Company.
Baker, K. (2010). *LMNO peas.* Beach Lane Books.
Base, G. (1986). *Animalia.* Harry Abrams.
Branley, F. M. (2000). *Snow is falling.* HarperCollins.
Branley, F. M. (2006). *Air is all around you.* HarperCollins.
Briggs, R. (1978). *The snowman.* Random House.
Brown, M. W. (1995). *A child's goodnight book.* HarperFestival.
Brown, M. W. (1995). *Goodnight moon.* HarperFestival.
Brown, M. W. (1995). *Big red barn.* HarperFestival.
Bryan, S. (2007). *A boy and his bear.* Arcade Publishing.
Cameron, P. (1961). *I can't said the ant.* Scholastic.
Carle, E. (1974). *My very first book of shapes.* HarperCollins.
Carle, E. (1997). *Have you seen my cat?* Aladdin.
Carle, E. (1999). *From head to toe.* Harper Festival.
Carle, E. (2005). *Does a kangaroo have a mother too?* HarperCollins.
Carle, E. (2007). *Eric Carle's ABCs.* Grossett & Dunlap.
Carle, E. (2007). *Slowly, slowly, slowly said the sloth.* Puffin Publishing.
Christelow, E. (1989). *Five little monkeys jumping on the bed.* Clarion Books.
Cole, J., & Calmenson, S. (1991). *The eensty, weentsy spider.* HarperCollins.
Cousins, L. (1999). *Maisy's bedtime.* Candlewick.
Cousins, L. (1999). *Maisy dresses up.* Candlewick.
Cousins, L. (1999). *Maisy's pool.* Candlewick.
Cousins, L. (2001). *Maisy goes shopping.* Candlewick.
Cousins, L. (2010). *Maisy goes to preschool.* Candlewick.
Cousins, L. (2010). *Maisy takes a bath.* Candlewick.
Crews, D. (1993). *School bus.* Greenwillow.
Crews, D. (1995). *Freight train.* Scholastic.
Crews, D. (1995). *Ten black dots.* Greenwillow.
Cowley, J. (1998). *Nicketty-nacketty noo-noo-noo.* Mondo Publishing.
Day, A. (1991). *Carl's summer vacation.* Simon & Schuster Books for Young Readers.
Day, A. (1991). *Good dog, Carl.* Simon & Schuster Books for Young Readers.
Day, A. (1997). *Carl's birthday.* Farrar, Straus & Giroux
DePaola, T. (1988). *Hey diddle diddle.* Puffin.
Dewdney, A. (2005). *Llama, llama red pajama.* Viking.
Ehlert, L. (1989). *Eating the alphabet: Fruits and vegetables from A to Z.* Harcourt Brace.
Ehlert, L. (1990). *Color farm.* Harper Collins.
Ehlert, L. (1990). *Growing vegetable soup.* Voyager Books.
Ehlert, L. (1992). *Planting a rainbow.* HMH Books for Young Readers.
Ernst, L. (1996). *The letters are lost.* Puffin.
Fleming, D. (1996). *Lunch.* Square Fish.

Fox, M. (1997). *Time for bed.* Harcourt Brace.
Fox, M. (2010). *Ten little fingers. Ten little toes*. HMH Books for Young Readers.
Gaiman, N. (2008). *The dangerous alphabet book*. Harper Collins.
Glazer, T. (1995). *On top of spaghetti.* Harcourt Brace.
Guarino, D. (1997). *Is your mama a llama?* Scholastic.
Hoban, T. (1978). *26 letters and 99 cents?* Greenwillow Books.
Hoban, T. (1978). *Is it red? Is it yellow? Is it blue?* Greenwillow Books.
Hoban, T. (1986). *Red, blue, yellow shoe.* Greenwillow Books.
Hoban, T. (1992). *Fish eyes: A book you can count on.* Greenwillow Books.
Hoban, T. (1996). *Shapes, shapes, shapes.* Greenwillow Books.
Hoban, T. (1997). *Exactly the opposite.* Greenwillow Books.
Hoban, T. (1997). *Is it larger? Is it smaller?* Greenwillow Books.
Hoban, T. (2000). *Cubes, cylinders, cones, and spheres.* Greenwillow Books.
Hoberman, M. A. (1998). *Miss Mary Mack.* HMH Books for Young Readers.
Hoberman, M. A. (2000). *The seven silly eaters.* HMH Books for Young Readers.
Hoberman, M. A. (2002). *The eensy, weensy spider.* LB Kids.
Intriago, P. (2011). *Dot.* Margaret Ferguson Books.
Isadora, R. (1992). *City seen from A to Z.* Greenwillow Books.
Jenkins, P. B. (1991). *Let's read and find out: A nest full of eggs*. HarperCollins.
Johnston, S. T. (1999). *Alphabet city*. Puffin (Caldecott Honor Book).
Jones, C. (1998). *This old man.* HMH Books for Young Readers.
Jordan, H. (2000). *Let's read and find out: How to grow a seed*. HarperCollins.
Jorgenson, G. (1995). *The crocodile beat.* Illustrated by Patricia Mullins. Simon & Schuster Children's Publishing.
Kellogg, S. (1997). *Jack and the beanstalk*. HarperCollins.
Kontis, A. (2006). *AlphaOops: The day Z went first.* Candlewick.
Langstaff, J. (1991). *Oh a-hunting we will go*. Aladdin.
Lear, E. (2005). *A was once an apple pie.* Orchard Books.
Lee, S. (2008). *The wave*. Chronicle Books.
Lehman, B. (2004). *The red book*. Houghton Mifflin.
Lehman, B. (2006). *Museum trip*. Houghton Mifflin.
Lies, B. (2008). *Bats at the library*. Houghton Mifflin.
Litwin, E. (2011). *Pete the cat: I love my white shoes*. HarperCollins.
Litwin, E. (2013). *Pete the cat and his four groovy buttons*. HarperCollins.
Lobel, A. (1981). *On Market Street*. Greenwillow Books.
London, J. (1998). *Froggy goes to school.* Puffin.
London, J. (1998). *Froggy rides a bike*. Puffin.
London, J. (2003). *Froggy eats out*. Puffin.
London, J. (2004). *Froggy goes to the doctor*. Puffin.
London, J. (2007). *Froggy's sleepover.* Puffin.
London, J. (2008). *Froggy learns to swim*. Puffin.
London, J. (2010). *Froggy goes to camp*. Puffin.
Martin, B. (1970). *Brown bear, brown bear, what do you see?* Henry Holt & Company.
Martin, B. (1997). *Polar bear, polar bear, what do you hear?* Henry Holt & Company.
Martin, B. (1998). *Here are my hands.* Henry Holt & Company.
Martin, Jr., B. (2006). *"Fire! Fire!" said Mrs. McGuire.* Harcourt.
Martin, B., & Archambault, J. (1989) *Chick chicka boom boom*. Simon & Schuster.
Martin, J. (1992). *Carrot, parrot.* The Trumpet Club.
Mayer, M. (1993). *A boy, a dog, a frog and a friend.* Dial.
Mayer, M. (2003). *A boy, a dog, and a frog*. Dial.
Mayer, M. (2003). *Frog goes to dinner*. Dial.
Mayer, M. (2003). *Frog on his own*. Dial.
Mayer, M. (2003). *Frog, where are you*? Dial.
Mayer, M. (2003). *One frog too many*. Dial.
McLimans, D. (2006). *Gone wild: An endangered animal alphabet*. Walker Childrens.
McPhail, D. (1989). *Animals A to Z*. Scholastic.
Meddaugh, S. (1995). *Martha speaks*. HMH Books for Young Readers.
Musgrove, M. (1992). *Ashanti to Zulu: African traditions*. Puffin Books (Caldecott Honor Book).
Neitzel, S. (1994). *The jacket I wear in the snow*. Greenwillow.
Norwith, J. (1999). *Take me out to the ball game*. Aladdin.

Numeroff, L. (1991). *If you give a moose a muffin.* HarperCollins.
Numeroff, L. (1998). *If you give a pig a pancake.* HarperCollins.
Numeroff, L. (2008). *If you give a cat a cupcake.* HarperCollins.
Numeroff, L. (2010). *If you give a mouse a cookie.* HarperCollins.
Palotta, J. (1989). *The yucky reptile alphabet book.* Charlesbridge.
Palotta, J. (1999). *The airplane alphabet book.* Charlesbridge.
Palotta, J., & Thomason, B. (1992). *The vegetable alphabet book.* Charlesbridge.
Pelletier, D. (1996). *The graphic alphabet book.* Scholastic (Caldecott Honor Book).
Pinkney, J. (2009). *The lion and the mouse.* Little, Brown Books for Young Readers.
Pinkney, J. (2013). *The tortoise and the hare.* Little, Brown Books for Young Readers.
Peek, M. (1988). *Mary wore her red dress.* HMH Books for Young Readers.
Peek, M. (1981). *Rollover! A counting song.* HMH Books for Young Readers.
Peet, B. (2008). *The caboose got loose.* HMH Books for Young Readers.
Pfeffer, W. (1994). *Let's read and find out: From tadpole to frog.* HarperCollins.
Pfeffer, W. (1996). *Let's read and find out: What's it like to be a fish.* HarperCollins.
Raffi. (1988). *Down by the bay.* Crown Books.
Raffi. (1989). *Five little ducks.* Crown Books.
Raschka, C. (2011). *A ball for Daisy.* Schwartz & Wade.
Reidy, J. (2013). *Too purply.* Bloomsbury.
Rinker, S. D. & Lichtenheld, T. (2011). *Goodnight, goodnight construction site.* Chronicle Books.
Rockwell, A. (2008). *Let's read and find out: Clouds.* HarperCollins.
Rohmann, E. (1997). *Time flies.* Dragonfly Books.
Schwartz, A. (1999). *Old MacDonald.* Scholastic.
Sendak, M. (1991). *Chicken soup with rice: A book of months.* HarperCollins.
Seuss, Dr. (1963). *Dr. Seuss' alphabet book.* Random House.
Slate, J. (2001). *Miss Bindergarten gets ready for kindergarten.* Puffin.
Showers, P. (1991). *Let's read and find out: How many teeth.* HarperCollins.
Showers, P. (1997). *Let's read and find out: Sleep is for everyone.* HarperCollins.
Sobel, J. (2006). *Shiver me letters: A pirate ABC.* HMH Books for Young Readers.
Stevens, J. (1995). *Tops and bottoms.* Harcourt Brace.
Tafuri, N. (1991). *Have you seen my duckling?* Greenwillow.
Thompson, B. (2010). *Chalk.* Marshall Cavendish Children's Books.
Trapani, I. (1994). *Twinkle, twinkle, little star.* Charlesbridge.
Trapani, I. (1996). *I'm a little teapot.* Charlesbridge.
Trapani, I. (1998). *Mary had a little lamb.* Charlesbridge.
Trapani, I. (1999). *Row, row, row your boat.* Charlesbridge.
Trapani, I. (2001). *Baa, baa, black sheep.* Charlesbridge.
Trapani, I. (2004). *How much is that doggie in the window?* Charlesbridge.
Tullet, H. (2011). *Press here.* Chronicle Books.
Van A., C. (1987). *The Z was zapped: A play in twenty-six acts.* HMH Books for Young Readers.
Walsh, E. S. (1995). *Mouse count.* HMH for Young Readers.
Walsh, E. S. (1995). *Mouse paint.* HMH for Young Readers.
Weeks, S. (2002). *Mrs. McNosh hangs up her wash.* HarperCollins.
Westcott, N. (1990). *The lady with the alligator purse.* Little, Brown Books for Young Readers.
Westcott, N. (1992). *Peanut butter and jelly: A play rhyme.* Harcourt.
Westcott, N. (1993). *There's a hole in the bucket.* Lippincott.
Wiesner, D. (1991). *Freefall.* HarperCollins.
Wiesner, D. (2011). *Tuesday.* Houghton Mifflin.
Willems, M. (2003). *Don't let the pigeon drive the bus.* Hyperion Press.
Williams, S. (1989). *I went walking.* HMH for Young Readers.
Williams, S. (1989). *Let's go visiting.* HMH for Young Readers.
Wilson, K. (2009). *Bear snores on.* Harcourt.
Wood, A. & Wood, B. (2003). *Alphabet mystery.* Blue Sky Press.
Yolen, J. (2009). *How do dinosaurs say I love you?* Blue Sky Press.
Yolen, J. (2000). *How do dinosaurs say goodnight?* Illustrated by Mark Teague. Blue Sky Press.
Yolen, J. (2007). *How do dinosaurs go to school?* Illustrated by Mark Teague. Blue Sky Press.
Ziefert, H. (2012). *ABC dentist.* Blue Apple Books.
Ziefert, H., & Ehrlich, F. (2008) *A bunny is funny.* Blue Apple Books.
Zelinsky, P. O. (1990). *The wheels on the bus.* Dutton Publishing.

chapter 4

Beginning Readers in the Letter Name–Alphabetic Stage of Spelling

Source: Huda Bazyan

Source: View Apart/Shutterstock

At age 6, Kelly was beginning to struggle at school. Although she concentrated with great difficulty on the letters in each word, she was unable to read the first-grade list of spelling words. Meanwhile, it appeared to her that the children around her were reading and writing with ease. In order to accommodate Kelly's individual needs, her teacher worked with the school reading specialist, and together they determined that Kelly needed additional instruction to master the sounds and letters of the alphabet before working with typical first-grade spelling words. Kelly's reading teacher designed lessons based on what she already knew and what she was ready to learn. She began by sorting pictures into categories with the same beginning sound, hunted for words with those same beginning consonants, played games with beginning sounds, wrote short sentences, and read and reread familiar books. Once beginning sounds were mastered, they moved to working with word families (*cat*, *bat*, *fat*) to learn about short vowels. Over time, with instruction based on her individual needs, Kelly became confident and able to read and write grade-level material comfortably.

This chapter is devoted to beginning readers like Kelly in the letter name–alphabetic stage of spelling. The word study approach, founded on research, is built around the idea that children make the greatest progress possible if we teach lessons based on a child's individual strengths and needs. In this chapter, we discuss the common characteristics of children's reading, writing, and spelling at this stage (Table 4.1), examine common spelling features and how to talk about them with your child, learn a series of games and activities to support word study at home, and understand how to make connections among spelling, reading, and writing.

Stage Overview: Beginning Readers in the Letter Name–Alphabetic Stage of Spelling

Reading

As children progress from the emergent stage of reading to the beginning stage, they have developed a basic understanding of many of the early literacy concepts discussed in the previous chapter and outlined in Table 4.2. Nevertheless, children need additional instruction and experience to master most of these skills and to be able to apply them in new books and situations.

Oral language, concepts, and vocabulary are continuously developed throughout all stages of literacy development; however, beginning readers must also work to master critical early literacy skills in order to read, write, and spell effectively, including phonological awareness, phonemic awareness, phonics, alphabet recognition, concepts about print (CAP), concept of word (COW), and sight word development. Although children at this stage already have a base of knowledge, they are still working to deepen and refine their **phonological awareness**, the ability to identify and reflect on sounds in the spoken language. Most beginning readers at the letter name-alphabetic stage have already begun to develop phonological awareness, but it is important to continue reinforcing these skills to support reading development. At this stage, students should be able to break spoken words into syllables (*por-cu-pine*), identify and produce rhyming words (*cake* and *lake*), and identify the beginning sounds in words (*cake* starts with /k/). A subcategory of phonological awareness known as **phonemic awareness** also becomes very important. Phonemic awareness involves attention to individual speech sounds within words. At first, children have partial phonemic awareness and can only segment the first sound in a word, but over time, they learn how to divide all the sounds within a word (*frog* = /f/ /r/ /o/ /g/) and blend isolated sound units into words (/c/ /a/ /p/ = *cap*). Research has demonstrated that phonemic awareness improves a child's ability to recognize words, read,

TABLE 4.1 Beginning Readers and Writers in the Letter Name–Alphabetic Stage of Spelling

Reading Characteristics	• Typically, kindergarten to third-grade students • Rely on memory, familiar sentence patterns, picture clues, and early decoding skills to begin reading • Develop a stable concept of word (ability to match spoken words to print) • Read slowly and word by word • Read aloud • Use fingerpointing to help reading
Writing Characteristics	• Use letters to represent sounds in writing • Writing is labored as children work to listen for sounds • Short pieces that take a long time to create • Writing is phonetic and highly dependent on sounds • Begin to spell common words correctly • Begin to use correct spacing consistently • Random mix of upper- and lower-case letters while working towards standard capitalization • Begin to use (and overuse) punctuation • Repetitive writing frequently focused on self
Spelling Characteristics	• Apply the alphabet literally, using the names of the letters to spell sounds, such as *U* for *you*, *YN* for *when*, and *GP* for *jeep* • Spell phonetically, representing the most prominent sounds in syllables, such as *DADE* for *daddy* • Omit silent letters like the *e* in *came*, spelling it CAM
Common Spelling Errors	• *B, BD, BAD* for *bed* • *S, SP, SEP, SHEP* for *ship* • *L, LP, LOP, LOMP* for *lump* • *B, BK, BAK* for *back* • *FT, FOT, FLOT* for *float* • *JN, JV, JRF, DRIV* for *drive* • *YN* for *when* • *BAKR* for *baker*
Instructional Focus	• Beginning and final consonants (_**t**a**p**_, _**b**u**n**_, _**p**e**n**_, _**r**u**b**_**)** • Blends (_**sl**ip_, _**fl**at_, _**pr**op_) and digraphs (_**sh**op_, _**th**at_, _**ch**ick_, _wi**sh**_, _pa**th**_**)** • Same-vowel word families (-*at*, -*ap*, -*an*) • Mixed-vowel word families (-*at*, -*it*, -*ot*) • Short vowels (_c**a**p_, _l**i**st_, _t**o**p_, _p**e**st_, _r**u**n_) • Affricates (_**dr**um_, _**tr**uck_) • Preconsonantal nasals (_bu**mp**_, _we**nt**_, _ri**ng**_, _si**nk**_)

TABLE 4.2 Early Literacy Development Skills

Oral Language, Concepts, and Vocabulary	The understanding that words represent ideas and concepts and can be used to share thoughts and experiences with others
Phonological Awareness (PA)	The ability to identify and reflect on sounds within spoken words including syllables, rhyme, and single sounds
Phonemic Awareness	The recognition of the smallest units of sounds within words (the words *cat* and *ship* both have three phonemes or units of sound: /c/ - /a/ - /t/ and /sh/-/i/-/p/)
Phonics	The systematic relationship between letters and sounds
Alphabet Recognition	The ability to identify and name upper and lower case letters
Concepts about Print (CAP)	A set of understandings about how books are organized (front to back, page turning, titles, illustrations), how print is oriented on the page (top to bottom and left to right), and how other features of print (bold, italics, punctuation) relate to how print is read
Concept of Word (COW)	The ability to match spoken words with printed words, as demonstrated by the ability to point to each word of a memorized text accurately
Sight Words	Printed words stored in memory that can be identified immediately, "at first sight," without having to use decoding strategies to figure out the word. Words become fastened to memory by matching speech sounds and meaning to their representations in spelling.

write, and spell (National Reading Panel, 2000). **Phonics** combines the skills of phonemic awareness and alphabet knowledge as children learn the actual letter–sound correspondences that ultimately leads to the ability to sound out or decode words, the process that allows words to become stored in memory. Once stored in memory, words that were previously figured out only by decoding now become **sight words**, words that can be easily recognized at first sight.

Children refine their understanding of **concepts about print** (CAP) early in the beginning stage of reading. As described in Chapter 3, concepts about print include a set of understandings about how books are organized (front to back page turning, titles, illustrations), how print is oriented on the page (top to bottom and left to right), and features of print such as punctuation and capitalization. CAP also includes a conceptual understanding of the difference between letters and words. In other words, a child can point to individual words and letters when asked.

Beginning readers have developed a stable **concept of word** (COW), the ability to correctly point to each word in the text as they reread or recite familiar text, such as a nursery rhyme. In a familiar rhyming book like *Five Little Monkeys Jumping on the Bed* by Eileen Christelow, children can point to the words using their memory for the rhyming pattern, their knowledge of beginning sounds, and automatic recognition of the letters representing those sounds. COW is a watershed skill, one that must be mastered in order to read.

Beginning readers' development of phonological awareness, phonics, and concept of word leads to amassing a sight word vocabulary and ultimately to reading for meaning. Sight words are words the student can identify immediately at first sight without guessing, using pictures, sounding out, or using any other decoding strategies. At first, beginning readers may only know a handful of words that they have seen very frequently, such as their name and common words like *cat* or *like*. However, as they see the same words over and over and as they learn about how letters and sounds work (phonics), practice sounding them out and decoding them, they begin to remember them when they see them and their sight vocabulary increases.

A large store of sight words makes it possible to read fluently and to devote attention to comprehension rather than to figuring out unknown words.

Beginning readers are working to master the early literacy skills discussed in this chapter and in Chapter 3 in order to transition from dependence on simple predictable reading materials, such as *Five Little Monkeys Jumping on the Bed,* to less predictable beginning reading materials, such as the *Elephant and Piggie* series by Mo Willems. The latter text no longer repeats a pattern or a common refrain. Readers at this stage gradually rely less on memory of predictable text and more on their ability to figure out unfamiliar words using a variety of decoding strategies. As they start to remember words, these sight words become like welcomed stepping stones as they wade through text, word by word, often sound by sound.

Although beginning readers have acquired a solid concept of word, they tend to be slow, word-by-word readers. Children at this stage use partial clues such as the beginning letters and sounds that are familiar, along with pictures to identify words. As partial alphabetic readers (Ehri, 1997), children know something about consonants, but they lack the vowel knowledge needed to sound out words or easily store words in memory. From the earlier example of *Five Little Monkeys Jumping on the Bed,* the word *monkeys* might be recognized out of context by virtue of several letters in the word (*m – k,* or perhaps *m–y*). In another story or context, however, these partial phonetic cues alone will not be sufficient to read the words.

Beginning readers read aloud. It is necessary for them to say the words out loud by moving their mouths in order to fully process and recognize words. Pointing to each word is natural and desirable at this stage. It helps children keep their place on the page and encourages them to look more carefully at the letters in each word, which in turn helps them remember words as sight words.

FIGURE 4.1 Writing Sample: Letter Name–Alphabetic – Caroline

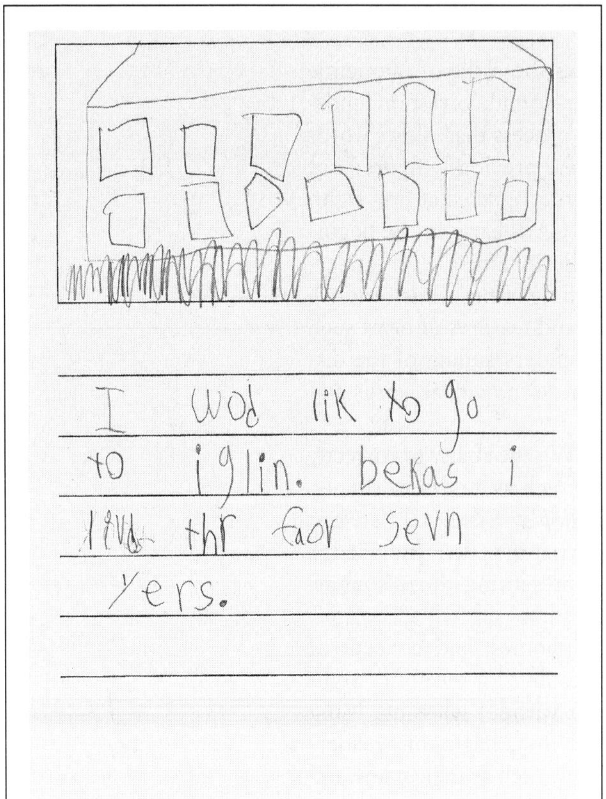
I wod lik to go
to iglin. bekas i
livd thr faor sevn
yers.

Source: Copyright © by Pearson Education, Inc. Used with permission of Michele Picard.

Writing

As with reading, the writing of beginning readers is very labored and often painstakingly slow. Children at this stage are working to break apart and listen to the sounds in words, remember the letters that go with each sound, and record those letters with correct letter formation. Young children often talk to themselves as they write, trying to identify and form the letters and sounds in the words they use in their writing. In that process, they may forget their original idea because they get so caught up with isolating and recording the sounds in each word. Compositions tend to be short, perhaps a few sentences with accompanying drawings. It is also common to see very repetitive pieces as children learn to write using the words and patterns with which they are familiar, such as *I like to ....* Beginning writing reflects an egocentric focus as children write mainly about themselves and their own experiences. Beginning writers often use a random combination of both upper and lower case letters, particularly early on in the stage. As they progress, they use a more conventional application of capital letters, although some errors in capitalization and letter formation (such as *b/d* reversals) are likely to persist for some time. Correct spacing between words develops early in the stage. Children also begin to experiment with punctuation as they learn how to write in complete sentences. They often overuse punctuation as they become aware of it, such as adding a period to the end of every line of writing or even in between every word.

In Figure 4.1, Caroline, a letter name–alphabetic speller, writes, "I would like to go to England because I lived there for seven years." Her story is a single sentence. She uses one letter for one sound. For example, she spells *LIK* for *like*, *LIVD* for *lived*, *YERS* for *years*, and *BEKAS* for *because*. She uses invented spelling, identifying the sounds and letters that are most prominent in words, as in her use of *INGLN* for *England*. Caroline also uses a few sight words, such as *I*, *go*, and *to*.

In Figure 4.2, Ethan, another first-grader, has written about himself as a superhero in the piece titled *Superhero Me*. The writing contains several ideas or sentences, but lacks any punctuation except at the end and contains a mix of upper- and lower-case letters. Ethan has correctly spelled several high-frequency or common sight words, including *the*, *I*, *me*, *play*, and *like*. He has used what he knows about letters and sounds to *invent* the spellings of words he does not have stored in memory. He has correctly represented beginning and ending consonant sounds, with the exception of *KAN* for *can* and *KOOL* for *cool* (reasonable approximations, because *C* and *K* can make the same beginning sound). Ethan has also correctly used several **blends** (two or more letters with distinct sounds that blend together). In this case, Ethan uses the blends *bl-* in *blue* and *dr-* in *dress*. He is using some short vowel sounds in his spelling of *dress* as *DRES*, but he is inconsistent in other words, using but confusing vowels in his spelling of *feel* as *FIL*. Ethan is at the end of this stage, because he is using quite a few patterns such as *oo* for *U* and adds the letter *E* to *look (LOOKE)* to mark the long vowel (although incorrectly).

FIGURE 4.2 Writing Sample: Letter Name–Alphabetic – Ethan

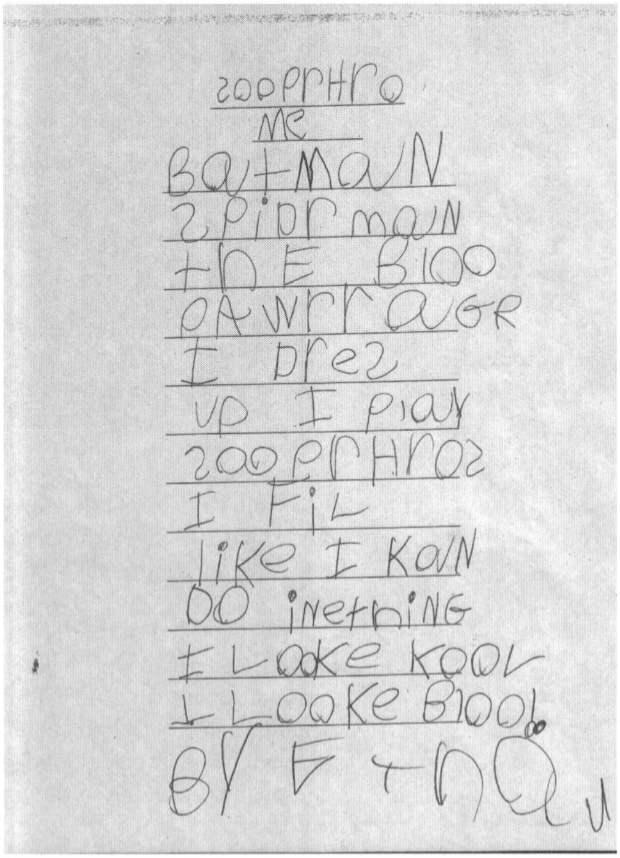

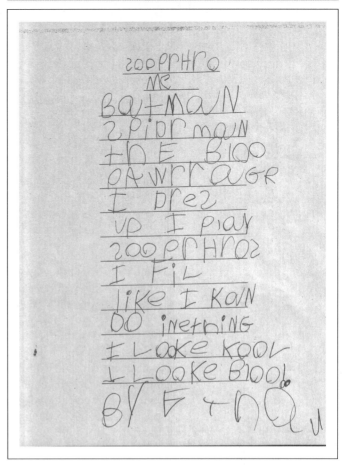

Ethan's story: "Superhero Me – Batman Spiderman the blue Power Ranger I dress up I play superheroes I feel like I can do anything I look cool I look blue! By Ethan"

Source: From *"Words Their Way for Parents: How to Support Your Childs Phonics, Spelling, and Vocabulary Development, 1st Ed."* by Ethan. Copyright © 2018, by Alison Meadows.

Spelling

As described in the section on writing, the letter name–alphabetic stage spelling is a very deliberate effort. The process of spelling words usually involves the repeated steps of stretching out the sounds in a word, identifying each of the sounds (phonemic awareness), associating each sound with a written letter (phonics), deciding whether the letter should be uppercase or lowercase (concepts about print), and finally remembering how to form the letters correctly. In general, children at this stage only record one sound for each letter that they hear. The name of the stage is appropriately named, as children are literally using the name of the letters to spell. For example, they are likely to spell the word *jeep* as *GP*, because the letter name for the *G* sound is "jee." Also, they are likely to spell the word *when* as *YN* because the letter name for *Y*, when pronounced as "why," contains the /w/ sound at the beginning. Table 4.3 lists how each letter of the alphabet is named.

TABLE 4.3 Names of the Letters of the Alphabet

A ay	H aitch	O oh	V vee
B bee	I ie	P pee	W doubleyoo
C see	J jay	Q kyoo	X ecks
D dee	K kay	R are	Y wie
E ee	L el	S es	Z zee
F ef	M em	T tee	
G gee	N en	U yoo	

In a developmental approach to spelling, teachers use children's invented spellings as a way to determine

TABLE 4.4 Characteristics of Letter Name–Alphabetic Spelling

Common Spelling Errors	What Do Children Know?	What Do Children *Use but Confuse*?	What Is Absent from Children's Spelling?
B, BD, BAD for *bed* *S, SP, SEP, SHEP* for *ship* *L, LP, LOP, LOMP* for *lump* *B, BK, BAK for back* *FT, FOT, FLOT* for *float* *GV, JV, JRF, DRIV* for *drive* *YN* for *when* *BAKR* for *baker*	• Beginning and ending consonants • Directionality (write from left to right) • Some known sight words (*the, is*) • Frequently occurring short vowel words (*cat, dog*) • Spaces between words • Many short vowels and some consonant blends and digraphs • High-frequency long vowel words (*like, name, nice*)	• Letter name–sound matches • Short vowels • Consonant blends and digraphs • Harder blends with R and L (*tr, gr, pl, bl*) • Preconsonantal nasals	• Vowels • Complete blends and digraphs • Silent letters • Most long vowel patterns or silent vowels

what they *know*, what they *use but confuse*, and what is *absent*. Put another way, teachers identify which spelling features children use consistently, inconsistently, or not at all. Table 4.4 describes the continuum of spelling characteristics in the letter name–alphabetic spelling stage.

WHAT DO CHILDREN DO OR SPELL CORRECTLY AT THIS STAGE? Although these letter name–alphabetic spellers are early in their development of literacy skills, there are some things that they already can do. Unlike emergent learners who were writing with random marks or letters, children at this stage are beginning to use phonological awareness and letter–sound correspondence (phonics) to record their messages. Children begin to use consonants accurately at the beginnings and endings of words, perhaps spelling *bed* as *BD* and *ship* as *SP.*

WHAT DO CHILDREN "USE BUT CONFUSE" AT THIS STAGE? Letter name–alphabetic spellers begin to learn letter combinations known as **blends** and **digraphs**. As a reminder, *digraphs* are two consonants that represent one sound: *ch*, *th*, *sh*, or *wh*. *Blends* are two consonants that blend together while each retains their independent sound (*pl* in *plant*, *br* in *brick*). At first, these are represented only partially in their spelling, such as *FG* for *frog* or *SP* for *ship*. The correct spelling of these blends and digraphs is studied through both picture and word sorts.

Short vowels are the most persistently confused patterns throughout the letter name–alphabetic stage. Every vowel (*a*, *e*, *i*, *o*, and *u*) has two sounds, commonly referred to as *long* and *short*. The long vowel "says its letter name" and is usually spelled or "marked" by an additional vowel, such as a silent *e* at the end. In contrast, short vowel sounds are not contained in their letter names but are most commonly represented with a single letter. Short vowels, similar to the consonants, are associated with individual sounds, such as *a* in *cat*, *e* in *bed*, *i* in *bib*, *o* in *fox*, and *u* in *bug*. Early in this stage, children have difficulty attending to the vowel sound in the middle of words, but once they have the phonological awareness to isolate the middle sound, they commonly confuse the different short vowel spelling by using letter names that when pronounced, sound closest to the short vowel sound they were trying to represent. For example, the pronunciation of the letter name *A* is closer to the short *e* vowel sound (*eh*, as in *Ed*) than the letter name *E*, so children in the early to middle part of this stage frequently spell short *e* words with an *a* (*BAD* for *bed*). Short vowels are studied through same-vowel word families, mixed-vowel word families, and regular short vowel sorts, which are discussed later in the chapter.

Two additional sounds typically confused in the letter name–alphabetic stage include **affricates** and **preconsonantal nasals**. Both features are studied during the latter part of the letter name–alphabetic stage. The *affricate sound* is the sound at the beginning of words like *chop, jump, germ, trap*, or *drive*. Learning to spell the affricate sounds entails learning a set of consonant digraphs (*ch*) and blends (*dr, tr*) that are particularly difficult to spell because of the way they are formed in the mouth. The affricate blends include *dr* as in *drive* and *tr* as in *trip*. As you pronounce each of these words, notice that they sound more like *gr* and *chr* rather than the letters used, which is exactly how letter name–alphabetic spellers may spell them (*GRIV* for *drive, CHRIP* for *trip*). Children at this stage also use but confuse preconsonantal nasals, or words in which an *m* or *n* precedes a final consonant, as in the words *camp, hand*, and *think*. They are called *nasals* because air escapes through the nose when producing the sound. After mastering short vowels, these last few sounds are taught later in the letter name–alphabetic stage. Lack of understanding of preconsonantal nasals can also be seen in Ethan's writing in Figure 4.2 as he writes *RAGR* for *ranger*. Ethan neglects to use the preconsonantal *n* in *ranger*.

WHAT IS ABSENT AT THIS STAGE? Letter name–alphabetic spellers eventually master the ability to segment and represent all the sounds in a word (complete phonemic awareness), but they usually omit silent letters, such as the final letter *E* in *cave, make*, or *rate*. They are not yet aware that it is often necessary to use additional letters to signal long vowel sounds (*mop/mope, pan/pain, lit/light*). When they attempt to spell two- or three-syllable words, vowels may also be omitted in final syllables, as Ethan did when he spelled *SPIDR* for *spider*. These patterns are studied in the later stages of spelling development. The letter name–alphabetic stage focuses primarily on one-syllable short vowel words with consonant digraphs and consonant blends.

Understanding Picture and Word Sorts

Regardless of what kind of phonics or spelling instruction your child receives at school, you can support them by establishing a word study routine at home and providing fun and purposeful activities to support their learning. Your child may bring home sorts from school, or you may want to supplement classroom instruction with sorts. Ready-to-print sorts and directions for how to do the sorts can be found in the book *Word Sorts for Letter Name–Alphabetic Spellers* (Johnston, Bear, Invernizzi, & Templeton, 2014). The examples of sorts described in this chapter come from this book.

In the *Let's Talk About It* section, we use one sort example to describe how to pose questions and guide purposeful conversations as you talk about the sounds, patterns, and meaning in words. In the *Sort Support* section, we explain what you and your children need to know about specific spelling features. This gives you the tools to help your child understand the way words work in spelling and reading at this stage.

Let's Talk About It!

Effective word study is based on comparing and contrasting words as a way to focus children's attention on a specific spelling feature. **Spelling features** are letters or combinations of letters that represent sound and pattern units in English. For example, the blend *pl* as in *plan* and the digraph *sh* as in *shack* represent spelling features studied in this stage of development. Children sort words into groups and talk about their similarities and differences. Instead of memorizing sounds or rules, your child categorizes words and pictures and discovers generalizations as they think about what's the same and what's different in each category. Discovery is facilitated through purposeful contrasts, questioning, and discussion. Discussions around sorts and spelling patterns focuses on a series of fundamental questions used across stages (Figure 4.3).

FIGURE 4.3 Let's Talk About It! Guiding Questions

Let's Talk About It!

1. How are the pictures or words alike in each category?
2. Are there any pictures or words that do not fit? Why?
3. What do you learn from this sort? What are the big ideas or the underlying generalizations you can learn from this sort?

FIGURE 4.4 Mixed Short Vowel Family Sort

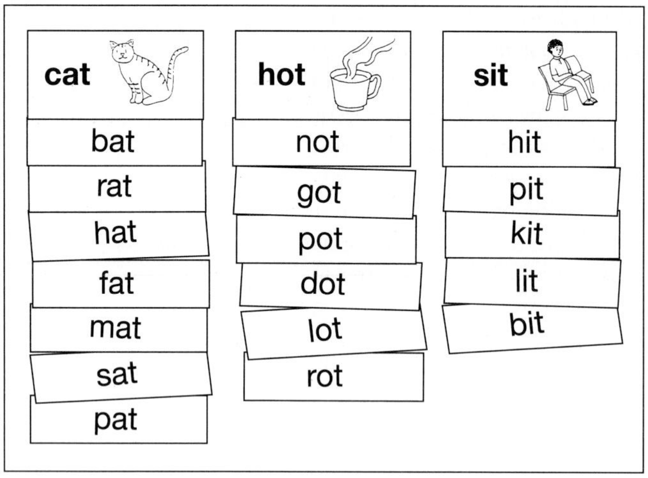

Let's talk about an example at the letter name–alphabetic stage. This example is a mixed-vowel word family sort that is designed to reinforce the idea of word families and to focus attention on the short vowel sound because the ending consonants are all the same, in this case the letter *t*. Let's sort and talk about it using the following words:

> *cat, hat, not, bit, bat, fat, pit, lit, got, lot, fit, pot, mat, cot, sit, dot, pat, rat, sat, hot, hit, kit, rot, that*

As discussed in Chapter 2, you begin by making sure your child can either read all the words or identify each of the pictures. It should be noted that with rhyming families, children often rely on the pattern to help them read individual words. When you put all the *-at* family words together, reading *-at* words becomes more automatic. This is one of the reasons we begin with word families instead of mixed vowels. Next, select a few of the words to talk about their individual word meanings. Together, *sort* the words into the categories as shown in Figure 4.4. Once you have completed the sort, *check* to make sure all the words are placed correctly in each category by asking your child to read each column aloud. Next, *reflect* by talking about the sort with your child using the three guiding questions outlined in Figure 4.3.

HOW ARE THE PICTURES OR WORDS ALIKE IN EACH CATEGORY? Using the sort represented in Figure 4.4, you and your child consider and discuss the similarities and differences across and within the sort. All of the words end with *t*, so it is necessary to look at and consider the vowel in the middle of the words. The sort includes three different short vowel sounds: short *a* as in *cat*, short *i* as in *sit*, and short *o* as in *hot*. In each column, all of the words are in the same **word family**, meaning that they have the same ending chunk of a middle vowel sound and ending sound. All of the words in the same word family also rhyme.

ARE THERE ANY PICTURES OR WORDS THAT DO NOT FIT? WHY? All words in this sort fit into one of the three word family categories. There are not any oddballs included in this particular sort. Oddballs are more common beginning in the later parts of the letter name-alphabetic stage.

WHAT DID YOU LEARN FROM THIS SORT? WHAT ARE THE BIG IDEAS OR THE UNDERLYING GENERALIZATION YOU CAN LEARN FROM THIS SORT? Next, you and your child address the third and perhaps the most important question. The studied feature of mixed-vowel word families has several underlying principles (Figure 4.5).

FIGURE 4.5 Examples of Underlying Generalizations: Mixed-Vowel Word Families Sort

Examples of the Big Ideas or Underlying Generalizations: Mixed-Vowel Word Families Sort

- ✓ All words have vowels.
- ✓ Words with the same word family rhyme and end in the same two letters.
- ✓ Children can use chunking to read and spell additional words.
- ✓ Each short vowel makes a different sound.
- ✓ We can stretch words out to hear the middle short vowel sound.
- ✓ We can blend the beginning sounds (onset) and the rime (the vowel and what follows) to read words.

First, all of the words in each category have the same two final letters, known as a **rime**, and represent the same ending sounds or chunk. Second, words with the same endings are considered part of a word family because they rhyme. The idea that word chunks can be repeated allows the student to spell unfamiliar words in the same family. For example, if a child can spell *cat*, *hat*, and *mat*, he or she can also apply the *–at* chunk in words such as *flat*, *chat*, and *brat*. The application of word knowledge from known to unknown words is called *generalization* and is at the heart of word study.

Sort Support: What You and Your Child Need to Know at the Letter Name–Alphabetic Stage

At each stage of spelling, it is helpful to understand which spelling features are commonly *used but confused*, as this is the focus of instruction. In this section, *Sort Support* provides insight into the general concepts that spellers learn at the letter name–alphabetic stage. Each description provides a definition, examples, and a few spelling concepts or big ideas within each unit of study. This helps you feel confident talking about how words work with your child.

During the prior emergent stage, children should have mastered alphabet recognition and developed a basic understanding of letter sounds. At the beginning of the letter name–alphabetic stage, children review beginning consonant sounds. The letter name–alphabetic stage examines the following main features, described in more detail as follows:

- Beginning and final consonants (***tap***, ***bun***, ***pen***, ***rub***)
- Blends (***slip***, ***flat***, ***prop***) and digraphs (***shop***, ***that***, ***chick***, ***wish***, ***path***)
- Same-vowel word families (*-at/-ap/-an*)
- Mixed-vowel word families (*-at/-it/-ot*)
- Short vowels (*cap*, *list*, *top*, *pest*, *run*)
- Affricates blends (***drum***, ***truck***)
- Preconsonantal nasals (***bump***, ***went***, ***ring***, ***sink***)

Features are studied in the sequence listed above in addition to the study of **high-frequency** words throughout the stage. Make sure to be on the lookout for high-frequency words in every sort throughout this stage, then notice and discuss these words as they are discovered. By the end of the letter name–alphabetic stage, children should be able to spell the vast majority of single-syllable short vowel words correctly.

BEGINNING CONSONANT SOUNDS During the emergent stage, children learn to identify the beginning sounds, usually consonants, in words. A review of the beginning consonant sounds is beneficial early in the letter name–alphabetic stage. Children at this stage may contrast as many as four letter sounds per sort. Letters that are similar in formation (*b/d/p*) are generally taught separately, as are letters that have similar sounds, such as *F* and *V*. Beginning consonant sorts include all pictures to sort with a **header** that includes the upper- and lower-case letter with a **key picture**. See Figure 4.6 for an example of a beginning consonant picture sort. As needed, specific sorts can also be created to clarify lingering confusions, such as the similar-sounding *b* and *p*, the visually similar *b* and *d*, or letters frequently confused based on their names (*y* and *w*).

FIGURE 4.6 Sample Sort: Beginning Consonants

TABLE 4.5 Examples of Blends and Digraphs

	Types of Blends and Digraphs	Examples
Beginning Blends	*l*-blends: *bl-, cl-, fl-, pl-, gl-*	*black, clump, flash, plant, glad*
	r-blends: *gr-, tr-, pr-, br-, cr-, dr-, fr-*	*grab, truck, prop, brag, crib, drip, fresh*
	s-blends: *sc-, sk-, sm-, sn-, sw-, st-, sl-, sp-*	*scab, skunk, small, snap, swim, stuck, slug, spell*
Ending Blends	*l*-blends: *-ld, -lp, -lf, -ld, -lk*	*cold, help, self, bald, milk*
	r-blends: *-rd, -rk*	*hard, shark*
	s-blends: *-st, -sk, -sp*	*last, whisk, wisp*
	other: *-pt, -ft, -ct*	*rapt, sift, pact*
Beginning Digraphs	*sh-, ch-, th-, wh-*	*shut, chick, thin, when*
Ending Digraphs	*-sh, -ch, -th*	*fish, much, bath*

Overall, children at this stage are learning several important concepts. First, there are two types of letters: consonants and vowels and each represents at least one sound. Some consonants represent more than one sound, such a *G* in *giraffe* and *gold* or *C* in *call* and *cent*. Similarly, sometimes a sound such as the /k/ sound in *cage* and *kite* can be made by two different letters; the letters *C* and *K*. Children also learn to segment (divide) and blend sounds in individual words; this skill begins as an aural skill and is later used to spell and read.

BLENDS AND DIGRAPHS Once children have developed firm understanding of the sound or sounds represented by each consonant, they are ready to examine what happens when two consonants come together. **Blends** are two consonants that you blend or read together, but each keeps its own distinct sound. In contrast, **digraphs** are two consonants that make a new single sound. Consonant digraph patterns include *sh-* as in *shape*, *ch-* as in *church*, *th-* as in *think* and *wh-* as in *whale*. Blends and digraphs can be found both at the beginning of words and at the ends of words as showcased in Table 4.5.

Although it is not necessary for children to understand the terms *blend* and *digraph*, it is important for them to recognize and read them in words. At this stage of spelling development, children continue to work with beginning-sound picture sorts (Figure 4.6) because the number of words they can read is limited. Later in the letter name–alphabetic stage, vowel sorts include words with blends and digraphs at both the beginnings and ends of words.

Figures 4.7 and 4.8 showcase sample sorts for blends and digraphs. Sorting allows students the opportunity to distinguish among single consonants, blends, and digraphs.

SAME-VOWEL WORD FAMILIES In the letter name–alphabetic stage, children study three different types of word sorts focused on short vowels: same-vowel word families (all short *a*, such as words spelled with *-an*, *-at*, and *-ap*), mixed-vowel word families (families with different vowels, such as words spelled with *-in*, *-an*, *-un*), and short vowel sorts without the support of a rhyming family (short *a*, *e*, *u* words). Same-vowel word family sorts often include both the word and a picture to provide children with additional

FIGURE 4.7 Sample Sorts: Digraphs

FIGURE 4.8 Sample Sorts: Blends

support, because they usually do not yet know how to read many words (Figure 4.9). Same-vowel word family sorts review ending sounds because the middle vowel is the same throughout the sort. Previously, consonant sounds were studied only in beginning-sound picture sorts, so same-vowel word family sorts encourage children to extend that knowledge to ending sounds. These sorts also introduce the idea that words with the same word family also rhyme. This idea is key to generalizing spellings to other words not included in the sort. If *can*, *van*, and *fan* all end in *–an*, then *plan* and *scan* must also end in *–an*, because they belong to the same rhyming family.

FIGURE 4.9 Sample Sort: Same-Vowel Word Families

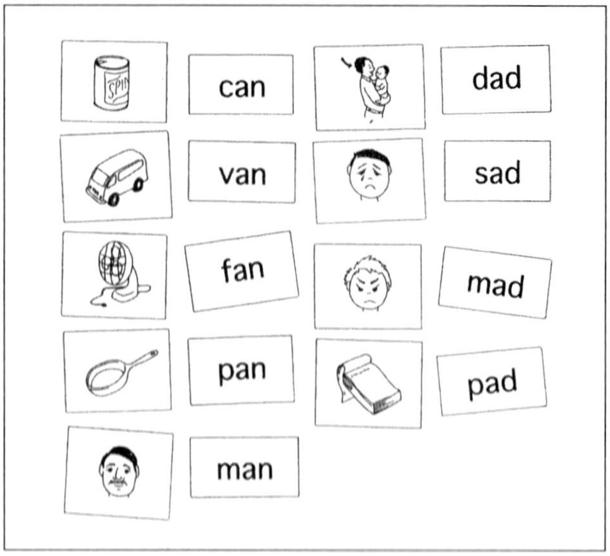

MIXED-VOWEL WORD FAMILIES Once children become familiar with word families and rhyme, they are ready to move into mixed-vowel word family sorts. Mixed-vowel word family sorts look very similar to the same-vowel word family sorts. Instead of using words with the same short vowel (all short *a* words), mixed-vowel sorts focus on two or

FIGURE 4.10 Sample Sort: Mixed-Vowel Word Families

can	pin	sun
man	fin	run
pan	chin	bun
fan	win	fun
tan	grin	
van	thin	
plan	skin	
than		
run		

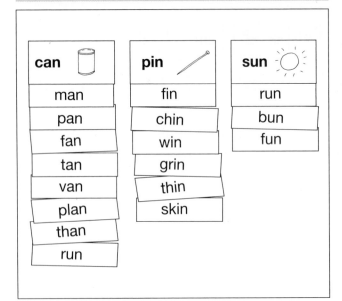

FIGURE 4.11 Sample Sort: Short Vowels

cat	sock	*oddball*
jam	job	was
wag	fox	for
cab	got	
sad	hop	
ran	lot	
map	mom	
ham	top	
bag	box	
had	mop	
	hot	

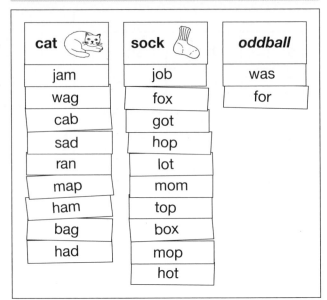

three different short vowels. Each short vowel family continues to rhyme or to have the same final ending letter, as in *pan* for *-an*, *pin* for *-in*, and *fun* for *-un* (Figure 4.10). Keeping all the ending consonants the same focuses attention on the short vowel sound in the middle of words. Mixed-vowel word family sorts usually include words with a few pictures because most children in need of this instruction can't read many words yet.

In mixed-vowel word family sorts, children learn that each short vowel makes a distinct sound, and that words with the same two final letters rhyme and allow us to generate similar spellings easily. If we know how to read and spell *pan*, we also know *can, Dan, fan, man, ran, tan*, and *van*. If we know how to read and spell *fin*, we also know *pin, tin*, and *bin*.

SHORT VOWELS After learning about short vowels in same-vowel and mixed-vowel word families, children are ready for the more challenging study of short vowel sorts without the support of rhyme, and to learn about the consonant-vowel-consonant (CVC) pattern seen in words like *cap* or *run* (Figure 4.11). Short vowel sorts allow children to refine their understanding of the five short vowel sounds: *a* as in *hat*, *i* as in *pig*, *e* as in *beg*, *o* as in *rot*, and *u* as in *fun*. It should be noted, however, that short vowel sounds vary. For example, the short *a* sounds in *map*, *hand*, and *pal* are all slightly different because they are influenced by the consonant sounds that surround them.

ODDBALLS Short vowel sorts also introduce the concept of oddballs. In this case, **oddballs** are words that look like the CVC pattern but do not have the expected short vowel sound. For example, the words *saw* and *was* have the letter *a* in the middle, but they do not have the short *a* sound heard in *hat*. Often, oddballs studied at this stage are high-frequency words that are encountered regularly in daily reading. Oddballs are important to include in word sorts because their presence demands flexibility in thinking. For example, the word *for* follows the CVC pattern associated with the short vowel sound, so if children were sorting visually only, they would want to put it under the short *o* column with words like *pot*, *mop*, and *sock*.

AFFRICATES An **affricate** is a linguistic term referring to a sound that is created by forcing air through a small closure in the mouth, creating friction. Although we do not expect you to be a linguist, it is helpful to know that affricate sounds are challenging to spell because many letters and letter combinations create the affricate sound; *dr, tr, ch, j*, and *g* can all create an affricate sound, as does the letter name for *H* (pronounced "aitch"). So the blend *tr* in *trap* sounds and feels more like *jr* or *chr* as in *chrap*. Children at the letter name–alphabetic stage spell based on the pronunciation of the name of the letters, but this strategy does not work for them with affricates (*GRIV* for *drive*, *CHRIP* for *trip*). Affricate sorts compare the affricate to other similar sounds and compare the affricate blend (*tr*) to the individual sounds in the blends (*t*, *r*) to help them see the differences in letter combinations. Ultimately, letter name-alphabetic spellers will be able to distinguish among similar-sounding words that begin with affricate blends and digraphs, as shown in Figure 4.12.

FIGURE 4.12 Sample Sort: Affricates

PRECONSONANTAL NASALS A **preconsonantal nasal** refers to a nasal-sounding consonant, an *m* or *n*, that precedes the final consonant, as in *jump*, *hand*, *bump*, *sink*, and *ring*. The vowel is nasalized as air escapes through the nose during pronunciation. Although preconsonantal nasals are considered a kind of final consonant blend, their difficulty makes them worthy of study as a distinct spelling feature. Preconsonantal nasals are difficult to hear, and children frequently leave a letter out (*BUP* for *bump*, *HAD* for *hand*). Preconsonantal nasals are studied through word sorts at the end of the letter name-alphabetic stage. Figures 4.13 and 4.14 show how these preconsonantal nasals can be grouped by the ending blend.

Spelling Strategies

Parents and teachers can help children learn to use different strategies to spell unknown or familiar words whose spellings have not been mastered. Some strategies are more useful than others, depending on the stage of development in which your child is performing (Dahl et al., 2003; Ehri, 1997; Williams & Lundstrom, 2007). Emergent and letter name–alphabetic spellers, for example, are highly dependent on sound and letter–sound

FIGURE 4.13 Sample Sort: Preconsonantal Nasals

-ng	-mp
rang	camp
sing	imp
bring	pump
sang	stamp
gang	lump
hung	jump
thin	bup
king	lamp
ring	ramp
swing	stump
gang	plump

FIGURE 4.14 Sample Sort: Preconsonantal Nasals

-nt	-nd	-nk
went	send	bunk
pant	stand	blank
print	sand	trunk
want	land	wink
hunt	wind	stink
spent	bend	drink
		pink
		bank
		thank
		think

correspondences. Invented spelling or the sound-it-out strategies are perfectly appropriate at this stage.

Following are some additional strategies parents can use to help their children spell unknown or familiar words whose spellings can be elusive. Strategies are listed from the earliest stage use to the most advanced.

USE INVENTED SPELLING As discussed previously, *invented spelling* is when students use their best judgment to spell unknown words, spelling using the letters, sounds, and patterns that the child has already learned. Invented spelling does not mean that the child randomly guesses at how to spell words, but rather applies what he or she has already learned to spell with reasonable approximations. Encouraging children to use invented spelling in their daily writing for unknown words complements the developmental idea that children should be taught on their individual **instructional level**, not too easy and not too hard. The same should apply for the spelling in their daily writing.

SOUND-IT-OUT Once a child has identified a word to spell, parents can teach young children to stretch out and isolate the sounds in the word. Ask, "What's the first sound that you hear?" The child repeats the initial sound, identifies the letter, and writes it. Repeat the process until the child has recorded only the sounds that he or she hears. This strategy is most appropriate for young readers and writers in the emergent and letter name–alphabetic stages.

KNOW IT IN A SNAP **High-frequency words** fall into two categories—those that can be identified phonetically, such as *but, can, if, with, be, me, did, into, that,* and *yes*, and others that must be learned more through memory and experience, such as *saw, said, there, are, your,* and *their*. It can be helpful to explain that many words are decodable, meaning that they can be divided into sounds, whereas others need to be known in a snap. You may also need to combine this strategy with the sound-it-out. For example, if your child wants to spell the word come, you can can ask which two sounds are heard—the *c* and the *m*. Then provide the other letters. It is helpful for children to know that while identifying sounds and chunks are valuable strategies, there are some words that depend on memory.

CHUNK KNOWN WORD PARTS Your child may know how to spell part of a word and be unsure of other parts. Encourage him or her to "spell the parts you know." For example, your child may know the beginning letter combinations, such as *sh-, th-, ch-, bl-,* or the end of a rhyming family, such as *–og, -ip, -at*. Teach children to tackle the parts of words that are known and then to concentrate on the unknown portion. This is appropriate for children in the middle of the letter name–alphabetic stage of spelling and through the upper levels.

USE ANALOGY *Analogy* is the use of rhyming words to determine the spelling of an unfamiliar word. Encourage your child to think of a word that is already known and consider the spelling for the rhyming word. For example, if we know how to spell the word *hop*, we can spell other words that rhyme by changing the beginning sound or blend. Spelling *hop* correctly leads us to spell the words *top, shop, chop, mop,* and *stop*.

Word Study with Parents, Tutors, and School Volunteers

In this section, we share specific examples of how you can support the development of word knowledge for children at the letter name–alphabetic stage. These are in addition to the routines and essential techniques described in detail in Chapter 2. You may remember from Chapter 3 that children may also still need to be working on phonological awareness and

FIGURE 4.15 Follow the Path

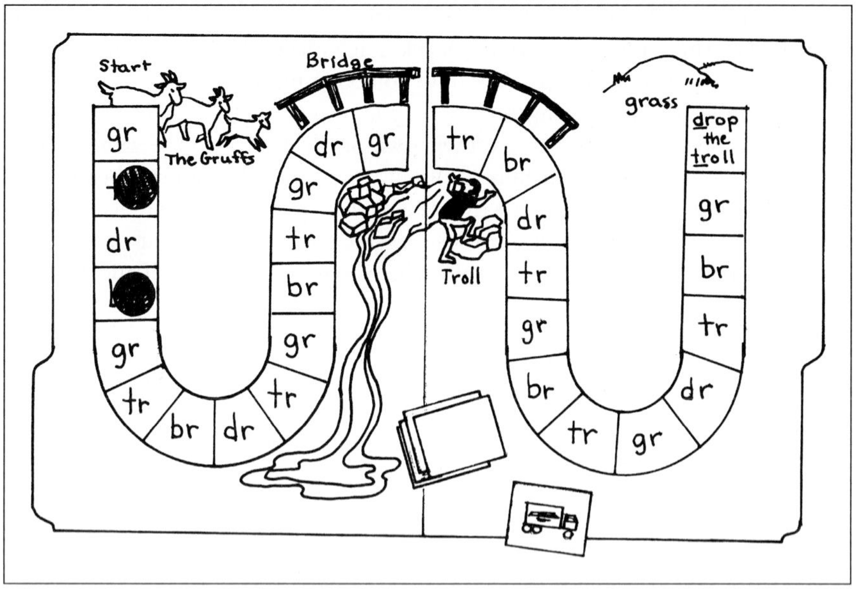

alphabet knowledge. For fun games and activities to reinforce these essential skills, refer to Chapter 3 on emergent learners.

Follow the Path Games

A follow the path game is created using a board game format (Figure 4.15) and works much like the familiar game of Candyland®. This is a great way to practice the letters and sounds you have been studying and can be a fun family activity. These games can be created to use with just about any feature you are studying with your child using the templates provided in the Appendix. Use the templates to glue a path of your choice on a file folder or large piece of construction paper. Decorate the game board with color, stickers, pictures, or a theme. Label each space on the path with one of the letters or patterns you are studying. For example, when studying short vowels you might have all the spaces marked with *a* or *i* in order to play the game with the short *a*/short *i* sort. Children love to create these games with you. You can use coins, chips, or pieces from other games as the markers for each player. Use your child's sort to play the game. Place all the cards face down in a stack. Each player draws a card in turn and moves the playing piece to the next space on the path that has the matching feature. Variations include having each player spell the word out loud or naming another word with the same pattern before moving to the next space. You can make a new game for each pattern your child studies, or you can have blank game boards laminated and then simply write the new features in with a dry-erase marker each time your child works with a new sort.

Bingo

Bingo is a popular and familiar game. This activity can be adapted to use with any spelling feature. Children in the letter name–alphabetic stage may play this game with beginning sounds, blends, and short vowels. *Bingo* can also be used with rhyming pictures or sight words. Create your own Bingo card with 9 or 16 squares (3 × 3 or 4 × 4). Figure 4.16 shows a game prepared to review the *s*-blends.

FIGURE 4.16 Bingo

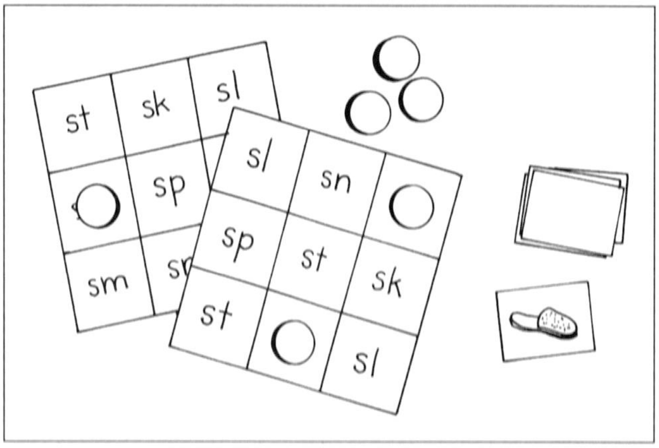

You also need some kind of marker, such as coins, chips, beans, or pasta. Use your child's sort to create the Bingo cards by writing, drawing, or sticking down the pictures on the Bingo card. Each person selects a different Bingo card and several markers or pieces. Use your child's sort to play the game. Place all the cards face down in a stack. Each player draws a card in turn and covers the space with the matching feature. Play until someone fills a row or the entire card with markers and remember to shout "Bingo!"

In a variation called Spello, children create their own Spello boards in the same style as *Bingo* using the template found in the Appendix. Call out words with the patterns being studied (such as word families or short vowels) to write wherever they choose on the blank Spello board. After the board has been filled, call out the words again as your child uses tokens to cover words as they are called out. When a row or the whole board is covered, yell out "Spello!"

Memory

Memory is a common children's game in which two or more players try to match two cards with the same picture, sound, or spelling feature (initial sounds, short vowel word family *-at*). Children play this using their word or picture sort. Turn all the cards from one sort face down spread out on the floor or a table. Partners take turns flipping over two cards and reading the words or naming the pictures. If they match by feature (same beginning sound or same word family), the player may take the pair. Players take turns looking for pairs of words with matching features until all the cards are gone.

Match!

Children look for matches in beginning sounds or word families in this game similar to *Slap Jack*. This game is played with two people. Each player has half the deck of pictures or words. Children turn a picture card face-up from their deck at the same time. When two cards are turned up from the same sound or family, they make a match, and the first person to recognize and say "Match!" gets the pair. If the words or pictures do not match, another set is turned over until a match occurs.

Build, Blend, and Extend

Children build words with letters and word families in this activity designed to reinforce phonemic awareness and the blending of sounds. Build, Blend, and Extend also encourages children to use analogy as a spelling strategy with word families ("If I can spell *cat*, then I can spell *fat*").

Create a set of cards with beginning sounds (*b*, *m*, *st*, *ch*) and word families (*at*, *ap*, *ig*) based on the patterns your child is studying (Figure 4.17). Guide your child to build words by putting together beginning sounds and word families (*m* and *at*) and then blend the sounds to read the word ("Mmmmmmm, aaaaaaaat, mat"). Extend the activity by asking your child to change one part to make a new word ("How can you change *mat* to *sat*?"). When playing Build, Blend, and Extend with your child, focus initially on one word family. As you child increases word knowledge, you can try word families with the same vowel (*-at*, *-ap*, *-an*) and later word families with different vowels (*-at*, *-it*, *-ot*). As your child learns beginning blends (*st*, *br*, *pl*) and digraphs (*sh*, *ch*, *th*), these can be included too. Commercial products similar to Build, Blend, and Extend can also be readily purchased.

FIGURE 4.17 Build, Blend, and Extend

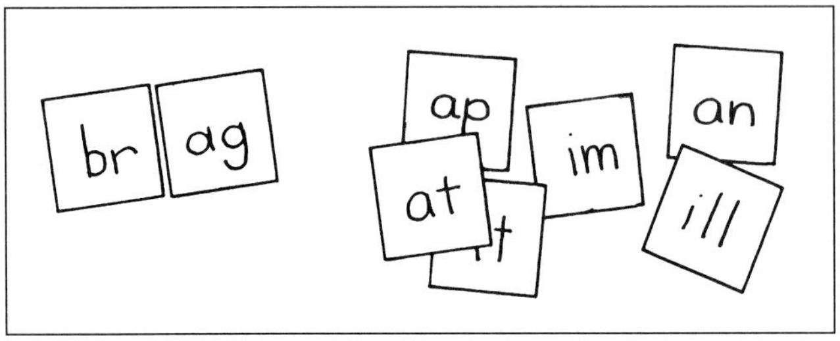

Word Family Wheels and Flip Books

Wheels and flip charts are fun for young children to play with independently or with a friend. The wheels and flip charts are used to reinforce blending the beginning sound with the ending chunk to read words in word families they

FIGURE 4.18 Word Family Wheels and Flip Books

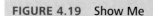

FIGURE 4.19 Show Me

have sorted, as shown in Figure 4.18. Children practice reading the word family wheels and flip books as fast as they can. This activity builds confidence and automaticity. You can create your own word family wheels and flip books, or you can also purchase ready-made versions from educational suppliers.

Show Me

This activity is a favorite with children who are learning word families and short vowels. Give your child a folder with an assortment of letter cards. There are three pockets in which the letters can be placed to make short vowel words, as shown in Figure 4.19. You ask your child to use the letter cards to spell a short vowel word such as *mat*, *hat*, or *hot*. Once he or she is ready, you call out, "Show me." The emphasis of the game is to create different words with manipulative letter cards for practice. You can start by using words that are in the same families, such as *bad*, *sad*, or *mad*, in which your child focuses primarily on changing the initial consonants. Move on to a different family and different vowels. For example, you could follow this sequence: *mad*, *mat*, *hat*, *hot*, *pot*, *pet*. Add cards with digraphs or blends to spell words such as *ship* or *fast*.

To create a Show Me game, to make the folder, cut paper into approximately 7- × 5-inch rectangles. Fold up a 1-inch section along the long side and then fold the whole thing into overlapping thirds. Staple at the edges to make three pockets (see Figure 4.19). Print an assortment of consonant letters on the top half of each index card to use in the pocket folder. A useful assortment of letters for this activity includes the five short vowels and *b*, *d*, *f*, *g*, *m*, *n*, *p*, *r*, and *t*. Too many consonants can be hard to manage.

Making Words with Cubes

FIGURE 4.20 Making Words with Cubes

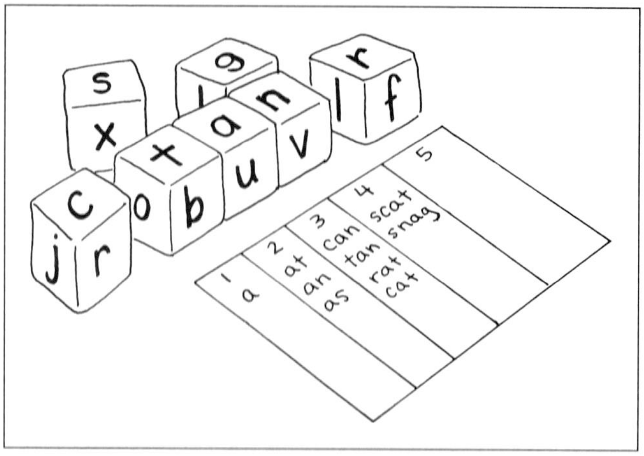

Short vowel words are built with letter cubes in this game. It can be used for other vowels as well. Letter cubes can be found in many games such as *Boggle* and *Perquackey*. Be sure to put all the vowels on a single cube so vowels show up in every roll. In pairs, players take turns being the Player and the Recorder. The Recorder writes the words made by the Player. A Player shakes the cubes, spills them out onto the table, and then starts a timer. Whatever letters land face-up must be used to make words. The Word Maker moves the cubes to create words and spell them to the Recorder. The cubes can then be moved around to make more words. The Recorder writes the words in columns by the number of letters in the words (Figure 4.20). When the time ends, the players check the words for accuracy. To create a score, count the total number of letters used in each word. Children quickly realize that the bigger the words they make, the greater the score.

Roll the Dice

This game is for two to four players to reinforce word families. To play this game, you need to either purchase word family dice at an educational supply store or purchase blank dice or small blocks on which you write "Roll Again," "Lose a Turn," and four contrasting word families (*an*, *ap*, *ag*, and *at*) as shown in Figure 4.21. Players take turns rolling the dice with the word families. If it lands on a word family, the player must come up with a word for that family and record it on a piece of paper. Each player keeps a list of his or her own words and can use a word only once, although someone else may have used it. If a player is stumped or lands on "Lose a Turn," the die is passed to the next person. If the student lands on "Roll Again," he or she takes another turn. The person who records the most words at the end of the allotted time wins. You may also play in teams. Each team has its own die and a Recorder. The first person of each team rolls the die and quickly calls out an appropriate word. The Recorder writes the word on the paper. The Player hands the die to the next Player and the list of words grows until a predetermined amount of time expires. The team with the most words wins. The game may also be played with six word families and without the "Lose a Turn" and "Roll Again" options.

FIGURE 4.21 Roll the Dice

FIGURE 4.22 Go Fish!

Go Fish!

This version of the classic *Go Fish!* card game can be used to review word families. Create a deck of 32 cards with four words from each of eight different word families written on them (*that*, *bat*, *fat*, and *hat*). Write each word at the top left of the card so that the words are visible when held in the hand (Figure 4.22). Deal five cards to each Player and place the remaining cards in a facedown stack. The first Player asks any other Player for a match to a card in his or her hand: "Do you have any words that rhyme with *hat*?" If the Player receives a matching card, he or she may put the pair down and ask again. If the other Player does not have the card requested, he or she tells the first player to "Go fish!" which means draw a card. Play continues until one Player runs out of cards. Go Fish! can also be adapted for beginning sounds and blends using pictures, or it can be used with vowel patterns.

Guess My Word

Guess My Word game is played with a sort to increase understanding of both word meaning and pattern. Partners play this word guessing game with their sort. Put all of the picture or word cards face down in a stack between the partners. On each turn, a Player takes a card from the stack without letting his or her partner see the card, and then gives clues about the word meaning and spelling feature. For example, for the word *frog*, the clues might include: "It is a small green animal. It rhymes with *dog*. It starts with the same sound as *frame*." The Player keeps giving clues until the partner guesses the word.

Commercial Products

There are many commercial and educational products readily available that can support word knowledge and literacy development. The key to selecting products that will help your child is making sure that you have the spelling stage and patterns being studied in mind. Word games for children include *Boggle*, *Perquackey*, *Scrabble Junior*, *What's Gnu?*, *Hedbanz* (vocabulary), and *Bingo*. There are also many applications for electronic devices, including smartphones, that support the word study.

Supporting Reading and Writing

Reading and writing are closely related and development in one area contributes to another. They can be seen as two sides of the same coin—a reader consumes the written word, whereas a writer produces it. In this section, we explore how to promote reading and writing and how to make connections to spelling.

Reading

During the letter name–alphabetic stage, children transition from dependence on simple and predictable reading materials that they read with support to less predictable beginning reading materials. With less predictable materials, readers must rely on an expanding sight vocabulary and the ability to figure out unfamiliar words using a variety of decoding strategies. Parents can support this transition by reading to and with their children in combination with word study.

READING ALOUD TO YOUR CHILD It is important to continue reading aloud to your child throughout the elementary grades. Select books to read aloud that would be too difficult for him or her to read independently but are age-appropriate in content and interesting to your child. Children love being immersed in stories through both picture books such as *Chrysanthemum* by Kevin Henkes, about a young child who is teased about her name, or chapter books such as *Fantastic Mr. Fox* by Roald Dahl, about a clever fox who outsmarts three farmers and protects his family. Reading aloud to children helps build language skills, vocabulary, and background knowledge. Make the read aloud interactive by inviting comments and questions from your child. Encourage connections to the characters and themes. Ask your child questions and encourage him or her to share thoughts and reactions to the reading. Remember that this is a conversation. Keep it fun! Select a wide variety of genres to read together, including nonfiction and poetry. Award-winning nonfiction writers such as Seymour Simon (*Global Warming, Hurricanes, Volcanoes, Earthquakes*), and Sy Montgomery (*The Snake Scientist, The Tarantula Scientist, The Tapir Scientist*) are masters at engaging students with fascinating facts, full-color photographs, and tales of adventure. Reading aloud and talking about information books will also build your child's vocabulary, background knowledge, and overall interest in reading and the world around them.

Poetry also offers opportunities for language play and discussion. Young children love Shel Silverstein (*Where the Sidewalk Ends* and *Falling Up*) and Jack Prelutsky (*Be Glad Your Nose Is On Your Face and Other Poems: Some of the Best of Jack Prelutsky*), as well as Langston Hughes (*The Dream Keeper and Other Poems*) and Eloise Greenfield (*Honey, I Love*). Many picture books are also written in rhyme, such as Bill Peet's collection of picture books (*The Caboose Who Got Loose, Cyrus the Unsinkable Sea Serpent*) or renditions of famous poems like *Casey at the Bat* by Ernest Thayer. Choose a regular daily reading time with your child. Reading before bed can be an enjoyable time to spend time with your child and finish the day with comfort and conversation. See Figure 4.23 for sources

FIGURE 4.23 Recommended Book Lists for Young Readers

Association for Library Service to Children (ALSC) Notable Books for Children (annual)
http://www.ala.org/alsc/awardsgrants/notalists/ncb

Caldecott Medal and Honor Books
http://www.ala.org/alsc/awardsgrants/bookmedia/caldecottmedal/caldecotthonors/caldecottmedal

Theodore Geisel Award
http://www.ala.org/alsc/awardsgrants/bookmedia/geiselaward/geiselabout

American Library Association (ALA) Coretta Scott King Award Books
http://www.ala.org/emiert/cskbookawards

International Literacy Association Children's Choices
http://www.literacyworldwide.org/get-resources/reading-lists/childrens-choices-reading-list

Jim Trelease Handbook of Read Alouds
http://www.trelease-on-reading.com

Capitol Choices: Noteworthy Books for Children and Teens
http://www.capitolchoices.org

National Science Teachers Association (NSTA) Outstanding Science Trade Books, K-12
http://www.nsta.org/publications/ostb

National Book Foundation National Book Awards
http://www.nationalbook.org/nba2014.html

of award-winning books for young readers. Also, be sure to speak with your child's teacher, school, and public librarians for their recommendations.

BEGINNING READER TEXTS Reading aloud to your child eliminates the need for your child to identify the word on the page and allows him or her to focus exclusively on meaning. When our children read to us, however, our focus shifts from conversation and background building to also include ways to identify words. Beginning readers cannot read very much without some kind of support. Support can come from two sources: the text and a knowledgeable reader who serves as a partner such as a teacher, tutor or parent. First, let's consider the text.

There are three types of books used primarily with beginning readers at the letter name–alphabetic stage: predictable readers, decodable readers, and beginning readers (Brown, 2000). Rather than choosing only one type of text as being the best for beginning readers, each of these types of texts has specific purposes for teaching based on the needs of the children (Table 4.6). Although all three kinds of texts provide some common structures (pictures that support the text, simple sentence structures, simple or familiar plot), each type of these texts provides a different kind of support to the beginning reader that helps them gradually make progress in their reading ability (Fountas & Pinnell, 2010).

TABLE 4.6 Types of Text for Beginning Readers

Type of Text	Characteristics	Purposes	Examples
Predictable Text	• Familiar topics and language • Phrases or sentences repeat • Pictures support the content • Simple sentence structures • Limited number of pages and words • Familiar or simple plot	• Help children develop print awareness and concept of word • Build word recognition	• *Brown Bear, Brown Bear* by Bill Martin and Eric Carle • *I Went Walking* by Sue Williams • *Katy Wore Her Red Dress* and *Henry Wore His Green Sneakers* by Merle Peek and James Cross Giblin
Decodable Text	• Text controlled to emphasize common spelling patterns and chunks (*cat, mat*) plus high-frequency words (*said, was*) • Emphasis on words that are phonetically regular • Pictures support the text • Simple sentence structures • Familiar or simple plot	• Help children apply phonetic matches between letters and sounds; increases word recognition skills • Help children recognize high-frequency words	• Bob Books by Scholastic • The Wright Phonics Readers by Wright Group • Phonics Readers • *Reading A to Z* website (decodable readers) • Phonics Readers by Steck-Vaughn
Beginning Leveled Readers	• Familiar genre, theme, text structure, content • Stories are not predictable or patterned • Words are not selected based on their spelling pattern (such as is the case with decodable books) • Simple one- and two-syllable words, with high-frequency words and decodable words • Limited text on each page and in the text as a whole	• Refine word-recognition skills and automatic word recognition • Work toward comprehension of longer text	• *Little Bear* by Else Holmelund Minarik • *Frog and Toad* by Arnold Lobel • *Reading A to Z* website (Leveled readers) • *Elephant and Piggie* series by Mo Willems

Predictable readers. Predictable texts are based on repeated phrases and language patterns, such as in *Brown Bear, Brown Bear* by Bill Martin:

> *Brown bear, brown bear, what do you see?*
> *I see a red bird looking at me.*
> *Red bird, red bird, what do you see?*
> *I see a white cat looking at me.*

This repeated pattern helps beginning readers to figure out new words. **Predictable books** support development of print awareness and concept of word and help build fluency through word recognition. In our experience, parents have sometimes expressed concern that children have memorized the predictable text and are not really reading. We commonly remind parents that memory and pattern are intentional devices to provide children with support as they develop a solid concept of word and accrue a sight word vocabulary. Memorizing the text and cueing off the initial consonants allows the student to begin to read by tracking the words and paying attention to the meaning.

Decodable readers. In contrast to predictable texts, decodable texts do not repeat sentences and phrases. Decodable readers are controlled to specifically include a set of spelling patterns so that readers have a limited burden of decoding new words. For example, in the sentence "The fat cat sat on a mat," most of the words require knowledge of the *–at* chunk, but not other phonetic combinations. Decodable readers are uniquely designed to teach phonetic patterns in words and are sometimes called **phonics readers**. They tend to focus on the child's ability to recognize or decode words and less on a meaningful story structure. Each page generally has a single sentence and picture support. Although some decodable text is available for purchase to the general public, they are more commonly purchased by a school system, including readers such as *The Wright Skills Decodable Books*, *Bob Books* by Scholastic, and *Phonics Readers* by Steck-Vaughn, and books available on the *Reading A to Z* website. Decodable texts provide an opportunity to exercise students' phonics knowledge gleaned from word study, but they often fall short in terms of interest and rich vocabulary.

Beginning readers. The third and most common type of text made available to your child is the beginning-leveled reader. These are more challenging than either decodable or predictable texts and they increase in difficulty. **Leveled readers** or books start with short sentences that include both sight words and decodable words along with illustrations or photographs. Characteristics of text at this early stage include a familiar genre (fiction, nonfiction, poetry), familiar content supported by picture information, simple sentences, and vocabulary that is commonly within a child's oral-speaking vocabulary. Words are generally one or two syllables (early in the stage) with easy and phonetically regular letter–sound relationships. Texts have a consistent layout of words and illustrations and are usually short (Fountas & Pinnell, 2010). As texts increase in difficulty, the sentences get longer, more sentences occur on each page, and the illustrations are not as closely tied to the text.

As parents, it is important to understand that all three types of texts provide deliberate support to your child and that your child's school may use a combination of these texts. Most important, you can support your child by reading and rereading these types of familiar texts.

Personal readers. A fourth type of text that is useful for beginning readers is called a **personal reader** (Bear, Caserta-Henry, & Venner, 2004). Rather than published books, personal readers are homemade or school-made collections of familiar short pieces of text, such as songs, rhymes, dictated stories and excerpts from texts, that are stored in folders or binders and available for children to read and reread (Figure 4.24). As children reread these pieces, they develop letter–sound knowledge and build automatic word recognition, fluency, rhyme, and concept of word, as well as general world knowledge.

You can make your own personal reader using simple reading materials. Nursery rhymes like *Humpty Dumpty* or *Little Miss Muffet* and songs like *The Itsy Bitsy Spider* or *Happy Birthday* might already be familiar to your child or easily learned. Many of these can be found at online resources where you can print out illustrated versions. You can also create your own one-page

FIGURE 4.24 Personal Reader with Word Bank

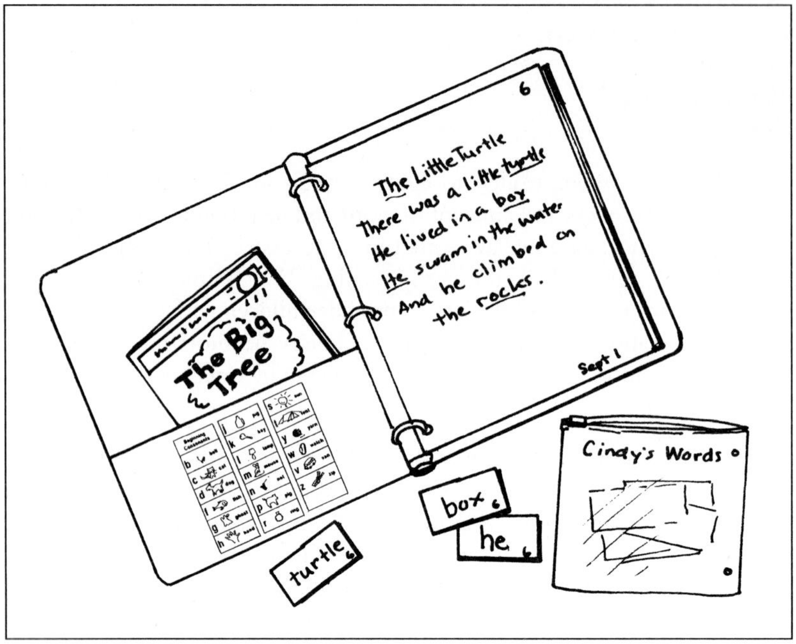

copies using a simple, enlarged font. Sing the song or recite the rhyme until it is familiar to your child, and then point to the words as you slow it down and read it to them. Then ask your child to point to the words as they read it with you and then on their own. These one-page copies can be illustrated, colored, and added to the personal reader.

GUIDING YOUR CHILD'S READING In addition to the deliberate support of predictable, decodable, and beginning leveled readers, parents can provide side-by-side support by learning a several simple strategies described next.

Book introductions Before reading, parents can learn to introduce a book by flipping through the pictures and asking the child to note what is happening on the pages while intentionally noting any unfamiliar words. Parents may introduce the book using the language of the text and anticipate difficult words and concepts (Clay, 1991). For example, if you see a picture of a moose, it may be helpful to say, "Is that a moose? or Look at that moose," knowing that the child will need to read the word moose which is a tricky word.

Choral and echo reading Parents can support beginning readers by sharing the reading. You may encourage your child to read the text with you in unison in a practice known as **choral reading**. Another strategy for beginning readers is to read the text aloud and ask your child to echo or repeat the reading immediately following your reading of each page, known as **echo reading**. It is especially useful when children are developing concept of word, learning letters and sounds, and beginning sight words. At this stage, children need the support of memory to read and track the same text that you have read first. As your child becomes a more capable reader, she or he relies less on predictable text and choral and echo-reading support and relies more on letter–sound knowledge, sight word vocabulary, and decoding skills.

Partner or buddy reading As your child becomes more confident reading, you may encourage your child to read one page and allow you to read the next. Reread text taking turns.

Talking about reading When you and your child have finished reading, talk about the book. Be sure to have a natural and genuine conversation, and avoid asking lots of specific questions; rather, ask your child to retell or summarize what the text was about. Ask open-ended questions, such as "What was your favorite part?" "Did something surprise you?" "What did you think of the characters?"

TABLE 4.7 Prompts to Help Children Figure Out Unknown Words

Prompts	Explanation
Don't say anything!	Give the child time to think and work it out if they are struggling. Don't be too quick to supply the right answer, and avoid interruption when possible.
"Try that again."	If your child makes a mistake, you might point to it and ask him or her to try it again.
"Did that make sense?" or *"Something isn't right. Can you try that again?"*	Parents can use this prompt when children read through a sentence and do not realize that they read the word incorrectly.
"What is the first letter sound(s)?"	Once your child knows beginning sounds, draw attention to the first letter(s).
"Look at the picture. Does the first letter of that word match the picture?"	This prompt might be helpful for beginning readers when reading text with illustrations.
"Sound it out. Look at each of the letters."	This can be a useful prompt, if and only if the word can be sounded out and your child has the necessary knowledge about letters, sounds, and patterns. It is important to recognize that not all words are decodable, and this prompt is commonly overused. For example, it is useful with the word *pig* (p/i/g), but not the word *one*. Explain that some words can be sounded out and others cannot. Use the prompt when appropriate.
"Do you see a part of the word that you know?"	Parents can focus attention on parts of the word that are familiar to children. You can cover beginning blends, endings, or prefixes to show the child the potentially familiar part of the word. For older children, parents can encourage their children to break the word into known parts, or to locate the prefix, the suffix, or the base word to assist with the identification of the word.
"Read the sentence and try that word again" or *"Let's reread the sentence up to here and use the first few letters to start to say the word."*	This prompt encourages the child to get a running start, to consider the complete meaning of the sentence to provide context for the unfamiliar word as well as the beginning sounds of the challenging word.
"Skip the word, read to the end, and then come back and try it. What would make sense?"	This strategy is particularly helpful with older readers.
Give the word. Tell the child.	Sometimes none of the prompts listed above will help and it's best to supply the word to avoid long interruptions and frustration. For example, the last word of the sentence, "*The road was rough*" is both impossible to sound out and not suggested by context. You might say something like, "That is a hard word. It says "rough."

What to say when your child doesn't know a word. Another form of side-by-side support that commonly occurs between parents and children is the support you provide when your child doesn't recognize or mispronounces a word. As you listen to your child read, consider asking your child to identify the unfamiliar word using specific supportive prompts (Johnston, Invernizzi, Juel, & Lewis-Wagner, 2009), as seen in Table 4.7.

Increasing sight vocabulary. One of the primary goals of beginning readers is to develop a body of words they know automatically without hesitation. The irony is that sight words become sight words by virtue of having sounded them out many times before, mapping the spelling to pronunciations and meanings, and seeing them over and over. Sorting known words is one of the best ways to cultivate a sight word vocabulary—a corpus of words that your child can identify "at first sight" without having to decode it again. As children learn to read, this sight vocabulary is especially important so that they can focus their attention on understanding the meaning of the text rather than figuring out every word.

An effective way to manage growing a sight vocabulary is through the use of a **word bank**, a physical collection of words on little cards and stored on a ring, in a box, or in a plastic bag. Known words are collected from your child's reading and printed neatly on the cards. With each new book read, 1–3 words are selected to add to the word bank. The key to successful word banks is to let your child choose words that they can read. When the child sees the word on the card out of context, they might not remember it, but they are able to recall the context of the book to help them remember the word. If your child doesn't remember a word bank word, find it in the book and have your child match it up. That process, along with including word bank words in the word sorts, helps your child remember them. At least some of the words selected for the word bank should be high-frequency words and that help children in reading other text (*can, like, see, the, blue, girl, what, many*). But word bank words should also include words with special meaning or high interest to the child (*dinosaur, princess, sister*, siblings' names) as well as decodable words that match the spelling features you are sorting in word study. Avoid giving your child a stack of commercial flashcards to be learned. Words in a child's word bank are selected from familiar contexts and are then used in word sorts and the other word games described later. Table 4.8 lists some fun ways to practice word bank words. All of these activities focus on repeated practice reading the words automatically in isolation, matching them back in the text, and analyzing their spellings as relate to pronunciations and meaning. If a word continues to be forgotten, just take it out of the word bank.

Children typically use word banks until they have 150 to 200 known words. At this point, they have usually become more fluent readers as a result of their growing word knowledge

TABLE 4.8 Word Bank Games

Knock Knock	Place the entire collection of word bank words face down in a pile or spread out. The child knocks on each card, then flips the card over and says the word in the following pattern: "Knock, knock! Who's there? *Like*!" This game can also be modified to Doorbell – "Ding dong! Who's there? *Like*!" If the word is read correctly the child keeps the card; if not the card is turned upside down for another try.
Pick Up (also known as ***I Spy*** or ***I'm Thinking of …***)	Lay out a collection of 5–10 word cards face-up. Include some words that your child confuses, along with familiar but similar words. Call out words for your child to find. You can call them out by the full word, sound and pattern clues, or meaning clues. For example, "Pick up a word that starts with /s/ and rhymes with *cat*" or "I am thinking of a word that starts like *play*" or "I spy a word from the book *I Like Dogs*."
Memory	This is a variation of the classic game that can be played with the word bank or a word sort. Choose 8–15 words from the word bank and create a second set of cards. Turn all the cards face down and spread out on the floor or a table. Partners take turns flipping over two cards and reading the words. Players take turns looking for matches until all the cards are gone.
Word Hunts	Ask your child to search through the entire word bank for words with a particular feature—for example, words that start with *T*, words that end in *M*, or words that have an *O* in them. You can also focus on concepts—for example, words that name animals, words that name people, color words, or things in a house. Working with a word bank is designed to provide multiple opportunities for the child to read and reread the words accurately and automatically.

(Johnston, Invernizzi, Juel, & Lewis-Wagner, 2009). It can be fun to set a goal of collecting a certain number of words and planning a celebration when reaching the goal. You can use a chart to track the progress on the way to 150 or 200 words.

Writing

As noted in the previous section, reading and writing—and therefore spelling—are reciprocal processes. When we write, we use our knowledge of spelling—sound, pattern, and meaning—to record our thoughts and ideas. In the previous emergent stage of development, writers are often unable to read what they have written because they lack or have limited letter-to-sound correspondences. Students in the letter name–alphabetic stage can usually read what they write depending on how completely they spell, and their writing is generally readable to anyone who understands the logic of their letter–name strategy.

Ellie, a first-grader, shares her thoughts about winter in the example shown in Figure 4.25. Ellie represents most beginning and ending single consonants as in her spelling of *LK* for *like* and *WR* for *wear*, but the blend in *snow*, spelled *SO*, is incomplete. Many vowels are missing, although she does included some that "say their name" as in *MAK* for *make* and *SO* for *snow*. She substitutes *a* for short *i* in *mittens* and *i* for short *o* in *hot*. Notice how she used the letter *h* to represent the *ch* digraph in *chocolate* (spelled *HIKLT*) because the name of the letter ("aitch") has the sound she is trying to represent. Correctly spelled words like *Mom* and *the* are probably familiar sight words.

FIGURE 4.25 Ellie Writes about Winter

I like winter. I make a snowman in the snow. I wear mittens. Mom makes me hot chocolate.

Children's invented spellings should be valued at this stage so that they can write about the topics that are important to them. At the same time, parents can begin to remind their children what they have learned in word study by gently urging them to listen for additional sounds in words. Although students cannot be expected to edit for the correct spellings of all the words they use in their writing, they should be prompted to use what they have learned in word study when they write. The rule of thumb is this: Hold them accountable for spelling features that have been taught, but don't penalize them for inventing spellings that they haven't studied yet.

SOUND BOARDS Sound boards (Figure 4.26) are references for letter name–alphabetic spellers that can be used in writing. These charts display a key word and picture for each letter–sound match, helping children internalize the associations. Sound boards help your child find the letters that stand for the sounds needed in their writing. When your child is writing a letter, story, list, or joke and wants to know how to spell a word, encourage him or her to stretch out the sounds and identify the letters that represent those sounds. Use the sound board to find the appropriate letter sound(s). Remember that at this stage, it's best to allow your child to do the heavy lifting of sounding a word out and finding the appropriate letter or letters to match. The goal is for your child to make use of the knowledge gained through word sorting in writing.

FIGURE 4.26 Sound Boards

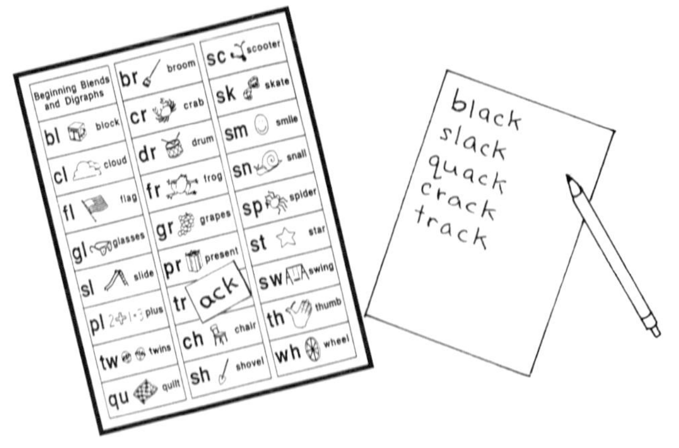

DICTATIONS OR SILLY SENTENCES Dictations are sentences or a few sentences that are called out by one person and written by another. In word study, a teacher, tutor, parent, or partner creates a short sentence that includes at least one word from the word study sort, while the other person records the sentence. Dictations allow a child to concentrate on applying what he or she knows about spelling in a fun and quick way. Silly sentences can be created with several words from the weekly word sort. For example, following the *-an* and *-at* rhyming word family sort, letter name-alphabetic spellers might be asked to write, "The fat cat sat in the tan van" (Johnston, Invernizzi, Juel, & Lewis-Wagner, 2009). Dictations can also be used to practice reading.

PRACTICAL WRITING Children benefit from a wide variety of writing experiences that allow them to express their ideas for purposeful reasons. Encourage your child to write for a variety of reasons. Write letters, jokes, reports, stories, comics, and top-10 fact lists about areas that interest your child. Ask your child to review writing assignments from school. Write about the books you read together at home. Consider keeping a journal, either individually or as a family. Encourage your child to share his or her writing with friends and family. Guide your child to email, text, blog, or tweet friends and family members with you. As with reading, the more your child writes, the better his writing will become.

A BRIEF SUMMARY

In this chapter, we described characteristics typical of beginning readers in the letter name–alphabetic stage of development; provided guidance on understanding picture and word sorts, described a wide variety of games and activities for word study at home, and discussed ways to connect reading, writing, and spelling with your child. In Chapter 5, we focus on children described as transitional readers and writers in the within word pattern stage of spelling development.

REFERENCES

Brown, K. J. (2000). What kind of text—For whom and when? Textual scaffolding for beginning readers. *Reading Teacher*, *53*(4): 292–307.

Bear, D. R., Caserta-Herny, C., & Venner, D. (2004). *Personal readers and literacy instruction with emergent and beginning readers*. Berkeley, CA: Teaching Resource Center.

Clay, M, M. (1991). Introducing a new storybook to young readers. *The Reading Teacher*, *45*, 264–273.

Dahl, K. L., Barto, A., Bonfils, A., Carasello, M., Christopher, J., Davis, R., Erkkila, N., Glander, S., Jacobs, B., Kendra, V., Koski, L., Majeski, D., McConnell, E., Petrie, P., Siegel, D., Slaby, B., Waldbauer, J., & Williams, J. (2003). Connecting developmental word study with classroom writing: Children's descriptions of spelling strategies. *Reading Teacher*, *57* (4): 310–319.

Ehri, L. C. (1997). Learning to read and learning to spell are one and the same, almost. In C. A. Perfetti, L. Rieben, & M. Fayol (Eds.), *Learning to spell: Research, theory, and practice across languages* (pp. 237–269). Mahwah, NJ: Lawrence Erlbaum.

Fountas, I. C., & Pinnell, G. S. (2010). *The continuum of literacy learning* (Grades PreK to 8): *A guide to teaching*, 2nd ed. Portsmouth, NH: Heinemann.

Johnston, F. R., Invernizzi, M., Juel, C., & Lewis-Wagner, D. (2009). *Book Buddies: A tutoring framework for struggling readers*. New York, NY: The Guilford Press.

Johnston, F. R., Invernizzi, M., Bear, D. R., & Templeton, S. (2014). *Words their way: Word sorts for letter name-alphabetic spellers*. New York: Pearson Publishing.

National Reading Panel (US), National Institute of Child Health, & Human Development (US). (2000). *Report of the national reading panel: Teaching children to read: An evidence-based assessment of the scientific research literature on reading and its implications for reading instruction: Reports of the subgroups*. National Institute of Child Health and Human Development, National Institutes of Health.

Williams, C., & Lundstrom, R. P. (2007). Strategy instruction during word study and interactive writing activities. *Reading Teacher*, *61*(3): 204–212.

CHILDREN'S LITERATURE REFERENCES

Ahlberg, A., & Ahlberg, J. (1986). *Each peach pear plum*. Puffin.
Brown, M.W. (1947). *Goodnight moon*. Harper Brothers.
Bruel, N. (2005). *Bad kitty*. Roaring Book Press.
Donaldson, J. (2003). *Room on the broom*. Puffin.
Guarina, D. (1989). *Is your mama a llama?* Illustrated by Steven Kellogg. Scholastic.
Greenfield. E. (1986). *Honey, I love*. HarperCollins.
Henkes, K. (2008). *Crysanthemum*. Mulberry Books.
Hughes, L., & Pinkney, B. (2007). *The dream keeper and other poems*. Knopf Books for Young Readers.
Kirk, D. (2007). *Miss Spider's tea party*. Scholastic.
Kontis, A. (2012) *AlphaOops! The day Z went first*. Candlewick.
Lionni, L. (1990). *The alphabet*. Dragonfly Books.
Lobel, A. (2003). *Frog and Toad are friends*. HarperCollins.
Martin, B. (1967). *Brown Bear, Brown Bear, what do you see?* Henry Holt & Co.
Martin, B., & Archambault, J. (1989). *Chicka chicka boom boom*. Simon and Schuster.
Maslen, B. L., & Maslen, J. R. (2006). *Bob books*, Set 1: Beginning Readers. Scholastic.
McMullen, J., & McMullen, K. (2006). *I stink!* Harper Collins.
Minarik, E. H., & Sendak, M. (1978). *Little Bear* (An *I Can Read* Book). Harper Trophy.
Montgomery, S., & Bishop, N. (2013). *The tapir scientist: Saving South America's largest animal*. Houghton Mifflin Harcourt Publishing.
Montgomery, S., & Bishop, N. (2007). *The tarantula scientist*. Houghton Mifflin Harcourt Publishing.
Montgomery, S., & Bishop, N. (2013). *The snake scientist*. Houghton Mifflin Harcourt Publishing.
Pearson, D. (2003). *Alphabeep: A zipping, zooming ABC*. Holiday House.
Peek, M., & Giblin, C. J. (1998). *Katy wore her red dress and Henry wore his green sneakers*. Houghton Mifflin Co.
Peet, B. (1982). *Cyrus the unsinkable sea serpent*. Houghton Mifflin Co.
Peet, B. (1980). *The caboose who got loose*. Houghton Mifflin Co.
Prelutsky, J. (2008). *Be glad your nose is on your face and other poems: Some of the best of Jack Prelutsky*. Greenwillow Books.
Seuss, Dr. (1963). *Dr. Seuss's ABC*. Random House.
Silverstein, S. (1974). *Where the sidewalk ends*. HarperCollins.
Silverstein, S. (1987). *Falling up*. HarperCollins.
Thayer, E. L., & Polacco, P. (1997). *Casey at the bat*. Puffin.
Simon, S. (2013). *Global warming*. Harper Collins Publishers.
Simon, S. (2007). *Hurricanes*. Harper Collins Publishers.
Simon, S. (2006). *Volcanoes*. Harper Collins Publishers.
Simon, S. (2006). *Earthquakes*. Harper Collins Publishers.
Weston, M. (2002). *Jack and Jill and Big Dog Bill: A phonics reader (Step into Reading)*. Random House Books for Young Readers.
Willems, M. (2014). *An Elephant and Piggie book: Waiting is not easy*! Disney-Hyperion.
Williams, S., & Vivas, J. (1990). *I went walking*. HMH Books for Young Readers.
Wilson, K. (2002). *Bear snores on*. Margaret K. McElderry Books.
Wood, A., & Wood, B. (2003). *Alphabet mystery*. Blue Sky Press.
Yolen, J. (2000). *How do dinosaurs say goodnight?* Blue Sky Press.

chapter 5

Transitional Readers in the Within Word Pattern Stage of Spelling

Source: Amble Design/Shutterstock

Source: Anna Baynum

In the second grade, 8-year-old Caleb came home and told his mother that he was "not a smart boy." He had received an *N* for "Needs improvement" on his report card. He sobbed and explained that in kindergarten and first grade he used to be "good at it," meaning spelling and reading. In Caleb's class, all students were given the school-wide second-grade spelling list that began with basic long vowel words with a silent *e* (*gate*, *home*). Caleb had learned the rule that "a silent *e* makes the vowel say its name" and could easily remember the rule, but not when to use it. The weekly second-grade spelling lists quickly began to include words with long vowels with varying patterns (*same*, *wait*, *stay*, *weigh*). Caleb began to really struggle.

As a hard-working student, Caleb completed all of the assigned exercises, such as writing the words three times and fill-in-the-blank sentences, and he tried his best to memorize all of the words. On the weekly quiz, however, Caleb rarely met with success as the preset spelling lists became increasingly difficult. Although his parents reassured him that he was still a "smart boy" and encouraged him to bring home his spelling work to practice, Caleb shared that reading was also becoming more difficult. In the past, he had loved reading and felt confident and secure reading aloud; now, he felt it was a chore.

At this point, his parents spoke with the teacher to express concern. They worked together to create a plan and agreed that Caleb would join a small group of students working on phonics through word study with the school reading specialist. Caleb still needed practice learning the difference between short and long vowel sounds and understanding when to apply the silent *e* correctly.

The reading specialist focused exclusively on word study and explicitly demonstrated through categorization or sorting activities how vowels sounds are spelled. After six weeks, the classroom teacher and reading specialist began to see improvement in Caleb's reading, writing and spelling. Just as builders secure a solid foundation before building a house, students must master early spelling features related to sound before examining more complicated long vowel patterns that include additional silent letters.

This chapter is all about transitional readers like Caleb in the within word pattern stage of spelling, most typically found in first through mid fourth grade. Caleb initially struggled in second grade because he had not mastered the early features of the within word pattern stage needed to be successful in his school's curriculum. With the help of the school reading specialist using developmental word study instruction, Caleb did master these skills and was able to rediscover success and confidence in reading and writing.

In this chapter, we discuss the common characteristics of students in reading, writing, and spelling at this stage (Table 5.1), examine common spelling features and how to talk about them with your child, learn a series of games and activities to support word study at home, and understand how to make connections across spelling, reading, and writing.

Stage Overview: Transitional Readers and Writers in the Within Word Pattern Stage of Spelling

Reading

Teachers and parents may find transitional readers and writers in the middle-to-late part of first grade, but they are found mostly in first through early fourth grade classrooms. Many struggling readers in this stage are also found in the middle- and high-school settings (Flanigan, Hayes, Templeton, Bear, Invernizzi, & Johnston, 2011). Transitional readers are able to recognize many words automatically, and can begin using strategies to read (decode)

TABLE 5.1 Characteristics of Transitional Readers and Writers

Transitional Readers and Writers in the Within Word Pattern Stage of Spelling	
Reading Characteristics	• Typically first- to mid fourth grade students • Read short chapter books • Gradually shift to silent reading over the course of the stage • Read with increased fluency and expression • Read books with more text and fewer pictures • Recognize most single-syllable words easily
Writing Characteristics	• Spell most high-frequency words correctly • Write multiple paragraphs and pages • Spell short vowel words correctly • Write with increasing fluency, voice, expression, and organization • Elaborate their ideas by adding information
Spelling Characteristics	• Spell most single-syllable short vowel words correctly • Spell most beginning consonant digraphs (*th, sh, ch, wh*) and two-letter consonant blends (*pr, bl, st*) correctly • Attempt to use silent long vowel markers (*NALE* for *nail*) • Spell many high-frequency words correctly and automatically (*the, they, and, I, like, from*)
Common Spelling Errors	• *SNAIK* for *snake* • *FELE* for *feel* • *FLOTE* for *float* • *BRIET* for *bright* • *SPOLE* for *spoil* • *CHUED* for *chewed* • *SEET* or *SETE* for *seat* • *NALE* for *nail* • *CRALL* or *CRAUL* for *crawl* • *TROPE* for *troop*
Instructional Focus	• Single-syllable words • Common and less-common long vowel patterns (*rain, right*) • *R*-influenced vowels (*car, fur, corn*) • Ambiguous vowels that are neither long nor short (*boil, shout, caught*) • Complex consonant clusters (*dge* vs. *ge*, *tch* vs. *ch*) • Homophones

or identify unfamiliar words. Readers at this stage depend less on illustrations and are more focused on the individual words. They begin to read silently, a milestone for readers, and can read faster silently than when they read out loud. Not all students at this stage, however, are exactly alike. There is a continuum of skills demonstrated in reading, writing, and spelling as they move through this transitional period of literacy development.

Early in the stage, students are able to read easy short chapter books and progress to series books with more text. These simple series books, such as *Frog and Toad* (Lobel, 1970–1979) and *Henry and Mudge* (Rylant, 1987–2006), build fluency and confidence in our readers. Transitional readers then progress to even more text in series such as *Franny K. Stein: Mad Scientist* by Jim Benton, *The Magic Tree House* (Pope-Osborne, 2000–2015), *Stories Julian Tells* and *Stories Hughey Tells* (Cameron, 1981–2013), and *Time Warp Trio* series by Jon Scieszka (1991–2015).

Short chapter books move from pictures on each page, large amounts of white space, large print, and a limited number of sentences to fewer illustrations, greater quantities of text, and smaller font (Table 5.2). It is common for students reading at the transitional level

TABLE 5.2 Characteristics of Books for Transitional Readers

Type of Text	Characteristics	Examples
Early Transitional Books	• Illustrations on each page • Large amounts of white space on a page • Limited number of sentences in a large font • Sentences begin and finish on the same page • Repetition of characters' names • Repetition of high-frequency words (*look, mom, next, then, said*) • Use of single-syllable *decodable words* (words that are phonetic or can be sounded out) • Up to three to five chapters	*Henry and Mudge* series (Cynthia Rylant) *Fox All Week* series (James Marshall) *Frog and Toad* (Arnold Lobel) *Amanda Pig* series (Jean van Leeuwen) *Ling and Ting* (Grace Lin)
Late Transitional Books	• Illustrations interspersed throughout the text instead of every page • Some white space on every page • Smaller typeface • Sentences no longer begin and end on the same page • Longer amounts of text; includes five or more chapters • Plot and character development continues throughout book	*Junie B. Jones* series (Barbara Park) *The Magic Tree House* series (Mary Pope Osborne) *Stories Julian Tells* (Ann Cameron, 1981–2013) *Stories Hughey Tells* (Ann Cameron, 1981–2013) *Time Warp Trio* series (John Sciezka) *Franny K. Stein: Mad Scientist* series (Jim Benton) *Ruby and the Booker Boys* series (Derrick Barnes) *Keena Ford* series (Melissa Thompson) *Get Ready Gabi* series (Marisa Montes and Joe Cepeda) *Carver Chronicles* (Karen English and Laura Freeman)
Graphic Novels	• Detailed illustrations with dialogue and speech captions • Comic book style • Story is highly dependent on illustrations	*Bone* by Jeff Smith *Amulet* series (Kazu Kibuishi) *Captain Underpants, Super Diaper Baby,* and *The Adventures of Ook and Gluk* series (Dav Pilkey) *Binky the Space Cat* series by Ashley Spires *Dragonbreath* series by Ursula Vernon *Frankie Pickle* series by Eric Wight *Lunch Lady* series by Jarrett J. Krosoczka *Babymouse* series by Jennifer Holm and Matthew Holm *Balloon Toons* series by various authors

to check out stacks of books from the same series because they are easy to read, and they take pride in the volume of books that they can read. Reading *every* book in a series becomes a motivating goal. Series books provide consistent characters and familiar story lines. The deliberate design of these books provides a high level of support for the transitional reader. Finishing each chapter allows students to feel a sense of accomplishment, reaching mini-milestones before finishing the entire book.

Graphic novels, another type of series written in the style of comic books, have become hugely popular in recent years, and are particularly appealing to transitional readers because the amount of text is limited and pages are primarily detailed illustrations. Stories are generally fast-paced and visually interesting. The *Bone* series by Jeff Carpenter, *Amulet* series by Kazu Kibuishi, and the widely known *Captain Underpants*, *Super Diaper Baby*, and *The Adventures of Ook and Gluk* series by Dav Pilkey are all examples of graphic novels for transitional readers. They are high interest, are funny, and contain familiar characters and story lines that keep readers reading.

Writing

Just like reading, writing also becomes more fluent during this period of development because students can accurately and automatically spell many words, including high-frequency words (*was, what, because, there, know*). The physical act of writing is performed with greater speed and less conscious attention (Nagy, Berninger, Abbott, Vaughan, & Vermeulen, 2003). Increased fluency gives transitional writers more time to concentrate on ideas and vocabulary, which may account for the greater sophistication in the way writers express their ideas at this stage. Students begin to write for a variety of purposes, including letters, emails, blogs, or journals at home, and nonfiction reports, journal entries, essays, and poems at school. Narrative stories at this stage tend to go on and on and on (*and then . . ., and then . . .*) as students include everything that might be important. Finally, children begin to use punctuation and other aspects of grammar, usage, and mechanics correctly. They begin to plan and organize their writing, and revise and edit with guidance from teachers and parents.

FIGURE 5.1 Writing Sample: James

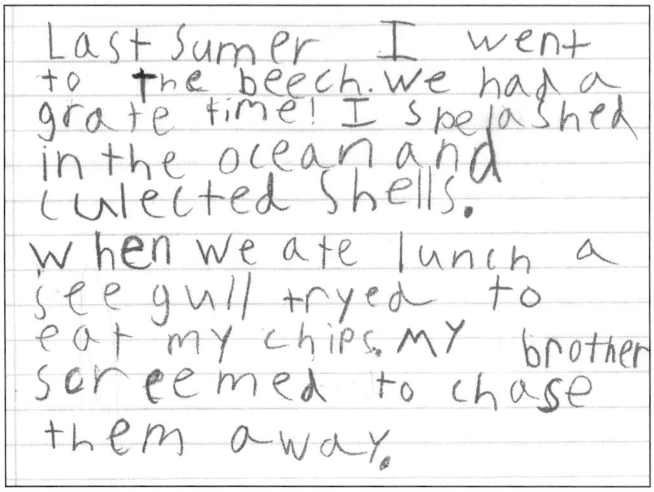
Last Sumer I went to the beech. we had a grate time! I spelashed in the ocean and culected shells.
when we ate lunch a see gull tryed to eat my chips. MY brother screemed to chase them away.

Source: Michelle Picard

In Figure 5.1, James, a third-grade student, writes about a day at the beach. He spells single-syllable short vowel words such as *last*, *chips*, *shells*, and *lunch* correctly. He also spells high-frequency words such as *I*, *the*, *when*, *went*, *and*, and *them* correctly. His misspellings focus on the long vowels. He spells *BEECH* for *beach*, *GRATE* for *great*, and *SCREEMED* for *screamed*. James understands that long vowels are often spelled with more than one vowel; however, he is using but confusing the long vowel patterns. James spells *chase* and *away* correctly; both represent common long vowel patterns for the letter *a* (*a*-consonant-*e* for *chase* and *ay* in *away*).

Vocabulary

Estimates vary, but students in the early grades can, on average, add 10 to 15 new words a week to their oral language vocabularies (Biemiller, 2005). The influence of listening to books read aloud—which introduces concepts, ideas, and vocabulary—makes a powerful difference in the amount of vocabulary children acquire. Reading and vocabulary are highly correlated, and we see that that one influences the other. Parents can support vocabulary growth through conversations, explanations, and reading with their children. At this stage, children experience great gains in both written and spoken vocabulary.

TABLE 5.3 Characteristics of Within Word Pattern Spelling

Common Spelling Errors	*What Students Do Correctly*	*What Students Use But Confuse*	*What Is Absent*
SNAIK for *snake* *FELE* for *feel* *FLOTE* for *float* *BRIET* for *bright* *SPOLE* for *spoil* *CHUED* for *chewed* *SEET* or *SETE* for *seat* *NALE* for *nail* *CRALL* or *CRAUL* for *crawl* *TROPE* for *troop*	• Consonants, blends, digraphs • Short vowels in CVC words (*sat, stop, leg, trick*) • *R*-influenced CVC words (*car, for, her* • Spell known sight words (*the, at, I , like*)	• Silent letters in long vowel patterns (CVCe such as *cake, like, spoke*) • Common long vowels CVVC (*boat, street, rain*) • Less common long vowel patterns (*veil, gauge, table*) • *R*-controlled vowels (*fear, steer, pier, fare*) • Ambiguous vowels (*boy/boil, crawl, caught*) • Complex consonant clusters (*fudge/cage, match/church*)	• Inflected endings (*-ing, -ed, -es, -s*) • Consonant doubling (*shopping, mopping, hopping*) • Complex consonant units (*switch, smudge)* • Open and closed syllables (*human, butter*) • Accented syllables (*mistake, repeat*) • Unaccented syllables (*competition*) • Prefixes and suffixes (*pre-, mis-, -dis, -un, -ly, -ed, -ing*)

Spelling

Spelling and reading (decoding/word recognition) become much more automatic at this stage. Transitional writers know the alphabet, are able to form letters automatically, use a large number of high-frequency words, can spell single-syllable short vowel words correctly, and are willing to spell longer words to the best of their abilities. When in doubt, they use invented spelling or their best guess—not unlike adults before they use spell check.

The spelling development of children across the within word pattern stage is summarized in Table 5.3. Children in this stage explore the **pattern layer** of English spelling. This requires a higher degree of abstract thinking because they face two tasks at once. They must not only identify the sounds in the word, but must also choose from a variety of patterns that represent the sound, which usually involves silent letters as part of the vowel spelling (*cute*, ***through***, *suit*) or special consonant patterns (*lodge*, ***itch***).

WHAT DO STUDENTS SPELL CORRECTLY? At this stage, children's phonemic awareness (or ability to isolate and identify sounds) is well developed. They spell consonants, blends (*bl*, *pr*, *st*), and digraphs (*sh*, *th*, *ch*) correctly. Within word pattern spellers have also mastered the use of single-syllable short vowel words (CVC) including those influenced by the letter *r*, such as *car*, *star*, *her*, and *for*. Children can isolate the vowel sounds in the middle of words, but learning the variety of ways those vowel sounds in the word can be spelled is challenging.

WHAT DO STUDENTS "USE BUT CONFUSE"? Within word pattern spellers understand that one letter is no longer sufficient to spell long vowel sounds. Early in this stage, children learn the difference between the sounds of short and long vowels, and then the basic long vowel pattern of adding a silent *e* to the end of words. They begin to recognize that, in order to have a long vowel, there is a need for another silent letter or *marker* that may not have a sound of its own. Later, children learn the many different variations for spelling vowel sounds.

Consider the word *made*, as in "I *made* cake for dessert." A student in the letter name–alphabetic stage might write *MAD* and believe that the letter *A* makes the long vowel sound because the letter name *A* says its name. The within word pattern speller recognizes a need for another letter to "mark" the *A* as long, and may spell *made* by inserting an extra vowel within the word such as *MAID*, *MAED*, or *MAYD*. This "extra letter" is referred to as a **long vowel marker**. With many long vowel patterns to choose from, spellers at this stage must focus on common and uncommon long vowel patterns and under which conditions they should be used.

Within word pattern spellers are focused on long vowel patterns. For example, there are several ways to spell the long *a* sound, including *a* as in *table*, *a*-consonant-*e* (CVCe) as in *make*, *ai* as in *rain*, *ay* as in *play*, *ei* as in *veil*, *eigh* as in *eight*, *ea* as in *steak*, and *au* as in *gauge*. Children learn which patterns are common and which are uncommon. They also learn that some vowel patterns are usually at the end of a word, such as *ay* in *play*, whereas others are in the middle. As children acquire greater understanding of long vowels, they use but confuse and then explore silent consonants (***k**now*, ***w**rong*, ***g**nat*), complex consonant clusters (*ma**tch***, *do**dge***, ***scr**ap*), *r*-controlled vowels (*glare*, *four*, *pure*, *board*), and ambiguous vowels, vowels that are neither long nor short (*boy*, *boil*, *pause*, *paws*).

WHAT IS ABSENT? Within word pattern spellers are not yet able to manage many spelling patterns in multisyllabic words. They are not yet aware that it is sometimes necessary to add or delete letters when adding endings (*swimming*, *daring*) or to double the consonant in the middle of words to maintain the short vowel sound (*bubble*, *winner*). These syllable patterns are studied in the next stage of spelling development. The within word pattern stage focuses primarily on single-syllable words. It is a fairly lengthy stage for most students that requires carefully sequenced instruction.

Understanding Picture and Word Sorts

Regardless of what kind of phonics or spelling instruction your child receives at school, you can provide support by establishing a fun word study routine at home. Your child may bring home sorts from school, or you may want to supplement classroom instruction with word sorts and activities. Ready to print sorts and directions for how to use them can be found in the book *Word Sorts for Within Word Pattern Spellers* (Invernizzi, Johnston, Bear, & Templeton, 2016). The examples of sorts described in this chapter come from this book.

In the *Let's Talk About It* section, we use one sort example to describe how to pose questions and guide purposeful conversations as you talk about the sounds, patterns, and meaning in words with your child. In the *Sort Support* section we explain what you and your children need to know about specific spelling features at the within word pattern stage. This provides the tools to help your child understand the way words work in spelling and reading at this stage.

Let's Talk About It!

A word study approach to spelling encourages students to categorize words by contrasting sounds, spelling patterns, and word meanings in order to make generalizations about words. Encourage your child to share their ideas, notice sounds and spelling patterns associated with each group, and explain their own thinking and observations. Purposeful questioning and guided discussion is needed to recognize and learn the underlying principles of the English spelling system. To support your conversation, Figure 5.2 lists a few fundamental questions.

In an ongoing study of long vowels, children study all of the different ways to spell each long vowel sound, including patterns that are common and those that are less frequent. Typically, children at this stage begin by comparing words with short and long vowels. For example, in the study of short and long *e*, there are several ways to spell long *e* (*ee* as in *heel*, *ea* as in *steam*, *ie* as in *thief*, *e*-consonant-*e* as in *scene*, and *e* as in *me*). Initially, children compare

FIGURE 5.2 Let's Talk About It! Guiding Questions

Let's Talk About It!

1. How are the pictures or words alike in each category? How are they different?
2. Are there any pictures or words that do not fit? Why?
3. What do you learn from this sort? What are the big ideas or underlying generalizations you can learn from this sort?

Additional Questions for Consideration

4. Which spelling patterns are more frequent? Less frequent?
5. Is each spelling pattern more commonly found at the beginning, middle, or end of the word?
6. Does meaning influence the spelling of these words?

short *e* to the most common long *e* patterns, which are *ee* as in *street* and *ea* as in *meat*. Let's sort and talk about it using the following words:

> *been, clean, dress, feet, heat, jeep, keep, leaf, less, mean, next, sleep, sweep, team, teeth, vest, web, weak, week, west, wheat, when*

We begin with a sound sort by sorting the words into two groups by the vowel sound—in this case short *e* ("eh") and *long e* ("eeeee"), as seen in Figure 5.3. Students in the within word pattern stage of spelling recognize that sound is no longer enough to determine the spelling of a word. As you review the sort, you and your child are likely to notice that there is one word, *been*, that doesn't seem to fit in either category (depending on pronunciation). This is addressed later as an oddball.

Once your child has sorted words into categories by vowel sound, you should ask if your child notices that there are different patterns in the long vowel category. If not, you can point out that some words have the long vowel pattern *ee* as *sweep*, and others have *ea* as in *clean*. Sort the long vowel words into pattern categories together, as seen in Figure 5.4. Once you have completed the sort, guide the conversation with Questions 1–3 in Figure 5.2.

FIGURE 5.3 Within Word Pattern Sound Sort: Long and Short *e*

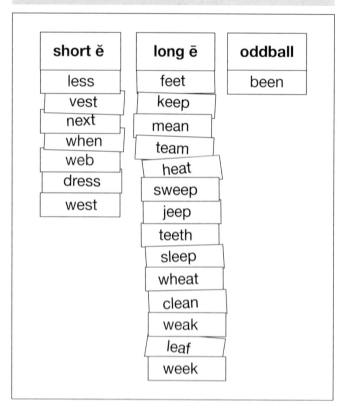

short ĕ	long ē	oddball
less	feet	been
vest	keep	
next	mean	
when	team	
web	heat	
dress	sweep	
west	jeep	
	teeth	
	sleep	
	wheat	
	clean	
	weak	
	leaf	
	week	

HOW ARE THE PICTURES OR WORDS ALIKE IN EACH CATEGORY? HOW ARE THEY DIFFERENT? Ask how the words are alike in each column. For example, in the first column, all the words have a short *e* sound and the pattern of only one vowel. The vowel is surrounded by at least two consonants (CVC). The column labeled "*ee*" has words with the same long vowel sound and the same pattern. This is also true for the column headed "*ea*." It is important to note that at the within word pattern stage, there are often two reasons for each of these categories—sound and pattern. All of the long vowel words in this sort include either short *e* or a long *e* sound, but are represented with different spelling patterns, specifically *ee* as in *feet* and *ea* as in *meal*.

ARE THERE ANY PICTURES OR WORDS THAT DO NOT FIT? WHY? While sorting, you and your child may also notice words that don't quite seem to fit. In word study, these are known as **oddballs**.

FIGURE 5.4 Within Word Pattern Sort: Long *e* Spelling Patterns

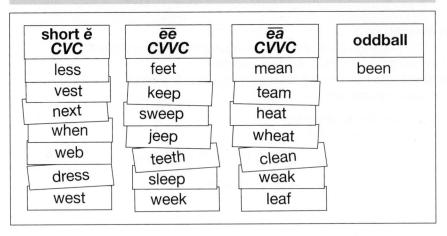

short ĕ CVC	ēē CVVC	ēā CVVC	oddball
less	feet	mean	been
vest	keep	team	
next	sweep	heat	
when	jeep	wheat	
web	teeth	clean	
dress	sleep	weak	
west	week	leaf	

This sort includes the oddball *been*. Discuss with your child why the word *been* does not fit the categories. The word *been* has the long pattern *ee* as in *street*, but it does not have the same sound. Some people pronounce the word *been* as *bin*, which is also another word meaning a container or receptacle. In this case, *been* and *bin* could be homophones, just as the words *week* and *weak* are homophones in this sort.

WHICH SPELLING PATTERNS ARE MORE FREQUENT? LESS FREQUENT? This discussion is not based directly on the sort, but rather on the study of the spelling patterns across the week. Although recognizing the different spelling patterns for long vowels is important, it is equally important for children to understand the conditions and frequency in which each spelling pattern works. You can support your child by asking which spelling patterns are more frequent. To answer the question, gather or consult a list of words with each of the patterns. For example, if you collect words from your child's reading or consult a phonics list, such as those found in the appendix of *Words Their Way: Word Study for Phonics, Spelling and Vocabulary*, you will find that the *ee* (*street*) and *ea* (*meal*) patterns for long *e* are both quite common, whereas other patterns are less common, such as *ie* as in *thief*.

Alternatively, you can check the sort support section in this text and take our word for it! To underscore the point, Table 5.4 showcases the results of a review of spelling patterns analyzed in more than 17,000 words (Fry, 2004) showing that the spelling features *ee* and *ea* are more common than the *ie*. This information is helpful when attempting to spell an unfamiliar word. Your child can narrow his or her choices to the more-common vowel patterns. For example, if your child is unsure of how to spell the word *fleet* (as in a *fleet* of ships), an educated guess based on frequency suggests that the pattern will be either *ee* or *ea*, but not the less-frequent patterns of *ie* as in *thief*, *y* as in *happy*, or *e*-consonant-*e* as in *these*.

TABLE 5.4 Frequency of Long e Patterns

Number of Words with Various Long *e* Patterns in the Most Common 17,000 Words (Fry, 2004)	
Long *e* (*ea*)	249
Long *e* (*ee*)	245
ie as in *field*	62

IS EACH SPELLING PATTERN MORE COMMONLY FOUND AT THE BEGINNING, MIDDLE, OR END OF THE WORD? When you draw attention to where each pattern is found in a word, your child will soon notice that both long *e* patterns are found in the middle of the words. As you and your child examine words with the long *e* sound and hunt through text to find more examples, however, you may also discover four additional patterns: *e*-consonant-*e* as in *scene*, two-syllable words ending in *y* as in *happy*, *ie* as in *thief*, and *e* as in *me*. Ask your child where these spelling patterns can be found. You may notice that *y* (*silly*, *pretty*) and single final letter *e* (*he*, *she*, *me*) words consistently occur at the end of a word, whereas the *e*-consonant-*e* pattern in *scene* represents a middle sound. Noticing the position of spelling patterns helps your child generalize spelling patterns to unfamiliar words.

DOES MEANING INFLUENCE THE SPELLING OF THESE WORDS? As discussed earlier, you and your child will discover that a word's meaning provides information as to which vowel pattern to use. **Homophones**, words that sound the same but have different spellings and different meanings, such as *peek* and *peak*, are impossible to spell without learning the meaning of each one. The sound of the words does not provide a clue, nor does the pattern. In this sort, you may notice the words *week* and *weak*. They both sound the same, yet have different meanings. Only the meaning of the word and memory provide the information to the correct spelling. Reflecting on and discussing these meanings and the spelling patterns assigned to each one underscores the principle that we cannot depend exclusively on sound or pattern to learn to spell; rather, we must attend to sound, pattern, and meaning.

WHAT DO YOU LEARN FROM THIS SORT? WHAT ARE THE BIG IDEAS OR THE UNDERLYING GENERALIZATIONS OF THIS SORT? This is perhaps the most important question to be discussed. The long *e* word study lesson highlighted in Figure 5.4 has a several big ideas, summarized as follows:

- The letter *e* can represent both long and short vowel sounds.
- Short *e* is generally represented in a consonant-vowel-consonant (CVC) pattern such as *bed* and *shed*. *CVC* refers to the fact that the consonants surround the vowel.
- Long vowel sounds can be represented with more than one pattern.
- Long *e* can be represented by spelling patterns such as *ee* as in *sheet*, or *ea* as in *stream*.
- The spelling patterns *ee* as in *sweep* and *ea* as in *meal* are common, whereas others are less frequent.
- Meaning is also an indication of which spelling pattern to use, as in the example of the homophones *week* and *weak*.

In summary, learning to spell words occurs by examining spelling patterns and reflecting on their relationships to sound and meaning. *Let's Talk About It* emphasizes the role of conversation and reflection based on sorting. Encourage your child to notice sounds and patterns and then explain similarities and differences across groups to help them understand and apply the big ideas to less familiar words. All learners, both young and old, must examine words critically to discover how spelling features work. Your role is to provide the developmentally appropriate support in the form of sorting and discussing five key ideas at this stage: sound, pattern, meaning, position, and frequency.

Sort Support: What You and Your Child Need to Know at the Within Word Pattern Stage

At each stage of spelling, it is helpful to understand which spelling features are *known*, which are commonly *used but confused*, and which are *absent*, as discussed earlier in the chapter. In this section, *Sort Support* provides insight into the general and specific concepts that spellers learn at the within word pattern stage, whether your child is engaged in a word study or a traditional spelling or decoding program.

Children in the within word pattern stage use but confuse vowel patterns (Invernizzi, Abouzeid, & Gill, 1994). They no longer spell *boat* sound by sound to produce *BOT*, but instead use a variety of spelling combinations such as *BOTE*, *BOWT*, *BOOT*, or even *BOAT* as they experiment with the possible patterns for the long *o* sound. When children begin to use more than one letter to represent a vowel pattern, they are ready for instruction with long vowels. The discussion and examples in this section are provided to help you feel confident talking about how words and spelling features work with your child. We explore the following:

- Common long vowel patterns
- Less-common long vowel patterns

FIGURE 5.5 Sample Sort: CVCe Common Long Vowels

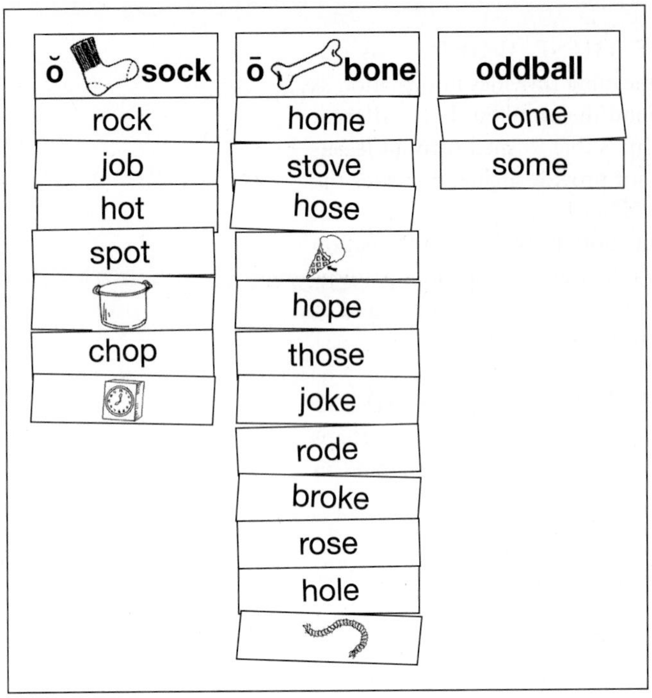

- *R*-influenced vowel patterns
- Diphthongs and other ambiguous vowel sounds
- Complex consonants
- Homophones

COMMON AND LESS COMMON LONG VOWEL PATTERNS Every vowel (*a, e, i, o, u*) has two sounds, commonly referred to as **long** and **short**. Most students early in the stage easily notice that adding a silent *e* to the end of a short vowel word makes the vowel say its name. They see that the addition of the silent *e* changes the short vowel sound into a long vowel sound: *tap* becomes *tape*, *hop* becomes *hope*, and *cub* becomes *cube*. The silent *e* pattern, also known as the CVCe pattern (consonant-vowel-consonant-silent *e*), is the most common long vowel spelling for *a, i, o,* and *u*. An example sort can be seen in Figure 5.5. Another very common long vowel pattern is the consonant-vowel-vowel-consonant (CVVC) pattern, as in *rain, bean, boat,* and *fruit*. A third common long vowel pattern includes words that end in a vowel sound represented as CV or CVV (*lay, chew, cry*). As students become familiar with common long vowel patterns, less-common patterns are introduced. In a study of long *e*, for example, children first learn about *ee* as in *street*, *ea* as in *stream*, and later add on *ie* as in *thief*, *e*-consonant-*e* as in *these*, *y* as in *happy*. You and your child continue to discuss sound, pattern, meaning, frequency, and position. Table 5.5 offers examples of common and less-common long vowel patterns. See Figure 5.6 for an example of a common long vowel pattern sort.

As you and your child explore, you will discover a number of underlying generalizations. To begin, long vowel patterns can be spelled in a number of different ways and often include a second vowel that is silent and "marks" the first. Long vowel patterns include CVCe (*make, stripe, bike, these,* and *cute*), CVVC (*boat, rain, street,* and *fruit*), and CVV (*play, blow,* and *tie*). Some long vowel spelling patterns are more common than others, as indicated in Table 5.5. Although long vowel patterns usually occur in the middle of a word, specific patterns consistently appear at the end, such as *ay* as in *tray*, *ow* as in *blow*, and *y* as in *cry*. Finally, the meaning of a word also helps determine spelling. There are many long vowel homophone pairs, for example, with the same pronunciation but different spellings and meanings (*pair/pear, stake/steak*).

R-INFLUENCED VOWELS In English, the letter *R* influences or affects the way the preceding vowel is pronounced. For example, compare the pronunciation of the vowels in *bar* and *bad*. The vowel in *bar* is influenced by the letter *R*, which is so strong that it is impos-

TABLE 5.5 Common and Less-Common Long Vowel patterns

	Common Long Vowel Patterns	Less-Common Long Vowel Patterns
Long *a*	*a-e (make), ai (rain), ay (play)*	*ei (eight, veil), ey (prey), ea (steak)*
Long *e*	*ee (street), ea (heat), e (me)*	*ie (chief), e-e (theme), y (happy)*
Long *i*	*i-e (tribe), igh (fight), y (sky)*	*i followed by nd or ld (mind, child)*
Long *o*	*o-e (pole), oa (toast), ow (snow)*	*o followed by two consonants (cold, most, jolt)*
Long *u*	*u-e (tube), oo (moon), ew (blew)*	*ue (blue), ui (suit)*

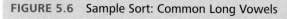

FIGURE 5.6 Sample Sort: Common Long Vowels

ŏ CVC	ō CVCe	$\overline{oa}$ CVVC	$\overline{ow}$ CVV	oddball
stock	**froze**	**coal**	**show**	lose
long	globe	coach	blow	
	Rome	roast	grow	
	close	oat	flow	
	wrote	loaf	throw	
		roam	row	
			mow	
			know	

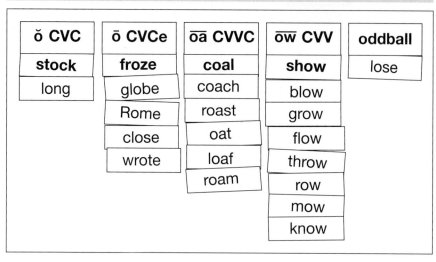

sible to separate the vowel sound from the *r* sound. Teachers sometimes refer to this concept as the "bossy *r*." Table 5.6 provides several examples of *r*-influenced vowels and an example sort can be seen in Figure 5.7. Some other consonants can also have a similar influence on vowels. The consonant sound of *l* is lost in a word like *talk*, but it is part of the vowel sound, which is neither long nor short. When *w* precedes *a*, *ar*, and *or*, the vowel takes on a very different sound, as in *wand*, *war*, and *word*. In other words, vowel sounds can be influenced (changes the sound) when followed by certain consonants (*r*, *l*, *w*). It is also important to note that some *r*-influenced vowels follow the same patterns as short and long vowels (*car/care*, *fir/fire*, *her/here*, *purr/pure*); however, the sound is still *r*-controlled. Like long vowels, some ***r*-influenced** patterns are more common or more frequent than others. For example, there are many words with *are* and *ire* but few with *ure*. *R*-controlled spelling patterns can be found at the beginning (*arm*), middle (*start*), or end (*far*) of a word. There are many homophones among *r*-influenced vowel patterns (*fare/fair*, *here/hear*, *four/fore*). Meaning must be considered when spelling such words.

TABLE 5.6 Examples of *R*-Influenced Vowels

Vowel	*R*-Influenced Examples
A	*ar (car), are (care), air (fair)*
E	*er (her), eer (deer), ear (hear), ear (learn)*
I	*ir (shirt), ire (tire)*
O	*or (for), ore (core), our (pour), oar (boar)*
U	*ur (burn), ure (pure)*

FIGURE 5.7 Sample Sort: *R*-Influenced Vowels

ar	*are*	*air*	oddball
part	**care**	**hair**	pear
start	pare	fair	wear
harm	stare	pair	bear
sharp	square	chair	where
dark	bare	stair	heart
shark	fare		
	hare		

DIPHTHONGS AND OTHER AMBIGUOUS VOWELS The group of vowel sounds known as **ambiguous vowels** includes those that are neither long nor short. They include a variety of patterns that represent a range of sounds, such as *ou* in *cough*, *though*, and *could*. A few common ambiguous vowels include *oo* (*moon*) and *oo* (*book*); *oy* (*boy*) and *oi* (*boil*); *ow* (*brown*) and *ou* (*cloud*); and *aw* (*crawl*), *au* (*caught*), *al* (*tall*) and *o* (*dog*). You and your child may notice that some ambiguous vowel patterns are more common than others. For example, *au* (*pause*) and *aw* (*paw*) are more common than *ough* (*bought*). Position is also helpful to determine which ambiguous vowel to use. The vowel patterns *oi* as in *boil*, *ou* as in *cloud*, and *au* as in *caught* are usually in the middle

FIGURE 5.8 Sample Sort: Ambiguous Vowels

aw	*au*
saw	**caught**
paw	cause
straw	fault
lawn	pause
claw	sauce
draw	taught
yawn	haul
hawk	launch
crawl	vault
drawn	haunt
shawl	
drawn	
raw	
law	

TABLE 5.7 Examples of Complex Consonants

Complex Consonants	Examples
Silent beginning consonants	*kn (knot), wr (wrap), gn (gnat)*
Three letter blends	*scr (scratch), str (stretch), spr (spring), spl (splat,) squ (square)*
Three letter blends with digraphs	*thr (threat), shr (shred), squ (square)*
Hard/soft *c* and *g*	hard *c (cash)* vs. soft *c (cell)*, hard *g (gone)* vs. soft *g (germ)*
Complex ending consonant clusters	*dge (edge)* vs. *ge (cage), tch (match)* vs. *ch (march), ck (quick)* vs. *k (strike)*
Final consonants with silent *e*	*-ce (peace), -se (please), -ze (prize), -ve (leave)*

position of single-syllable words, whereas vowel patterns *oy*, *aw*, and *ow* are usually in the middle or final position, as in *bowl*, *boy*, and *claw*. An ambiguous vowel sort can be seen in Figure 5.8.

COMPLEX CONSONANTS **Complex consonants** refer to a variety of consonant sounds and consonant clusters that are more complicated than the simple two consonant digraphs and blends learned in the previous stage. Examples of complex consonant patterns can be seen in Table 5.7 and include silent initial consonants, triple blends, and other complex consonants.

You and your child learn that some uncommon spelling patterns include silent consonants (*kn*, *wr*, *gn*), which are frequently found in homophones (*right/write*, *know/no*). In addition, words can begin with three-letter blends or digraphs (*spr*, *thr*), which should be blended together as one chunk when reading. They learn that both *c* and *g* have two sounds—the hard sound (/k/) as in *cat*, *cup*, and *cot* as opposed to the soft sound (/s/) in *cider*, *cent*, and *cycle*; the hard sound as in *gap*, *goat*, or *grumble* as opposed to the soft sound (/j/) as in *gentle*, *giant*, and *gym*. The sound of both *c* and *g* is determined by the vowel that follows (Figure 5.9). When the letters *i*, *e*, or *y* follow the letter *c*, the consonant sound is soft, as in *cider*, *cent*, and *cycle*. When the letter is followed by *a*, *o*, or *u*, the consonant sound is hard, as in as in *cap*, *cod*, or *cup*. The same is true for the letter *g*. When followed by *i*, *e*, or *y*, the consonant sound is soft, as in *gentle*, *giant*, or *gym*, and it is a hard sound when followed by *a*, *o*, and *u*, as in *gap*, *gone*, and *gum*.

FIGURE 5.9 Sample Sort: Complex Consonants Hard and Soft C and G

Hard *c*	**Soft *c***	**Hard *g***	**Soft *g***
card	**city**	**gave**	**giant**
code	center	golf	gem
cart	circle	guess	gym
cub	circus	guest	gentle
calf	cell	guide	ginger
	cent		gist
	cycle		

When exploring ending complex consonant clusters (*ch/tch*, *ge/dge*), children learn that each is associated with the preceding vowel sound. The consonant cluster *–tch* is usually used in single-syllable words and has a short vowel, as in *pitch*, *catch*, and *lodge*. The spelling feature *–ch* is usually used in single-syllable words that are not short, as in *beach* and *church*. The consonant cluster *–dge* is usually used in single-syllable words with a short vowel, as in *fudge*, *badge*, and *ridge*. The consonant cluster *–ge* is usually used in single-syllable words without short vowels, as in *large* and *age*. These vowels may be long, ambiguous, or *r*-controlled.

At this stage, you and your child should revisit the final /k/ sound, which has three spellings, associated with

TABLE 5.8 Examples of Homophone Pairs

Homophone Pairs					
eye/I	*flu/flew/flue*	*in/inn*	*fir/fur*	*blue/blew*	*red/read*
tail/tale	*wood/would*	*to/too/two*	*see/sea*	*rap/wrap*	*mail/male*
lead/led	*know/no*	*knot/not*	*one/won*	*stair/stare*	*wail/whale*
which/witch	*dear/deer*	*steel/steal*	*days/daze*	*hay/hey*	*tacks/tax*
genes/jeans	*hour/our*	*heard/herd*	*horse/hoarse*	*sight/site/cite*	*doe/dough*
you/ewe	*write/right*	*your/you're*	*ate/eight*	*groan/grown*	*die/dye*
dew/do/due	*threw/through*	*way/weigh*	*throne/thrown*	*son/sun*	*be/bee*
pair/pear/pare	*so/sew*	*new/knew*	*tea/tee*	*wait/weight*	*nose/knows*
by/buy/bye	*he'll/heel/heal*	*hole/whole*	*male/mail*	*meet/meat*	*stake/steak*
bear/bare	*hair/hare*	*maid/made*	*sea/see*	*scene/seen*	*or/oar*
sail/sale	*board/bored*	*flour/flower*	*chili/chilly*	*cereal/serial*	*hire/higher*

the previous vowel sound. The consonant cluster *–ck* is usually used in single-syllable words with a short vowel, as in *luck* and *check*. The consonant sound *k* is represented by either *k* or *ke* in single-syllable words with vowels that are not short, as in *cook*, *rake*, and *bark*. These vowels may be long, ambiguous, or *r*-controlled. Finally, observe how words ending in *-ce* (*dance*), *-ge* (*edge*), *-ve* (*leave*), and *-se* (*sense*) have a silent *e* associated with the consonant rather than the vowel.

HOMOPHONES **Homophones**, words that sound alike but are spelled differently, have different meanings, such as *bear/bare*, *pane/pain*, and *forth/fourth*. A study of homophones helps explain the many vowel spellings in single-syllable words and increases vocabulary knowledge. Homophones inevitably turn up in any study of vowel patterns and are included in word sorts throughout the within word pattern stage, but an intensive look at homophones late in the stage can also be useful. In these sorts, students match and compare homophone pairs. Children focus not only on the vowel patterns, but also on the meaning of the words. Examples of homophone pairs and triads are in Table 5.8.

Spelling Strategies

Children in the within word pattern stage have a growing store of known words they can spell accurately, including many high-frequency words, but there are still many words they don't know how to spell. Accept your child's best spelling efforts, but also make it clear that they are accountable for spelling word features that have been formally studied, and that they should use a variety of strategies to spell words they do not know. Children often forget to use what they already know to figure out something new. Keep in mind that there is a continuum of spelling strategies, and some strategies are more useful than others, depending on the stage of development in which your child is performing (Dahl et al., 2003; Ehri,1997; Williams & Lundstrom, 2007). Below are three strategies, specific to this stage of development, to use when your child asks you how to spell a word or when you notice that they have made a mistake.

USE ANALOGY Analogy is the use of rhyming words to determine the spelling of an unfamiliar word. Encourage your child to think of a word that is already known and consider the spelling for the rhyming word. For example, if we know how to spell the word *night*, we can also spell the words *might*, *right*, *fight*, and *slight*. Of course, not all rhyming words have the same patterns. For example, the word *spite* also rhymes with *night*.

USE THE "BEST BET" STRATEGY While sorting and studying vowel patterns, children may notice that one pattern often has more examples than another. Encourage your child to think about the most common pattern that he or she knows first and to consider what is the "best bet." For example, if your child wants to spell the word *splay*, as in, "A butterfly *splayed* its wings before taking flight," prompt your child to consider, "What patterns do I know to spell long *a*? Which pattern is the most common at the end of a word?" Next, they might recognize that *ay* is the only common pattern at the end of a word or syllable. So, the best bet is to use *ay* for *splay*. The "best bet" strategy demonstrates a shift from relying predominantly on the sounds of the language to the many patterns that are used in words. It is important for your child to shift thinking to include pattern and later meaning.

ENCOURAGE STUDENTS TO TRY A WORD SEVERAL WAYS: HAVE-A-GO Teach your child to attempt spelling a word before asking for help, and offer positive feedback on what they try. Encourage them to try it different ways in order to identify which one might "look right." Is it *coach* or *coche*? Australians Parry and Hornsby (1988) described this popular strategy as "have-a-go," and various forms have been developed. Have-a-go is a visual memory approach—asking oneself "Does it look right?" and is best combined with the thoughtful reflection about how words work, as noted in previous strategies, including best bet, spelling by syllable, and using affixes and roots. For example, if you want to spell the word *come*, you may begin with asking the student to identify the sounds in the word. The letter sounds /c/ and /m/ are both easily identifiable; however, it is also a word that requires us to use memory to spell.

Word Study With Parents, Tutors, and School Volunteers

In this section, we share specific examples of how you can support the development of word knowledge for children in the within word pattern stage of spelling. These are in addition to the routines and essential techniques described in detail in Chapter 2. The routines and essentials are a great place to start, either to complement a school word study program or to start your own at home. Remember that all of the sorts, games, and hands-on activities are designed to have children play with words in isolation as well as within reading and writing. Effective programs ask our children to build and sort words, read and write words, and play games to work toward an automatic recognition and use of words. All aspects of literacy must be integrated to gain word knowledge.

Word Study Notebooks

A **word study notebook** is an essential tool in the within word pattern stage, and provides an organizational structure and documentation of student work. Schools that implement word study ask their students to use the notebooks to record their sorts and the series of interactive activities in which they engage over the week. If your child maintains a notebook, encourage him or her to bring it home once a week so that you are able to review their study and also to reinforce what is being learned. If your child does not have a word study notebook, start one at home! The sturdy stitched composition notebooks with a hard marbleized cover work well. You may use the notebook to record weekly activities, such as word hunts, writing sorts, speed sort records, illustrations of key vocabulary terms, and written reflections, or simply to collect interesting words and phrases.

Children are encouraged to generate collections of homophones, multiple-meaning words, and **idioms** with illustrations and explanations. Idiomatic phrases, a group of words that have a meaning that is not transparent by the literal meaning, such as to "go bananas" or "have ants in your pants," are abundant and often a cause of confusion. Collecting, illustrating, and discussing common phrases is fun and often humorous. It is also especially interesting to learn of their origins. Common idioms are highlighted in Table 5.9. There are literally hundreds of idioms to explore!

Multiple-meaning words are also important, and are quite prolific as well! Even common words such as the small word *run* have multiple meanings. It can mean to move one's legs quicker than walking, to move quickly as with a stream, to photocopy or produce by copying, to publish a story in the media, to have a tear or pull in a woman's stocking, to enter an election, or a series of good plays in a sporting event. Encourage your child to consider multiple meanings and talk about the different contexts in which words are used.

TABLE 5.9 Common Idioms

Common Idioms	Explanations
"a drop in the ocean"	inconsequential, a small part of something
"butterflies in my stomach"	a feeling of nervousness
"break a leg"	good luck
"hit the nail on the head"	to be exact, precise, correct
"keep an eye on him"	watch someone or something carefully
"over the moon"	to be elated, happy, excited
"piece of cake"	something is easy
"sitting on the fence"	not making a firm decision between two choices
"take a rain check"	to delay an offer until another time
"you can't judge a book by its cover"	appearances are not always what they seem
"water under the bridge"	things in the past are no longer important

Word Study Uno

Word Study Uno is a version of the popular card game Uno for three to four players. Create a set of at least 27 word cards by writing words in the upper left corners of blank cards using the patterns that you and your child have been studying (or use your child's actual sort). For example, if your child is working on long *o* patterns, create word cards that have *o*-consonant-*e* (*hope*), *oa* (*roam*), and *ow* (*show*) combinations. Also, create four each of the following cards: Skip, Draw Two, and Wild.

To play, deal five cards to each player. The remaining cards are placed in a deck face down and the top card is turned face up to start the discard pile. Players take turns playing cards that match the pattern of the face-up card or playing one of the special cards (Skip, Draw 2, Wild). For example, if the beginning card is *boat*, the first player could put down *soap*, *road*, or *goat* or play a special card. The Skip card indicates that the next player loses a turn. The Draw 2 card forces the next player to pick two cards from the pile without playing any cards. Slightly different from traditional Uno, whenever a Wild, Draw 2, or Skip card is played, the player can select the category. A player who cannot put down a card must draw from the pile. A player who has only one card remaining must yell, "Uno!" If the player forgets, another player can tell the player with one card to draw another card. The first player to run out of cards wins the game.

Guess My Category

Guess My Category is played using a large set of word cards with a variety of vowels and vowel patterns. In each round, one player displays word cards one at a time that fit a "secret" category. It is the other players' job to try to guess the category. For example, your child might put out the words *home*, *goat*, and *show*, and you would need to guess that all the words are long *o* words. Or your child might put out the words *rain*, *clean*, and *suit*, and you would need to guess that all the words have the CVVC long vowel pattern. The guesser can also try to guess the category by proposing other words, such as asking, "Would *grade* fit in your category?" The rules of the game can be expanded to include semantic (types of birds) and grammatical (nouns) categories. There are no limits to the kind of categories your child might be able to create, all of which will build a growing word consciousness.

Word Operations (or Change a Word Part)

Give your child a word and then ask him or her to add, drop, or change one or two letters at a time to create a new word. Typically, consonants, blends, and digraphs are exchanged at the beginning (*ship* to *chip* to *flip*) or the end (*card* to *carp*), but vowels can also be exchanged (*green* to *groan* to *grain*). Take turns and model how to change one letter in the word to create a new word. Here is a string of words that could be played: *space, pace, place, lace, race, trace, track, rack, crack, lack, slack, sack, Mack, mask, ask, task, bask, base, vase, case, cast, last, lass, glass, grass, brass, brash, trash, crash,* and *cash.*

Vowel Concentration

Vowel Concentration is played the traditional way, but players look for pairs of words with the same sound and pattern. Prepare a set of word cards for a particular vowel pattern. Players may use their set of words they cut out for the week, but they should not be able to read the word through the back of the card. Remove oddballs because they are not likely to make a pair. Players turn all the words face down in a rectangle formation. The first player turns over two word cards. If they have the same vowel sound and pattern (such as *fort* and *north*), the player keeps both cards and adds them to the point pile. The player can take another turn before play passes to the next player. The game ends when all matches have been made. The winner is the player with the most word cards in the point pile.

Vowel Rummy

Up to four players may play Vowel Rummy. You need 35 to 45 cards. A good starting combination is five cards for each short vowel in the CVC pattern for a total of 25 cards, plus five cards for each long vowel in the CVCe pattern (except for long *e*, because there are so few words in that category), for a total of 20 more cards. You can also include Wild cards.

Five cards are dealt to each player and the rest are turned face down in a deck. Players look in their hands for pairs or three, four, or five of a kind. Each player has one chance to discard unwanted cards and draw up to four new cards from the deck to keep a hand of five cards. For example, a player might be dealt *bone, rope, that, wet, rake.* This player may want to discard *that, wet,* and *rake,* and draw three other cards to possibly create a better hand.

The possible combinations are one pair (*that, camp*); two pairs (*that, camp, bone, rope*); three of a kind (*bone, rope, rode*); four of a kind (*bone, rope, rode, smoke*); three of a kind plus a pair (*bone, rope, rode, hat, rat*); or five of a kind (*bone, rope, rode, smoke, note*). Players lay down their hands to determine the winner of the round. The winner is determined in this order: Five of a kind (this beats everything), four of a kind, three of a kind plus a pair, two pairs, three of a kind, and finally one pair. In the case of a tie, players can draw from a deck until one player comes up with a card that breaks the tie. Play continues by dealing another set of cards to the players. The player who wins the most rounds is the winner.

Declare Your Category!

Declare Your Category! is for two to five players (three is optimal) and works best with players who have some experience playing games. In this game, players guess the first player's category. Create a deck of 45 word cards with a variety of vowels and vowel patterns. Make at least four cards with any one pattern.

Seven cards are dealt to each player and the remainder is placed face down in a deck. Players lay out their seven cards face up. The first player turns up a key card from the deck (e.g., *home*) and looks for a word in his or her hand to match in some way. It might have the same sound and/or spelling pattern (either *o*-consonant-*e* or *VCe*); for example, *soap, bone,* or *gave.* The match is laid down for all to see and the player announces, "Guess my category." Play moves to the next person, who must search his or her hand for a similar match. Players can pass when they wish. The player who started the category keeps the sorting strategy a secret. Play keeps going until the last player to put a card down declares the category.

If the person who set up the category does not think the next player has put down an acceptable card, he or she can send a card back and give that player another chance. Mistakes are discussed at the end of each round. The player who plays the last card has to declare the category to win and keep all of the cards. If the player is wrong, the previous player gets a chance to declare the category. At the end of each round, students are dealt enough cards to get them back to seven. The winner of the round turns up a card from the pile and makes up the next category. Play continues until the deck is empty. The player with the most cards wins.

Homophone Dictionaries

Children love learning about homophones. Once homophones have been introduced through sorting known words, encourage your child to create a personal or family homophone dictionary. Work together to collect pairs or trios of homophones, create pictures, and provide context by including either a sentence or a child-friendly definition. This could be a section of the word study notebook or a separate journal or notebook. This dictionary can then become a reference for spelling homophones.

Homophone Rummy

Children play this card game with homemade Homophone Rummy cards. Parents prepare several sets of homophone pairs (52 cards, 26 pairs). Parents should select words with which children have some familiarity. Write the words in the upper left corner of the cards, as shown in Figure 5.10. Deal each player seven cards and begin the game with each player checking their hands for already existing pairs. Pairs can be laid down in front of the player, who must give the meaning for each word or use it in a sentence that makes the meaning clear. The remainder of the deck is placed in a central location and the first card is turned face up beside it to form a discard pile. Each player draws from either the deck or the discard pile. Any new pairs are laid down and defined. The player must then discard one card to end the turn. Note: If a card is taken from the discard pile, all the cards beneath it are also taken, and the last card picked up must be used to make a pair. The game is over when one player has no cards left. The person yells, "Rummy!" Then the pairs are counted up to determine the winner.

FIGURE 5.10 Homophone Rummy

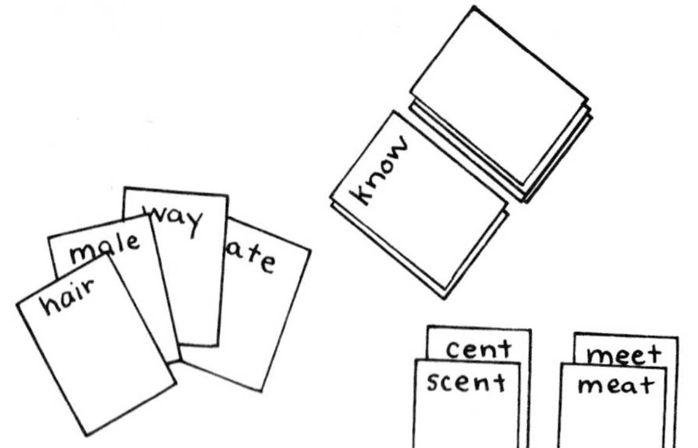

Homophone Win, Lose, or Draw

Homophone Win, Lose, or Draw resembles charades and is fun to play as a family or with a group of friends. Players work in teams to draw and guess each other's words that are homophones. To prepare, write homophones on cards and then divide your group into two teams. To play, a card is pulled from the deck and shown simultaneously to the selected artists for each teams. Each artist must draw a picture representing the given homophone, which requires understanding a homophone's spelling and meaning. As the artists draw, their teammates call out possible answers. When the correct word is offered, the artist calls on the team to spell both words in the pair. A point is awarded to the team that provides the correct information first. Continue the same process while rotating artists with each round.

Books That Feature Homophones and Homographs

There are many books for children that focus on homophones and homographs, including the ones listed in Figure 5.11. **Homographs** are words that are spelled the same and pronounced differently with different meanings ("There is *lead* in that paint" vs. "She *lead* the team to victory"). These creative books are highly engaging for children, thanks to the

FIGURE 5.11 Books with Homophones and Homographs

Books with Homophones and Homographs

1. Barretta, G. (2007). *Dear Deer: A Book of Homophones*. Henry Holt and Company.
2. Cleary, B. (2014). *A Bat Cannot Bat, a Stair Cannot Stare: More about Homonyms and Homophones*. Millbrook Press.
3. Cleary, B. (2014). *How Much Can a Bare Bear Bear: What Are Homonyms and Homophones?* First Avenue Editions.
4. Ghigna, C. (1999). *See the Yak Yak*. Random House.
5. Gwynne, F. (1988). *A Chocolate Moose for Dinner.* Aladdin.
6. Gwynne, F. (1988). *The King Who Rained.* Aladdin.
7. Gwynne, F. (1998). *A Little Pigeon Toad.* Aladdin.
8. McKinney, L. (2014). *They're Nuts: Another Homophone Book*. Tate Publishing.
9. Parish, H. (2007). *Amelia Bedelia under Construction.* Greenwillow Books.
10. Parish, P. (1993). *Thank You Amelia Bedelia*. Harper Collins.
11. Presson, L. (1999). *A Dictionary of Homophones.* Barron's Educational Series.
12. Terban, M. (2007). *Eight Ate: A Feast of Homonym Riddles*. HMH Books for Young Readers.

FIGURE 5.12 The Race Track Game

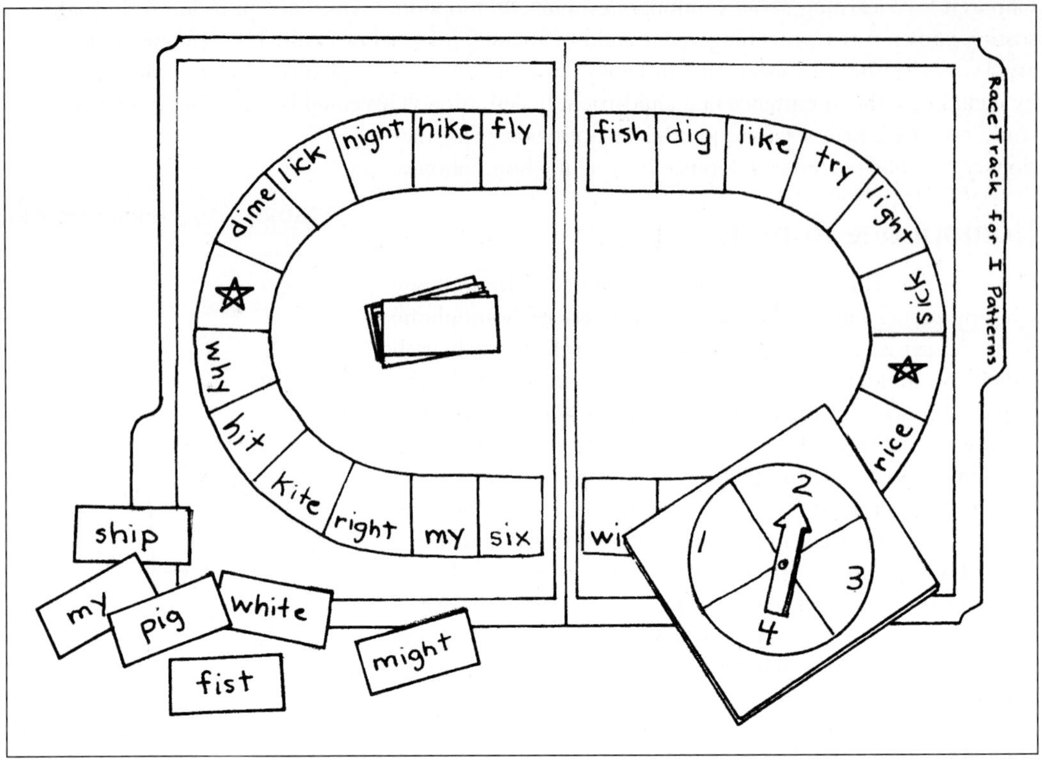

often funny situations that occur when mixing or misusing homophones. For example, each page in *Chocolate Moose for Dinner* (Gwynne, 1988) illustrates an example of confusing the meanings of homophones *moose* and *mousse*; the classic *Amelia Bedelia* series by Peggy Parrish includes many examples of homophone confusions, such as when Amelia gets out her sketchpad when reminded to "draw the drapes." Homographs are also fun to examine at this stage through books such as *The Dove Dove: Funny Homograph Riddles* by Marvin Terban, and *Zoola Palooza: A Book of Homographs* by Gene Beretta.

Follow-the-Path Games

Follow-the-path games, such as the Racetrack Game (Figure 5.12) and the Train Station Game (Figure 5.13), are useful for additional practice with common and uncommon spelling patterns. Using a template to create a game board and write in the words that your child has been studying. Also incorporate special squares on the game board. For example, in the Train Station Game, you can use the following:

1. Car on the track. Lose one turn.
2. You pass a freight train. Move ahead 2 spaces.
3. Tunnel blocked. Go back 1 space.
4. You lost your ticket. Go back two spaces.

The game can be played with up to four players. Each player selects a game piece. The first person then spins or rolls the die and moves the appropriate number of spaces. Students pronounce the word they land on and identify the vowel. If the player has studied the long vowel pattern within each long vowel, ask them to say the pattern. For example, "*Nail* is a long *a* with a CVVC pattern." In addition, players must say another word containing the same vowel sound to stay on that space. Play continues in this fashion until someone reaches the end.

FIGURE 5.13 The Train Station Game

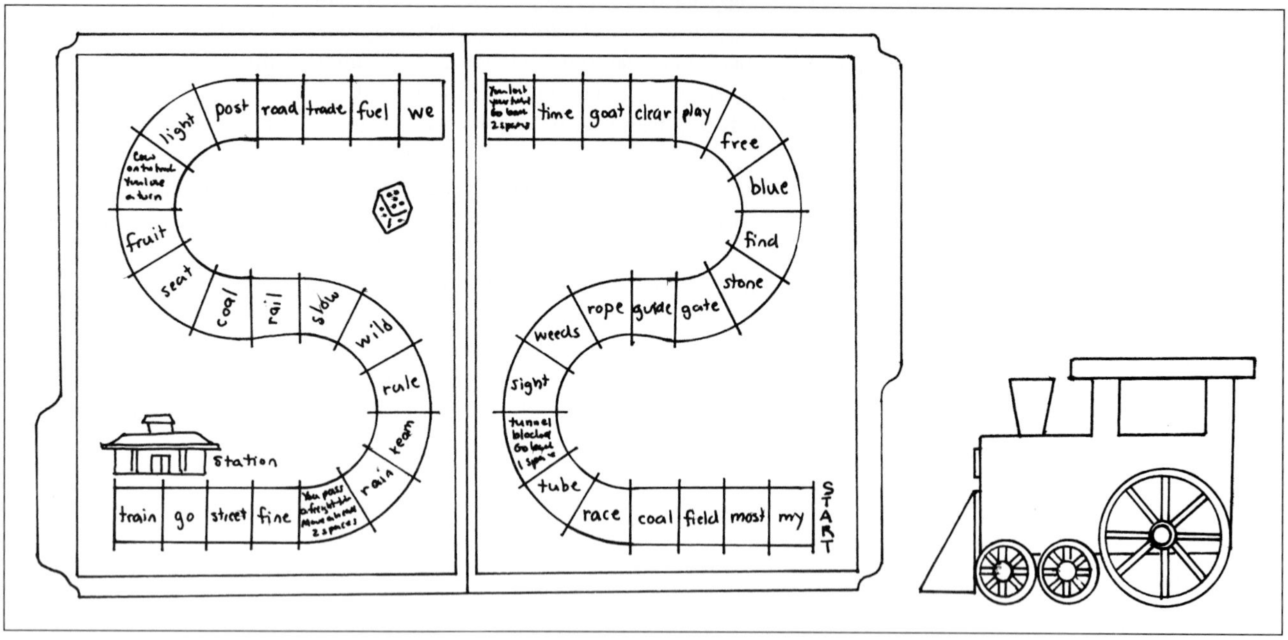

The Spelling Game

The Spelling Game is for two to four players. It can be used for any feature and is easily changed by simply replacing the word cards. Use a follow-the-path game board. Leave the majority of the spaces blank except for a few spaces where you may write directions such as "Go Back 3," "Lose a Turn," and "Go Ahead 2 Spaces." Add playing pieces and a spinner or die. Children use their own collection of words for the week. On each turn, the player draws a card from the face-down stack of word cards. The player says the word to the first player, who must spell the word aloud. If the player spells the word correctly, he or she can spin or roll to move around the path. The winner is the first one to get to the end of the path. Another variation is to have players write the words on paper or dry-erase boards.

Supporting Reading and Writing

Reading

Consistent reading is crucial during this stage of development in school and at home. Following are a few suggestions to promote reading that interests and inspires!

SELECT BOOKS WITH YOUR CHILD Parents, tutors, and volunteers can provide deliberate support for children as they select books. Guide your child to select books that are interesting and accessible, meaning that concepts are familiar and age appropriate for your child. Teach your child to make good selections by browsing the cover and reviewing the back-cover summary and a few pages in the story. Ask your child to evaluate the choice. "Is this a book that would interest me?" "Is this an author that I know?" "Is this the genre I like to read?" After considering interest in the book, you and your child should briefly evaluate the level of text difficulty or readability. Recall our conversation in Chapter 1 about **instructional** and **independent levels**. We referred to the instructional level as the *strike zone*, neither too challenging nor too simple. Children at this stage are proud of their abilities to complete entire chapter books, and must be encouraged to read and reread comfortable text.

One helpful strategy for selecting an appropriate reading level is referred to as the *Goldilocks Rule*. This suggests that children should read or sample several pages and determine if the text is *too easy*, *too hard*, or *just right*. The judgment of "too difficult" may refer to decoding words, vocabulary, sentence structure, or general topic. By evaluating text, children learn to monitor their own understanding and make thoughtful choices. The Goldilocks Rule reminds children that not every book is a great fit, and they are in control of their choices.

Although readability is an important factor, it must also be noted that challenging books also have great value, especially nonfiction texts, which typically introduce topic-specific vocabulary and new text structures, including problem–solution, chronology, cause and effect, and enumeration (listing). As long as your child is interested in a topic or a book and is motivated to read and puzzle out the meaning of the text, and as long as he or she is not experiencing frustration, following their curiosity through books is a good thing! Parents must balance the need for children to enjoy readable and engaging texts in which they can read comfortably, and also a child's desire to read something that is potentially beyond their instructional level, especially with nonfiction or informational books.

MONITOR THE TIME YOUR CHILD READS AT HOME The amount of time children read is critical to their success (Anderson, Wilson, & Fielding, 1988). There are two simple actions you can take to increase the amount of time your children read. First, provide an abundance of high-interest reading materials that are easily accessible. Make it a point to have your home (or teaching space) filled with books, magazines, newspapers, electronic readers, comic books, and cookbooks. Keep reading material available in every room in the house, including the bathroom and in the car, so that you and your child are more likely to pick up a book. Books can be borrowed from libraries, schools, relatives, and friends. Second, have a regular reading time for at least 30 minutes each day. Many parents set up a family reading time after dinner and homework and before bedtime. Everyone has heard the practical expression, "Practice makes perfect." This holds true with reading too; the more children read, the better readers they become. Building a cycle of reading success, motivation, and momentum is essential to literacy development. Encourage your child to read on a daily basis. This daily reading may look different depending on the book, the day, or your child's age or mood. Daily family reading might include everyone reading silently from their own books, reading the same book independently and then talking about it, or taking turns reading pages from the same book. Make reading an enjoyable habit!

READ ALOUD TO YOUR CHILD Although transitional readers are excited to be reading on their own, it is equally valuable to read aloud to your child. Select a book that is at or above your child's independent reading level. This allows your child to experience a book without the challenges of decoding and allows a focus on understanding and enjoyment. There are many academic reasons to read aloud to children. Reading aloud increases a child's general knowledge, specific vocabulary, language, and knowledge of genre and the structures of fiction and nonfiction. It provides an example of fluent reading and pronunciation of new words.

Good children's literature is also one of the best starting places for vocabulary learning and is a much richer source than television or adult daily conversation (Hayes & Ahrens, 1988). Picture books and chapter books are full of new, rich vocabulary that is wrapped in complex sentences. There are typically more new words in a children's picture book than in several hours of television (Cunningham & Stanovich, 1997). Reading is the greatest source of vocabulary, knowledge, and language available. Rereading favorite books is also an excellent way to revisit ideas, language, and vocabulary.

Reading aloud also creates a shared and often cherished experience in which you both respond emotionally to the book, whether it is humorous, suspenseful, inspirational, tragic, or informative. This is true not only for parents, but also for teachers and tutors. The common story becomes a touchstone for other conversations and experiences. As parents and a former teachers, some of our fondest memories are of reading aloud with children of all ages.

TALK ABOUT READING Ask your children to share what they are reading and their thoughts about the reading. Good readers are constantly "making meaning" out of text, which teachers describe as *comprehension.* They make connections to previous experiences and to other books. Did you notice how the *Henry and Mudge* series and *Because of Winn-Dixie* both feature the importance of a dog as a child's best friend in both good times and bad? Does the Watson family in *The Watsons Go to Birmingham* by Christopher Paul Curtis remind you of our own family or another? How?

Ask children to share their thoughts about what has been read, and ask them to give examples from the book to support their thinking. Your goal is to encourage a love of reading and build understanding, but you do not want the conversation to feel like a quiz. It should reflect a genuine interest and conversation. Ask, "What's going on in your book right now?" "Has anything surprised you?" "What do you think will happen next?" "To which kind of reader would you recommend this book? Why?" Strive for that same natural feel that might be seen between two adults sharing a novel that only one of the persons has read. Enjoy reading and talking about reading with your children. If your child is reading about informational text, ask them to teach you about the subject, and ask about what the author's main purpose is in writing. What's the author's overall thinking? Why is wild weather so fascinating? What can we learn about a shark that is helpful to humans?

BUILD FLUENCY THROUGH POETRY AND REPEATED READINGS Reading fluently and expressively is an important goal of the transitional stage. Automatic word recognition and increasing knowledge of word patterns and parts are the keys to fluent and expressive reading. Reading and rereading familiar texts is one way to increase fluency; another is to read aloud or perform poetry, which naturally provides an authentic reason to read aloud. Select a poem and choose parts with your child to read the poem aloud. Imagine reading the poem "Invitation" from *Where the Sidewalk Ends* by Shel Silverstein. You and your child can take turns reading lines, but you may both choose to read the final two lines together: "Come In, Come In!" Poems are meant to be read aloud, and reading them aloud develops accuracy, appropriate speed, tone, and expression (fluency). Poetry is also a welcomed break from chapter books for many children because the pieces are shorter, and many offer humor or silly content that children enjoy.

Writing

At the transitional stage, children are finally able to produce writing with some ease. As we note with the writing sample earlier in the chapter, the volume of writing increases and multiple pages are produced. There are many fun ways to integrate writing into your family life that can get everyone involved. There is no need to give your child homework; instead, get inspired by your family's daily life, integrate writing when it comes naturally, and build a bridge to school writing assignments and projects.

ENCOURAGE YOUR CHILD TO WRITE FOR A VARIETY OF PURPOSES AND SHARE THEIR WRITING Write letters, jokes, reports, essays, stories, songs, comics, and top-10 fact lists about areas that interest your child. Ask your child to see their writing pieces and projects from school, and share these with family. Celebrate writing. Encourage your child to write about the experiences you share as a family. Consider keeping a journal, either individually or as a family, or between a tutor and student. Children are encouraged when someone else is writing in response to their own stories, poems, and comics. Also consider the integration of technology for sharing writing—email, blogs, Skype, and FaceTime all provide an extended audience for your child to share their thoughts. Remember, writers write for an audience!

PROVIDE INTERESTING WRITING MATERIALS Inspire your child to write by keeping a large variety of interesting writing materials available in a desk or writing area. Similar to our recommendation in reading, access to materials influences our decisions. Include different types of writing utensils (pens, pencils, colored pencils, markers, highlighters) and different types of paper (stationary, postcards, notebooks, notecards, journals, sticky notes). Children often get very excited when they are able to create a long book, so consider adding a stapler too. You will be amazed at the things your child will create! You may also consider electronic methods for writing and composition. Children as young as kindergarten have been known to dictate or retell familiar or novel stories into a smartphone, setting the stage for writing their own text.

EXPLORE WRITING ASSIGNMENTS FROM SCHOOL Although children are introduced to writing as early as kindergarten, academic, interdisciplinary writing begins to accelerate from third and fourth grade on. Build a bridge between home and school by actively asking your child to share writing assignments in all content areas, including science, history, and English. Review the directions or explanation from the teacher and ask your child to share their planning and writing. Ask if the writing meets all of the criteria provided by the teacher. Express interest in the topic and writing and give feedback. Do not change the writing or make corrections. Rather, share where you as a reader were interested and where you may have experienced confusion. Encourage your child to add information that strengthens an argument or adds detail to a story. The same can be said for editing—rather than correcting the writing, ask your child to review the piece looking exclusively for editing corrections in spelling, grammar, punctuation, and capitalization. Children become more proficient writers as they engage in writing for a variety of purposes and learn from knowledgeable teachers, tutors, parents and volunteers.

A BRIEF SUMMARY

In this chapter, we described characteristics typical of transitional readers in the within word pattern stage of development. We explored the spelling features specific to the stage; how to discuss sound, pattern, and meaning; and strategies to spell unknown words with our children. Finally, we shared a variety of activities to develop your child's word knowledge and overall literacy development. In Chapter 6, we focus on students described as *intermediate readers and writers in the syllables and affixes stage of spelling development.*

REFERENCES

Anderson, R. C., Wilson, P. T., and Fielding, L. G. (1988). Growth in reading and how children spend their time outside of school. *Reading Research Quarterly, 23*: 285–303.

Biemiller, A. (2005). Size and sequence in vocabulary development: Implications for choosing words for primary grade vocabulary instruction. In E. H. Hiebert (Ed.). *Teaching and learning vocabulary: Bringing research to practice* (pp. 223–242). Mahwah, NJ: Lawrence Erlbaum.

Cunningham, A. E., & Stanovich, K. E. (1997). What reading does for the mind. *Journal of Direct Instruction, 1*(2): 137–149.

Dahl, K. L., Barto, A., Bonfils, A., Carasello, M., Christopher, J., Davis, R., Erkkila, N., Glander, S., Jacobs, B., Kendra, V., Koski, L., Majeski, D., McConnell, E., Petrie, P., Siegel, D., Slaby, B., Waldbauer, J., & Williams, J. (2003). Connecting developmental word study with classroom writing: Children's descriptions of spelling strategies. *Reading Teacher, 57* (4): 310–319.

Ehri, L. C. (1997). Learning to read and learning to spell are one and the same, almost. In C. A. Perfetti, L. Rieben, & M. Fayol (Eds.). *Learning to spell: Research, theory, and practice across languages* (pp. 237–269). Mahwah, NJ: Lawrence Erlbaum Associates.

Flanigan, K., Hayes, L., Templeton, S., Bear, D. R., Invernizzi, M., & Johnston, F. (2011). *Words their way with struggling readers: Word study for reading, vocabulary, and spelling instruction, grades 4–12*. Boston, MA: Allyn & Bacon.

Fry, E. (2004). Phonics: A large phoneme–grapheme frequency count revisited. *Journal of Literacy Research, 36* (1): 85–98.

Hayes, D. P. & Ahrens, M. (1988). Vocabulary simplification for children: A special case of "motheres." *Journal of Child Language*, *15*: 395–410.

Invernizzi, M., Abouzeid, M., & Gill, T. (1994) Using students' invented spellings as a guide for spelling instruction that emphasizes word study. *Elementary School Journal*, *95* (2): 155–167.

Invernizzi, M., Johnston, F., Bear, D., & Templeton, S. (2009). *Word sorts for within word pattern spellers*. New York, NY: Pearson.

Nagy, W., Berninger, V., Abbott, R., Vaughan, K., & Vermeulen, K. (2003). Relationship of morphology and other language skills to literacy skills in at-risk second-grade readers and at-risk fourth-grade writers. *Journal of Educational Psychology*, *95*(4), 730–742.

Parry, J., & Hornsby, D. (1988). *Write on: A conference approach to writing*. Portsmouth, NH: Heinemann.

Williams, C., & Lundstrom, R., (2007). Strategy instruction during word study and interactive writing activities. *The Reading Teacher*, *61* (3): 204–212.

CHILDREN'S LITERATURE REFERENCES

Barretta, G. (2007). *Dear deer: A book of homophones*. Henry Holt & Company.

Baretta, G. (2011). *Zoola palooza: A book of homographs*. Henry Holt & Company.

Barnes, D. (2008). *Ruby and the Booker Boys series*. Scholastic.

Camerson, A. & Strugnel, A. (1989). *The stories Julian tells*. Random House.

Cleary, B. (2014). *A bat cannot bat, a stair cannot stare: More about homonyms and homophones*. Millbrook Press.

Cleary, B. (2014). *How much can a bare bear bear: What are homonyms and homophones?* First Avenue Editions.

English, K., & Freeman, L. (2014). *Carver chronicles series*. HMH Books for Young Readers.

Ghigna, C. (1999). *See the yak yak*. Random House.

Gwynne, F. (1988). *A chocolate moose for dinner*. Aladdin.

Gwynne, F. (1988). *The king who rained*. Aladdin.

Gwynne, F. (1998). *A little pigeon toad*. Aladdin.

Lin. G. (2011). *Ling and Ting series*. LB Kids.

Lobel, A. (2004). *Frog and Toad*. Harper Collins.

Marshall, J. (1995). *Fox all week*. Penguin Young Readers.

McKinney, L. (2014). *They're nuts: Another homophone book*. Tate.

Montes, M. & Cepeda, J. (2003). *Get ready for Gabi series*. Scholastic.

Osborne, P. M. (2001). *The magic tree house*. Random House.

Parish, H. (2007). *Amelia Bedelia under construction*. Greenwillow Books.

Parish, P. (1993). *Thank you Amelia Bedelia*. Harper Collins.

Park, B. (2001). *Junie B. Jones*. Random House.

Presson, L. (1999). *A dictionary of homophones*. Barron's Educational Series.

Pulver, R. & Reed, L.R. (2010). *Silent letters loud and clear*. Holiday House.

Pulver, R. & Reed, L.R. (2011). *Happy endings: A story about suffixes*. Holiday House.

Rylant, C. (1996). *Henry and Mudge*. Simon Spotlight.

Shaskan, T. S. (2008). *If you were a contraction*. Picture Window Books.

Silverstein, S. (2014). *Where the sidewalk ends*. Harper Collins.

Stead, T. & Ballester, J. (2011) *Should there be zoos?* Mondo Publishing.

Terban, M. (2007). *Eight ate: A feast of homonym riddles*. HMH Books for Young Readers.

Terban, M. (2008). *The dove dove: Funny homograph riddles*. HMH for Young Readers.

Thomson, M. (2009). *Keena Ford series*. Puffin Books.

chapter 6

Intermediate Readers and Writers in the Syllables and Affixes Stage of Spelling Development

Source: Amble Design/Shutterstock

Source: Michelle Picard

From an early age, Amiyah was an avid reader and writer. Her fourth-grade classroom was a supportive and challenging environment where she shared her passions of theater, mathematics, and reading. Once a month, she participated in a book club with her neighborhood friends. They read a collection of books, including *Walk Two Moons* by Sharon Creech, *Esperanza Rising* by Pam Munoz Ryan, *The True Confessions of Charlotte Doyle* by Avi, and *Brown Girl Dreaming* by Jacqueline Woodson. In class, Amiyah and her peers wrote stories, informational reports, reading-response journal entries, and social studies essays. Spelling instruction was an explicit part of her English Language Arts class.

Nick, a seventh grader, also in the intermediate stage of reading and syllables and affixes stage of spelling, enjoyed school as well. He spent his weekends playing basketball and video games, and spending time with his dog and friends. Together they shared book recommendations and swapped favorite books such as *The Lightening Thief* by Rick Riordan and graphic novels, including the *Bone* series by Jeff Smith and the *Amulet* series by Kazu Kibuishi. At the middle-school level, the number of writing assignments increased and Nick was responsible for essays in science, social studies, and English, lab reports, journal entries, audiovisual presentations, persuasive writing, and some narrative pieces. For Nick, spelling instruction (and decoding) was emphasized less than during elementary school, while the need to synthesize reading and research in writing increased. Although both Amiyah and Nick are at different ages and have different reading interests, they both benefit from a developmental approach to word study and written word knowledge. Explicit and systematic instruction in written word knowledge develops increased vocabulary, reading comprehension, and writing fluency.

This chapter is devoted to intermediate readers in the syllables and affixes stage of spelling, typically found in third through eighth grades. Note that this is a broad range as a result of the varied experiences with language, literacy, and instruction in which children participate. A child who has reached this stage in third or fourth grade has different interests and experiences than a child in middle school.

As in previous chapters, this chapter contains information about the common characteristics of students in reading, writing, and spelling at this stage (Table 6.1), examines common spelling features and how to talk about them with your child, introduces a series of games and activities to support word study at home or in a tutorial setting, and discusses how to make connections among spelling, reading, and writing.

Stage Overview: Intermediate Readers and Writers in the Syllables and Affixes Stage of Spelling

Reading

As students expand their word knowledge, they are able to read more fluently and for longer stretches of time in varied kinds of texts, allowing them to further develop vocabulary, background knowledge, and ultimately, reading comprehension. This is an important shift as readers in the upper-elementary and middle school grades are expected to read widely from textbooks and other informational text. There is a greater emphasis on academic content area subjects such as science and social studies. In Table 6.2, we provide a glimpse into typical books for intermediate readers across two grade level clusters, because there is a significant maturational difference between these children, despite their common spelling stage.

TABLE 6.1 Characteristics of Intermediate Readers and Writers in the Syllables and Affixes Stage of Spelling

Reading Characteristics	• Typically third- to eighth-grade students • Read fiction and nonfiction texts ranging from third- to eighth-grade level • Focus on nonfiction texts • Read with fluency and expression • Background knowledge, experience, and vocabulary significantly affect comprehension • Word knowledge closely tied to vocabulary growth • Word recognition (and spelling) focused on polysyllabic words
Writing Characteristics	• Write for a variety of purposes (reports, essays, journals, stories) • Write with increased organization, fluency, and expression • Provide supporting information and detail • Use sophisticated and specialized vocabulary
Spelling Characteristics	• Spell most single-syllable short- and long vowel words correctly • Make errors in polysyllabic words at the point where syllables meet • Spell most high-frequency words correctly
Common Spelling Errors	• *SHOPING* for *shopping* • *ATEND* for *attend* • *KEPER* for *keeper* • *SELLER* for *cellar* • *CONFUSSHUN* for *confusion* • *PLESHURE* for *pleasure* • *AMAZZING* for *amazing* • *PERRAIDING* for *parading*

Instructional Focus	• Introducing polysyllabic words
	  ○ Compound words (*hotdog, sunshine*)
	  ○ Homophones (*cereal/serial, flour/flower, medal/meddle*)
	  ○ Homographs (to own a ***rec**ord* vs. to *re**cord*** an album)
	• Inflected endings
	  ○ Plurals (*flower**s**, church**es**, cherr**ies***)
	  ○ Adding *-ed* and *-ing* (*jump**ed**, jump**ing***)
	  ○ Comparatives and superlatives (*fast**er**, thinn**est***)
	• Syllable juncture—where syllables meet
	  ○ Open Syllables (*o/pen, cre/ate*)
	  ○ Closed Syllables (*slip/per, mem/ber, riv/er, laugh/ter*)
	• Vowel patterns in accented syllables
	  ○ Long vowels in accented syllables (*mist**ake**, t**oa**ster*)
	  ○ *R*-controlled vowels in accented syllables (*m**ar**ble, rep**air***)
	  ○ Ambiguous vowels in accented syllables (*f**ou**ntain, l**au**ndry*)
	• Vowel patterns in unaccented syllables (*troub**le**, doct**or**, sudd**en***)
	• Exploring consonants
	  ○ Hard and soft consonants (***c**ent/**c**rate, **g**ym/**g**arden*)
	  ○ Silent consonants (***w**ritten, **k**nuckle, r**h**ythm*)
	  ○ Other unique consonant patterns (*dol**ph**in, lau**gh**ter, **qu**estion*)
	• Affixes
	  ○ Prefixes (***pre**view, **mis**understood*)
	  ○ Suffixes (*grace**ful**, happi**ness***)

TABLE 6.2 Examples of Fiction and Informational Text

	Upper Elementary (Grades 3–5)	Middle School/Young Adult (Grades 6–8)
Realistic Fiction	*Diary of a Wimpy Kid* by Jeff Kinney *Because of Winn Dixie* by Kate DiCamillo *Bridge to Terabithia* by Katherine Paterson *Hatchet* by Gary Paulsen *Dyamonde Daniel* series by Nikki Grimes	*Out of My Mind* by Sharon Draper *Peak* by Roland Smith *The Secret Sky: A Novel of Forbidden Love in Afghanistan* by Atia Abawl *Thirteen Reasons Why* by John Asher *Mockingbird* by Kathryn Erskine *Esperanza Rising* by Pam Munoz *The Boy in the Black Suit* by Jason Reynolds *Crossover* by Kwame Alexander
Fantasy Fiction	*Tales of Despereaux* by Kate DiCamillo *The Lightning Thief* by Rick Riordan *The Bad Beginning* by Lemony Snicket	*Holes* by Louis Sachar *The Hunger Games* by Suzanne Collins *Harry Potter* series by J.K. Rowling
Historical Fiction	*Number the Stars* by Lois Lowry *The Watsons Go to Birmingham* by Christopher Paul Curtis *The Mighty Miss Malone* by Christopher Paul Curtis	*90 Miles from Havana* by Enrique Flores-Galbis *A Long Walk to Water* by Linda Sue Park *The Book Thief* by Markus Zusak *Walk Two Moons* by Sharon Creech *Fever 1793* by Laurie Halse Anderson *Brown Girl Dreaming* by Jacqueline Woodson *Out of the Dust* by Karen Hesse
Science Fiction	*The City of Ember* by Jeanne DuPrau *Coraline* by Neil Gaiman	*The Ear, the Eye, and the Arm* by Nancy Farmer *The House of Scorpion* by Nancy Farmer *The Giver* by Lois Lowry
Graphic Novels	*Bone* by Jeff Smith *Redwall: The Graphic Novel* by Brian Jacques *City of Light, City of Dark* by Avi	*American Born Chinese* by Gene Luen Yang *Amulet: Book One—The Stonekeeper* by Kazu Kibuishi *Anya's Ghost* by Vera Brosgol
Informational Text	*Let It Shine: Stories of Black Women Freedom Fighters* by Andrea Davis Pinkney *The Right Word: Roget and His Thesaurus* by J. F. Bryant *Hurry Freedom: African Americans in Gold Rush California* by Jerry Stanley	*Bomb: The Race to Build and Steal the Worlds' Most Dangerous Weapon* by Steve Sheinkin *Chew on This: Everything You Didn't Want to Know about Fast Food* by Eric Schlosser and Charles Wilson *Breaker Boys: How a Photograph Helped End Child Labor* by Michael Burgan

Writing

Intermediate writers become increasingly confident and fluent in their writing and are able to work on longer pieces over many days. The ability to spell the vast majority of words they need for writing allows them to focus more attention on the meaning they are trying to convey. You are likely to hear *voice* in their writing, as well as an increased awareness of their

FIGURE 6.1 Thomas's Reflection on an Essay

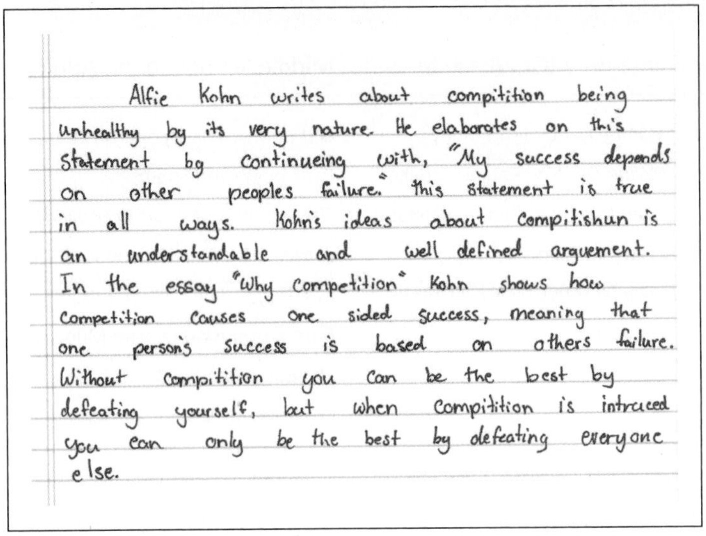

Alfie Kohn writes about compitition being unhealthy by its very nature. He elaborates on thi's statement by continueing with, "My success depends on other peoples failure." this statement is true in all ways. Kohn's ideas about Compitishun is an understandable and well defined arguement. In the essay "Why Competition" Kohn shows how Competition causes one sided success, meaning that one person's success is based on others failure. Without compitition you can be the best by defeating yourself, but when compitition is intruced you can only be the best by defeating everyone else.

Source: From *"Words Their Way for Parents: How to Support Your Childs Phonics, Spelling, and Vocabulary Development,* 1st Ed.". Copyright © 2018, by Michelle Picard.

audience. Intermediate writers are expected to revise their written work, write many different pieces of writing across genres, and edit for accuracy of spelling and punctuation.

Thomas, a middle school student, reflects on an essay written by Alfie Kohn about competition (Figure 6.1). Thomas's spelling suggests that he is in the early syllables and affixes stage. Notice that he spells *competition* as both *COMPITITION* and *COMPITISHUN.* He is clearly relying on the ineffective strategy of sounding out syllables, rather than pairing the related words *compete* and *competition*. He spells *ARGUEMENT* for *argument* and *CONTINUEING* for *continuing*. Both errors are typical early in the stage as he is uncertain when to drop the letter *e* when adding the inflected ending *–ing* or the suffix *–ment*. Thomas also demonstrates a solid command of the spelling features in the previous within word pattern stage. Single-syllable short vowel and long vowel words are spelled correctly, as are high-frequency words (*then*, *you*, *by*, *but*, *about*, *without*).

Spelling

At the intermediate stage of writing, children like Thomas are able to write with ease, having moved from invented spelling to conventional spelling. In writing, they focus on their message and revisit spelling during the editing and revision stage. Word study instruction prior to this point focused on vowel and consonant patterns in single-syllable words to build a foundation for the polysyllabic words studied here, much in the same way the basic math facts build a foundation for long division. Table 6.3 provides a summary of what students know, what they use but confuse, and what is still missing in the syllables and affixes stage.

WHAT DO CHILDREN DO OR SPELL CORRECTLY AT THIS STAGE? Children at this stage are capable spellers and have automated many components of conventional spelling (correct spelling). They recognize and use blends (***blend***, ***slip***), digraphs (***sh**ort*, ***ch**ur**ch***), and short (*pl**a**nt*, *w**i**n*) and long vowels (*l**i**k**e***, *str**ee**t*, *b**oa**t*, *t**u**b**e***, *n**igh**t*) in one-syllable words and many polysyllabic words. They automatically recognize and spell many sight words, such as *because*, *they*, and *was*.

WHAT DO CHILDREN "USE BUT CONFUSE" AT THIS STAGE? Early in this stage, your child is ready to learn or may already be using but confusing the principles of doubling when adding an inflectional ending, such as *–ing*. Children may wonder why we

TABLE 6.3 Characteristics of Syllables and Affixes Spelling

Common Spelling Errors	What Do Children Know?	What Do Children *Use But Confuse*?	What Is Absent from Children's Spelling?
SHOPING for *shopping* *ATEND* for *attend* *KEPER* for *keeper* *SELLER* for *cellar* *CONFUSSHUN* for *confusion* *PLESHURE* for *pleasure* *AMAZZING* for *amazing* *PERRAIDING* for *parading*	• Blends, digraphs, short vowels (*bl, sl, tr, th, ch, sh*) • Short vowels in CVC words (*grab, sip, lent*) • Long vowel patterns in one-syllable words (*br**ai**d, str**i**pe, fl**oa**t*) • Complex consonant units in one-syllable words (*stre**tch**, do**dge**, lu**ck***) • Spell known sight words correctly (*they, because, and, without*)	• Doubling and *e*-drop with inflectional endings (*sho**pp**ing, mo**pp**ing, amazing, having*) • Syllable juncture: open- and closed-syllable patterns (*cap/tive, bub/ble*) • Vowel patterns in accented syllables (***kee**per, par**ade***) • Vowel patterns in unaccented syllables (*bott**le**, doct**or***) • Some suffixes and prefixes (*atten**tion**, **pre**tend*)	• Few things are completely missing • Schwa vowel sound in the middle of words • More challenging prefixes • Use of word derivations to aid in spelling

double the final consonant in *mop* to *mopping*, but in *ask* do not double the *k* to spell *asking*. They explore doubling when adding inflected endings (*-ing*, *-ed*) before an examination of this principle *within* words. The study of open and closed syllables reveals when to double or not to double within words continues to be an important point (*dri**bb**le*, *di**nn**er*).

Children also use but confuse some of the vowel patterns that they know well in one-syllable words but have less experience applying in polysyllabic words. For example, children may spell *LOANSOME* for *lonesome*, *COMPEET* for *compete*, or *REFRANE* for *refrain*. Children at this stage also experiment with unaccented syllables that are difficult to hear, as in the spellings *CATTEL* for *cattle* or *JOURNEL* for *journal*. Finally, they learn to add prefixes and suffixes (***non**fiction*, ***in**complete*, ***fore**shadow*, *brav**er***, *happ**iest***, *sunn**y***) correctly when spelling words and recognize not only the influence of the spelling, but also meaning.

WHAT IS ABSENT AT THIS STAGE? At this stage of spelling development, there are few spelling patterns completely missing. Still, this stage introduces a new point in word analysis, which is the syllable. Confusions as noted above reside at the points of juncture or within the **accented** or **unaccented** syllable. Spellers at this stage are not yet using related word pairs to help with spelling trickier words. For example, if you know how to spell *confuse*, you know how to spell *confusion*; if you know *compose*, you have insight to *composition*. Children must learn to apply their previous understandings of singe-syllable words in polysyllabic words and extend their understanding of accented and unaccented syllables. It should also be noted that students become aware of when they are misspelling words and will rely on spell check or the substitution of another word for their writing.

Vocabulary

In the intermediate stage of reading and writing in the syllables and affixes stage of development, your child's reading becomes the primary source of new vocabulary. This is especially true in content areas such as science and social studies. However, learning words from context cannot be left to chance. Parents, tutors, volunteers, and teachers need to take an active role in making sure that vocabularies are growing steadily. Remember that your own enthusiasm and curiosity about words can be contagious!

TABLE 6.4 Differences between Generative and Specific Vocabulary Instruction

Generative Word Study Approach	Specific Individual Word Approach
• Focus on how spelling and meaning connect • Focus on underlying generalizations about how spelling features and word parts affect spelling, parts of speech, and overall word meanings • Focus on strategies to determine spellings and meanings of words • Knowledge of a word part provides insight to multiple words	• Focus on specific words • Recognition that there are levels of understanding (recognition, levels of familiarity, understanding of multiple meanings and connotations, and actual use) • Useful to teach words in a specific context followed by multiple exposures, uses, and experiences with the individual word • Knowledge of single word provides insight to that form and meaning of the word
Example: graph ("to write") *graph, paragraph, autograph, graphics, topography, bibliography, calligraphy, choreographer, seismograph*	Example: physics vocabulary *acceleration, force, kinetic energy, momentum, conservation, inertia, mass, gravity, speed, velocity, potential energy*

There are two different overall ways to develop vocabulary: a **generative approach** and **specific approach** (Table 6.4). Both are important. The focus of a word study approach is primarily *generative*. The study of word parts, **prefixes, suffixes, root words**, and parts allows us to learn the meaning of a part and how it influences the spelling and meaning of multiple words. For example, when we understand that the prefix *un-* means *not*, you can generate a whole new cadre of words, such as ***un****fair*, ***un****able*, ***un****afraid*, ***un****reliable*, ***un****common*, ***un****believable*, and ***un****selfish*. All mean "the opposite of" or "not," like the **base word**. If you are *unafraid*, you are *not* afraid.

A generative approach to vocabulary development and spelling encourages children and adolescents to examine how words and word parts are related by base word. For example, if you know the word *courage*, meaning "mental or moral strength," you can also learn the words *courage****ous***, ***dis****courage*, ***dis****courag****ing***, ***dis****courag****ingly***, ***en****courage****s***, ***en****courag****ing***, and ***en****courage****ment***. By understanding both the base word and how common **affixes** influence meaning, we can learn many related words and their spellings. As noted in Chapter 2, word study follows the adage, "*If you give a man a fish, he eats for a day. If you teach a man to fish, he eats for a lifetime.*" Generative vocabulary instruction is about learning a strategy to expand vocabulary for a lifetime.

The teaching of individual words, *specific* words, is also important in growing your child's vocabulary. We all consider individual meanings of words in our reading, especially those central to the topic. In a study of oceans in a middle-school science class, students need to learn specific vocabulary, such as *continental shelf*, *intertidal zone*, *drift*, *tide*, *upwelling*, *turnover*, *reef*, *plankton*, and *trench*. Vocabulary knowledge and reading comprehension are highly correlated (Cunningham & Stanovich, 1991); therefore, it is imperative that we utilize both generative and specific approaches to vocabulary development.

Understanding Polysyllabic Word Sorts

Regardless of what kind of vocabulary or spelling instruction your child receive at school, you can support him or her by establishing a word study routine at home and providing purposeful activities to support learning. Your child may bring home sorts from school, or you may want to supplement classroom instruction with word sorts and activities. Ready-to-print sorts and directions for how to use them can be found in the book *Word Sorts for Syllables and Affixes Spellers* (2016) by Johnston, Invernizzi, Bear, and Templeton. The examples of sorts described in this chapter come from this book.

In the *Let's Talk About It* section, we use one sort example to describe how to pose questions and guide purposeful conversations as you talk with your child about the sounds, patterns and meanings of words. In the *Sort Support* section, we explain what you and your child need to know about specific spelling features through key underlying principles. This gives you the tools to help your child understand the way words work in spelling and reading at this stage.

Let's Talk About It

At the beginning of the syllables and affixes stage of development, adolescents explore inflected endings, specifically the affixes *–ing* and *–ed*. When a writer or speller adds either the suffix *–ed* or *–ing*, there are three conditions that may result. First, you may "just add" the ending, as in *jump* to *jumping* or *jumped*. Second, you may drop the final *e* in words that end with this silent letter and add the ending, as in *skate* and *skating* or *skated*. Finally, you may double the final consonant in the word and add the inflected ending, as in *jog*, *jogging*, and *jogged*. The real question becomes, "Under which condition or circumstance do you apply these principles? When do you drop a silent *e*? When do you double a final consonant? When do you just add the suffix?" Let's talk about it!

Recall from earlier chapters that we always begin by modeling and guiding our children as they categorize words, in this case by the three conditions as shown in Figure 6.2. Note that the sorting is only the first step. Categorizing the words by visual patterns requires little thought; it is the discussion of *why* words work the way that they do that separates word study from other approaches. And so, we ask the essential questions outlined in Figure 6.3.

HOW ARE THE WORDS ALIKE IN EACH CATEGORY? HOW ARE THEY DIFFERENT? After sorting the words into three categories, we ask, "What is the same and what is different in each of the categories?" In the first column in the "Just Add" category, the speller has literally affixed or added the suffix *–ing*, meaning, "to be in the act of." The

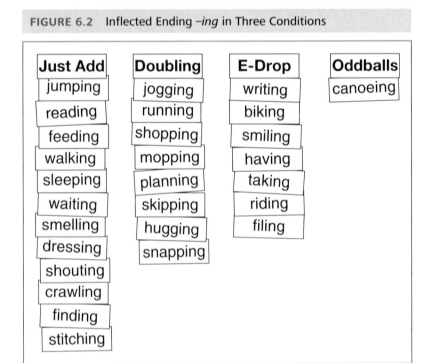

FIGURE 6.2 Inflected Ending *–ing* in Three Conditions

Just Add	Doubling	E-Drop	Oddballs
jumping	jogging	writing	canoeing
reading	running	biking	
feeding	shopping	smiling	
walking	mopping	having	
sleeping	planning	taking	
waiting	skipping	riding	
smelling	hugging	filing	
dressing	snapping		
shouting			
crawling			
finding			
stitching			

FIGURE 6.3 Let's Talk About It! Guiding Questions

Let's Talk About It! Basic Questions

1. How are the words alike in each category? How are they different?
2. Are there any words that do not fit? Why?
3. What do you learn from this sort? What are the big ideas or underlying generalizations you can learn from this sort?

base word stands alone and the suffix is affixed. Note that these words have both short and long vowels—but none of them have a CVCe pattern. In the "Doubling" (final consonant) category, each of the words includes a second final consonant added to the base when *–ing* is affixed in order to keep the short vowel sound. In the "*e*-Drop" column, the base word ends in *e*, and this vowel was dropped prior to adding the *–ing*, as in *have* to *having*. Note that all three conditions require us to examine the point of **syllable juncture**, the point at which the word has more than a single syllable.

ARE THERE ANY WORDS THAT DO NOT FIT? WHY? Note that words ending with a double letter such as *smell* and *dress* are often an initial source of confusion. Both words have a double final consonant, and children may place the words in the doubling column. Once they review the words, however, and understand that the speller did not actually *add* an additional consonant to maintain the vowel, they realize that *smell* and *dress* must be placed in either the **oddballs** category, because they look like they have been doubled, or to the "Just Add" category. Both decisions are reasonable as long as the child can explain why. In this sort the word *canoeing* is an oddball because we do not drop the final *e* when adding *-ing*.

WHAT DO YOU LEARN FROM THIS SORT? WHAT ARE THE BIG IDEAS OR UNDERLYING GENERALIZATIONS YOU CAN LEARN FROM THIS SORT? In this sort, we learn that the majority of words only require us to add the suffix *–ing* to the base word. Words that end in *e*, such as *have* or *make*, drop the final *e* before adding the suffix *– ing* with remarkable consistency. In other words, spellers must almost always drop the *e* before adding the *–ing*. There are few exceptions. *Canoeing* is one such example. Finally, this sort illustrates when to double the final consonant. Students must learn what is frequently referred to as the *1-1-1 condition*—you double the final consonant if the word meets three criteria:

- Is 1 syllable
- Contains 1 short vowel
- Has 1 final consonant

The reason a double consonant is needed is to protect or preserve the short vowel sound in the base word. So, for example, the word *mop* becomes *mopping* if you double the final consonant. If we affix *–ing* without doubling the consonant, the vowel becomes a long *o* and a completely different word of *moping*. There are several pairs to contrast to make this teaching point directly (Figure 6.4).

FIGURE 6.4 Sample Sort: Pairs to Contrast When Introducing Doubling

Single consonant	*Double consonant*
hoping	hopping
taping	tapping
pining	pinning
griping	gripping
striping	stripping
moping	mopping
waging	wagging

Sort Support: What You and Your Child Need to Know at the Syllables and Affixes Stage

The Sort Support section provides a definition, some examples, and a few spelling concepts or big ideas within each unit of study. This helps you feel confident talking about how words work with your child. We explore seven areas of spelling:

1. Polysyllabic words
2. Inflected endings
3. Open and closed syllables
4. Vowels in accented syllables
5. Vowels in unaccented syllables
6. Consonants
7. Affixes

EXPLORING POLYSYLLABIC WORDS We begin study in this stage with an exploration of basic polysyllabic words. These initial categories are types of words they have encountered in prior stages, but now with more than one syllable: *compound words*, *homophones*, and *homographs*.

Compound words. **Compound words** are created when two smaller words are joined to make a new word with a new meaning, such as *blacktop* or *shellfish*. They may also include words with more than two syllables, such as *butterfly*, *overflow*, or *understand*. You and your child should study compound words at this stage of development for two reasons: to learn that it is the meaning and spelling of both words that leads us to spell compound words correctly, and the study lays the foundation for explicit attention to syllables.

Homophones. As a reminder, **homophones** are words that sound the same, but are spelled differently and have different meanings (*boulder*, *bolder*). You and your child should revisit homophones in this stage to include polysyllabic homophones, such as *idol/idle*, *principal/principle*, and *stationary/stationery*. Keep in mind that sound does not assist us in spelling homophones; however, the frequency of a pattern and the meaning of words may help us remember the spelling.

Homographs. **Homographs** are words that are spelled alike but whose meanings and parts of speech change with a shift in accent, as in "Re**cord** your expenses" or "Keep a **rec**ord of your expenses." Accent or stress in pronunciation affects the meaning of the word, as does the context of the written passage. Also note, the stress or accent in a homograph relates to the part of speech. Homographs accented in the first syllable are typically nouns, as in, "The Gobi **Des**ert is located in Asia," whereas stress in the second syllable is typically a verb, as in, "He de**sert**ed the army and was arrested." Exceptions do exist, as with the word *minute*, which can be an adjective (Minute Man) or a noun (Wait one minute!). To study these words, sort them by adjectives and nouns, then note where the accent or stress falls. A few additional examples are represented in Table 6.5.

TABLE 6.5 Common Homographs

Homographs	Examples
***rec**ord (n), re**cord** (v)*	*It is a good idea to re**cord** your expenses so you have a **rec**ord of them.*
***con**duct (n), con**duct** (v)*	*His **con**duct was in good standing.* *The maestro con**duct**ed the orchestra.*
***sub**ject (n), sub**ject** (v)*	*In school there are a number of interesting **sub**jects.* *She sub**ject**ed herself to a two-week course boot camp for physical fitness.*
***per**mit (n), per**mit** (v)*	*He earned his drivers **per**mit.* *The teacher per**mit**ted her students to use the Internet for the assignment.*
***des**ert (n), de**sert** (v)*	*The Gobi **Des**ert is located in Asia.* *He de**sert**ed the army and was arrested.*

INFLECTED ENDINGS **Inflected endings** (*–s*, *–es*, *ed*, *–ing*, *–er*, and *–est*) are connected to a base word to indicate verb tense, number, or degree of comparison. Although inflectional endings have been used in oral language since preschool years, studying them in spelling introduces children to base words and suffixes as well as the rules that govern spelling changes. When spelling words with inflected endings, it is important to think about the spelling of the base word.

Plurals. A **plural** is a word that refers to more than one (*book/books*, *church/churches*). The most common suffix students learn to use is the plural, adding *-s* even when the sound it represents varies, as in *cats* (/s/) and *dogs* (/z/). When making a noun plural, the basic pattern is to add an *-s* at the end of the word, but there are a few conditions that vary. The inflected ending *–es* is used to form a plural when words end in *ch*, *sh*, *ss*, *s*, and *x*. Adding *–es* to a word usually adds a syllable (*dish* to *dishes*). When words end in the letter *-y*, change the *-y* to *-i* before adding *–es*, as in *baby* to *babies*, or *cherry* to *cherries*; however, if the *-y* is preceded by a vowel, the *-y* remains and an *-s* is added (*monkeys*, *turkeys*). Words that end with a final *-f* or *-fe* change to *-v* and add *-es* (*wife* to *wives*, *wolf* to *wolves*). Finally, some words take a new form when made plural (*goose* to *geese*, *mouse* to *mice*). Of course, none of these "rules" typically stick in students'

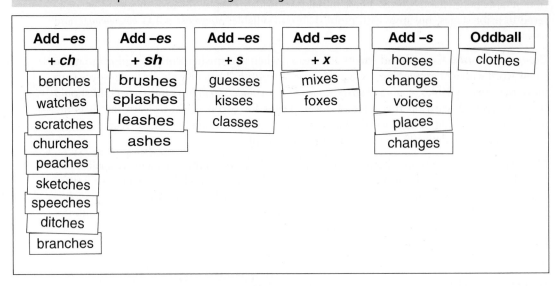

FIGURE 6.5 Sample Sort: Plural Endings: Adding *-es*

Add *-es* + *ch*	Add *-es* + *sh*	Add *-es* + *s*	Add *-es* + *x*	Add *-s*	Oddball
benches	brushes	guesses	mixes	horses	clothes
watches	splashes	kisses	foxes	changes	
scratches	leashes	classes		voices	
churches	ashes			places	
peaches				changes	
sketches					
speeches					
ditches					
branches					

minds, but through the process of comparing and contrasting words by sound, pattern, and meaning, students discover and remember these consistencies. For example, Figure 6.5 shows how the spelling of the base word is the key to knowing whether to add just *-s* or *-es* to make a word plural.

Adding –ed and –ing. As described in detail through the *Let's Talk About It* example, **inflected endings** are suffixes, which provide insight into the word's part of speech. The suffixes *–ed* and *–ing* change the tense of the base word (*jump, jumping, jumped*) but do not change the meaning or part of speech. When spelling words with *–ed* and *–ing*, there are three basic conditions, also known as the 1-1-1 principle discussed in the previous section. Finally, spellers learn to drop the *-e* when the base word ends with a silent *e* (*have/having, make/making*). There are a handful of exceptions, such as words that end with *-x* or *-w*, that never double (*taxing, showed*).

Later in this stage, your child learns that two-syllable words accented on the *second* syllable follow the same general principles as discussed earlier (*admitted, destroying, misplaced, applies*). Two-syllable words accented on the first syllable do not require doubling the final consonant when adding *–ed* or *–ing* (*cancel/canceled, trumpet/trumpeted*). Most important, consider the spelling of the base word when adding inflected endings.

Comparatives and superlatives (-er/-est). Adjectives ending in *–er* are referred to as **comparative**, whereas words ending in *–est* are referred to as **superlative**. The suffixes *–er* and *-est* function in the same way as *–ed* and *–ing*. Spellers use the *e-drop, doubling, no change,* and *change y to i* principles when adding *–er* or *–est* to a base word as in *cheaper, braver, bigger,* and *sillier.* The suffix *–er* is added to base words when comparing two things, and *–est* when the comparison involves more than two. In teaching comparatives and superlatives, it is helpful to compare and contrast categories of better and best, as shown in Figure 6.6.

FIGURE 6.6 Sample Sort: Comparatives and Superlatives

Base word	+ *er*	+ *est*
tall	taller	tallest
thin	thinner	thinnest
small	smaller	smallest
brave	braver	bravest
funny	funnier	funniest
curly	curlier	curliest
flat	flatter	flattest

OPEN AND CLOSED SYLLABLES Syllable types can be described as open or closed. It is key for children at this stage to examine open and closed syllables because many of the spelling patterns they study are focused on

TABLE 6.6 Five Open and Closed Syllable Types

Open Syllable Types A syllable that ends with a long vowel sound, spelled with a single vowel letter.		**Closed Syllable Types** A syllable with a short vowel, spelled with a single vowel letter, ending in one or more consonants.	
Label	Examples	Label	Examples
V/CV* (open)	*lazy, coma, beacon, bacon*	**VCCV*** (closed)	*skipping, button, rubber* (doublets, same letter) *chapter, window, garden* (two different consonants)
VV (open)	*create, riot, liar*	**VC/V** (closed)	*river, robin, cover, planet*
		VCCCV (closed)	*laughter, pilgrim, instant, complain*

*Most common patterns.

sound and patterns at the *syllable juncture*, or the place where two syllables come together. **Open syllables** end in a long vowel sound (***ti**/ger*, ***rea**/son*), whereas **closed syllables** have a short vowel and end with a consonant sound (***pen**cil*, ***rab**bit*). Table 6.6 describes five syllable types. Open syllables follow two patterns: VCV (***o/pen*** or ***hu/man***) or VV (*cre/ate*, *ri/ot*); the syllable is divided after the long vowel. Closed syllables follow four patterns: VCCV doublets (*slipper, million, sudden*), VCCV different consonants (***mem/ber***, ***pen/cil***, ***num/ber***), VCV (***riv/ er***, ***rob/in***), and VCCCV (***laugh/ter***, ***ath/lete***). Closed syllables that follow the VCCV pattern across the syllable are divided between the consonants, as in ***din/ner*** or ***win/ter***. When spelling words with three or more consonants at the juncture, it is helpful to remember that certain consonant blends and digraphs work together and are never divided, such as *th*, *gh*, and *dr*.

The first two syllable patterns, the open V/CV pattern and the closed VC/CV pattern, are the most frequent. The third pattern, the closed VC/V pattern, with only a single consonant at the juncture after a short vowel (*nev/er*, *pan/ic*), occurs less frequently, except in certain spelling environments; syllables ending in *v*, for example, almost never double. As your child may have learned in earlier sorts, frequency of individual word patterns can help you select the most likely pattern when trying to spell a word.

The fourth pattern, the closed VCCCV pattern, includes words that have a consonant digraph or blend at the syllable juncture (*ath/lete*, *hun/dred*). In the last pattern, the open VV pattern, each vowel contributes a sound; the word is usually divided after the first long vowel sound (*cre/ate*, *li/on*), so it is another example of an open syllable. In open syllables with two vowels, the VV pattern is divisible, as in ***po/et***, ***cre/ate***, and ***gi/ant***. It is helpful to understand how to syllabicate or to divide syllables in order to spell and read words.

VOWEL PATTERNS IN ACCENTED SYLLABLES Long vowel, *r*-controlled, and ambiguous vowel patterns are revisited in polysyllabic words at this stage. Studying vowel patterns in the accented syllable calls attention to the stressed syllable, which is where most of the information is. Almost everything your student has learned about vowel patterns in single-syllable words can be seen in the accented syllable. Figure 6.7 showcases short and long *a* patterns in multisyllabic words.

FIGURE 6.7 Sample Sort: Vowel Patterns in Accented Syllables

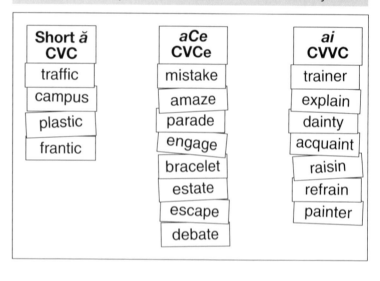

Short ă CVC	***aCe* CVCe**	***ai* CVVC**
traffic	mistake	trainer
campus	amaze	explain
plastic	parade	dainty
frantic	engage	acquaint
	bracelet	raisin
	estate	refrain
	escape	painter
	debate	

Long vowel patterns in accented syllables. In most words with two or more syllables, one syllable is emphasized, **stressed**, or **accented** more than the others. Long vowel patterns in the stressed syllable function the same way in single-syllable and polysyllabic words. The vowels remain long. Examples include *ai (rain/main**tain**), a-consonant-e (gate/mis**take**), ay (bay/cr**ay**on), igh (fight/**ligh**tning), ee (beep/**stee**ple), ea (meat, de**feat**), oa (boat/**float**ation), ow (stow/**row**boat), u-e (huge/con**clude**)*, and other common long vowel patterns.

R-influenced vowels in accented syllables. **R-influenced vowels**, vowels immediately followed by the letter *r* as in *star, bird, her, for,* and *fur,* also function in the same way in polysyllabic words, such as *garden, merchant, circle, fortuitous,* and *burden* in the stressed syllable. Words with *–ar* and *–or* are easiest to spell, because they sound so consistently like the name of the letter *R* (*star, garden, tar*) or, in the case of *–or,* like the little word *or* (*tornado, fortune*). Words with *–er, -ir,* and *–ur* are difficult, however, because they all sound alike (*bird, curd, herd*); sound is no clue at all. These words must be grouped together by the spelling pattern (*-er, -ir, -ur*) and remembered.

Ambiguous vowels in accented syllables. **Ambiguous vowels**, neither long nor short, are vowel sounds represented by a variety of different spelling patterns or vowel patterns that represent a wide range of sounds (*ou* in *cough, through,* and *could*). They function the same in the accented syllable in polysyllabic words as with *ou* as in *outlandish, ow* in *coward, au* in *caulking,* and *aw* as in *awkward.*

VOWEL PATTERNS IN UNACCENTED SYLLABLES In the **unaccented** or **unstressed syllable**, the vowel sound is often not clearly long or short, and is therefore more difficult to spell. The unclear vowel sound heard in the unstressed syllable is often represented by the **schwa** sound (the upside down *e* in a dictionary). Although sound does not provide any clues in spelling the schwa or the final unaccented syllable (*an**gle**, an**gel**, me**tal**, ci**vil**, fer**tile***), some patterns are much more frequent than others. For example, *–le* as in *angle* is more frequent than *–il* as in *civil, -el* as in *angel,* or *–al* as in *final.* Likewise, *–er* as in *swimmer* or *smaller* is more common than *–ar* as in *beggar* or *–or* as in *actor.* When unsure of spelling in the unaccented syllable, encourage your child to use his or her *best bet* based on spelling frequency and knowledge of the word's part of speech and meaning. You and your child should also note that nouns related to people usually end in *–er,* as in *dancer* and *writer,* or *–or,* as in *actor* or *editor.* Adjectives used in a comparison usually end in *–er,* as in *smaller* and *brighter,* or *–ar,* whereas descriptive adjectives as in *popular* or *similar* end in *–ar.* Table 6.7 showcases some common final unaccented syllables.

TABLE 6.7 Final Unaccented Syllables

Final Unaccented Syllable	Examples
-er, -or, -ar	*super, actor,* and *sugar*
-le, -el, -al, -il, -ile	*angle, angel, metal, civil,* and *fertile*
-en, -an, -in, -on, -ain	*sudden, human, basin, apron,* and *captain*

EXPLORING CONSONANTS There are a variety of more complicated consonant patterns explored in this stage, include hard and soft consonants, silent consonants, ending /k/ sound, and other unique consonant patterns. Students encounter these words in more mature text.

Hard and soft consonants. The letters *c* and *g* each have two different sounds, a soft sound and a hard sound. The words *circus* and *garage* illustrate both the soft and the hard sound in each word. The first *c* in *circus* is soft, as in *cycle,* and the second *c* is hard, as in *cap,* and the first *g* in *garage* is hard like *gap,* and the second *g* is soft like *budget.* The letters *c* and *g* are both soft when followed by the letters *e, i,* or *y,* as in *center, circle, cycle,* or *gentle, giant,* and *gymnast.* The letters *c* and *g* are both hard when followed by the letters *a, o,* or *u,* as in *capital, contest, custom,* or *gaping, gossip, gutter.* This general principle is true not only in the initial position, but in the final syllable; the letters *c* and *g* are soft in *notice, distance,* and *sentence* and *gadget, budget,* and *surgeon,* and hard in *traffic* and *cynic* and *fatigue* and *plague.*

Silent consonants. You and your child should simply take note of common silent letters, such as the silent *p* in *psychology, pneumonia,* and *psalm.* Many silent letters are found in families, such as the *wr-* family (*wrist, wrong,* and *wrinkle*) or the *kn-* family (*knife, knapsack,* and *knowledge*).

Other silent letters exist as a result of the words that are related to them. For example, the silent *n* in *autumn* seems unnecessary, until you connect it with the word *autumnal*, where you hear the *n*; the pairs *bomb/bombard* and *sign/signal* work the same way. This concept of **spelling–meaning connections** is discussed in more detail in Chapter 7.

Sounds of /k/ Spelled ck, ic, and x. The /k/ sound as in *kite* can be spelled by three spelling patterns when the sound comes at the end of a word: *-k* as in *shake*, *-ck* as in *shock*, and *-ic* as in *magic*. The /ks/ sound as in *relax* is spelled with an *x*. The pattern *–ck* is used when the syllable has a short vowel as in *quick* and *pickle*. Most words that end in *–ic* are two-syllable (non-compound) words in which the accent or stress is on the first syllable.

Other unique consonant patterns. Three additional digraphs include *ph* as in *phenomenal*, *gh* as in *rough*, and *qu* as in *queasy*. They are not common. The digraph *ph* represents the sound /f/ as in the beginning of the word ***ph**rase*, or in the middle of the word *al**ph**abet*. The digraph *gh* may represent the sound like /f/ at the end of words like *tou**gh*** and *enou**gh***. It may also be silent in the middle of words like *dau**gh**ter* and *tau**gh**t*. The digraph *qu* sounds like /kw/ as in ***qu**easy* and ***squ**irrel*.

AFFIXES: PREFIXES AND SUFFIXES Although prefixes and suffixes, collectively known as **affixes**, may be introduced as early as kindergarten, older children benefit from studying how these word parts influence spelling and meaning. Even young children understand that meaning of the prefix *re-* meaning *again* in words like ***re**wind*, *retie*, and ***re**write*. In this stage of development, we explore the most common affixes and how there is a spelling–meaning connection. Affixes influence the meaning of a word.

A **prefix** is a word part attached to the beginning of a **base word** or **root**, whereas a **suffix** is attached to the end of a base word or root. Both types of affixes change the meaning of a word. For example, the comparison of *active*, meaning "ready to engage in activity," to *inactive*, meaning "not active," are complete opposites. Some affixes are far more common than others; for example, *pre-*, *mis-*, *dis-*, and *un-* account for 58% of the affixed words in English. In addition to affecting meaning, suffixes also often denote the part of speech. The word *kind* is an adjective and becomes a noun with the suffix *–ness*, as in *kindness*. When spelling and reading, it is helpful to identify affixes and their meanings. A few common affixes are outlined in Tables 6.8 and 6.9. When studying these words, it is helpful to sort them by their affixes and

TABLE 6.8 Common Affixes: Prefixes

Prefixes	Meaning	Examples
in-	not	inactive, inaccurate, inefficient, inoperable, insecure
un-	un	unkind, unfair, unbelievable, unable, uncommon, unequal
dis-	apart, away	discomfort, discourage, disable, disappear, disarm, disclose
mis-	wrong, ill	mislead, misguide, misunderstood, misbehave, misconduct
re-	again	rewrite, revise, rekindle, rebound, recall, recharge, recycle
pre-	before	preview, preschool, precursor, prehistoric, precook, pregame

TABLE 6.9 Common Affixes: Suffixes

Suffixes	*Meanings*	*Examples*
-ful	full of	careful, cheerful, colorful, fearful, powerful, youthful
-ness	the state of being, having the quality of	kindness, awareness, closeness, firmness, goodness
-less	without	thoughtless, ageless, breathless, careless, painless
-ment	the means or result or an action	payment, government, agreement, replacement
-ly	having or full of	lovely, quickly, strongly, badly, barely, closely, costly

then discuss not only the meaning of the word, but also how the affix changes the meaning of the base word.

Spelling Strategies

As discussed in previous chapters, supporting your child with spelling strategies is dependent on the stage of development in which your child is performing (Dahl et al., 2003; Ehri, 1997; Williams & Lundstrom, 2007). The following strategies are recommended.

USE THE "BEST BET" STRATEGY This strategy is helpful beginning in the within word pattern stage and into the upper-level stages. The strategy is based on your child's knowledge of vowel patterns' frequency and position. As your child becomes familiar with which patterns are more common, he or she can determine the *best bet* for a specific spelling. For example, there are always more long *u* words spelled with the feature *u-consonant-e*, as in *rude*, than those spelled with the feature *ui*, as in *fruit*. This strategy may also be applied in the syllables and affixes stage—especially with long vowels in the accented syllable as they function in the same way. They should also consider what they know about syllables and word parts to determine a best bet for their spelling.

SPELL BY SYLLABLE When you encounter an unknown word, encourage your child to consider each syllable and the syllable types that make up a word. For example, accented syllables are rarely problematic, because we are familiar with the patterns in single-syllable words. The long *a* sound in *rain* is the same as in a polysyllabic word, such as *maintain*. Unaccented syllables, however, are more challenging and must be considered in terms of related words and frequency. For example, when faced with the unaccented syllable of *–le* or *–el*, as in *ramble* or *bushel*, it is helpful to know that *–le* is far more common. Isolating the syllable is a helpful strategy. It is also helpful to identify whether the spelling is in an open or a closed syllable. As you and your child have discovered, open syllables end with a long vowel sound, as in *la/zy* (V/CV) and *cre/ate* (VV), and closed syllables have a single short vowel ending in one or more consonants, as in *skip/ping* and *chap/ter* (VCCV), *riv/er* (VC/V), and *pil/grim* (VCCV). These differences aid us with spelling unfamiliar words.

USE PREFIXES, SUFFIXES, AND ROOTS (WORD PARTS) Breaking words into syllables for reading and spelling is an effective strategy. Equally valuable is identifying and breaking apart the word by known word parts or meaning units. Specifically, identify and spell prefixes, suffixes, and familiar roots. The word *predetermined*, for example, can be divided into the prefix *pre-*, base word *determine*, and suffix *–ed*. The word *antidisestablishmentarianism*, one of the longest words in the English language, is not as difficult to spell when you consider the word parts: *anti-dis-estab-lish-ment-arian-ism*. Ask, "Do you recognize the prefix?" "The suffix?" "Base word or root?" In the example *antidisestablishmentarianism*, there are actually multiple prefixes (*anti-* and *dis-*) and suffixes (*-ent* and *–ism*). Encourage your child to break the word into word parts and concentrate on each known part. This strategy is useful in the upper three stages of development.

CHECK FOR A SPELLING-MEANING CONNECTION Words are related by spelling and meaning. If you know how to spell the word *medicine*, for example, you can also spell (or least have a lead on the spelling of) the words *medicinal*, *medic*, and *medicines*. Each of the words is related to "healing" from the Latin root *medicina* and retains a similar spelling and meaning. Likewise, if you know how to spell *define*, you may also be able to spell *defines*, *defining*, *defined*, *definition*, *definitions*, *undefined*, *indefinite*, *indefinitely*, *indefinable*, *redefines*, *redefining*, and *redefined*. This is referred to as the *spelling–meaning connection* (Templeton, 2002).

ENCOURAGE STUDENTS TO TRY A WORD SEVERAL WAYS: HAVE-A-GO In school, children often learn to try spelling a word several ways and to look at which one looks right. For example, is it *SPALLING*, *SPELING*, or *spelling*? Is it *NECCESSARY*,

NECESARY, or *necessary?* This strategy is called "Have-a-go," and was originally described by Australians Parry and Hornsby (1988). This strategy is best combined with the thoughtful reflection about how words work, as noted in previous strategies, including best bet, spelling by syllable, and using affixes and roots.

USE SPELLING DICTIONARIES AND DIGITAL RESOURCES Let's be honest—few of us turn to a thick, heavy dictionary to look up the spelling of a word if other resources are more easily available, like spell check or asking the person beside you. We want our children to avoid settling for incorrect spelling or selecting simpler words based on the ease of their spelling. But the information in dictionaries can also be informative. Encourage your child to use both hardcopy and electronic dictionaries as resources not only to spell a word, but also to understand what it means and how that word evolved over time in language.

USE SPELL CHECK Some educators and parents worry that using spell check discourages children from learning to spell. There is no evidence to support this claim. If children and adolescents are using word-processing software, teach them how to use spell check but also to be aware of its shortcomings. Point out that homophone errors are not likely to be caught (*hear, here*), similarly spelled words are often skipped (*fat/fate, cut/cute*), and that unusual proper names may be incorrectly identified as misspellings. For most competent spellers, errors are often the result of poor typing skills, but it is also the case that students may not know how to spell a word. Spell check may help in either case. Explain to your child that underlined errors may be corrected right away or ignored until the editing stage.

Word Study With Parents, Tutors, and School Volunteers

In this section, we share specific examples of how you can support the development of word knowledge for children in the intermediate stage of reading and syllables and affixes stage of spelling. The routines and essential techniques discussed for this stage may be used to complement a school word study program or increase word consciousness and study outside of school.

Word Study Notebooks

At the upper stages of spelling and vocabulary development, teachers often require students to keep a word study notebook. Notebooks may include weekly word study routines (writing sorts, word hunts, and reflections), collections of prefixes, suffixes, and roots, and collections of idiomatic expressions and interesting words. If children maintain notebooks, encourage them to share their work weekly and talk about what they are learning. If not, consider starting a vocabulary notebook, which focuses on a collection of interesting types of words and word parts. Table 6.10 includes several interesting word types, word parts, and word phrases that are fun to explore and will increase your child's vocabulary.

The use of a vocabulary word study notebook also provides an opportunity for you and your child to talk about breaking words apart when he or she encounters unfamiliar words in reading, writing, or spelling. Figure 6.8 provides a useful sequence for reading or spelling challenging words.

Strategies and Activities to Develop Academic Vocabulary

At this stage of development, your child will be introduced to more and more vocabulary in specific subject areas. Therefore, we include three helpful techniques to help your child learn academic vocabulary.

TABLE 6.10 Types of Interesting Words, Word Parts, and Phrases

Type of Words	Definition	Examples
Collective Nouns	A noun that appears singular in form, but denotes a group	*batch, cluster*
Homophones	Words that sound the same, but have different spellings and meanings	*gait/gate, see/sea, pedal/peddle/petal*
Homographs	Words that are spelled identically but have different pronunciation and meanings	*record – "I have a record of the Beatles"* or *"Did you record the television show?"*
Idioms/ Idiomatic Phrases	Phrases or expressions that mean something other than a literal meaning	*"It's raining cats and dogs"* or *"She has butterflies in her stomach."*
Puns	A play on words or a joke based on words with multiple meanings	*"The weatherman who forecasted snow in July is a bit of a flake."*
Oxymorons	A play on words with contradictory terms	*jumbo shrimp* or *plastic silverware*
Prefixes	A word part attached to the beginning of a base word or root and that change the meaning of a word	*pre-, mis-, dis-, un-*
Suffixes	A word part attached to the ending of a base word or root and that indicate the part of speech.	*-ness, -ment, -ly, -ic*
Word Parts/ Roots	A Greek or Latin root that forms the base of a word	*graph* as in *graphic, photograph* *spect* as in *spectacles, spectacular,* and *inspection*

FIGURE 6.8 Breaking Words Apart

1. Examine the word for meaningful parts—base word, prefixes, or suffixes.
   - If there is a prefix or suffix, take it off so you can find the base.
   - Look at the base to see if you know it or if you can think of a related word (a word that has the same base).
   - Reassemble the word, thinking about the meaning contributed by the base, the suffix, and then the prefix. This should give you a more specific idea of what the word is.
2. Try out the meaning in the sentence; check if it makes sense in the context of the sentence and the larger context of the text that is being read.
3. If the word still does not make sense and is critical to the meaning of the overall passage, look it up in the dictionary.
4. Record the new word in the word study notebook to be reviewed over time.

FIGURE 6.9 Semantic Map about Animals

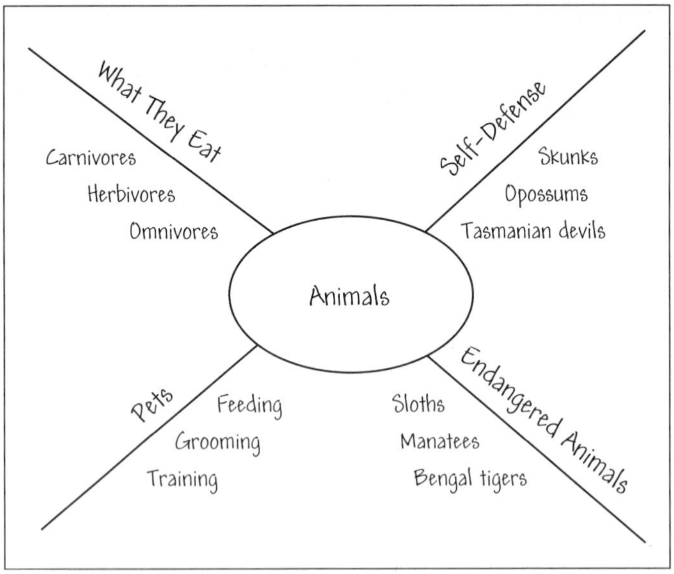

CONCEPT AND SEMANTIC MAPS A semantic map is a visual representation of a word and related words and ideas. Once you have identified a key vocabulary word, you and your child should generate a list of related terms and then organize them into categories, as is shown in Figure 6.9 around the concept of animals. As your child learns more about the concept, he or she can add words and phrases to the map in another color. Ultimately, our children can use semantic maps independently to provide structure to studying a topic.

FIGURE 6.10 Frayer Model Example: *Opinion*

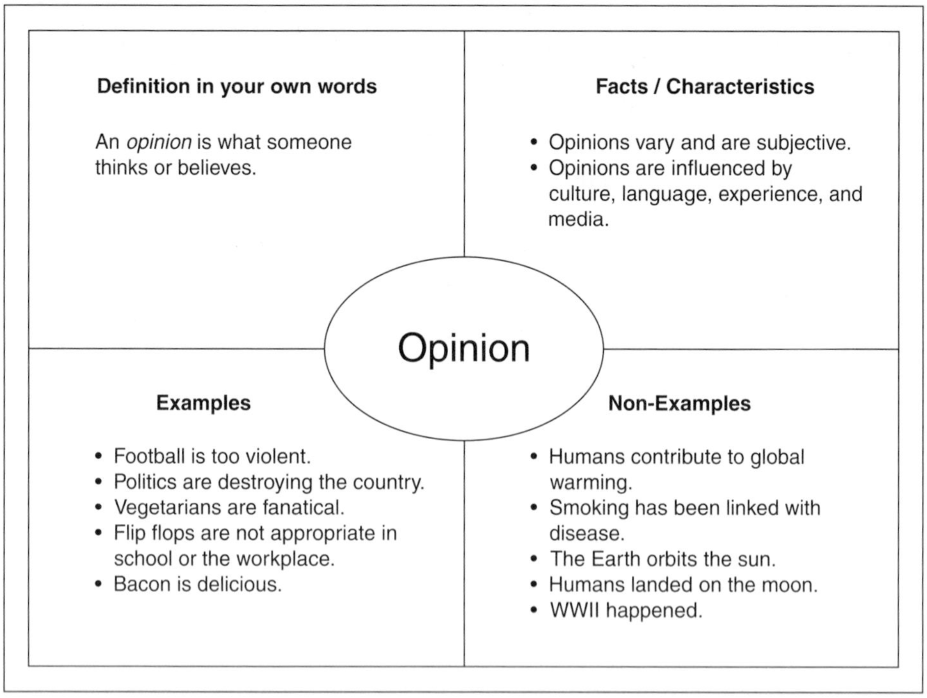
Definition in your own words
An opinion is what someone thinks or believes.
Facts / Characteristics
• Opinions vary and are subjective.
• Opinions are influenced by culture, language, experience, and media.
Opinion
Examples
• Football is too violent.
• Politics are destroying the country.
• Vegetarians are fanatical.
• Flip flops are not appropriate in school or the workplace.
• Bacon is delicious.
Non-Examples
• Humans contribute to global warming.
• Smoking has been linked with disease.
• The Earth orbits the sun.
• Humans landed on the moon.
• WWII happened.

FRAYER MODEL The Frayer model provides a graphic organizer that includes a word's definition, facts and characteristics of the word, examples and non-examples (Frayer, Frederick, & Klausmeier, 1969). It was designed to demonstrate deep understanding about a single word. See Figure 6.10 for an example using the word *opinion*.

LIST-GROUP-LABEL List-Group-Label is a straightforward vocabulary strategy. First, list all of the terms and phrases in a single unit of study or topic; often these words are boldfaced in textbooks. Next, sort this list into groups, and create a title or label for each category that reflects how the words are related. It can be helpful to create your initial list on cards or sticky notes. The act of categorizing specific vocabulary terms requires discussion and a nuanced understanding of how words are related. Finally, you and your child may need to gather additional information on specific terms that were challenging to define and sort. An example from the study of the Civil War is listed in Figure 6.11. This strategy requires thoughtful discussion and understanding of terms and their relationships to one another.

Strategies and Activities to Develop Spelling

In addition to word study supports described in Chapter 2, there are a number of games that can be played to support spelling instruction. We include three additional types of games here.

CARD GAMES Most card games can be adapted into creative spelling games. For example, *Crazy Eights*, *Solitaire*, *Rummy*, *Memory*, *Concentration*, and *Go Fish!* can all be played with the right deck of spelling cards. Create a deck of cards with the spelling features under study, and apply the same rules as one of the games mentioned here. In general, the spelling pattern is substituted for the suit in regular deck of cards. For example, if you are playing *Go Fish!* with inflected endings, one partner might ask for a "Just add *–ing*" or an "*e*-drop with *–ing*" to make a match and the game continues. Card games are great for two to four players.

FIGURE 6.11 List-Group-Label: Key Terms for the Civil War

People	Military Terms	Illness	Places	Key Events
Abraham Lincoln	battery	dysentery	North	Emancipation Proclamation
General Grant	regiment	scurvy	South	Gettysburg Address
General Lee	garrison	typhoid	plantation	Underground Railroad
Harriet Tubman	sentry		Ford's Theater	assassination at Ford's Theater
John Wilkes Booth	bayonet		Gettysburg	South secession
Yankee	cannons		Mason-Dixon line	
Confederate	musket		border states	
rebel				
abolitionist				

BOARD GAMES Board games are a common way to support spelling development in a family fun way! You can create a board game or use another game board from a commercial game for any spelling feature. Create a deck of cards with the words and specifically the spelling features under study. Figure 6.12 illustrates the Double Scoop board game. Players take turns reading the spelling words in a sentence and the second player spells the word. For

FIGURE 6.12 *Double Scoop* Board Game

FIGURE 6.13 *Apple and Bushel* Board Game

example, "The bunny was hopping down the road" requires the speller to double the letter *p* to avoid spelling *hoping*. The first player to reach the double scoop wins.

Similarly, in Figure 6.13, in the Apple and Bushel game, students draw cards (the spelling sort of the week based on *–el* and *–le* endings) and are asked to spell the word correctly. If you spell *angel*, for example, the player moves to the next space with *–el*.

PREFIX SPIN In Prefix Spin, create a spinner with multiple prefixes. Each person has a piece of paper and a pencil. Set the timer for 60 seconds and then the players generate as many words as they can in the allotted time (Figure 6.14). After sharing the list, the person with the most words acquires a point. The process repeats. If a player lands on the same prefix, the players must come up with new words in order to earn additional points and play continues. Winner has the most points from the total number of turns.

FIGURE 6.14 Prefix Spin

Supporting Reading and Writing

Reading

There are many ways to support readers and writers at each stage of development. We encourage readers to review the recommendations below as well as a few from previous stage chapters.

READ ALOUD TO YOUR CHILD Once children learn to read, we see a marked decline in reading aloud to children, both at school and by parents. As parents ourselves, we urge you not to miss out on this extraordinary opportunity to read to your child. Reading aloud creates a common experience and a bond between parents and children. Sharing read-alouds promotes empathy, language development, and an understanding of new concepts and situations.

We recommend reading a book at a reading level that is greater than the one your child experiences independently. This allows the child to hear sophisticated language and ideas and develops background knowledge and knowledge of different genres or types of text. If your child is a teenager, this admittedly becomes more of a challenge! As adolescents see their independence and autonomy as paramount, the following suggestions may help you find greater success.

LISTEN TO AUDIOBOOKS Many of us have enjoyed family car trips while listening to the audiobook versions of favorites, such as the *Harry Potter* or *The Hunger Game* series. Recently, Newberry award–winning author Kwame Alexander read aloud his own title, *Booked*. A professional voice reading a favorite text is an entertaining and educational experience. E-readers or smartphones that provide easy access to audiobooks are a wonderful way to engage children in books that appear challenging or to create a less-demanding situation to experience a text.

KEEP IT SOCIAL Reading, like so many things in our lives, is social! How many of you are more likely to exercise if someone is meeting you at the gym or for a walk? Are you more likely to read the latest novel if your book club is meeting? The same is true for your child or young adult. Keep it social. Ask your child what he or she is reading, and consider reading one of the same books. Consider hosting a book club.

With the encouragement of her mom, one of our daughters hosted a monthly book club from third to sixth grade. A book was selected, purchased, and shared. The girls gathered to talk about it with their own genuine questions and thoughts, while they also shared humor, conversation, and brownies. Similarly, author Jon Scieszka shared how he hosted a boy's night for his son's friends and dads. They played basketball, ate pizza, and talked about books. Scieszka created the website *Guys Read* to promote reading among boys and men.

The amount of time our children engage in reading is strongly correlated with vocabulary development and overall reading achievement (Cunningham & Stanovich, 1991). We want to identify time and opportunity for reading.

DISCUSS VOCABULARY Encourage your child to notice new and interesting words. If your child has a tablet computer, such as a Kindle, looking up words in a dictionary has never been easier. With the touch of a screen, your child has access to the word's meaning as well as the origin and history. Discuss new and interesting words over dinner.

SUPPORT ACADEMIC READING IN SCHOOL Children in the upper-elementary and middle-school grades are increasingly introduced to informational text, both at school and at home. Although teachers and tutors address the fundamental differences in strategies to read informational text and fiction, it is helpful to acknowledge the differences at home as well. Children benefit from direct instruction with text structure. For example, informational texts are filled with distinct text features designed to help the reader understand. Headings, bold or italicized print, photographs, graphs, illustrations, maps, charts, and diagrams are all useful tools, if you know how to use them along with the body of the text. Also, there is typically a table of contents, glossary, and index in informational text. Children benefit from direct instruction and experience with the structure of different texts.

Writing

Whereas writing at home is perhaps less intuitive than reading, it is important to support your child in writing, particularly in academic writing. Although students at this age do not readily seek out adult help with their writing, parent or tutor guidance can be very beneficial. We offer the following recommendations in addition to those discussed in earlier chapters.

ASK YOUR CHILD TO SHARE WRITING FROM SCHOOL It's important to be aware of what types of writing are being conducted at the school. Is your child writing an essay, a lab report, a narrative story, or a persuasive essay? Ask to see their writing assignments, and engage in a conversation with your child about his or her writing.

PROVIDE FEEDBACK FOR REVISION ON ORGANIZATION AND COMPOSITION One of our daughters suggested to her brother, "If you want to make the paper better and still have it be your own, ask mom. If you *just* want the paper to be better, ask Dad." Although we laughed at this comparison, it makes the important point that the goal is to make the *writer* better, not the *piece*. When you provide feedback about your child's written piece, we suggest that you consider some of the basic questions: Is the main idea clearly stated? Is it well organized? Does it make sense to the reader? Are there supporting examples and details? Also, remember that editing revisions are most helpful if they address the spelling features that the child has mastered or is using but confusing.

A BRIEF SUMMARY

In this chapter, we described characteristics typical of intermediate readers and writers in the syllables and affixes stage of development. We spent considerable time exploring the understanding of what you and your child need to know about spelling at this stage, and provided a wide variety of games, activities, and practices to promote literacy development.

In Chapter 7, we focus on children described as advanced readers and writers in the derivational relations stage of spelling development.

REFERENCES

Cunningham, A. E., & Stanovich, K. E. (1991). Tracking the unique effects of print exposure in children: Associations with vocabulary, general knowledge, and spelling. *Journal of Educational Psychology, 83*, 264–274.

Dahl, K. L., Barto, A., Bonfils, A., Carasello, M., Christopher, J., Davis, R., Erkkila, N., Glander, S., Jacobs, B., Kendra, V., Koski, L., Majeski, D., McConnell, E., Petrie, P., Siegel, D., Slaby, B., Waldbauer, J., & Williams, J. (2003). Connecting developmental word study with classroom writing: Children's descriptions of spelling strategies. *Reading Teacher, 57* (4): 310–319.

Ehri, L. C. (1997). Learning to read and learning to spell are one and the same—almost. In C. A. Perfetti, L. Rieben, & M. Fayol (Eds.). *Learning to spell: Research, theory, and practice across languages* (pp. 237–269). Mahwah, NJ: Lawrence Erlbaum Associates.

Frayer, D., Frederick, W. C., & Klausmeier, H. J. (1969). *A schema for testing the level of cognitive mastery*. Madison, WI: Wisconsin Center for Education Research.

Johnston, F., Invernizzi, M., Bear, D. R., & Templeton, S. (2004). *Word sorts for syllables and affixes spellers*. New York, NY: Pearson.

Parry, J., & Hornsby, D. (1988). *Write on: A conference approach to writing*. Portsmouth, NH: Heinemann.

Templeton, S. (2002). Effective spelling instruction in the middle grades: It's a lot more than memorization. *Voices from the Middle, 9*(3), 8–14.

Williams, C., & Lundstrom, R., (2007). Strategy instruction during word study and interactive writing activities. *The Reading Teacher, 61*(3): 204–212.

CHILDREN'S AND YOUNG ADULT LITERATURE REFERENCES

Abawl, A. (2015). *The secret sky: A novel of forbidden love in Afghanistan.* Philomel Books.
Alexander, K. (2015). *Crossover*. HMH Books for Young Readers.
Anderson, L. H. (2002). *Fever 1793.* Simon & Schuster Books for Young Readers.
Asher, J. (2011). *Thirteen reasons why*. Razorbill.
Avi. (2002). *The true confessions of Charlotte Doyle.* Scholastic.
Avi & Floca, B. (2013). *City of light, city of dark.* Graphix.
Bauer, M.D. (2012). *Little dog lost.* Atheneum Books for Young Readers.
Brosgol, V. (2014). *Anya's ghost*. Square Fish Publishing.
Bryant, J. F. (2014). *The right word: Roget and his thesaurus.* Eerdman's Publishing.
Burgan, M. (2011). *Breaker boys: How a photograph helped end child labor.* Compass Point Books.
Clements, A. (1998). *Frindle.* Atheneum Books for Young Readers.
Collins, S. (2014). *The hunger games.* Scholastic.
Creech, S. (2001). *Love that dog.* HarperCollins.
Creech, S. (2011). *Walk two moons.* HarperCollins.
Curtis, C. P. *(2000). The Watsons go to Birmingham.* Laurel Leaf.
DiCamillo, K. (2006). *Tales of Despereaux.* Candlewick.
DiCamillo, K. (2009). *Because of Winn-Dixie.* Candlewick.
Draper, S. (2012). *Out of my mind.* Atheneum Books for Young Readers.
DuPrau, J. (2004). *The city of ember*. Yearling.
Erskine, K. (2011). *Mockingbird.* Puffin.
Farmer, N. (2012). *The ear, the eye, and the arm.* Atheneum Books for Young Readers.
Farmer, N. (2014). *The house of scorpion.* Atheneum Books for Young Readers.
Flores-Galbis, E. (2012). *90 miles from Havana.* Square Fish Publishing.
Gaiman, N. (2012). *Coraline.* HarperCollins.
Gene, L. Y. (2008). *American-born Chinese*. Square Fish Publishing.
Giff, P. R. (1999). *Lilly's crossing.* Bantam Doubleday Dell.
Hesse, K. (2009). *Out of the dust.* Great Source Publishing.
Jacques, B. (2007). *Redwall: The graphic novel.* Philomel.
Kenney, J. (2007). *Diary of a wimpy kid*. Amulet Publishing.
Kibuishi, K. (2008). *Amulet: Book one—The stonekeeper.* Graphix.
Lowry, L. (2011). *Number the stars.* HMH Books for Young Readers.
Lowry, L. (2014). *The giver.* HMH Books for Young Readers.
Park, L. S. (2011). *A long walk to water.* HMH Books for Young Readers.
Paterson, K. (2004). *Bridge to Terabithia.* HarperTeen.
Paulsen, G. (2006). *Hatchet.* Simon & Schuster Books for Young Readers.
Pinkney, A. D. (2013). *Let it shine: Stories of black women freedom fighters.* HMH Books for Young Readers.
Riordan, R. (2014). *The lightning thief.* Disney-Hyperion.
Rowling, J. K. (1999). *Harry Potter* series. Scholastic.
Ryan, P. M. (2002). *Esperanza rising*. Scholastic.
Sachar, L. (2000). *Holes.* Yearling Publishing.
Schlosser, E. & Wilson, C. (2007). *Chew on this: Everything you didn't want to know about fast food.* HMH Books for Young Readers.
Sheinkin. S. (2012). *Bomb: The race to build and steal the world's most dangerous weapon*. Flash Point.
Smith, J. (2004). *Bone.* Cartoon Books.
Smith, R. (2008). *Peak.* Harcourt.
Snicket, L. (1999). *The bad beginning.* HarperCollins.
Stanley, J. (2000). *Hurry freedom: African Americans in gold rush California.* Crown Books for Young Readers.
Van Draanen, W. (2003). *Flipped.* Ember Publishing.
Wissinger, T.W. (2013). *Gone fishing: A novel in verse.* HMH Books for Young Readers.
Woodson, J. (2014*). Brown girl dreaming.* Nancy Paulsen Books.
Zusak, M. (2007). *The book thief.* Alfred A. Knopf.

chapter 7

Advanced Readers and Writers in the Derivational Relations Stage of Spelling Development

Source: Amble Design/Shutterstock

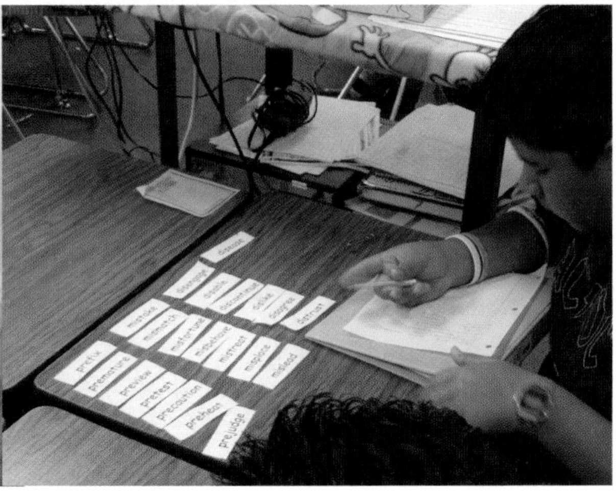

Source: Madden/Pearson Education, INC.

Have you ever watched the Scripps National Spelling Bee? Children study for years to participate in this highest-level spelling competition. Students who are very successful in spelling competitions know how to use sound, pattern, and most importantly meaning to help them spell familiar or new words. You may frequently hear the competitors asking several questions before attempting to spell the words, including "What is the definition?" "Can you use it in a sentence?" "What is the part of speech?" "What is the language of origin?" "Are there any alternate pronunciations?" Notice that these questions all revolve around word meaning. Children who excel at this competition are able to use their knowledge of word roots and derivations to help them figure out the spelling of words. Take for example *gesellschaft* (guh-zel-schahft), the winning word spelled by 2016 National Spelling Bee co-champion Nihar Janga. Although this word is unfamiliar, knowledge that this word originates in German helped Nihar with some of the difficult sounds to identify, such as the /j/ sound at the beginning spelled with *ge*, and the /sh/ spelled with *sch*, as both of these spellings are common to German words. Although most of us will never compete in this national event, all children and adults can actively use knowledge of word derivations to help them spell unknown words. This skill is the focus of the derivational relations stage.

The name *derivational relations stage* refers to the relationship between words and their origins. For example, the words *derive*, *derivative*, *derivation*, and *derivational* are all related to the Latin verb *derivare*. Students learn that we derive related words by adding prefixes and suffixes to a base word or root. Exploring words in this stage draws on extensive experiences in reading and writing, and has more to do with vocabulary development than simply spelling.

In this chapter, you will read about the common characteristics of students in reading, writing, and spelling at the derivational relations stage (Table 7.1), examine common spelling features and how to talk about them with your child, learn a series of games and activities to support word study at home or in a tutorial setting, and understand how to make spelling–meaning connections in reading and writing.

Stage Overview: Advanced Readers and Writers in the Derivational Relations Stage of Spelling

Children in the derivational relations stage are found in upper-elementary school, middle school, high school, and into adulthood. They are fairly competent spellers; however, misspellings such as *INDITEMENT, ALEGED, IRELEVANT*, and *ACCOMODATE* do occur among highly skilled and accomplished readers and writers. Exploring the logic underlying correct spellings of these words not only helps individuals learn and remember the correct spelling, but more important, leads to a deeper understanding and appreciation of spelling–meaning connections as well. This understanding and appreciation leads in turn to the growth of vocabulary.

Reading

Advanced reading is influenced by many factors including word knowledge (word recognition, decoding strategies, spelling, and vocabulary), comprehension strategies, interest, motivation, background knowledge and experience, and knowledge of the particular subject or genre. Our children are reading books that range from *Because of Winn-Dixie*, the story of a stray dog by Kate DiCamillo, to Maya Angelou's first memoir, *I Know Why the Caged Bird Sings*, which shares the hardships she faced growing up in the South during a time of segregation. *Bomb: The Race to Build and Steal the World's Most Dangerous Weapon* by Steven Sheinkin,

TABLE 7.1 Characteristics of Advanced Readers and Writers in the Derivational Relations Stage of Spelling

Reading Characteristics	• Advanced readers • Typically fifth- to twelfth-grade students • Read fiction and nonfiction texts for a variety of purposes • Focus on nonfiction texts in subject areas • Background knowledge, experience, and vocabulary significantly affect comprehension • Read with fluency and expression
Writing Characteristics	• Proficient writers • All of the preceding characteristics • Write responses that are sophisticated and critical
Spelling Characteristics	• Derivational relations spellers • Spell most words correctly • Make errors on rare words derived from Latin and Greek
Common Spelling Errors	• *SOLEM* for *solemn* • *OPISISION* for *opposition* • *COFUDENSE* for *confidence* • *CRITASIZE* for *criticize* • *CLOROFIL* for *chlorophyll* • *COMOTION* for *commotion* • *AMMUSEMENT* for *amusement* • *DOMINENCE* for *dominance*

Instructional Focus	• Affixes (prefixes and suffixes)
	• Consonant and vowel alternations
	  ○ Consonant alternations (*sof**t**/sof**t**en, crum**b**/crum**b**le*)
	  ○ Vowel alternations
	    ▪ Vowel alternations long to short (*c**a**ve/c**a**vity*)
	    ▪ Vowel alternations to schwa (*def**i**ne/def**i**nition, hab**it**/hab**it**at*)
	    ▪ Vowel alternation with change in accent when adding suffixes (*moral/morality*)
	• Predictable spelling changes in consonants and vowels (*expl**ai**n/expl**a**nation*)
	• Greek and Latin roots
	• Advanced suffixes (*-ible* vs.*-able*)
	• Assimilated or absorbed prefixes (***imm**ature, **ill**egal*)

an award-winning piece that details the race to create the atomic bomb, is one example of a nonfiction selection appropriate for this stage of development.

Table 7.2 lists texts that are typically read during this stage. These selections also illustrate the significant differences in age-appropriate content and sophistication of reading tasks. As parents and educators, it is important that we know our young adults as individuals with preferences in reading, and work to support the match between their interests and books while simultaneously expanding their world through varied texts and experiences.

TABLE 7.2 Middle and High School Reading Selections

	Middle School Grades 6–8: Young Adult	High School Grades 9–12: Young Adult
Realistic Fiction	*The Secret Sky: A Novel of Forbidden Love in Afghanistan* by Atia Abawl *Thirteen Reasons Why* by John Asher *Mockingbird* by Kathryn Erskine *Crossover* by Kwame Alexander	*The Perks of Being a Wallflower* by Chbosky *Monster* by Walter Dean Myers *Speak* by Laurie Halse Anderson *Whale Talk* by Chris Crutcher *The Fault in Our Stars* by John Green
Fantasy Fiction	*Holes* by Louis Sachar *The Hunger Games* by Suzanne Collins *Harry Potter* series by J.K. Rowling *The Maze Runner* by James Dashner *Divergent* series by Veronica Roth	*Fahrenheit 451* by Ray Bradbury *The Inheritance* series by Christopher Paolini *Daughter of the Lioness* by Tamora Pierce *Feed* by M. T. Anderson *The Hero and the Crown* series by McKinley
Historical Fiction	*90 Miles from Havana* by Flores-Galbis *Fever 1793* by Laurie Halse Anderson *Brown Girl Dreaming* by Jacqueline Woodson *Out of the Dust* by Karen Hesse	*Sold* by Patricia McCormick *The Help* by Kathyrn Stocket *Hang a Thousand Trees with Ribbons: The Story of Phyllis Wheatley* by Ann Rinaldi *The Breadwinner* by Deborah Ellis
Science Fiction	*The Ear, the Eye, and the Arm* by Nancy Farmer *The House of Scorpion* by Nancy Farmer *The Giver* by Lois Lowry	*Dune* by Frank Herbert *Life as We Know It* by Susan Beth Pfeffer *The Fifth Wave* by Rick Yancey *Cinder* by Marissa Meyer
Graphic Novels	*American-Born Chinese* by Gene Luen Yang *Anya's Ghost* by Vera Brosgol *March* by John Lewis and Andrew Aydin	*Maus I: A Survivors Tale: My Father Bleeds History* by Art Spiegleman *The Complete Persepolis* by Marjane Satrapi
Informational Text	*Bomb: The Race to Build and Steal the World's Most Dangerous Weapon* by Steve Sheinkin *Chew on This: Everything You Didn't Want to Know about Fast Food* by Eric Schlosser and Charles Wilson *Breaker Boys: How a Photograph Helped End Child Labor* by Michael Burgan	*The Devil in the White City: Murder, Magic, and Madness at the Fair That Changed America* by Erik Larson *Into the Wild* by Jon Krakauer *The Port Chicago 50: Disaster, Mutiny, and the Fight for Civil Rights* by Steve Sheinkin *Almost Astronauts: 13 Women Who Dared to Dream* by Tanya Lee Stone

An understanding of how words work in spelling, reading, and writing contributes significantly to the reading of complex text. As advanced readers explore Greek and Latin roots, they learn how the smallest units of meaning (suffixes, prefixes, and roots) are combined to generate new words. Understanding word parts is a generative process that allows readers to learn multiple words instead of just one word at a time. For example, from the Latin stem *spect*, which means "to look at," we get *inspect*, *spectator*, *speculate*, *spectacular*, *spectacles*, and so on. Linguists estimate that more than 90% of science and technology vocabulary is generated from Latin and Greek roots (Green, 2008). Students who understand the generative process are in a position to analyze and understand the academic vocabulary that they encounter in the reading materials of middle and high school. Reading materials are the primary place students encounter these words because they simply are not used in everyday conversations.

Writing

The writing of middle and high school students is highly dependent on instruction and experiences. In schools and at home, children write for a variety of academic and social purposes, including essays, research papers, journal entries, poems, short stories, lab reports, and reflections in response to films, books, conversations, speeches, and multimedia presentations. Socially, they engage in texts, tweets, blogs, and social media groups. Many teachers encourage their students to share social media reading posts, engage in online book clubs, and use blogging for research and learning. Each form of writing must be understood to write effectively in each of the contexts.

In Figure 7.1, at the direction of his middle school civics teacher, Jamal writes a letter to his senator about a current topic of interest. As you review the letter, you may notice substantive differences from the writing samples in the previous chapters with respect to organization, expression, grammar, and conventions. Jamal writes a well-organized letter with supporting statements for his point of view. With regard to spelling, most words are correct, and three words are spelled incorrectly (a corrected version was submitted for the assignment). The words *illogical*, *irresponsible*, and *accommodate* are all examples of assimilated or absorbed prefixes. For example, the word *illogical* comes from adding the prefix

FIGURE 7.1 Letter to a Senator from a Tenth-Grade Student

Dear Senator Warner,

My name is Jamal Smith and I am a tenth grader at Summer Hill High School. I am writing to you to encourage you to support the creation of a national single payer health system in the United States.

As you may or may not know, a single payer health system, a single public agency is in control of organizing care for citizens, while private organizations are still the ones to deliver service. For example, if someone were sick, a public system would provide their insurance coverage, while the doctors would have the control over keeping their patients in a healthy condition without being involved with the government themselves.

In the United States, we spend two times as much money as many other countries on our health care, but still do not have better infant mortality rates or life expectancies than countries with less expensive systems. This is **ilogical** for a country of such wealth. Much of the money that our country currently spends on healthcare is used to pay for advertising and the salaries of people who work in billing departments for insurance companies. It is **iresponsible** for so much of the money to go toward tasks that are not directly related to care and health. With a single payer system, we would get rid of private insurance companies that currently spend more time and money competing with each other than they do to take care of people who buy their healthcare insurance. Such a system would also rid us of the paperwork and expensive administrative staff needed to settle finances with healthcare companies. Are there currently any companies working towards such a plan? I would hope that such an idea would be at least considered for the United States, as our healthcare system is definitely in trouble. We need to maximize our resources and **acomodate** the needs of our citizens.

Thank you for your time and consideration of this plan for a single payer healthcare system. I can only hope that you will look at the advantages and disadvantages of this proposal. Thank you in advance for you efforts.

Sincerely,

Jamal Smith

Source: From *"Words Their Way for Parents: How to Support Your Childs Phonics, Spelling, and Vocabulary Development, 1st Ed."* by Jamal Smith. Copyright © 2018, by Michelle Picard.

in- (meaning *not*) to the base word *logical*. Try saying *in-logical* and then *illogical* to see why, over time, the last letter (*n*) of the prefix was assimilated to match the first letter of the base word for easier pronunciation. Because the first *l* is part of the prefix and the second *l* is part of the base, both *l*s must be present in the spelling. Failing to use the double letters called for in assimilated prefixes is where many advanced spellers make mistakes.

Vocabulary

Growth in the academic vocabulary students need to achieve in school subjects like science and social studies accelerates dramatically during the derivational relations stage. Their vocabulary grows through wide reading and study in specific content areas, and this leads to significant vocabulary and conceptual growth. Equally important is *generative knowledge*, the process by which meaningful word parts combine.

Spelling

Table 7.3 summarizes the characteristics of spellers in this stage. At first glance, misspellings at the derivational relations stage appear similar in type to those at the syllables and affixes stage. In contrast to the two-syllable words in which these errors occur in the syllables and affixes stage, however, derivational relations errors occur primarily in words of three or more syllables.

Spellers at this stage can usually find spelling errors in their own written work, and they can seek assistance through spell check, a dictionary, or a friend, or they might change the word to one they know how to spell. Nevertheless, unedited spelling and spelling inventories give us insight into what our children understand about spelling and word parts.

WHAT DO CHILDREN DO OR SPELL CORRECTLY AT THIS STAGE? Most words are spelled correctly, including vowel patterns in the **accented syllable** of longer words, such as the long *o* spelling patterns: *o-consonant-e as* in ***dispose***, *ow* as in ***bestow*** and ***towboat***, and *oa* as in ***roadway***. They have also mastered *doubling* and *e-drop* before adding suffixes such as *–ing* or *–er*. Knowledge of prefixes, suffixes, and roots continues to expand; the derivational relations speller may already know how to spell high-frequency suffixes such as *-ment* or *–ly*, but they are still learning the nuances in derivational relations in more complex endings, such as *-ence* or *–ance*, for example (see Table 7.3).

TABLE 7.3 Characteristics of Derivational Relations Spelling

Common Spelling Errors	What Students Do Correctly	What Students Use But Confuse	What Is Absent
SOLEM for *solemn* *OPISISION* for *opposition* *COFUDENSE* for *confidence* *CRITASIZE* for *criticize* *CLOROFIL* for *chlorophyll* *COMOTION* for *commotion* *AMMUSEMENT* for *amusement* *DOMINENCE* for *dominance*	• Spell most words correctly • Doubling and *e*-drop at syllable juncture (*shopping, mopping, amazing, having*) • Vowel patterns in accented syllables (*keeper, parade*) • Common Latin suffixes and prefixes (*pre-, bio-, -ly, -ment*) • Spelling constancy of most bases and word	• Unstressed vowels in derivationally related pairs (*confide to confident*) • Some suffixes and prefixes • Other spelling–meaning connections (*criticize/critic*) • Some Greek letter–sound relationships (*emphasize*) • Greek and Latin elements • Absorbed prefixes (*succession, illiterate*) • Advanced Latin suffixes (*dependence*)	No features are completely absent

WHAT DO CHILDREN "USE BUT CONFUSE" AT THIS STAGE? Spellers struggle with **unstressed** vowel patterns in multisyllabic words. For example, when faced with a word such as *confident*, a derivational relations speller may spell the unaccented second syllable with a *u*, as in *CONFUDENT* because that is the sound they hear. However, when taught to think about the meaning of the base word or **derivationally related** words, they come to realize that *confide*, with the long *i* sound, is used to form *confident* and *confidence;* the *i* is retained to signal its relationship in meaning despite the changes in sound. Spellers also use but confuse other spelling–meaning connections, such as the silent *n* in *solemn* (from *solemnity*) or the assimilated prefix in *opposition* (from *ob* + *position*), or other Greek and Latin elements, such as the *ch* or *ph* in *chlorophyll* (see Table 7.3).

Understanding Polysyllabic Word Sorts

Let's Talk About It!

Regardless of what kind of vocabulary or spelling instruction your child receives at school you can support them by establishing a word conscious home ready to explore spelling and vocabulary. Your child may bring home sorts from school or you may want to supplement classroom instruction with word sorts and activities. Ready to print sorts and directions for how to use them can be found in the book *Word Sorts for Derivational Relations Spellers* (Templeton, Johnston, Bear & Invernizzi, 2016). The examples of sorts described in this chapter come from their book.

In Chapter 1, we discuss a derivational relations sort that examines the difference between when we use the suffix *–ible* and the suffix *–able*. You may remember that we followed a process in which we gathered words that end in *–ible*, such as *visible*, and those that end in *–able*, such as *dependable*. After reviewing or studying the collection of words, we came to the understanding that the suffix *–able* is usually added to words with a *base word*, a word that stands alone, such as *depend* in *dependable*, whereas *–ible* is usually added to words that only have a root or word part, such as *vis* in *visible*. Our discussion followed the guiding questions outlined in Figure 7.2. Sorting the words that end in *–able* and *–ible* is merely a visual task, but in order to understand the principle at work, students must pay attention to what comes before the suffix. The work is in the discussion that occurs during and after observation and analysis. A summary of the conversational points surrounding an *–ible* and *–able* sort might be as follows:

1. The suffixes *–ible* and *–able* sound alike when added to the ends of words (*visible, dependable*), so sound is not a clue to the spelling.
2. The suffix *–able* is usually added to words with a *base word*, a word that stands alone, such as *depend* in *dependable.*
3. The suffix *–ible* is usually added to words that have a word part that usually doesn't stand alone, such as *vis* in *visible.*
4. The suffixes *–ible* and *–able* both mean "having the power or skill of something."
5. The suffix *–able* is more common than the suffix *–ible.*

FIGURE 7.2 Let's Talk About It! Guiding Questions

Let's Talk About It!

1. How are the words in each category alike?
2. Are there any oddballs or words that do not fit? Why?
3. What do you learn from this sort? What are the big ideas (or the underlying principles) to be learned in this sort?
4. How does meaning influence the spelling of these words?

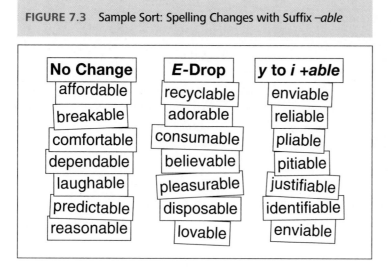

FIGURE 7.3 Sample Sort: Spelling Changes with Suffix *–able*

No Change	***E*-Drop**	***y* to *i* *+able***
affordable	recyclable	enviable
breakable	adorable	reliable
comfortable	consumable	pliable
dependable	believable	pitiable
laughable	pleasurable	justifiable
predictable	disposable	identifiable
reasonable	lovable	enviable

Exploring words that end in *–ible* and *–able* also reveals that that there are three main conditions under which a spelling change is made (Figure 7.3): *no change*, as in *dependable*; *e-drop*, as in *achievable*; and *y to I*, as in *variable*. Of course, these conditions review many of the principles learned in the syllables and affixes stage. The exploration of the suffixes *–able* and *–ible* leads to rich conversations about spelling and vocabulary.

Sort Support: What You and Your Child Need to Know at This Stage

Before we explore specific spelling features, it's important to understand that words that are related in meaning are often related in spelling as well, despite changes in sound (Chomsky, 1970; Templeton, 2004). If you are unsure of how to spell a word, considering other words that are similar in meaning and structure help you spell the related word. For example, if you know how to spell *compose*, you have a clue to spelling *composition*, even when the *o* in the second syllable changes to an **unaccented** vowel sound (*uh*). Vowel sounds often change or alternate as suffixes are added. Listen to the sound of the letter *i* as it changes in *preside* and *president*. These vowel alternations are studied during the derivational relations stage of spelling. Consonant sounds can also alternate, as in *hymn* and *hymnal*, in which the *n* is silent in the first word.

The discussion and examples in this section help you to feel confident talking with your child about how words and spelling features work (Moats, 2000; Templeton, Johnston, Bear, & Invernizzi, 2009). We explore the following:

1. Affixes (prefixes and suffixes)
2. Consonant and vowel alternations
3. Predictable spelling changes in consonants and vowels
4. Greek and Latin roots
5. Advanced suffixes
6. Assimilated prefixes

AFFIXES: PREFIXES AND SUFFIXES The spelling–meaning connection is introduced in a preliminary way in the primary grades through the introduction of prefixes such as *un-* in ***unfair*** and ***unkind***, and suffixes such as *-ly* in *lovely* and *friendly*. **Affixes** are important, because along with base words and word roots, they are the building blocks of an advanced vocabulary. Prefixes influence the spelling and meaning of words. For example, the prefix *pre-* means "before"; therefore, *prewrite* is to think and write before composing, *preview*

TABLE 7.4 Examples of Suffixes Indicating Parts of Speech

Nouns	Adjectives	Verbs
-ary (library), -ery (bravery), -ory (victory)	*-er (faster, lazier)*	*-ize (idolize)*
-ty (safety), -ity (activity)	*-est (fastest, laziest)*	*-ify (classify)*
-er (speaker), -or (creator)	*-ful (delightful)*	*-ate (decorate)*
-ian (guardian, musician)	*-less (painless)*	
-ist (artist)	*-ary (imaginary), -ory (satisfactory)*	
-ion (action)	*-ous (dangerous), -ious (furious)*	
-ence (confidence), -ance (brilliance)	*-ent (confident), -ant (brilliant)*	
-ency (emergency), -ancy	*-able (dependable), -ible (legible)*	

is to examine something before viewing it in its entirety, and *preheat* means to heat prior to cooking or baking. Suffixes, however, can also change the part of speech. For example, the verb *inspect* becomes the noun *inspector* with the addition of *–or*. Other examples may be seen in Table 7.4, where suffixes are categorized by parts of speech.

In addition to reviewing the use of common prefixes and suffixes as learned in the syllables and affixes stage, students at this stage of development explore advanced word parts, including the affixes outlined in Table 7.5. As always, you and your child should collect words, categorize them, and then analyze and discuss the words for commonalities in spelling and meaning.

Some of the affixes studied contain unique spelling patterns that must be examined closely in this stage. For example, the suffix pronounced "shun" can be spelled several ways, as in *protection*, *invasion*, and *admission*. This common suffix also causes a final consonant to change its

TABLE 7.5 Common Prefixes and Suffixes Studied at the Derivational Relations Stage

Prefixes	Meaning	Suffixes	Meaning
inter -	*between*	*-er/-or/-ian/-ist*	*people who do or believe*
intra-	*within*	*-ary/-ory/-ery*	*having to do with whatever it is affixed to*
counter-	*opposing*	*-crat/-cracy*	*rule; democracy – rule by the people*
anti-	*against*	*-ism/-ist*	*belief in; one who believes*
super -	*over, greater*	*-ity*	*quality*
ex-	*out, former*	*-al/ -ic*	*relating to, characterized by*
fore-	*before*	*-logy/-logist*	*science of; scientist*
post-	*after*	*-pathy/ -path*	*feeling emotion, suffer/disease*
pro-	*in front of*	*-phobia*	*abnormal fear*
sub-	*under*		
quadr-	*four*		
pent-	*five*		

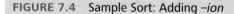

FIGURE 7.4 Sample Sort: Adding *-ion*

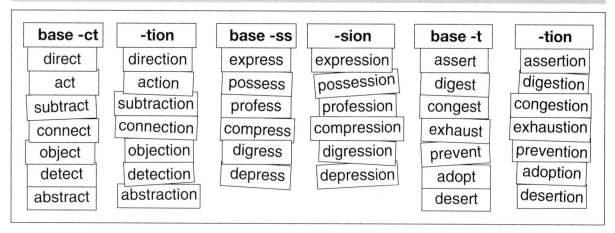

base -ct	-tion	base -ss	-sion	base -t	-tion
direct	direction	express	expression	assert	assertion
act	action	possess	possession	digest	digestion
subtract	subtraction	profess	profession	congest	congestion
connect	connection	compress	compression	exhaust	exhaustion
object	objection	digress	digression	prevent	prevention
detect	detection	depress	depression	adopt	adoption
abstract	abstraction			desert	desertion

sound; the final /t/ in *detect* changes to a /sh/ sound in *detection*. Vowel sounds can also alternate from long to short with the addition of the "shun" suffix; the vowel sound in the second syllable of *decide* changes from a long to a short vowel sound in the word *decision*. Hundreds of words in English end with this "shun" suffix, which means "act, process, or the result of an act," so a deep dive into derivationally related "shun" words pays big dividends. The generalizations that govern changes in spelling when this suffix is added are rather complex, but can be addressed early in the derivational relations stage because there are so many familiar words to examine. Children quickly discover that knowing how the base word is spelled gives a clue as to how the suffix should be spelled: *-ion*, *-tion*, *-sion*, or *-cian*. In order to spell the "shun" suffix, the ending of the base word must be considered. Like the suffix *-able* discussed earlier, it is important to pair the verb and noun forms of the words, such as *express* and *expression*. You and your child first learn that *–ion* can be directly added to the base word when ending in *–ct*, *–ss*, or *–t* (Figure 7.4), a condition referred to as "no change" or "just add" in word study.

Once you and your child have mastered the *no change* or *just add* conditions, you may explore the other conditions when adding *–ion*, as listed in Table 7.6. This exploration demonstrates that the question is really about the base word. How is the base word spelled and what letters does it end in? Although it can be overwhelming to consider the spelling changes that occur with *–ion*, remember to consider them in groups of words, as these groups are fairly predictable.

TABLE 7.6 Patterns for Adding Suffix *–ion*

Pattern with *–ion*	Examples
No change/just add *–ion*	collect/collection express/expression
Drop *–e* and add *–tion*	operate/operation seduce/seduction
Drop *–e* and add *–ion*	precise/precision immerse/immersion
Drop *–de* or *–d* and add *–sion*	explode/explosion comprehend/comprehension
Drop *–t* and add *–ssion*	admit/admission permit/permission

CONSONANT AND VOWEL ALTERNATIONS Another way to explore the spelling–meaning connection is to examine more directly how the sound of vowels and consonants change or alternate in related words. Despite these changes in sounds, the spelling often remains the same to preserve meaning. There are two types of alternations—consonants and vowels. Let's begin with consonant alternations.

Consonant alternations. Consonants that are silent in one word are sometimes "sounded" in a related word, as in the words *sign*, *signal*, and *signature*. This phenomenon is known as **consonant alternation**. A very common type of consonant alternation happens when *–ion* is added to words. Listen to how the sound of the letter *t* in *prevent* changes in *prevention*. The *t* now has the /sh/ sound. Other examples include /s/ to /sh/ in *compress* to *compression* and

TABLE 7.7 Silent Sounded Consonant Alternations

Silent	Sounded
bom**b**	bom**b**ard
colum**n**	colum**n**ist
condem**n**	condem**n**ation
de**b**t	de**b**it
resi**g**n	resi**g**nation
si**g**n	si**g**nal

/k/ to to /sh/ in *magic* to *magician*. You can see in Table 7.7 how a paired sort reveals the importance of the silent letters in the base words. This sort specifically addresses one of the reasons we have silent letters in English—that is, to signal a relationship in meaning even when the pronunciation changes.

Vowel alternations Words are related in spelling and meaning. When spelling an unknown word, it is helpful to think of a related word. Let's say your child is unsure of how to spell the word *pleasant*. Thinking about the word *please* is a big clue. Or how about the word *health*? Thinking of meaning and the base word *heal* can help you to spell *health*. Studying the vowel alternations in related words such as *cave/cavity*, *type/typical*, or *mine/mineral* helps develop the habit of thinking about spelling-meaning connections. **Vowel alternations** are a collection of word pairs in which the vowel alternates or changes with the addition of a suffix (Figure 7.5). In the pair *revise/revision*, note that the long *i* in the base word *revise* changes to a short *i* in the derived word *revision*.

Vowel alternations can be categorized into three groups: long to short, as in *cave* to *cavity*; long to **schwa**, which is a sound that is neither short nor long, as in *relate* to *relative*; or short to schwa, as in *allege* to *allegation*. Spellers in this stage may be stymied by the schwa sound if they are trying to spell purely based on sound. They must shift their attention from sound to meaning by collecting and matching word pairs and then categorizing the pairs by the nature of the vowel change: long to short (*precise/precision*), long to schwa (*admire/admiration*), or short to schwa (*metallic/metal*). The conversations about the consistent relationship between the spelling and meaning of the word pairs, no matter how the vowel sounds alternate, help your child make this shift.

PREDICTABLE SPELLING CHANGES IN CONSONANTS AND VOWELS After systematically exploring the derivational word pairs that share the same spelling, you can begin to examine related words in which both the sound and the spelling do change. Although this phenomenon seems to contradict the major principle of this stage, *words that share the same meaning often share the same spelling*, these changes are predictable and occur regularly in only a few families. The six groups of predictable spelling changes listed in Table 7.8 can be learned easily, because the exemplar pairs tend to form rhyming groups within each category. For example, within the long to short category, the words *receive/reception*, *deceive/deception*, and *conceive/conception* all rhyme and are all spelled the same way. In the long to schwa category, the spelling change

FIGURE 7.5 Sample Sort: Vowel Alternation—Long to Short

Long Vowel	Short Vowel
please	pleasant
mine	mineral
breathe	breath
revise	revision
nature	natural
cave	cavity
athlete	athletic
type	typical
crime	criminal
humane	humanity
ignite	ignition
precise	precision

TABLE 7.8 Predictable Spelling Changes in Consonants and Vowels

Shifts in Sound	Examples
Long to short	v**ai**n/v**a**nity, rec**ei**ve/rec**e**ption, ret**ai**n/ret**e**ntion
Long to schwa	expl**ai**n/expl**a**nation, excl**ai**m/excl**a**mation
/sh/ to /s/	fero**c**ious/fero**c**ity, preco**c**ious/preco**c**ity
/t/ to /sh/	permi**t**/permi**ss**ion, transmi**t**/ transmi**ss**ion
/t/ to /s/	silen**t**, silen**c**e, absen**t**/absen**c**e
/d/ to /zh/	explo**d**e/explo**s**ion, deci**d**e/deci**s**ion

of the long *a* in *explain* from *ai* to the schwa sound in the derived word *explanation*, also occurs in *exclaim/exclamation* and *proclaim/proclamation*.

GREEK AND LATIN ROOTS **Word root** is the term that is used to introduce the concept of Greek and Latin word parts. Word roots, in contrast to base words, usually cannot stand alone after all affixes have been removed, such as *chron* ("time") in *chronology* and *struct* ("build") in *restructure*. Some word roots can stand alone; most of them are Greek roots ending in vowels that have evolved as free-standing words over the years—words like *photo*, *auto*, *mono*, and the like. Regardless, the study of Greek and Latin word roots offers an incredibly rich terrain to explore and should begin in the upper elementary and middle grades and extend through high school and beyond.

The principle, *words are related in both spelling and meaning*, holds true for Greek and Latin roots as well and accounts for the generative nature of **spelling–meaning connections**. For example, the root *photo*, meaning "light," connects the following words: *photograph*, *photographs*, *photographing*, *photography*, *photographer*, *photosynthesis*, *photocell*, *photogenic*, *photocopier*, *telephoto*, and *photon*. Greek roots, such as *photo* and *graph*, may combine in different places in words—at the beginning (***photograph***), middle (***graphic***), and end (*tele**photo***). Latin roots, however, tend to stay in one place with prefixes and suffixes attached (**cred**ible, **cred**ence, in**cred**ible). After we understand these word parts and how they work, it may be helpful—as well as interesting—to point out this distinction between Greek and Latin roots. This section refers to Greek and Latin roots or elements.

We recommend that the exploration of Greek and Latin elements begin with those that occur with greatest frequency in the language and those that are most transparent in the words in which they occur. We begin with concrete, or almost obvious, meanings, such as the Greek roots *therm* (heat) as in *thermometer* and *photo* (light) as in *photograph*, and the Latin roots *spect* (to look) as in *spectacles*, *rupt* (to break, burst) as in *rupture*, and *dict* (to speak, say) as in *diction*. Finally, it is worth noting that *academic vocabulary*, words specific to fields of study in science, history, and mathematics, frequently include Greek and Latin roots, as in *geometry*, *geography*, *microbiology*, *aerodynamics*, *astrophysics*, *thermodynamics*, *monarchy*, and *democracy*. In Tables 7.9 and 7.10, note some of the most frequent Greek and Latin roots.

TABLE 7.9 Common Greek Roots

Greek Root	Meaning	Example Words
audi	sound, to hear	audio, audiologist, audible
auto	self	automobile, automotive, autobiography, automatic
bio	life	biology, biologist, biography, autobiography, biopsy, biodegradable
geo	earth	geology, geophysics, geography, geothermal, geocentric, geode
graph	to write	graph, paragraph, autograph, digraph, graphics, topography, biography
path	feeling, suffer	pathos, empathy, sympathy, antipathy, apathetic, empathize, pathogen
photo	light	photograph, photographer, photographic, photosynthesis, telephoto
tele	far	telecast, telegraph, telegram, telescope, television, telethon, teleconference

TABLE 7.10 Common Latin Roots

Latin Root	Meaning	Example words
audi	sound, to hear	audio, audiologist, audible, inaudible, audiovisual, audition, auditorium
bene	well, good	benefactor, benevolent, beneficial, benefit, benign, benefactress, benediction
dic, dict	speak	dictate, diction, dictionary, predict, verdict, benediction, contradict, dedicate
jud	judge	judge, judgment, prejudice, judiciary, judicial, adjudicate, injudicious
man(u)	hand	manual, manure, manufacture, manicure, manuscript, emancipate
port	carry	porter, portfolio, portage, portable, export, import, rapport, report, support
scrib, script	to write	scribble, script, scripture, subscribe, transcription, ascribe, describe
vid, vis	to see	video, vista, visage, visit, visual, visa, advise, audiovisual, envision, invisible

ADVANCED SUFFIXES A handful of suffixes present occasional challenges even for advanced readers and writers. One such example is the connection between the suffixes *–ant/–ance* and *–ent/–ence*. If you know how to spell one word that ends in *–ent* and *–ence* or *–ant* and *–ance*, then you can figure out how to spell the word about which you're uncertain. For example, if you are uncertain whether a spelling is *DEPENDANT* or *dependent*, but you know the word *independence*, then *independence* is your clue to the spelling of *dependent*. The suffixes *-ent* and *–ence* are related, just as the suffixes *–ant* and *–ance* are related. In addition, note that words with *–ent* and *–ant* create adjectives and *–ence* and *–ance* create nouns (Figure 7.6). At this stage, sound is no longer a helpful clue; however, making the spelling–meaning relationship explicit is extremely helpful!

FIGURE 7.6 Sample Sort: Comparing *–ent/-ence* and *–ant/-ance*

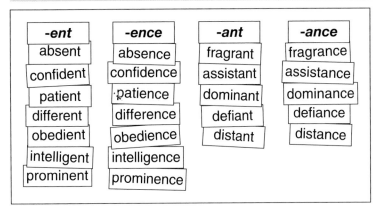

-ent	-ence	-ant	-ance
absent	absence	fragrant	fragrance
confident	confidence	assistant	assistance
patient	patience	dominant	dominance
different	difference	defiant	defiance
obedient	obedience	distant	distance
intelligent	intelligence		
prominent	prominence		

ASSIMILATED OR ABSORBED PREFIXES Prefixes are often obvious visual and meaning units that are easy to see and understand, as in *unlikely* or *inaccurate*. However, there is a group of prefixes that are somewhat disguised, as in the word *illegal*. The only clue to the prefix is the doubled letters. In an **assimilated prefix**, the sound and the spelling of the final consonant in the prefix was absorbed or assimilated into the base word. For example, the word *immobile* may have originally been *INMOBILE—in-* meaning *not* and *mobile* meaning *the ability to move freely*. Try saying *INMOBILE* three times fast! Although it's possible to pronounce *INMOBILE*, it's definitely awkward moving from the *n* to *m*. Over time, it became easier for people to leave out the *n* when pronouncing the word. The sound of the /n/ became absorbed into the /m/ sound at the beginning of the base word *mobile*. Before long, the spelling of the *n* changed to indicate the change in pronunciation—but it's important to remember that the letter didn't disappear. They knew it was necessary to keep the two letters in the prefix to indicate that it is a prefix. If the last letter of the prefix had been

TABLE 7.11 Examples of Assimilated Prefixes (*in-* and *com-*)

Assimilated from *in-*, Meaning *"not"*			Assimilated from *com-*, Meaning *"with" or "together"*		
il-	*im-*	*ir-*	*com-*	*col-*	*con-*
illiterate	immature	irrational	common	collection	conspire
illegal	immobile	irreparable	community	collide	connect
illogical	immortal	irregular	compress	collaborate	conclude
illegible	immodest	irreplaceable	compound	collapse	constellation
illicit	immigrant	irresistible	committee	collate	connote

dropped, then the making of the prefix might have been lost. Examples of assimilated prefixes can be seen in Table 7.11.

Assimilated prefixes may pose a significant spelling challenge for children because they depend on considerable prior knowledge about other basic spelling–meaning patterns, processes of adding prefixes to base words, and simple Greek and Latin roots. Most adults are unaware of this feature, but it can resolve many spelling dilemmas. The most common assimilated prefixes include *ad-* as in *adjacent* ("toward"), *com- as* in *committee* ("with"), *ex-* as in *expenditure* ("out"), *ob-* as in *obligation* ("to" or "against"), and *sub-* as in *substandard* ("under"). These prefixes often assimilate to base words and roots, resulting in doubled letters and spelling changes.

Spelling Strategies

Children and adolescents in the derivational relations stage can use a range of strategies outlined in previous chapters and included in frequently asked questions to spell unfamiliar words. At this stage, it is important that our children have moved beyond a strict reliance on sounds and that they know and apply the use of analogy, the spelling–meaning connection, consideration of the best bet, and the use of spelling resources.

Word Study With Parents, Tutors, and School Volunteers

In this section, we share specific examples of how you can support the development of word knowledge for children in the advanced stage of reading and derivational relations stage of spelling. The routines and essential techniques discussed for this stage may either complement a school word study program or increase **word consciousness** and study outside of school. Both vocabulary and spelling activities are presented.

Word Study Notebooks

Word study notebooks are an integral part of students' word learning beginning in the upper levels of word study including the within word pattern, syllables and affixes, and derivational relations stages. At the derivational relations stage, the word study notebook has shifted into more of a vocabulary notebook. If your child does not keep a word study notebook for school, you are encouraged to start one at home. Word study notebooks are used to keep a record of word sorts, *etymologies* (word histories), and collections of words such as homophones,

TABLE 7.12 Word Study Notebook Organization

Notebook Section	Description[1]
Section 1: Weekly Word Study Routines	A weekly record of sorts, reflections, and homework including words that consistently present spelling challenges
Section 2: Collections of Affixes and Roots	A collection of word parts along with their origins and meanings, as well as a list of many related words
Section 3: Collections of Interesting Words	A collection of interesting words, phrases, and vocabulary
Section 4: Content Vocabulary	A collection of terms from science, history, and other content areas

[1] For more details, see Chapters 2 and 6.

TABLE 7.13 Word Study Notebook Activities

Notebook Activity	Description[1]
Content and Semantic Maps	Brainstorm words and phrases related to a specific topic
Frayer Model	Analyze words by identifying the definition, facts and characteristics of the word, examples and non-examples
List, Group Label	Categorize words and concepts into groups

[1] For more information, see Chapter 6.

homographs, prefixes, suffixes, idioms, and content vocabulary words. A common school organization is depicted in Table 7.12. You may want to use the sections that make the most sense for you and your child. At this stage, we strongly recommend a vocabulary collection from both content knowledge–specific words and generative vocabulary word parts.

Strategies and Activities to Develop Vocabulary and Spelling

At the derivational relations stage, the work that children do in word study overlaps tightly with vocabulary work as the key focus on word and word-part meaning. Along with the basic organizational structure, many of the word study notebook activities used with syllables and affixes learners are also appropriate and engaging for learners at the derivational relations stage. The activities appropriate for both stages are described briefly in Table 7.13, and explained in more detail in Chapter 6.

WORD COLLECTION ROUTINE As children shift into the derivational relations stage, their focus on words becomes more refined with the new knowledge of word parts and word origins. A routine when collecting new and interesting words may be as follows:

- *Collect the word.* While reading, take notice of new and interesting words.
- *Record the word and a sentence.* Write the word, followed by the sentence in which it was used, the page number, and an abbreviation for the title of the book. (At times, the sentence may be too long. Write enough of it to give a clue to the meaning.) Think about the word's meaning.
- *Look at the word parts and think about their meanings.* Look at the different parts of the word—prefixes, suffixes, and base or root word. Think about the meaning of the affixes and the base or root.
- *Record related words.* Think of other words that are like this word, and write them underneath the part of the word that is similar.
- *Use the dictionary (purposefully but sparingly).* Look up the word in an online dictionary, read the various definitions, and in your own words, write the definition that best explains how the word has been used in the book you are reading. Look for other forms of the word and list them. Look at the origin of the word and add it to your notebook entry.

EXAMINE WORD ORIGINS Exploring the origins of words and the processes of word creation provides a powerful knowledge base for learning spelling and vocabulary, as well as

FIGURE 7.7 Web Resources about Words

Conduct an Internet search for the following resources:

- **American Corpus:** The Corpus of American English (Davies, 2008) is an invaluable online resource for locating related words in English. It may be used to search for the occurrence of words in different types of texts.
- **Etymology Online:** Useful for exploring word histories, this site includes accessible etymological information. The site's author, Douglas Harper, updates it on a regular basis.
- **OneLook:** A comprehensive dictionary website containing most of the major dictionaries that are available. This site also has excellent search capabilities for locating words that contain specific roots and affixes, as well as words that relate to a particular concept.
- **Real Spellers:** The educator who developed this website, Peter Bowers, shares lesson plans, lesson videos, and information about all aspects of English orthography; particularly strong are the morphological/etymological components.
- **Verbivore:** An excellent site for wordplay, containing many links to informative and engaging language and word sites.
- **Visual Thesaurus:** One of the most comprehensive interactive sites available. There is an annual subscription fee, but the benefits are more than worth the modest price.
- **Visuwords:** Similar in format to Visual Thesaurus, this site offers a more abbreviated web display. One significant feature is that, at the time of this writing, the site is free.
- **Wordsmith:** Subscribe for free and receive a new word in your inbox every day. Each week, words follow a particular theme. The categories of words discussed in this chapter—for example, eponyms and mythology—are represented.

for facilitating more effective reading and writing. **Etymology**, the study of word origins (from the Greek *etumon*, meaning "true sense of a word"), can develop into a lifelong fascination.

Another way to add interest to the study of word origins is to talk about words we have imported from other countries. A significant number of words have recently come into American English from other contemporary languages, primarily Spanish (*quesadilla, chili con carne*), but some from French (*bistro, a la carte*) and Italian (*al fresco, cappuccino*) as well. Many of these words revolve around food items, but there are many others if examined carefully with an eye to word consciousness. Over time, these "borrowed" words become so familiar that they don't strike us as foreign any longer and become a regular part of our vocabulary: *algebra* and *algorithm* from Arabic, *perfume* and *catalogue* from French, *ski* and *slalom* from Norwegian, *vigilante* and *macho* from Spanish, *karaoke* from Japanese, and *tomato* and *chocolate* from Native American languages.

FIGURE 7.8 Thinkmap for *Tranquil*

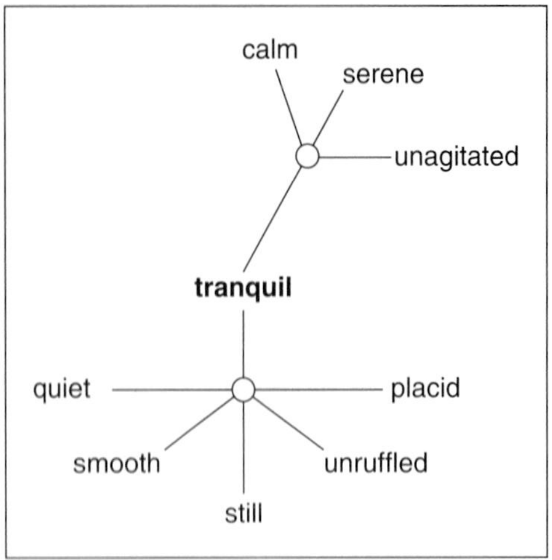

Source: From the Visual Thesaurus, http://www.visualthesaurus.com,

ONLINE RESOURCES FOR WORD STUDY The number of vocabulary- and word-themed websites seems to be increasing exponentially. Some of our favorites are listed and described under *Web Resources about Words* (Figure 7.7). One in particular, *Visual Thesaurus*, offers significant potential for students' explorations. Users type in a word, and the word is then presented in a "Thinkmap" web that displays the meaning relationships shared by the target word or concept and other terms. Clicking on any word in these web-based resources reveals definitions and examples in context, as well as a new web of relationships. Figure 7.8 shows the Thinkmap for the word *tranquil*. The group of terms above *tranquil* reveals the definition as it applies to individuals,

FIGURE 7.9 Word Tree: Words Grown from Base Words and Root Words

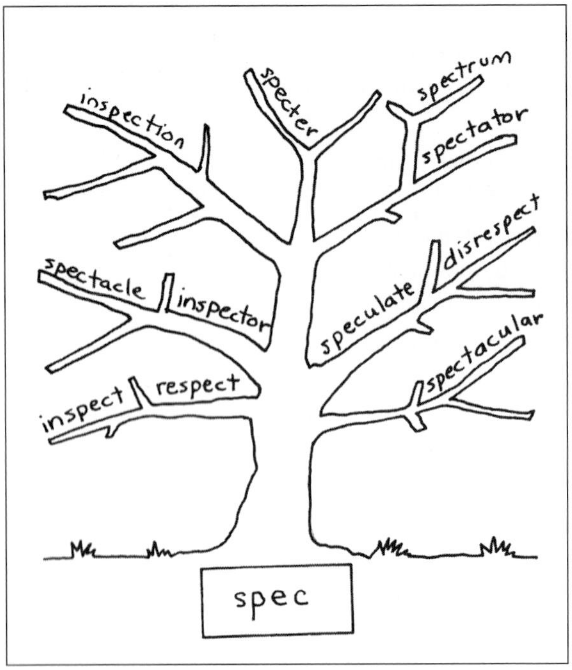

FIGURE 7.10 Growing Words: Knowing Word Parts and Meanings

Source: Copyright © Amigh Mariani. Used with the permission of Michelle Picard.

whereas the lower group describes *tranquil* in relation to a body of water. These visual representations provide children with a framework for exploring concepts in both breadth and depth.

WORD TREES In this activity, we explore how words "grow," building on and extending the understanding begun in the syllables and affixes stage of how word elements combine. You may wish to create or find an illustration of a tree. Next, decide on a base word or word root on which to focus. Your child writes the base word or word root at the bottom of the tree and thinks of as many forms of the word or related words as possible, and then writes them on the individual branches, as seen in Figure 7.9. These word trees can be kept in your child's word study notebook, on the refrigerator, or in a classroom or tutorial setting. Figures 7.10 and 7.11 illustrate two different ways to build vocabulary with a word root focus. In 7.10 each branch holds a few roots (dark green leaves) and the words related to those roots, while in 7.11 the root is the center of the flower surrounded by related vocabulary. Children genuinely enjoy watching the collection of their related words grow!

FIGURE 7.11 Word Roots and Related Words Posted in a Classroom

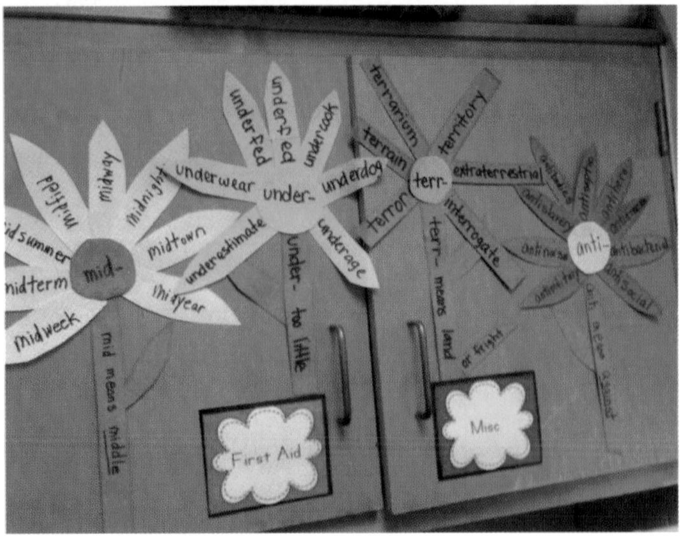

Source: Michelle Picard

BRAINBURST In Brainburst, players compete to brainstorm as many words as they can that are derived from the same root. This is a fun and challenging game to play as individuals or teams in a family. Prepare by writing different roots on cards that have a wide variety of possible derivations (*graph*, *phon*, *scope*, *aud*, *dict*, *port*, *tract*, *struct*, *spect*) and place them in a stack face down. Each player or team needs paper and pencil to record their words. Choose one root from the stack and start the timer for two to three minutes.

After the timer goes off, review the lists to check for words in common. The player or team with the most unique words is the winner. This game can also be played with common prefixes and suffixes.

WORD PART SHUFFLE Word Part Shuffle is a word-building activity. A child receives a stack of cards consisting of a majority of the most generative prefixes, suffixes, and word roots (Figure 7.12). The child then creates as many real words as possible using the word part cards.

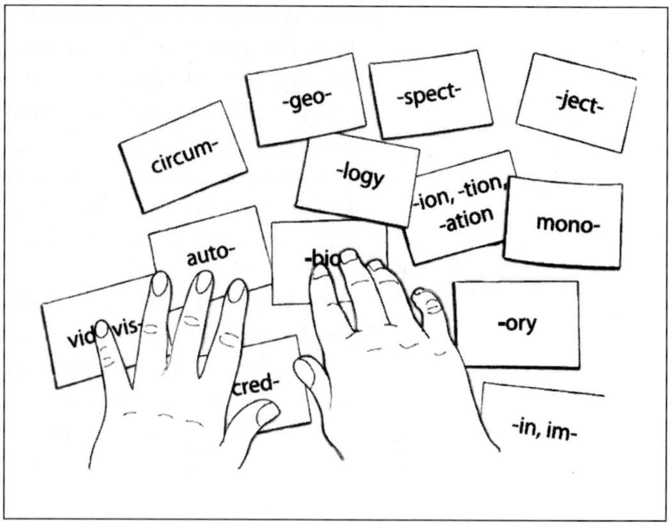

FIGURE 7.12 Word Part Shuffle Cards

VOCABULARY NOTECARDS Children and young adults select vocabulary words often from content-area subjects, such as history or science. Ask your child to prepare notecards on specific content vocabulary, including the definition, origin, and example (Figure 7.13). These can be used for studying in any content area. The more interactive vocabulary exploration is, the more memorable it is for our children and young adults.

laissez faire
/lay-zay fair/
definition: noninterference, lack of government intervention
origin: French laisser - to let + faire - to do
example: The teacher had a laissez faire attitude about chewing gum in school.

FIGURE 7.13 Notecard for *Laissez Faire*

SHADES OF MEANING Shades of Meaning requires us to think about the subtle differences between word meanings as they work with antonyms and synonyms. We begin by identifying two opposites, such as *hot/cold*, *brave/cowardly*, *old/young*, and *lazy/energetic*. Next, you and your child generate *synonyms*, words that are similar in meaning for the two opposites. Each word must then be compared to the two opposites and organized in a continuum from one word to the word opposite in meaning. For example, the words *balmy*, *frigid*, *chilly*, *boiling*, *frozen*, *tepid*, *hot*, *cool*, and *warm* could be arranged this way:

frigid frozen chilly cool tepid balmy warm hot

Encourage your child to begin with known synonyms and expand the continuum by using a thesaurus and online sites for synonyms to identify additional words. For example, *sweltering* and *steamy* could be added to our previous example. Where they are placed is a matter of opinion and is based on knowledge of the words. This game is particularly helpful in helping our children and adolescents to understand the nuances of words.

Supporting Reading and Writing

Reading

There are many ways to support readers and writers at each of the stages of development. We encourage readers to review the following recommendations as well as a few from previous chapters.

READ ALOUD AND SHARE AUDIOBOOKS Although reading aloud benefits people of all ages, we find that middle and high school age children are less amenable to being read to, specifically by their parents. Interestingly, the same does not appear to be the case for teachers, and we absolutely do recommend that teachers continue to read aloud in classrooms! We recommend that you read to your children as long as they are willing, and if they are not, we recommend that you consider listening to an audiobook together or individually. Listening to audiobooks, which are professionally produced, is a great benefit for everyone through the introduction of language, vocabulary, and content. They model fluent reading and expression, and allow us to engage in thinking and reflection followed by conversation with one another. Another benefit is that audiobooks are also available on many adolescents' digital devices with increasing accessibility. This allows books to compete with music, videos, games, and social media. Audiobooks are also valuable in introducing your child or adolescent to rich content knowledge, specifically in science and social studies.

PROMOTE LITERACY THROUGH DIGITAL DEVICES Digital devices—including computers, phones, and electronic readers—have changed the way we live and interact with the world. This is especially true of adolescents and young adults. Create easy access to books, audiobooks, and appropriate electronic media for your child to consume. The use and purchase of music skyrocketed when portable media players became affordable. Access to music required nothing more than a download. Make books, audiobooks, blogs, and electronic-literate mediums available to your young person and help them negotiate their use—or allow them to show you! Many public and school libraries have adopted electronic downloads as part of their book collections.

SHARE YOUR OWN READING AND ENGAGE IN THEIRS Another engaging way to join the reading life of your adolescent is to share your own reading. This may include news, blogs, Internet articles, magazines, and novels. Encourage your child or young adult to read some of the pieces that you find interesting, or better yet, ask your child or young adult what they are reading and read the same piece.

EXPLORE ACADEMIC READING AND VOCABULARY Children at this stage are asked to do large amounts of academic reading, usually in textbooks and articles, as well as large amounts of writing, most frequently in the form of essays or reports. You can build your child's stamina and understanding of these texts in two ways: by encouraging this type of reading at home and by increasing your child's knowledge of key academic vocabulary, by which we mean the types of words often found in textbooks across content areas, such as *analyze*, *demonstrate*, *comparison*, *differentiate*, *emphasize*, or *consistent*, as well as subject-specific vocabulary, such as government-related terms *democracy*, *oligarchy*, *monarchy*, *executive*, *judicial*, and *legislative*. Understanding these words helps comprehension of textbooks, articles, and passages across all content areas.

Writing

As discussed earlier in the chapter, types of writing increase in sophistication over the course of different ages and grade levels. There are different expectations of a young person who has reached either the middle or high school grade levels at the advanced reading and writing stage of development. Ideas presented in Chapter 6 are also appropriate to this stage of development. Specifically, continue to provide feedback for revising and editing within a writer's developmental stage, and make connections between the craft of writing and reading. Additional suggestions follow.

CELEBRATE AND SHARE WRITING Many parents save their child's writing, art samples, and artifacts from school. Although kindergarten artifacts tend to be far more common than a high school essay, we recommend as parents, tutors, and mentors that we value our teenager's writing by saving the best of it. If they have written for a literary magazine or prepared an important paper or blog post, let them know that you value it. Share writing with relatives; one of our families encouraged the teenagers to share college essays, an anniversary toast, and a passionate political post with relatives. If you are tutoring a student, be sure to build a portfolio with them to demonstrate their progress and work!

WRITE FOR AUTHENTIC AUDIENCES There are endless possibilities for young adults who want to connect with others by writing original pieces. Take some time to explore local and national opportunities. For example, Scholastic Publishing sponsors a national competition for writing and the arts. Student across the country are encouraged to submit original pieces in ten categories. Winners have their work published in an annual compendium.

EXPLORE ACADEMIC WRITING ACROSS DISCIPLINES Young adults are asked to engage in increasingly varied and sophisticated types of writing. In the middle grades, students are expected to write narration, description, expository, and persuasive pieces of writing across multiple subject areas. In high school, the expectations for critical analysis and writing to persuade, interpret, analyze, and evaluate increases and expectations rise. To support our young adults with academic and interdisciplinary writing, it is helpful to know what is assigned. Ask your child to share the writing assignment descriptions. Teachers usually provide the assignment in writing, along with either a checklist or a rubric that explains in detail the expectations for an effective piece. This is true not only in English with literacy essays, speeches, journal entries, and persuasive arguments, but also with essays in history and lab reports in science.

A BRIEF SUMMARY

In this chapter, we described characteristics typical of advanced readers and writers in the advanced stage of reading development. We spent considerable time exploring the understanding of what you and your child need to know about spelling at this stage, and provided a wide variety of games, activities, and practices to promote literacy development. In Chapter 8, we share frequently asked questions about word study and literacy development.

REFERENCES

Chomsky, C. (1970). Reading, writing, and phonology. *Harvard Educational Review, 40*(2), 287–309.

Green, T. M. (2008). *The Greek and Latin roots of English* (4th ed). Lanham, MD: Rowman & Littlefield Publishers.

Moats, L. (2000). *Speech to print: Language essentials for teachers*. Baltimore, MD: Paul H. Brookes.

Templeton, S. (2004). The vocabulary-spelling connection: Orthographic development and morphological knowledge at the intermediate grades and beyond. In J. F. Baumann & E. J. Kame'enui (Eds.), *Vocabulary instruction: Research to practice* (pp. 118–138). New York, NY: Guilford Press.

Templeton, S., Johnston, F., Bear, D. R., & Invernizzi, M. (2009). *Word sorts for derivational relations spellers*. Boston, MA: Allyn & Bacon.

REFERENCES FOR YOUNG ADULT LITERATURE

Abawl, A. (2015). *The secret sky: A novel of forbidden love in Afghanistan*. Philomel Books.

Alexander, K. (2014). *Crossover*. HMH Books for Young Readers.

Anderson, L. H. (2011) *Speak*. Square Fish.

Anderson, L. H. (2002). *Fever 1793*. Simon & Schuster Books for Young Readers.

Asher, J. (2011). *Thirteen reasons why*. Razorbill.

Burgan, M. (2011). *Breaker boys: How a photograph helped end child labor*. Compass Point Books.

Brosgol, V. (2014). *Anya's ghost*. Square Fish Publishing.

Chbosky, S. (2012). *The perks of being a wallflower*. MTV Books.

Collins, S. (2014). *The hunger games*. Scholastic.

Creech, S. (2011). *Walk two moons.* HarperCollins.
Cruther, C. (2009). *Whale talk*. Greenwillow Books.
Dashner, J. (2014). *The maze runner.* Delacorte Press.
Dean Myers. W. (2004). *Monster*. Harper Collins Publishers.
Ellis, D. (2015). *The Breadwinner*. Groundwood Books.
Erskine, K. (2011). *Mockingbird.* Puffin.
Farmer, N. (2012). *The ear, the eye, and the arm.* Atheneum Books for Young Readers.
Farmer, N. (2014). *The house of scorpion.* Atheneum Books for Young Readers.
Flores-Galbis, E. (2012). *90 miles from Havana.* Square Fish Publishing.
Gene, L. Y. (2008). *American born Chinese*. Square Fish Publishing.
Green, J. (2014). *The fault in our stars.* Penguin Books.
Haddon, M. (2004). *The Curious incident of the dog in the night-time.* Vintage Contemporaries.
Herbert, F. (1990). *Dune.* Ace.
Hesse, K. (2009). *Out of the dust.* Great Source Publishing.
Kibuishi, K. (2008). *Amulet: book one—the stonekeeper.* Graphix.
Krakauer, J. (1997). *Into the wild.* Anchor Books.
Larson, E. (2004). *The devil in the white city: Murder, magic, and madness at the fair that changed America*. Vintage.
Lewis, J., & A. Aydin. (2013). *March*. Top Shelf Publishing.
Lowry, L. (2014). *The Giver.* HMH Books for Young Readers.
McCormick, P. (2010). *Sold.* Disney Hyperion.
Meyer, M. (2013). *Cinder*. Square Fish.
Park, L. S. (2011). *A long walk to water.* HMH Books for Young Readers.
Pfeffer, S. B. (2008). *Life as we know it.* HMH Books for Young Readers
Rinaldi, A. (1996). *Hang a thousand trees with ribbons: The story of Phyllis Wheatley.* Gulliver Books.
Rowling, J. K. (1999). *Harry Potter* series. Scholastic.
Roth, V. (2014). *Divergent*. Katherine Tegen Books.
Ryan, P. M. (2002). *Esperanza rising*. Scholastic.
Sachar, L. (2000). *Holes*. Yearling Publishing.
Satrapi, M. (2007). *The complete Persepolis*. Pantheon.
Schlosser, E. & Wilson, C. (2007). *Chew on this: Everything you didn't want to know about fast food.* HMH Books for Young Readers.
Sheinkin, S. (2014). *The Port Chicago 50: Disaster, Mutiny, and the Fight for Civil Rights*. Roaring Brook Press.
Sheinkin. S. (2012). *Bomb: the race to build and steal the worlds' most dangerous weapon*. Flash Point.
Spiegleman, A. (1986). *Maus I: A survivors tale: My father bleeds history.* Pantheon.
Stone, T. L. (2009). *Almost astronauts: 13 Women who dared to dream*. Candlewick.
Stocket, K. (2011). *The help*. Berkley.
Van Draanen, W. (2003). *Flipped*. Ember Publishing.
Yancey, R. (2015). *The fifth wave*. Speak.
Woodson, J. (2014*). Brown girl dreaming.* Nancy Paulsen Books.
Zusak, M. (2007). *The book thief.* Alfred A. Knopf.

chapter 8

Frequently Asked Questions

Source: SpeedKingz/Shutterstock

Source: Wavebreakmedia/Shutterstock

Source: Amble Design/Shutterstock

Source: Bikeriderlondon/Shutterstock

Working with parents, tutors, school volunteers, teachers, and children throughout our collective careers, we offer the following frequently asked questions and responses. Although each of these concepts has been addressed in the body of *Words Their Way for Parents, Tutors, and School Volunteers*, we have found it helpful to compile and address the most common questions in one place for easy reference.

Frequently Asked Questions

1. Why is word study important?
2. Why do some people say that you shouldn't teach the names of the letters?
3. What order should we teach the alphabet letters?
4. If I allow my child to use invented or phonetic spelling, will he or she learn to spell incorrectly?
5. What if my child can sort the words correctly and gets them correct on the spelling test, but doesn't spell them correctly in writing?
6. How do I know if my child is making progress in spelling?
7. Should children progress through a stage in a single year?
8. In which stage should my child be performing to reach grade-level expectations?
9. Why don't we encourage children to just memorize the words?
10. Why don't we teach the "rules" of spelling?
11. Does word study work for English learners?
12. Does word study work for students identified with disabilities?
13. Does word study work for gifted students?
14. Will my child get tired of sorting?
15. What do I do if my child remains in the same stage and continues to get the same sorts?
16. When my child asks how to spell a word, should I tell him or her how to spell it? Should I correct his or her spelling?
17. How can I help my child when he or she does not know how to spell a word?
18. What if my child's school is not practicing developmental spelling?
19. What if my child mispronounces words? Will it affect reading and writing?
20. What should I do when my child cannot read a word?
21. How do I know if my child is reading on grade level?
22. How are reading levels described? What are the letters and numbers used to describe reading levels?
23. What affects my child's comprehension?
24. What can I do if my child is not reading on grade level?
25. Should we allow our child to be retained if he or she is not reading or writing on grade level?
26. How do I know if my child is dyslexic?

Question 1: Why Is Word Study Important?

An understanding of how written words represent sound, pattern, and meaning is critical to literacy achievement. Spelling predicts overall reading performance and is significantly correlated with word recognition and oral reading fluency (Cataldo & Ellis, 1988; Ehri & Wilce, 1987; Ellis & Cataldo, 1992; McCandliss, Beck, Sandak, & Perfetti, 2003; Zutell, 1992). Through active exploration and discussion, word study allows students to discover how sound, pattern, and meaning work in words and under which conditions. Knowledge of written words is also strongly correlated with vocabulary development and reading comprehension (Ehri & Rosenthal, 2007; Nagy, Berninger, & Abbot, 2003, 2006). Word study is designed to promote the acquisition of all these skills. In short, word study as a means to understanding how sound, pattern, and meaning work in words is important to learning to read, write, and spell.

The purpose of word study is twofold. First, word study increases the *specific* knowledge of words—the spellings and meanings of individual words. Second, students develop a *general* knowledge about how English spelling works to represent pronunciation and meaning. Through word study, students learn the regularities, patterns, and conventions of English needed to read and spell.

Question 2: Why Do Some People Say That You Shouldn't Teach the Names of the Letters?

Some reading programs teach children only the sounds of letters (such as /mmmmmmm/) and not the letter name (such as *M* or "em"). This may be the result of the fact that sounds are considered more important than the letter names or because educators think it is too confusing for children to learn both names and sounds. Both are, however, invaluable in learning to read and write.

Nearly all children learn the names of letters first from caregivers, siblings, games, television, videos, and the classic ABC song. To avoid using names feels awkward and artificial. At home and in classrooms, people need to be able to talk about letters easily and accurately, and the names make this possible.

Knowing the letter names can help children learn the sounds because most of the names include a sound associated with the letter. *B* ("bee"), *K* ("kay"), and *Z* ("zee") have their sounds at the beginnings of their names, whereas *F* ("eff"), *L* ("ell"), and *S* ("ess") have their sounds at the end. The names of vowel letters are the long sounds. Only the letters *H* ("aitch"), *W* ("doubleyou"), and the consonant *Y* ("wie") have no sound association, and not surprisingly, these letters are often the most difficult to learn. Letter names serve as the first reference point many children use when writing and explain some of the interesting invented spelling they create during the letter name–alphabetic stage. For example, students might spell *jeep* as *GEP*.

Question 3: What Order Should We Teach the Alphabet Letters and Their Sounds?

It is quite natural for children to learn the letters in their name first because they are the most personally important. Many children are interested in the letters in the names of family members and friends as well, and they provide a wide range of letters to learn. The letter names and sounds are often taught simultaneously. When a child spells his or her name with magnetic letters on the refrigerator, you may also point out the sounds that the letters make. For example, you could say, "Libby begins with /lllll/. The letter *L* makes the sound /lllll/. Can you find that letter?"

As we discuss in Chapter 3, there are many ways to learn the letter names and their corresponding sounds. Whereas learning to recognize and name the individual letters varies, the sequence for learning the letter sounds is more structured in school settings. We recommend that children first learn consonant sounds that are frequently occurring and have obvious differences, both visually and phonetically (sound and sight). Letters with similar sounds, such as /f / and /v/, are taught separately. Also, letters that are similar in formation, such as *b*, *d*, and *p*, are generally taught separately to reduce confusion.

Question 4: If I Allow My Child to Use Invented or Phonetic Spelling, Will He or She Learn to Spell Incorrectly?

The short answer is no. Children will not hold onto an incorrect spelling indefinitely. Invented or phonetic spelling is a child's approximation of what she or he knows about letters, sounds, and words. Rather than random attempts, children are using the letter names and sound associations that they are developmentally ready to understand. As children learn more about the way letters, sounds, and spelling patterns work in words, their spelling improves and moves toward conventional spelling. Parents can support this move by accepting children's best efforts and extending their knowledge by using many of the ideas and games introduced in this text.

Question 5: What If My Child Can Sort the Words Correctly and Gets Them Correct on the Spelling Test, But Doesn't Spell Them Correctly in His or Her Daily Writing?

When children write, they are also focused on generating ideas, organization, handwriting, and spelling. Children who are successful on a spelling test are completely focused on the letters, sounds, and patterns in the word—on the spelling. If these words are correct on an assessment, but not in daily writing, it is likely that their knowledge is still tentative and not automatic, which makes them vulnerable to the competing demands of writing. If they have not developed automaticity with the spelling features in their writing, they may need gentle reminders to use what they know.

If you know that your child has been successful on a spelling assessment with a specific spelling feature, point out the misspelled words in his or her daily writing and suggest that he or she take another look. In our experience as parents and teachers, the simple act of asking your child to check over the piece for spelling can be transformative. If additional support is necessary, underline words in pencil that are within your child's developmental stage and ask him or her to take a look at these specific words. In addition to drawing the connection between spelling and writing during composition, two useful instructional activities are the writing sort and the word hunt. Both activities, described in Chapter 2, make clear connections, provide practice among reading, writing, and spelling, and can be practiced at home and outside of school.

Question 6: How Do I Know If My Child Is Making Progress in Spelling?

As we discuss in Chapter 1, a child's developmental spelling stage can be assessed using a qualitative spelling inventory. This allows teachers not only to identify the student's stage of development, but also provides specific evidence of which spelling features have been mastered within each stage. Typically, schools that implement a developmental spelling program such as word study assess students at least three times a year—in the fall, midyear, and spring. This information can be shared during parent–teacher conferences and through other written communication. Consider making an appointment with your child's teacher to discuss your child's reading and spelling levels as well as their particular strengths and challenges.

Alternatively, parents can use the qualitative spelling and literacy checklist in Chapter 1 and the information learned from the stage chapters to identify the child's stage of development, and whether she or he is on par with grade-level expectations. Table 8.1 (recalled here from Chapter 1) provides a guide to typical spelling stages within a grade level and the end of year grade level expectations for that grade level.

TABLE 8.1 Spelling Stage Expectations by Grade Levels

Grade Level	Typical Spelling Stage Ranges within a Grade	End-of-Year Spelling Stage Goal
K	Emergent to Letter name–alphabetic	Middle letter name–alphabetic
1	Late emergent to Within word pattern	Early within word pattern
2	Late letter name–alphabetic to Early syllables and affixes	Late within word pattern
3	Within word pattern to Syllables and affixes	Early syllables and affixes
4	Within word pattern to Syllables and affixes	Middle syllables and affixes
5	Syllables and affixes to Derivational relations	Late syllables and affixes
6+	Syllables and affixes to Derivational relations	Derivational relations

Parents, tutors, and school volunteers can quantify growth in spelling by examining both the stage development and the acquisition of spelling feature knowledge. In other words, spellers demonstrate evidence of progressing through the five developmental stages: emergent, letter name–alphabetic, within word pattern, syllables and affixes, and derivational relations. In addition, there is a continuum of spelling feature knowledge that can be assessed to monitor progress. Table 8.2 showcases spelling features that are mastered within specific stages. The table is not exhaustive, but provides the focus for instruction at each stage. For

TABLE 8.2 Sample Spelling Features by Stage of Development

Stage of Development	Word Study Focus Spelling Feature Focus
Emergent	• Alphabet recognition (student is able to recognize all upper- and lower-case letters) • Alphabet formation (student is able to form all upper- and lower-case letters) • Letter sounds (student is able to associate at least one conventional sound with each letter)
Letter Name–Alphabetic	• Initial and final consonants, such as *b* in *boy* and *f* in *fan,* or *t* in *pet* and *m* in *gum* • Initial and final blends • Digraphs (two letters that make one sound, such as *sh*, *th*, *wh*, *ph*, *ch*, and *qu*) • Blends (two letters that blend together but keep two distinct sounds, including *l*-blends, such as *bl*, *cl*, and *fl*; *r*-blends, such as *gr*, *tr*, and *pr*; and final blends. such as *ft*, *rd*, and *st*) • Short vowel words, such as *cat*, *dog*, *lip*, and *pet*
Within Word Pattern	• Long vowel patterns, including common patterns, such as *aCe*, *ai*, *ay*, *ee*, *ea*, *e*, *iCe*, *igh*, *y*, *oCe*, *oa*, *ow*, *uCe*, *oo*, and *ew*, and uncommon patterns, such as *ei*, *ey*, *ie*, *eCe*, *i*, *o*, *ue*, and *ui*. • *R*-influenced vowels, such as *ar*, *air*, *er*, *ear*, *ir*, *ire*, *or*, *ore*, *ur*, and *ure* • Ambiguous vowels, such as *oi* in *spoil* and *oy* in *toy*; *aw* in *crawl* and *au* in *August* • Complex consonants, such as *dge* in *fudge* and *ge* in *cage*; *ch* in *church* and *tch* in *pitch*; *kn*, *wr*, *gn*, *thr*, *shr*, and *squ* • Homophones (two words with the same pronunciation, different spellings, and different meanings), such as *rain* and *reign*, *great* and *grate*, or *see* and *sea*
Syllables and Affixes	• Plurals with *–s* and *–es* endings, as in *books* and *dishes* • Unusual plurals, such as *geese* for *goose*, *knives* for *knife*, *fish* for *fish*, and *sheep* for *sheep* • Inflected endings, such as *–ing* and *–ed* • Compound words, such as *pancake*, *sidewalk*, and *bookcase* • Open and closed syllables, including open syllables, such as *o/pen* and *cre/ate*, and closed syllables, such as *slip/per*, *mem/ber*, *riv/er* and *laugh/ter*. • Vowel patterns in accented syllables • Final unaccented syllables, such as *beggar*, *barber*, *actor* • Two-syllable homophones, such as *pedal*, *petal*, and *peddle* • Homographs (two words that are spelled the same, pronounced differently, and have different meanings), such as the word *record*. "I have a Beatles **rec**ord" vs. "We need to re**cord** the song." • Simple prefixes, such as *un-* ("not"—*unlock*), *re-* ("again"—*remake*), *dis-* ("opposite"—*dismiss*) • Simple suffixes, such as *-y* ("like" or "tending toward"—*jumpy*), *-ly* ("like"—*gladly*)
Derivational Relations	• Additional study of prefixes and suffixes • Consonant and vowel alternation • Greek and Latin word elements • Advanced suffix study *-ible/-able*, *-ant/-ance*, *-ent/-ence*

additional information, please refer to the sort support section in each stage chapter or Appendix A: Sort Support. These sections are devoted to sharing what parents and their children need to understand and use at each stage of spelling development.

Question 7: Should Children Progress through a Stage in a Single Year?

Although some early stages might be mastered in a school year, others take two or more years to master, and we are all still in the last stage of spelling—derivational relations. In addition, students acquire word knowledge at different rates given different experiences with language, literacy, and instruction. Instead of using stages as benchmarks, look for progress by examining spelling features within a stage. For example, look for the mastery of beginning consonant sounds in the letter name–alphabetic stage before mastery of short vowels.

Question 8: In Which Stage Should My Child Be Performing to Reach Grade Level Expectations?

Word knowledge develops in a predictable continuum; however, students' acquisition of word knowledge varies. See Table 8.1 above for typical grade-level benchmarks for stage development.

Question 9: Why Don't We Encourage Children to Just Memorize the Words?

Rote memorization of words does not promote transfer of knowledge; transfer occurs when students can use what they have learned about the spelling of one word to spell another. Memorization alone is limiting because it assumes that words are learned one at a time, without understanding why words are spelled the way they are. In fact, to learn to read and spell the tens of thousands of words most high school graduates know, word learning must go beyond rote memory and include transfer of different sounds, patterns, and meanings or word parts to learn and use new words. This is why word sorting and reflection is central to the approach (Zutell, 1998). Rather than a rote memory perspective, word study promotes an active and reflective process. It exemplifies the proverb, "If you give a man a fish, he eats for a day. If you teach a man to fish, he eats for a lifetime."

Question 10: Why Don't We Teach the "Rules" of Spelling?

Rules are useful reminders for something we already know how to do; however, in spelling the rules are often unreliable. One often-cited researcher (Clymer, 1996) concluded that only 18 of 45 rules met his criteria of proving accurate at least 75% of the time, leading him to assert that many phonics rules were of "limited value" (Clymer, 1963, p. 255). For example, Clymer found that the rule describing two vowels together always make the sound of the first vowel to be true only 45% of the time in the words he sampled. More recently, Johnston (2001) analyzed 3,000 high-frequency words for grades three through nine and concluded that some vowel pairs are highly regular: *ay*, *oa*, *ee*, *ai*, and *ey* followed the "two vowels go walking" rule in 75% of the cases. Johnston argued that students can approximate the pronunciation of words when they can recognize vowel patterns such as CVVC, and then check themselves against the context and their own language knowledge. When children recognize vowel patterns as well as the most frequent sounds for these patterns, they can make better predictions about the pronunciation of unknown words. The ability to recite spelling rules does not ensure that students can apply them to read and spell new words. Rules are not a substitute for understanding.

Question 11: Does Word Study Work for English Learners?

Yes. Research studies have indicated that English learners develop spelling word knowledge according to the same developmental continuum as native English speakers do. Spelling errors among English learners continue to be as predictable as they are among native English speakers (Bear, Helman, Invernizzi, Templeton, & Johnston, 2007; Helman, 2004; Helman & Bear, 2007). As an example, students master consonants before vowel sounds in English. Our children's first language does, however, influence the way they learn to read and spell in English. If the child's first language has sounds that do not occur in English, or there are English sounds that are absent in their first language, more time and explicit instruction is necessary to teach those particular phonics features. For example, the sound of /sh/ as in *shell* does not exist in Spanish, so native Spanish speakers can be expected to need more time in mastering this particular phonics feature (Helman, 2004).

Question 12: Does Word Study Work for Students Identified with Disabilities?

Yes. Studies have included students with disabilities using this approach. Assessment-driven, developmentally appropriate word study instruction has been demonstrated to be effective with students with disabilities although more practice with each feature may be needed for some students (Invernizzi & Worthy, 1989; Sawyer, Lipa-Wade, Kim, Ritenour, & Knight, 1997).

Question 13: Does Word Study Work for Gifted and Other High-Achieving Students?

Yes. Developmental spelling is based on the idea of differentiating instruction for all students. High-achieving and gifted students particularly benefit from differentiated word study instruction. Because word study begins at students' instructional levels, high-achieving students don't have to experience lessons addressing concepts and features they have already mastered. At the more advanced levels, word study emphasizes Greek and Latin roots and their relationship to vocabulary instruction, as well as word histories, all of which can be fascinating for high-achieving learners.

Question 14: Will My Child Get Tired of Sorting?

As parents and educators, we have found that students do not tire of sorting—when the sort is at an appropriate level and is integrated with a wide variety of fun and purposeful word-learning activities. Sorting is designed primarily to be a thoughtful and reflective process in which students categorize words by spelling features and then come up with generalizations that support their thinking about words. For example, after sorting and sharing observations about the spelling features common to all words within a category, a student may discover that spellers use *–dge*, as in *fudge* and *ridge*, with words that are a single syllable and contain a short vowel, whereas *–ge* is more commonly used in words that do not have a short vowel sound such as *rage*, *gauge*, and *large*. Second, the sorting process is designed to develop *automaticity*. Students are encouraged to categorize words multiple times until they can do so effortlessly and discuss the logic behind their categories. Sorting does not become boring if it is coupled with the challenge of reflecting on the sort's use—what can be learned from the sort.

Question 15: What Do I Do If My Child Continues to Get the Same Sorts?

Although it is common for children to remain in a stage for more than a single year, they should not be working with the same sorts over and over. First, there are multiple resources in which parents, tutors, school volunteers, and teachers can find ready-made appropriate sorts focused on areas that children are using but confusing. We have mentioned several supplemental sorts in this text, and there are others. Teachers and parents may also elect to create new sorts using words from children's reading, as each of the authors of this book did during our own teaching days.

This is particularly important for older children, who are sometimes self-conscious of working with single-syllable words either in the letter name-alphabetic or within word pattern stages. For example, as a middle-school teacher, one of the authors created polysyllabic word sorts to teach long vowels to demonstrate to her students that they could learn long and ambiguous vowels in with longer words, and that their reading, writing, and spelling were linked. They need not repeat previous sorts. Finally, if children are not making progress, we recommend that you look at the quality and intensity of the program. Is there a weekly routine? Is the child provided with explicit instruction at least three times a week? Does your child engage in other activities, such as speed sorting, writing sorts, and word hunts? Are there discussions about the underlying generalizations based on the sorts? Sorting is one vehicle for reflection and study. To make progress, children need a comprehensive program that connects with reading and writing.

Question 16: When My Child Asks How to Spell a Word, Should I Tell How to Spell It? Should I Correct My Child's Spelling?

It is important to encourage children to use what they know when spelling and writing. If parents or teachers consistently provide the correct spelling before the child has used what he or she knows, they may become reluctant writers and spellers valuing correctness over the importance of conveying their own ideas. Rather than providing the spelling immediately, encourage your child to consider what they already know and give it a try. The next frequently asked question and response provide more detail on how to assist with stage-specific spelling support

With regard to editing written pieces—and specifically to correcting spelling—we do not recommend that parents, tutors, or volunteers correct all misspelled words. It is counterproductive to ask children to correct spellings that are beyond their developmental levels. Rather, we encourage you to ask your children to use the spelling patterns correctly that they have already learned. The one exception may be for a final published copy of a child's writing in school, in which case the teacher may provide corrections for all students.

Question 17: How Can I Help My Child When They Do Not Know How to Spell a Word?

Parents and teachers can help children learn to use different strategies to spell unknown or familiar words whose spellings have not been mastered. Some strategies are, however, more useful than others, depending on the stage of development in which your child is performing (Dahl, Barto, Bonfils, et al., 2003; Williams & Lundstrom, 2007). Emergent and letter name–alphabetic spellers, for example, are highly dependent on sound and letter–sound correspondences. Invented spelling or the sound-it-out strategy are perfectly appropriate at this stage. Within word pattern spellers, in contrast, are more likely to consider and use spelling patterns and the best bet strategy. Children at this stage consider the spelling patterns of words they already know how to spell, and consider how that feature may be generalized to other, less-familiar words. For example, a child may know how to spell the word *right*, and be able to generalize the *-igh* pattern to the spelling of *fight*, *might*, *light*, *flight*, and *bright*.

Although many students make these shifts naturally, there is practical evidence that explicit instruction in spelling strategy benefits all children and young adults. Following are strategies parents can use to help their children spell unknown or familiar words whose spellings can be elusive. Strategies are listed from the earliest stage use to the most advanced.

USE INVENTED SPELLING As discussed previously, *invented spelling* is when students use their best judgment to spell unknown words, spelling using the letters, sounds, and patterns that a child has already learned. Invented spelling does not mean that the child randomly guesses at how to spell words, but rather applies what he or she has already learned to spell with reasonable approximations. Encouraging children to use invented spelling in their daily writing for unknown words complements the developmental idea that students should be taught on their individual instructional level, not too easy and not too hard. The same should apply for the spelling in their daily writing.

SOUND-IT-OUT Once a child has identified a word to spell, parents can teach young children to stretch out and isolate the sounds in the word. Ask, "What's the first sound you hear?" The child repeats the initial sound, identifies the letter, and writes it. Repeat the process until the child has recorded only the sounds that he or she hears. This strategy is most appropriate for young readers and writers in the emergent and letter name-alphabetic stages.

KNOW IT IN A SNAP There are some words that simply cannot be spelled through the use of sound or analogy. High-frequency words fall into two categories—those that can be identified phonetically, such as *but, both, can, if, with, be, me, did, into, that,* and *yes*, whereas others must be learned through pure memory and experience, such as *saw, said, there, are, your,* and *their*. It can be helpful to explain that many words are *decodable*, meaning that they can be divided into sounds, whereas others need to be known in a snap. You may also need to combine this strategy with the sound-it-out. For example, if your child wants to spell the word *come*, you can can ask which two sounds are heard—the *c* and the *m*. Then provide the other letters. It is helpful for children to know that while identifying sounds and chunks are valuable strategies, there are some words that depend on memory.

CHUNK KNOWN WORD PARTS Your child may know how to spell part of a word and be unsure of other parts. Encourage him or her to "spell the parts you know." For example, your child may know the beginning letter combinations such as *sh-, th-, ch-*, or *bl-*, or the end of a rhyming family, such as *–og, -ip*, or *-at*. We teach children to look for the parts of words that are known and then to concentrate on the unknown portion. This is appropriate for children in the middle of letter name–alphabetic stage of spelling and through the upper levels.

USE ANALOGY *Analogy* is the use of rhyming words to determine the spelling of an unfamiliar word. Encourage your child to think of a word that is already known and consider the spelling for the rhyming word. For example, if we know how to spell the word *hop*, we can spell other words that rhyme by changing the beginning sound or blend. Spelling *hop* correctly leads us to spell the words *top, shop, chop, mop*, and *stop*, or if we can spell the word *night*, we can also spell the words *might, right, fight*, and *slight*. Of course, not all rhyming words have the same patterns. For example, the word *spite* also rhymes with *night*.

USE THE BEST BET STRATEGY While studying vowel patterns, children may notice that one pattern often has more examples than another. Encourage your child to think about the most common pattern that they know first, and then to consider what is their "best bet." For example, if your child wants to spell the word *splay*, as in "A butterfly splayed its wings before taking flight," prompt your child to consider, "What patterns do I know to spell long *a*? Which pattern is the most common at the end of a word?" Next, they may recognize that *ay* is the only common pattern at the end of a word or a syllable. So, the best bet is to use *ay* for *splay*. The best bet strategy demonstrates a shift from relying predominantly on the sounds of the language to the many patterns that are used in words. It is important for your child to shift thinking to include pattern.

ENCOURAGE STUDENTS TO TRY A WORD SEVERAL WAYS: HAVE-A-GO In school, children often learn to try spelling a word several ways and to look at which one looks right. For example, is it *SPALLING, SPELING*, or *spelling*? Is it *NECCESSARY,*

NECESARY, or *necesary*? This strategy is called "Have-a-Go" and was originally described by Australians Parry and Hornsby (1988). This strategy is best combined with the thoughtful reflection about how words work, as noted in previous strategies, including best bet and using affixes and roots.

SPELL BY SYLLABLE When considering an unknown word, in this stage of development, encourage your child to consider each syllable and the syllable types that make up a word. For example, accented syllables are rarely problematic, because we are familiar with the patterns in single-syllable words. The long *a* sound in *rain* is the same as in a polysyllabic word such as *maintain*. Unaccented syllables, however, are more challenging and must be considered in terms of related words and frequency. For example, when faced with the unaccented syllable of *–le* or *–el* as in *ramble* or *bushel*, it is helpful to know that *–le* is far more common. Isolating the syllable is a helpful strategy.

It is also helpful to identify whether the spelling is in an open or closed syllable. As you and your child have discovered, open syllables end with a long vowel sound, as in *la/zy* (V/CV) and *cre/ate* (VV), and closed syllables have a single short vowel ending in one or more consonants, as in *skip/ping* and *chap/ter* (VCCV), *riv/er* (VC/V), and *pil/grim* (VCCV). These differences aid us with spelling unfamiliar words.

USE PREFIXES, SUFFIXES, AND ROOTS (WORD PARTS) As suggested in the spell by syllable strategy, encouraging your child to break a word into syllables is an effective way to spell unknown words. Equally effective is to identify and break apart the word by known word parts or meaning units. Specifically, identify and spell prefixes, suffixes, and familiar roots. The word *predetermined*, for example, can be divided into the prefix *pre-*, base word *determine*, and suffix *–ed*. The word *antidisestablishmentarianism*, one of the longest words in the English language, is not as difficult to spell when you consider the word parts: *anti-dis-estab-lish-ment-arian-ism*. Ask, "Do you recognize the prefix? The suffix? The base word or root?" In the example *antidisestablishmentarianism*, there are actually multiple prefixes (*anti-* and *dis-*) and suffixes (*-ent* and *-ism*). Encourage your child to break the word into word parts and concentrate on each known part. This strategy is useful in the upper three stages of development.

CHECK FOR A SPELLING-MEANING CONNECTION Words are related by spelling and meaning. If you know how to spell the word *medicine*, for example, you can also spell (or least have a lead on the spelling of) the words *medicinal*, *medic*, and *medicines*. Each of the words is related to "healing" from the Latin root *medicina* and retains a similar spelling and meaning. Likewise, if you know how to spell *define*, you may also be able to spell *defines*, *defining*, *defined*, *definition*, *definitions*, *undefined*, *indefinite*, *indefinitely*, *indefinable*, *redefines*, *redefining*, and *redefined*. This is referred to as the *spelling–meaning connection* (Templeton, 2002).

USE SPELLING DICTIONARIES AND DIGITAL RESOURCES Let's be honest: few of us turn to a thick heavy dictionary to look up the spelling of a word if other resources are more easily available, like spell check or asking the person beside you. We want our children to avoid settling for incorrect spelling or selecting simpler words based on the ease of their spelling. Encourage your child to use both hardcopy and electronic dictionaries as resources not only to spell a word, but also to understand how that word is related to language and meaning.

USE SPELL CHECK Some educators and parents worry that using spell check discourages children from learning to spell. There is no evidence that this is true. If children and adolescents are using word-processing software, teach them how to use spell check, but also to be aware of its shortcomings. Point out that homophone errors (*bear*, *here*) are not likely to be caught; similarly, some misspellings are often skipped (*fat/fate*, *cut/cute*), and unusual proper names may be incorrectly identified as misspellings. For most competent spellers, errors are often the result of poor typing skills, but it is also the case that students may not know how to spell a word. Spell check may help in either case. Explain to your child that they may correct underlined errors right away, or ignore them until the editing stage.

Question 18: What If My Child's School Is Not Practicing Developmental Spelling?

This text helps you support your child's spelling and overall literacy development whether your child is in a school that practices developmental spelling or not. If your child is in a traditional program, you should begin by identifying your child's stage of spelling development. In Chapter 1, there is a brief description of each stage and it also includes a parent-friendly literacy checklist for reading and writing behaviors. You may also elect to administer and score a qualitative spelling inventory available in *Words Their Way: Word Study for Phonics, Vocabulary, and Spelling* (Bear, Invernizzi, Templeton, & Johnston, 2012). This is a simple spelling test scored from a qualitative perspective. Clear scoring guidelines are described in the text. Once you have successfully identified your child's stage, consider the essential sorts, techniques, and games presented in Chapter 2 and the chapter that corresponds to your child's stage of development.

Question 19: What If My Child Mispronounces Words? Will It Affect Reading and Writing?

If a child mispronounces words, such as *wabbit* for *rabbit*, *lello* for *yellow*, or *weaf* for *leaf*, parents, tutors, and volunteers are encouraged to repeat the child's word or phrase with the correct pronunciation. These types of articulation errors are common in young children and developmentally acceptable. In the early stages of literacy, speech patterns may affect spelling, as learners are dependent on the sound–symbol connection. It is not, however, a cause for concern, as language and literacy develop in tandem. If articulation errors persist past first grade, parents are encouraged to consult with the school staff or a speech therapist. Tutors and school volunteers should share their observations with the teacher or parent.

Question 20: What Should I Do When My Child Cannot Read a Word?

As you listen to your child read, you can support your child's reading using the suggestions and prompts in Table 8.3.

Question 21: How Do I Know If My Child Is Reading on Grade Level?

Most schools assess and monitor a child's reading level using both formal and informal reading assessments. There are standardized assessments, such as the Degrees of Reading Power (DRP), or the Reading Inventory (RI), and informal qualitative assessments, such as the Qualitative Reading Inventory (QRI), Developmental Reading Assessment (DRA), or the Phonological Awareness Literacy Screening (PALS). Most reading assessments are designed to measure a student's approximate grade level or the grade level at which students can read with accuracy and good comprehension. Teachers report the "typical grade level" at which your child is performing. It is critical that parents and tutors have a conversation with teachers about the child's reading level based on both assessments and their own classroom observations. Assessments of reading are a snapshot in time and should be considered as such. They are useful to support instruction and monitor progress.

Question 22: How Are Reading Levels Described? What Are the Letters and Numbers Used to Describe Reading Levels?

Individual teachers and school systems often use grade-level equivalencies to demonstrate progress in reading and also to level a classroom library to provide guidance to young chil-

TABLE 8.3 Prompts to Read Unknown Words

Prompts	Explanation
Don't say anything!	Give the child time to think and work it out if they are struggling. Don't be too quick to supply the right answer, and avoid interruption when possible.
"Try that again."	If your child makes a mistake, you might point to it and ask them to try it again.
"Did that make sense?" or *"Something isn't right. Can you try that again?"*	Parents can use this prompt when children read through a sentence and do not realize that they read the word incorrectly.
"What is the first letter sound(s)?"	Once your child knows beginning sounds, draw attention to the first letter(s).
"Look at the picture. Does the first letter of that word match the picture?"	This prompt might be helpful for beginning readers when reading text with illustrations.
"Sound it out. Look at each of the letters."	This can be a useful prompt, if and only if the word can be sounded out and your child has the necessary knowledge about letters, sounds, and patterns. It is important to recognize that not all words are decodable, and this prompt is commonly overused. For example, it is useful with the word *pig* (p/i/g), but not the word *one*. Explain that some words can be sounded out and others cannot. Use the prompt when appropriate.
"Do you see a part of the word that you know?"	Parents can focus attention on parts of the word that are familiar to children. You can cover beginning blends, endings, or prefixes to show the child the potentially familiar part of the word. For older children, parents can encourage their children to break the word into known parts, to locate prefix, suffix, or base word to assist with the identification of the word.
"Read the sentence and try that word again" or *"Let's reread the sentence up to here and use the first few letters to start to say the word."*	This prompt encourages the child to get a running start, to consider the complete meaning of the sentence to provide context for the unfamiliar word as well as the beginning sounds of the challenging word.
"Skip the word, read to the end, and then come back and try it. What would make sense?"	This strategy is particularly helpful with older readers.
Give the word. Tell the child.	Sometimes none of the prompts listed here help, and it's best to supply the word to avoid long interruptions and frustration. For example, the last word of the sentence *"The road was rough"* is both impossible to sound out and not suggested by context. You might say something like, "That is a hard word. It says 'rough.'"

dren in selecting appropriate text. In schools and educational materials, books are identified with varied leveling systems. If you refer to the back of a child's library book, you may find the letters *RL* on the back of the book. For example, *The A to Z Mysteries: The School Skeleton* by Ron Roy has the following note: RL: 2.6. This refers to the grade-level equivalent, the reading level of second grade in the sixth month. It is the level at which a child can read the book independently. Although reading comprehension is affected by a series of factors, reading level is a pure calculation of text factors. Reading formulas, such as the Fry, Dale-Chall, and the Flesch–Kincaid, use sentence length and word frequency to calculate a grade-level equivalency without regard to other factors that affect comprehension.

Other frameworks exist and are designed to monitor progress and to support text selection. Most notably, Irene Fountas and Gay Su Pinnell created a guided-reading leveling system in which books are leveled, in part, by readability formulas (grade-level equivalency), and in part by characteristics of the text (how much white space is on the page, vocabulary, concept development, genre). Books are identified or leveled using the letters from A to Z (Fountas & Pinnell, 2008). The Developmental Reading Assessment (DRA) and the Reading Inventory (RI) use different systems. The DRA uses numbers to indicate grade level proficiency. For example, second-grade levels include 18, 20, 24, and 28. The Reading Inventory quantifies reading levels into *Lexiles*. The Lexile framework uses a numerical scale from 100 to 1210. Lexiles are not very useful in the primary grades, but may be used in upper-elementary and secondary grades to indicate career and college readiness. Ask your child's teacher to explain your child's progress in terms of grade-level proficiency, and also ask which leveling system is used at the school or in the classroom. Most of all, remember that a reading level is a snapshot of proficiency and is variable, based on the many factors that affect comprehension.

Question 23: What Affects My Child's Comprehension?

According to the Rand report on reading comprehension (2002), reading comprehension is affected by a series of factors connected to three areas: the reader, the text, and the purpose, task, or activity in which the reading occurs. Each reader brings many proficiencies to the act of reading, including memory, motivation, background knowledge, vocabulary, and knowledge of specific comprehension strategies.

The text also influences a reader's ability to comprehend and is affected by complexity, length, conceptual knowledge, and vocabulary. And finally, the activity or purpose for reading also has an influence. Students who have a strong background knowledge and are motivated to read have stronger comprehension than a reader who is perhaps engaged in a high-stakes testing situation reading about something on which he or she has limited knowledge. Reading comprehension is affected by many factors over which parents, teachers, and students may exert influence. See Table 8.4 for an explanation of many factors that affect reading level and overall comprehension.

Question 24: What Can I Do If My Child Is Not Reading on Grade Level?

If your child is not reading on grade level, talk to the teacher and consider two questions, "What is being done in school to accelerate his or her learning in reading?" and "How can we support reading growth at home?" It is important that there is consistent communication between the school and home. The most important way to increase reading proficiency is to ensure that students are participating in instruction that matches his or her instructional level in word knowledge, fluency, and comprehension—not necessarily the grade level.

You can support your child's reading and word knowledge (spelling and word identification) by reinforcing word study as described in this text, and encouraging and monitoring the amount of reading in which your child engages. In order to progress in reading, children must engage in reading. Just as a soccer player, a runner, a musician, or an artist must spend the time with their craft, readers must spend time reading and thinking about his or her reading. Reading is a conversation between the reader and the author and is intended to teach, entertain, or inspire. You can support this process by reading with your child, or if the child is older, reading the same text. You can monitor how much time is spent reading at home and outside the classroom and talk about what he or she is learning or feeling about the text. Be sure that he or she is reading something of interest! Over time and with instruction, your child will increase reading interests and proficiencies. They will increase their general background knowledge, comprehension, vocabulary, and knowledge of specific genres, all which contribute to reading development.

Question 25: Should We Allow Our Child to Be Retained If He or She Is Not Reading or Writing on Grade Level?

The decision to retain a child can have profound consequences. Although educators have the best of intentions, the benefits of retention have not been supported by research. As a matter of fact, retention as a strategy to support student development and academic growth has consistently been shown to have a *negative effect* on student achievement (Hattie, 2009). Rather than a conversation on retention, parents are encouraged to have a conversation on how they and

TABLE 8.4 Factors That Affect Reading Level and Overall Comprehension

Characteristics of the Reader	
Phonological skills	In order to read in English, readers must have well-developed phonological awareness skills that allow them to apply phonics in reading.
Word recognition	Readers have varying degrees of ability to recognize or in the early stages to decode or recognize words on the page.
Cognitive capacities	Readers have specific cognitive capacities that affect understanding and comprehension, including short and long-term memory, attention, and critical analytical ability.
Knowledge	Readers have specific background knowledge and experiences that include knowledge of language, culture, genre, and vocabulary. All of these areas affect understanding in text.
Comprehension strategies	Proficient readers develop strategies to support comprehension, including the following: prediction, questioning, inference, summarization, synthesis, determining importance, visualization, and monitoring understanding.
Motivation	Motivation positively or adversely affects a reader's experience. Readers with high efficacy and belief in themselves as readers are more motivated to read and understand than those who believe reading is a chore.
Characteristics of the Text	
Text complexity	Text complexity is the intersection of factors that affect the text and the reader. A text is either complex or not complex, based on the alignment of skills of the reader and factors within the text.
Reading level	Reading levels considered statistically reliable are approximations of what is considered grade level based on sentence length, number of words, number of syllables in words, and other empirical pieces of information. Some reading leveling systems, such as the A to Z levels developed by Fountas and Pinnell (2008), are based predominantly on qualitative differences and well as statistical formulas.
Sentence and text length	The number of words in a sentence and in a text affect a reader's ability to read for meaning and connect ideas.
Vocabulary and conceptual knowledge	The use of vocabulary terms, whether they are familiar and commonplace or highly content-specific, affects the reader's level of understanding.
Organization and coherence	The overall structure and organization of a text affects a reader's ability to make meaning or understand. Coherence or the lack of coherence is another factor.
Genre	The structure of a text—specifically, the attributes of a specific genre—contribute to the challenge of a text. If a reader is familiar with cause and effect or the structure of a fairy tale, he or she is more likely to anticipate what is happening in a text.
Characteristics of Context or Conditions for Reading and Understanding	
Reading for pleasure Reading to learn Reading for high-stakes testing	The context in which we read affects understanding dramatically. There are significant differences in reading for pleasure in self-selected, high-interest text and text designed for high-stakes testing.

the school can work together to accelerate learning in reading and writing to meet and exceed grade-level expectations. This may include extended time with a reading specialist or focused lessons on word knowledge, fluency, reading, and writing, or attending summer school.

Question 26: How Do I Know If My Child Is Dyslexic?

Dyslexia is a specific learning disability primarily characterized by difficulty with word recognition, decoding, and spelling. The causes of dyslexia are complex but the general consensus from the research points to the phonological component of language, or the language components involved in processing speech sounds. Phonological aspects of language are highly heritable and sometimes occur in families. Dyslexia causes significant challenges in the academic environment and in severe cases necessitates special education services or accommodations.

The formal definition adopted by the International Dyslexia Association and also used by the National Institute of Child Health and Human Development (NICHD) explains that dyslexia

> *is characterized by difficulties with accurate and/or fluent word recognition and by poor spelling and decoding abilities. These difficulties typically result from a deficit in the phonological component of language that is often unexpected in relation to other cognitive abilities and the provision of effective classroom instruction. Secondary consequences may include problems in reading comprehension and reduced reading experience that can impede growth of vocabulary and background knowledge. (International Dyslexia Association, 2013, p. 3)*

There are many common myths about dyslexia (Bowman & Culotta, 2010). These include the misconceptions that dyslexia is a visual disorder marked by reversal of letters or seeing things backward. Reversals in writing, however, are very common in early literacy development, and often persist into second grade. It is essential that parents, tutors, school volunteers, and educators understand the differences between typical literacy development and the characteristics of dyslexia. If you have a serious concern about your child's literacy development, we recommend that you first consult with your child's teacher and the school reading specialist. For more information about dyslexia, see resources available from The International Dyslexia Association (www.interdys.org) or the American Dyslexia Association (www.american-dyslexia-association.com).

REFERENCES

Bear, D., Invernizzi, M., Templeton, S., & Johnston, F. (2012). *Words their way: Word study for phonics, vocabulary, and spelling instruction*. Upper Saddle River, NJ: Pearson.

Bear, D., Helman, L., Invernizzi, M., Templeton, S., & Johnston, F. (2007). *Words their way with English learners: Word study for phonics, vocabulary and spelling instruction*. Columbus, OH: Merrill/Prentice Hall.

Bowman, F. L., & Culotta, V. (2010). Myths about dyslexia. Retrieved from https://dyslexiaida.org/the-myths-and-truths-of-dyslexia

Cataldo, S., & Ellis, N. (1988). Interaction in the development of spelling, reading, and phonological skills. *Journal of Research in Reading, 11*, 85–109.

Clymer, T. (1963). The utility of phonic generalizations in the primary grades [with Comment]. *The Reading Teacher, 16*(4), 252–258.

Clymer, T. (1996). The utility of phonic generalizations in the primary grades. *The Reading Teacher, 50*(3), 182–187.

Dahl, K. L., Barto, A., Bonfils, A., Carasello, M., Christopher, J., Davis, R., & Williams, J. (2003). Connecting developmental word study with classroom writing: Children's descriptions of spelling strategies. *The Reading Teacher*, 310–319.

Ellis, N. C., & Cataldo, S. (1992). Spelling is integral to learning to read. *Psychology, Spelling, and Education*, 122–142.

Ehri, L. C., & Rosenthal, J. (2007). The spelling of words: A neglected facilitator of vocabulary learning. *Journal of Literacy Research, 39*(4), 389–410.

Ehri, L. C., & Wilce, L. S. (1987). Does learning to spell help beginners learn to read real words? *Reading Research Quarterly, 18*, 47–65.

Fountas, I., & Pinnell, G. S. (2008). *The continuum of literacy learning: Grades Prek–8*. Portsmouth, NH: Heinemann.

Hattie, J. (2009). *Visible learning: A synthesis of over 800 Meta-analyses relating to achievement*. London, UK: Routledge.

Helman, L. A. (2004). Building on the sound system of Spanish: Insights from the alphabetic spellings of English-language learners. *The Reading Teacher*, 452-460.

Helman, L. A., & Bear, D. R. (2007, November). Does an established model of orthographic development hold true for English learners? In *56th yearbook of the National Reading Conference* (Vol. 56, p. 266). National Reading Conference.

International Dyslexia Association (2013). Dyslexia in the classroom: What every teacher needs to know about dyslexia. Retrieved from http://eida.org/dyslexia-in-the-classroom.

Invernizzi, M., & Worthy, J. W. (1989). An orthographic-specific comparison of the spelling errors of LD and normal children across four levels of spelling achievement. *Reading Psychology, 10,* 173–188.

Johnston, F. R. (2001). The utility of phonic generalizations: Let's take another look at Clymer's conclusions. *The Reading Teacher, 55,* 132–143.

McCandliss, B., Beck, I. L., Sandak, R., & Perfetti, C. (2003). Focusing attention on decoding for children with poor reading skills: Design and preliminary tests of the word building intervention. *Scientific Studies of Reading,* 7(1), 75–104.

Nagy, W., Berninger, V. W., & Abbott, R. D. (2006). Contributions of morphology beyond phonology to literacy outcomes of upper elementary and middle-school students. *Journal of Educational Psychology, 98*(1), 134.

Nagy, W., Berninger, V., Abbott, R., Vaughan, K., & Vermeulen, K. (2003). Relationship of morphology and other language skills to literacy skills in at-risk second-grade readers and at-risk fourth-grade writers. *Journal of Educational Psychology, 95*(4), 730.

Parry, J. A., Hornsby, D., & Stott, D. (1988). *Write on: A conference approach to writing.* Portsmouth, NH: Heinemann Educational Publishers.

Sawyer, D., Lipa-Wade, S., Kim, J., Ritenour, D., & Knight, D. (1997). Spelling errors as a window on dyslexia. *Annals of Dyslexia, 49,* 137–159.

Snow, C. (2002). *Reading for understanding: Toward an R&D program in reading comprehension.* Santa Monica, CA: Rand Corporation.

Templeton, S. (2002). Effective spelling instruction in the middle grades: It's a lot more than memorization. *Voices from the Middle, 9*(3), 8–14.

Williams, C. & Lundstrom, R. P. (2007), Strategy instruction during word study and interactive writing activities. *The Reading Teacher, 61,* 204–212.

Zutell, J. (1992). An integrated view of word knowledge: Correlational studies of the relationships among spelling, reading, and conceptual development. *Development of orthographic knowledge and the foundations of literacy: A memorial festschrift for Edmund H. Henderson,* 213–230.

Zutell, J. (1998). Word sorting: A developmental spelling approach to word study for delayed readers. *Reading & Writing Quarterly: Overcoming Learning Difficulties, 14*(2), 219–238.

CHILDREN'S LITERATURE

Roy, Ron. (2009). *The A to Z mysteries: The school skeleton.* Random House.

APPENDIX A Sort Support for Spellers

<table>
<tr><th colspan="2">Sort Support for Letter Name–Alphabetic Stage of Spelling</th></tr>
<tr><th>Feature and Definitions</th><th>Big Ideas and Underlying Generalizations</th></tr>
<tr><td>Consonants

Consonant sounds are known for their noise and the way in which air is constricted as it is stopped and released or forced through the vocal tract, mouth, teeth, and lips.

Examples

b, c, d, f, g, h, j, k, l, m, n, p, q, r, s, t, v, w, x, y, z</td><td>✓ Letters represent sounds.
✓ There are two kinds of letters: consonants and vowels.
✓ Words that start with the same sound often start with the same letter.
✓ We can stretch words out to listen for just the beginning sound.
✓ Some letters represent more than one sound, such as G in giraffe and gold, or C in call and cent.
✓ Some sounds can be made with more than one consonant, such as the /k/ sound in cage and kite.</td></tr>
<tr><td>Blends and Digraphs

Blends. Two letters can work together to make a sound. We read these closely together, like st, pl, or br (blends).

Examples

s-blends: sp, sk, sm, sc, sn, sw
l-blends: pl, sl, bl, fl, cl, gl
r-blends: cr, fr, br, gr, tr, pr, br

Digraphs. Two letters together sometimes make a brand new sound, like sh, ch, or th (digraphs).

Examples

sh, th, ch, wh (ph, and qu are also digraphs)</td><td>✓ Blends are two consonants that you read or blend together but each keeps its own sound.
✓ Digraphs are two consonants that make a new single sound when combined.
✓ Two letters are needed to spell some sounds (sh, ch, th, wh).</td></tr>
<tr><td colspan="2">Short Vowels

Every vowel (a, e, i, o, and u) has two sounds, commonly referred to as long and short. The five short vowel sounds can be heard at the beginning of these five words: apple, Ed, igloo, octopus, and umbrella.</td></tr>
<tr><td>Same Vowel Word Families

A: -at, -an, -ap, -ag
E: -et, -en, -eg
O: -ot, -op, -og
I: -it, -in, ig, -ill
U: -ut, -un, -up, -ug</td><td>✓ Words with the same two letters at the end rhyme.
✓ Words have beginning, middle, and ending sounds.
✓ We can stretch words out to hear the beginning, middle, and ending sounds.
✓ Words can be spelled by sounding out or stretching the sounds and writing one letter for each sound.
✓ Words can be read by blending a beginning sound and the vowel followed by the same consonants, also called a rime.
✓ Words with the same word family (rime) also rhyme and end in the same two letters.</td></tr>
<tr><td>Mixed Vowel Word Families

A set of short consonant-vowel-consonant words that rhyme and have a single vowel, compared to another group of similar words with a different vowel.

Examples

-at, -ot, -it
-an, -in, -en, -un
-ad, -ed, -ab, -ob
-ap, -ip, -op, -ug
-ag, -eg, -ig, -og, -ug
-ill, -ell, -all
-ack, -ick, -ock, -uck
-ash, -ish, -ush</td><td>✓ Each short vowel makes a different and distinct sound.
✓ We can stretch words out to hear the middle short vowel sound.
✓ We can blend beginning sounds and word families to read words.
✓ Short vowels are usually between consonants (CVC).</td></tr>
<tr><td>Affricates

Speech sounds produced when the breath stream is stopped and released at the point of articulation. This includes the following sounds for /ch/, /sh/, /j/, and /tr/.

Examples

tr, dr, ch</td><td>✓ Some letter sound combinations are very hard to hear and don't seem to match the letters used to represent them (dr, tr).
✓ The blend dr sometimes sounds more like jr.
✓ The blend tr sometimes sounds more like chr.
✓ Affricates are usually in the beginning of words</td></tr>
</table>

Sort Support for Letter Name–Alphabetic Stage of Spelling	
Feature and Definitions	**Big Ideas and Underlying Generalizations**
Preconsonantal Nasals The letters *m* and *n* before the final consonant in a word such as in *think, camp,* and *sing. Nasals* are sounds produced when the air is blocked but escapes through the nasal cavity. **Examples** *-ang, -ing, -ong, -ung* *-ank, -ink, -unk* *-amp, -ump, -imp* *-mp, -ng, -nd, -nk*	✓ The preconsonantal nasal (*n* or *m*) is difficult to hear before a consonant because the second consonant sound tends to be much more prominent. ✓ The preconsonantal nasal affects the sound of the short vowel sound (*sat* vs. *sand*).

Sort Support for Within Word Pattern Stage of Spelling	
FEATURE	**Big Ideas and Underlying Generalizations**
Short and Long Vowels Every vowel (*a, e, i, o,* and *u*) has two sounds, commonly referred to as *long* and *short.* The long vowel "says its letter name." Short vowels are commonly represented with a single letter, with a few exceptions, such as *ea* in *bread.* **Common Long Vowels** Some vowel patterns are more common or frequently used than others. *A: aCe (cake), ai (rain)* *E: ee (street), ea (meat)* *I: iCe (bike), igh (light)* *O: oCe (broke), oa (boat)* *U: uCe (rude), ui (fruit)* **Less Common Long Vowels** Some vowel patterns are less common or less frequently used than others. *A: ay (play), ei (veil), eigh (eight), ea (steak), au (gauge)* *E: eCe, ie, y* *I: i (kind), y (fly)* *O: ow (show), o (told), oe (toe)*	**Sound** ✓ Many long vowel sounds can be spelled a number of different ways. **Pattern** ✓ There are many ways to spell long vowel patterns including CVV (*play, blow, tie*), CVVC (*boat, rain, street, fruit*), CVCe (*make, stripe, bike, these,* and *cute*). ✓ In the CVVC pattern, the second letter is often silent and marks the sound of the other one. **Frequency** ✓ Frequency of patterns is an important consideration in spelling words with long vowel sounds. ✓ Some long vowel spelling patterns are more common than others. For example, *ai* as in *train* is frequently represented in English, whereas the pattern *au* as in *gauge* is rare; *ee* as in *street* is commonly used, yet a single letter *e* as in *me* is less common. ✓ CVCe (*gate, line, home, tube*) and CVVC (*rain, steam, boat, suit*) are common long vowel patterns across most of the vowels. ✓ CVV (*play, blow, tie*) are familiar patterns, but are far less frequent. **Position** ✓ Position of patterns is an important consideration in spelling words with long vowel sounds. ✓ Although long vowel patterns may appear in the beginning, middle, or end of a word, specific patterns are consistently represented in one position. For example, *ay* as in *tray, ow* as in *blow,* and *y* as in *cry* are most frequently found in the final position of a word. **Meaning** ✓ Meaning helps determine spelling. There are many long vowel homophone pairs with the same pronunciation but different spelling and meaning (*pair/pear, stake/steak*).
R*-Influenced (controlled) Vowels** In English, *r* colors the way the preceding vowel is pronounced. For example, compare the pronunciation of the vowels in *bar* and *bad.* The vowel in *bar* is influenced by the letter *r.* ***Examples *-ar, -ir, -or, -ur* *-ar, -are, -air* *-er, -ear, -eer*	**Sound** ✓ Vowel sounds can be influenced (changes the sound) when followed by certain consonants (*r, l, w*). ✓ Some *r*-influenced vowels follow the same patterns as short and long vowels (*car/care, fir/fire, her/here, purr/pure*); however, the sound is influenced and becomes an *r*-controlled sound. **Pattern** ✓ There are many *r*-controlled patterns including: *ar* (*car*), *are* (*care*), *air* (*fair*); (*er, ir, ur*); *er* (*her*), *eer* (*deer*), *ear* (*hear*), *ear* (*learn*); *ir* (*shirt*), *ire* (*tire*); *or* (*for*), *ore* (*core*), *our* (*pour*), *oar* (*board*); *ur* (*burn*), *ure* (*pure*).

<table>
<tr><th colspan="2">Sort Support for Within Word Pattern Stage of Spelling</th></tr>
<tr><th>FEATURE</th><th>Big Ideas and Underlying Generalizations</th></tr>
<tr><td>-ir, -ire, -ier
-or, -ore, -oar
-ur, -ure</td><td>✓ Some r-influenced vowels follow the same patterns as short and long vowels (car/care, fir/fire, her/here, purr/pure); however, the sound is influenced and becomes an r-controlled sound.
✓ A reader, writer, speller must consider pattern and meaning when sound is insufficient.
Frequency
✓ Some r-influenced patterns are more common than others.
Position
✓ R-controlled spelling patterns refer to a vowel followed by the letter r (not those which have a vowel preceding the letter r).
✓ R-controlled spelling patterns can be identified at the beginning (arm), middle (start), or end (far) of a word.
Meaning
✓ There are many homophones among r-influenced vowel patterns (fare/fair, here/hear, four/fore). Pattern and meaning are the only elements that support a speller, reader, or writer in selecting the correct spelling for a homophone.</td></tr>
<tr><td>Ambiguous Vowels
A vowel sound represented by a variety of different spelling patterns or vowel patterns that represent a wide range of sounds.
Examples
oi (coil), oy (boy)
oo (soon), oo (good)
ou (sound), ow (brown)
aw (saw), au (caught)
wa (watch), al (small), ou (bought)</td><td>Sound
✓ Ambiguous vowel sounds are neither short nor long.
✓ The vowel sound can be influenced by other surrounding vowels or consonants.
Pattern
✓ Ambiguous vowel patterns include: oo (moon) and oo (book), oy (boy) and oi (boil), ow (brown) and ou (cloud), aw (crawl) and au (caught), al (tall) and o (dog).
Frequency
✓ Some ambiguous vowel patterns are more common than others.
Position
✓ The ambiguous vowel patterns oi as in boil, ou as in cloud, and au as in caught are usually in the middle position of single-syllable words.
✓ The ambiguous vowel patterns oy, aw, and ow are usually in the middle or final position, as in owl, boy, and claw.</td></tr>
<tr><td>Complex Consonants
Complex consonants include silent initial consonants, triple Blends, and other Complex Consonants. Complex consonant clusters in the final position are often influenced by the preceding vowel.
Examples
Silent beginning consonants
kn (knot), wr (wrap), gn (gnat)
Three letter blends
scr (scratch), str (stretch), spr (spring), spl (splat,) squ (square)
Three letter blends with digraphs
thr (threat), shr (shred), squ (square)
Hard/soft c and g
hard c (cash) vs. soft c (cell),
hard g (gone) vs. soft g (germ)
Complex ending consonant clusters
dge (edge) vs. ge (cage),
tch (match) vs. ch (march),
ck (quick) vs. k (strike)
Final consonants with silent e
-ce (peace), -se (please), -ze (prize), -ve (leave)</td><td>Sound, Pattern, Meaning
✓ Some uncommon spelling patterns include silent consonants (kn, wr, gn).
✓ Many of the words with the kn and wr patterns, which begin with a silent letter, are homophones (right/write, know/no).
✓ Words can begin with three letter blends or digraphs (spr, thr), which should be blended together as one chunk when reading.
✓ Both c and g have two sounds—the hard sound, as in cat, cup, and cot, and the soft sound, as in cider, cent, and cycle; the hard sound, as in gap, goat, or grumble, and the soft sound, as in gentle, giant, and gym.
• The soft or hard sound in both c and g is determined by the vowel that follows. When the letters i, e, or y follow the letter c, as in cider, cent, and cycle, the consonant sound is soft. When the letter is followed by a, o, or u, as in cap, cod, or cup, the consonant sound is hard.
• The same is true for the letter g. When followed by i, e, or y, as in gentle, giant, or gym, the consonant sound is soft, and it is a hard sound when followed by a, o, and u, as in gap, gone, and gum.</td></tr>
</table>

Sort Support for Within Word Pattern Stage of Spelling	
FEATURE	Big Ideas and Underlying Generalizations
	✓ Ending complex-consonant clusters (*ch/tch*, *ge/dge*) are associated with the preceding vowel sound. • The consonant cluster *–tch* is usually used in single-syllable words and has a short vowel, as in *pitch*, *catch*, and *lodge*. The spelling feature *–ch* is usually used in single-syllable words that are not short, as in *much* and *church*. • The consonant cluster *–dge* is usually used in single-syllable words with a short vowel, as in *fudge, badge,* and *ridge.* • The consonant cluster *–ge* is usually used in single-syllable words without short vowels, as in *large* and *age*. These vowels may be long, ambiguous, or *r*-controlled. ✓ The final /k/ sound has three spellings, associated with the previous vowel sound. • The consonant cluster *–ck* is usually used in single syllable words with a short vowel as in *luck and check.* • The consonant sound *k* is represented by either *k* or *ke* in single syllable words with vowels that are not short as in *cook, rake,* and *bark.* These vowels may be long, ambiguous or r-controlled. ✓ Words ending in *-ce* (*dance*), *-ge* (*edge*), *-ve* (*leave*), and *-se* (*sense*) have a *silent e* associated with the consonant rather than the vowel.
Homophones Words that sound alike but are spelled differently, and have different meanings. **Examples** *write/right, mite/might, waste/waist, pane/pain, sale/sail, ate/eight, way/weigh*	**Sound** ✓ *Homophones* are words that sound the same but are spelled differently (*mail/male*, *pear/pair/pare*) because they have different meanings. **Pattern** ✓ The different spellings are frequently common and less common long vowel patterns. **Meaning** ✓ The different spellings help the reader identify which meaning is intended, as does the context or meaning of the sentence. ✓ Homophones exemplify the interplay of sound, pattern, and meaning in English spelling (*ad/add, tacks/tax, sale/sale*). **Frequency** ✓ Homophones are extremely common in the English language

Sort Support for Syllables and Affixes Stage of Spelling	
FEATURE	Big Ideas and Underlying Generalizations
Compound Words Words made up of two or more words. They can be a single word or a hyphenated word. **Examples** *sunlight, bookshelf, blacktop, shellfish, cupcake*	**Pattern and Meaning** ✓ *Compound words* are created when two smaller words are joined to make a new word with a new meaning, such as *blacktop* or *shellfish*. ✓ Compound words have more than a single syllable. ✓ When spelling compound words, it is the meaning and spelling of both words that leads us to spell the word correctly. Some words have double consonants, such as *earring.*
Polysyllabic Homophones Words that sound alike, are spelled different, and have different meanings. Polysyllabic homophones have more than one syllable. **Examples** *petal/peddle, stationary/ stationery*	**Sound, Pattern, and Meaning** ✓ *Homophones* are words that sound the same but are spelled different and have different meanings (*boulder, bolder*). ✓ Sound does not assist us in the spelling of a homophone; however, the frequency of a pattern and the meaning of words may help us with the spelling. ✓ Homophones are the cause of many spelling errors in the English language.

Sort Support for Syllables and Affixes Stage of Spelling	
FEATURE	Big Ideas and Underlying Generalizations
Homographs Words that are spelled alike but have different pronunciations and different meanings **Examples** *Tear* a piece of paper or to shed a *tear;* *lead* someone along or the element *lead*.	**Sound, Pattern, and Meaning** ✓ *Homographs* are words that are spelled alike but whose meanings and parts of speech change with a shift in accent, as in "Record your expenses or have a record of your expenses." ✓ Accent or stress in pronunciation affects the meaning of the word, as does the context of the written passage. ✓ The stress or accent in a homograph relates to the part of speech. Homographs accented in the first syllable are typically nouns, whereas stress in the second syllable is typically a verb.
Plurals A word that refers to more than one.	**Sound** ✓ The sounds vary in a plural, as in *cats* (/s/) and *dogs* (/z/). ✓ With the exception of irregular plurals such as *fish*, the inflected endings *–s, -es,* and *–ies* represent the sound of the letter s. **Pattern** ✓ Add *-es* when words end in *ch, sh, ss, s,* and *x*. Adding *–es* to a word usually adds a syllable (*dish* to *dishes*). ✓ Change the *y* at the end of a word to *i* before adding *-es* when the word ends in a consonant +*y* (*baby* to *babies*), but not when it ends in a vowel +*y* (*monkeys*). ✓ Change words with a final *f* or *fe* to *v* and add *-es* (*wife* to *wives*, *wolf* to *wolves*). ✓ Some words take a new form when made plural (*goose* to *geese*, *mouse* to *mice*). **Meaning** ✓ Inflected endings change the number or tense of the base word *(-s, -ed, -ing)*, but do not change the meaning or part of speech. ✓ Plurals refer to more than one. ✓ When spelling words with inflected endings, it is important to think about the spelling of the base word.
Inflected Endings ***-ed* and *–ing*** An *inflectional ending* is a group of letters that represents a *morpheme,* a meaning unit, that changes the meaning of a word. **Examples** *-s, -ed, –ing*	**Sound** ✓ The suffix *–ed* can have three different sounds: the /t/ sound as in jumped, the /d/ sound as in planned, and the /ed/ sound as in waited. **Pattern** ✓ When adding *–ed* or *–ing,* there are three conditions: • Just add the ending to all other words. • Double the final consonant when the word is a single syllable, short vowel, and has a single final consonant (*batted, batting*). • Drop the *e* when the base word ends with a silent *e* (*have* to *having, make* to *making*). ✓ Words ending in *x* or *w* do not double (*boxed, chewed*). ✓ Spellers must add the letter *k* to words that end in *c* when adding *–ing* or *–ed* (*mimicking, mimicked*). ✓ Two-syllable words accented on ***second*** syllable follow the same general principles as discussed earlier: *admitted* and *admitting* (doubles), *admits* (just add), *applies, applied* (*y* to *i*), *destroyed, destroying, destroyer, destroys* (just add). ✓ Two-syllable words accented on anything other than the second syllable do not require doubling the final consonant when adding *–ed* or *–ing* (*cancel/canceled, trumpet/trumpeted*). **Meaning** ✓ The inflected endings are morphemes that provide insight into the word's part of speech. ✓ Inflected endings change the number or tense of the base word (*-s, -ed, -ing*), but do not change the meaning or part of speech.

Sort Support for Syllables and Affixes Stage of Spelling	
FEATURE	Big Ideas and Underlying Generalizations
Inflected Endings ***-er* and *–est*** An *inflectional ending* is a group of letters that represents a *morpheme,* a meaning unit, that changes the meaning of a word. The inflectional endings *–er* and *–est* are also known as *comparative* and *superlative.*	**Pattern** ✓ When spelling words with inflected endings, it is important to think about the spelling of the base word. ✓ The suffixes *–er* and *-est* function in the same way as *–ed* and *–ing.* Spell with the *e*-drop, doubling, no change, and change *y* to *i* principles when adding *–er* or *–est* to a base word as in *cheaper, braver, bigger,* and *sillier.* ✓ Add *–er* to the base words when comparing two things and *–est* when the comparison involves more than two. **Meaning** ✓ Adjectives ending in *–er* are referred to as comparative, whereas words ending in *–est* are referred to as *superlative.* ✓ In English, adjectives only take two inflected endings: the comparative *–er* and the superlative *–est.* ✓ The inflected endings *–er* and *–est* are morphemes and provide insight to the word's part of speech.
Open and Closed Syllables	**Sound** ✓ Open syllables end in a long vowel sound. ✓ Closed syllables have a short vowel and end with a consonant sound (*rab/bit* and *rac/ket*). **Pattern** ✓ Open syllables follow two patterns: VCV (***o/pe**n* or *h**u/ma**n*) or VV (*cr**e/a**te, **ri/ ot***); the syllable is divided after the long vowel. ✓ Closed syllables follow four patterns: VCCV doubles (*slipper, million, sudden*); VCCV different consonants (***mem/be**r, p**en/ci**l, n**um/be**r*); VCV (*r**iv/e**r, r**ob/i**n*); and VCCCV (*l**augh/te**r, **ath/le**te*). ✓ When spelling words with three or more consonants at the juncture, it is helpful to remember that certain consonant blends and digraphs work together, such as *th, gh.* and *dr*. ✓ Closed syllables that follow the VCCV pattern across the syllable are divided between the consonants, as in *d**in/ne**r* or *w**in/te**r.* ✓ In open syllables with two vowels, the VV pattern is divisible, as in *p**o/e**t, cr**e/a**te,* and *g**i/a**nt.* **Meaning** ✓ It is helpful to understand how to *syllabicate* (divide syllables) in order to spell and read words. **Frequency** ✓ The most common patterns are the open V/CV pattern (*s**ile**nt*) and the closed VC/CV pattern (*h**appe**n, c**onte**st*).
Accented Syllables Long, ambiguous, and *r*-controlled vowel patterns in accented syllables	**Sound and Pattern** ✓ In most words with two or more syllables, one syllable is emphasized, stressed, or accented more than the others. ✓ Long vowel patterns (*ai, a-e, ay, igh, i-e, y, ee, ea, y, oa, ow, o-e, oe, u-e, ue*) in the stressed syllable function the same way in single-syllable and polysyllabic words. The vowels remain long. ✓ Long, *r*-controlled, and abstract vowels previously studied can be spelled the same ways in the stressed syllables of multisyllabic words. ✓ The same inflected ending principles apply to words with an accented syllable, such as *admitting*.

Sort Support for Syllables and Affixes Stage of Spelling	
FEATURE	**Big Ideas and Underlying Generalizations**
Unaccented Syllables The syllable in a word that gets little emphasis and may have an indistinct vowel sound, such as the first syllable in *about*, the second syllable in *definition*, or the final syllables in *doctor* or *table*. **Schwa** A vowel sound in English that often occurs in an unstressed syllable, such as the /uh/ sound in the first syllable of the word *above*.	**Sound** ✓ In the unaccented or unstressed syllable, the vowel sound is often not clearly long or short, and is therefore more difficult to spell. ✓ The unclear vowel sound heard in the unstressed syllable is often represented by the *schwa* sound (the upside down *e* in a dictionary). **Pattern** ✓ There are many patterns for the schwa sound. ✓ Sound does not provide any clues in spelling the unaccented syllable (*ang**le***, *ang**e**l*, *met**al***, *civ**il***, and *fert**ile***). **Meaning** ✓ When unsure of spelling in the unaccented syllable, you and your child are encouraged to use their *best bet* based on spelling frequency and knowledge of the word's part of speech and meaning. **Frequency** ✓ Some patterns are more frequent than others; for example, *–le* as in *angle* is more frequent than *–il* as in *civil*, *-el* as in *angel*, and *–al* as in *final*. Likewise, *–er* as in *swimmer* or *smaller* is more common than *–ar* as in *beggar* and *–or* as in *actor*.
Exploring Consonants	**Sound** ✓ Some consonants are silent. ✓ Silent letters are often found in families, such as the *kn-* family (*knead, knew, knight, knife, knuckle, knell, knock, knob,* and *knowledge*), or the *wr-* family (*wrist, wrote, wrinkle, write, wretch, wreath, wry, wren,* and *wrong*). **Pattern** ✓ Some silent letters are present due to a related word, such as the pairs *bomb/bombard, autumn/autumnal,* and *sign/signal*. ✓ The letter *h* is silent in *ch* when it represents the sound /k/, as in *kite*, *cat*, or *chorus*. Notice that *ch* as in *church* is a diagraph with two letters representing a new sound, whereas *ch* as in *chorus* provides the hard sound of *c* and the *h* is silent. ✓ The silent letter *t* is often followed by *–le* or *–en,* as in *bristle* or *soften.* **Meaning** ✓ Many letters became silent as a result of the influence of another language. Consider the earlier example of *sword* and Old English.
Sounds of /k/ Spelled *ck, ic,* and *x*	**Sound and Pattern** ✓ The /k/ sound as in *kite* can be spelled by three spelling patterns: *-k* as in *shake*, *-ck* as in *shock*, and *-ic* as in *magic*. The /ks/ sound as in *relax* is spelled with an *x*. ✓ The pattern *–ck* is used when the syllable has a short vowel, as in *quick* and *pickle*. ✓ Most words that end in *–ic* are two-syllable words.
Other Unique Consonant Patterns	**Sound and Pattern** ✓ The digraphs *ph* and *gh* are not common. ✓ The digraph *ph-* represents the sound /f/, as in *phrase* and *alphabet* in the initial and middle positions in a word. ✓ The digraph *gh* may represent the sound like /f/, as in *tough* and *enough*. It may also be silent, as in *daughter* and *taught*. ✓ The digraph *qu* sounds like /kw/, as in *queasy* and *squirrel*.

Sort Support for Syllables and Affixes Stage of Spelling	
FEATURE	Big Ideas and Underlying Generalizations
Affixes: Prefixes and Suffixes An *affix* is a term that refers to prefixes and suffixes. A *prefix* is a morpheme, a group of letters that represents a unit of meaning, that is affixed to the beginning of a base word or root and changes the overall word's meaning. **Examples** *pre-, re-, mis-, dis-* A *suffix* is a morpheme, a group of letters that represents a unit of meaning, that is affixed to the ending of a base word or root and changes the overall word's meaning. Suffixes often indicate the part of speech of a word. **Examples** *–ness, -ic, -ment, –ly*	**Sound** ✓ Affixes influence the form or derivation of a word. **Pattern** ✓ An *affix* is a suffix or prefix attached to a base word or root. A *prefix* is attached to the beginning of a base word or root, whereas a suffix is attached to the end of a base word or root. ✓ A prefix is a morpheme attached to the beginning of a word (prewrite). ✓ A suffix is a morpheme attached to the end of a word (happiness). ✓ A *base word* is a complete word and can stand alone, such as *depend* or *graph*, to which prefixes or suffixes are added. ✓ A *root* is a word part of Greek origin that is often combined with other roots to form words such as *telephone* (*tele* and *phone*). **Meaning** ✓ Affixes affect the meaning of the word and/or the part of speech; therefore, knowing the meaning of the prefixes and suffixes can help you understand vocabulary: *-ful* means "full of," *–less* means "without," and *un-* means "the opposite of" or "not." **Frequency** ✓ Some affixes are more common than others; for example, *pre-, mis-, dis-,* and *un-* account for 58% of the affixed words in English. **Related Words** ✓ Affixes influence the meaning of a word and demonstrate a spelling–meaning connection. For example, if you can spell *courage,* you can spell *courageous, courageously, encourage, encourages, encouraging, encouraged, encouragement, discourage, discouraging, discouragingly,* and *discouragement.*

Sort Support for Derivational Relations Stage of Spelling	
FEATURE	Big Ideas and Underlying Generalizations
Affixes: Prefixes and Suffixes An *affix* is a term that refers to prefixes and suffixes. A *prefix* is a morpheme, a group of letters that represents a unit of meaning, that is affixed to the beginning of a base word or root and changes the overall word's meaning. **Examples** *pre-, re, -mis-, dis-* A *suffix* is a morpheme, a group of letters that represents a unit of meaning, that is affixed to the ending of a base word or root and changes the overall word's meaning. Suffixes often indicate the part of speech of a word. **Examples** *–ness, -ic, -ment, –ly*	**Sound** ✓ Affixes influence the form or derivation of a word, such as *demand* and *demanding* or *popular* and *popularity*. **Pattern** ✓ An *affix* is a suffix or prefix attached to a base word or root. ✓ A *prefix* is a *morpheme* (meaning *unit*) attached to the beginning of a word, such as *pre-* in *prewrite*. ✓ A *suffix* is a *morpheme* (meaning *unit*) attached to the end of a word, as *–ness* in the word *happiness*. ✓ A base word is a complete word and can stand alone, such as *depend* or *graph,* to which prefixes or suffixes are added. **Meaning** ✓ Affixes affect the *meaning* of the word and/or the part of speech; therefore, knowing the meaning of the prefixes and suffixes can help you understand spelling and vocabulary: *-ful* means "full of," *–less* means "without," and *un-* means "the opposite of" or "not." ✓ Suffixes specifically change the part of speech. ✓ The suffixes *-al, -ic,* and *–ial* are suffixes that often signal adjectives derived from nouns, such as from *fiction* to *fictional,* or from *hero* to *heroic.* ✓ The suffix *–ment* creates nouns out of verbs, meaning "the result of," as in *pay/payment, argue/argument, govern/government.*

Sort Support for Derivational Relations Stage of Spelling	
FEATURE	Big Ideas and Underlying Generalizations
	Frequency ✓ Some affixes are more common than others; for example, *pre-*, *mis-*, *dis-*, and *un-* account for 58% of the affixed words in English. **Related Words** ✓ Affixes influence the meaning of a word and demonstrate a spelling–meaning connection. For example, if you can spell *courage*, you can spell the following derived forms: *courageous, courageously, encourage, encourages, encouraging, encouraged, encouragement, discourage, discouraging, discouragingly,* and *discouragement*.
Adding Suffix *–ion* A *suffix* is a morpheme, a group of letters that represents a unit of meaning, that is affixed to the ending of a base word or root and changes the overall word's meaning. Suffixes often indicate the part of speech of a word.	**Sound Pattern** ✓ The suffix *–ion,* pronounced "shun," can be spelled several ways, as in *protection, invasion, admission,* and *musician.* **No Spelling Change** ✓ Base words that end in *–t, –ct,* or *–ss* do not require a spelling change. The suffix *–ion* is simply affixed, as in *digest, traction, expression*. ✓ Base words that end in *–ic* add *–ian,* as in *magician* and *politician*. **Drop *e*** ✓ Base words that end in *–te* drop the *e* and add *–ion,* as in *translate* to *translation*. ✓ Base words that end in *–se* drop the *e* and add *–ion,* as in *confuse* to *confusion*. ✓ Base words that end in *–ce* drop the *e* and add *–tion,* as in *reduce* to *reduction* **Add *–sion*** ✓ Base words that end in *–d, –de,* and *–it* drop those letters and add *–sion* or *–ssion* (*decide/decision, admit/admission*). **Frequency** ✓ More words end in *–tion* than *–sion* or *–ian*. ✓ Words that end in *–ian* are less common and usually refer to a person, such as a *musician* or *politician*. **Other** ✓ Sometimes *–ation* is added to the base word, which causes little trouble for spellers because it can be heard, as in *transport/transportation*. ✓ With some word pairs (base word and derived form) the stress and therefore the pronunciation may shift stress, as in the following pairs: ***cel**ebrate/cele**bra**tion, ex**agg**erate/exagge**ra**tion,* and *il**lus**trate/illus**tra**tion.*
Consonant Alternations The process in which the pronunciation of consonants changes in derivationally related words, whereas the spelling does not change (e.g., the silent to sounded *g* in the words *sign* to *signal*; the /k/ to /sh/ pattern in the words *music* and *musician).*	**Sound and Meaning** ✓ Words are related in meaning and spelling despite differences in sound, as in *sign* to *signal* or *bomb* to *bombard.* ✓ When spelling unknown words, it is helpful to think of a related word, as in *crumb* and *crumble* or *muscle* to *muscular*. ✓ It is also helpful to consider multiple underlying generalizations when spelling unknown words, as described with the addition of *–ion* and *–ian,* or the understanding that the letter *c* is either soft or hard when followed by different vowels. ✓ Consonants may shift from a silent to sounded, as in *sign* to *signal, autumn* to *autumnal,* or *bomb* to *bombard.* ✓ Consonants may shift from /t/ to /sh/ or /k/ to /sh/ when adding *–ion,* as in *connect* to *connection* or *music* to *musician*. ✓ Consonants may shift from /k/ to /s/ when the letter *c* is followed by the letters *e, i,* or *y,* as in *critic* to *criticize* or *political* to *politicize.* ✓ Consonants may shift from /s/ to /sh/, as in *prejudice* to *prejudicial.*

Sort Support for Derivational Relations Stage of Spelling	
FEATURE	Big Ideas and Underlying Generalizations
Vowel Alternations The process in which the pronunciation of vowels changes in derivationally related words, whereas the spelling does not change (e.g., the long-to-short vowel change in the related words *crime* and *criminal*; the long-to-schwa vowel change in the related words *impose* and *imposition*).	**Sound and Meaning** ✓ Words are related in meaning and spelling despite differences in sound, as in *cave* to *cavity.* ✓ When spelling unknown words, it is helpful to think of a related word, as in *major* to *majority.* ✓ Vowel sounds can be described as long, short, or schwa (*r*-controlled and ambiguous vowels also exist, but are not discussed here). ✓ Vowel sounds can change in related word pairs, such as *cave* to *cavity.* ✓ Vowel sounds can change from **long to short** in related word pairs**,** as in *cave* to *cavity* or *sign* to *signal.* ✓ Vowel sounds can change from **long to schwa** in related word pairs, as in *major* to *majority* or *relate* to *relative.* ✓ Vowel sounds can change from **short to schwa** in related word pairs, as in *allege* to *allegation* and *malice* to *malicious.* **Sound with Suffixes** ✓ Vowel sounds can change in related word pairs when adding suffixes when the **accent** changes. ✓ Vowel sounds can change in related word pairs from **schwa to short** with *–ity,* as in *mental* and *mentality.* ✓ Vowel sounds can change in related word pairs from **long to short** with *–cation,* as in *apply* and *application.* ✓ Vowel sounds can change in related word pairs from **long to schwa** with *–ation,* as in *declare* and *declaration.*
Predictable Spelling Changes Some vowel alternations require a change in spelling, and these tend to be predictable.	**Sound, Pattern, Meaning** ✓ Predictable spelling changes in consonants and vowels follow six patterns: 1. Vowel sounds can change from **long to short** in related word pairs, as in *rec**ei**ve/rec**e**ption.* The word families with *ei* to *e* and *ai* to *a* are predictable examples. 2. Vowel sounds can change from **long to schwa** in related word pairs, as in *expl**ai**n/expl**a**nation.* 3. Vowel sounds can change from **/sh/ to /s/** in related word pairs, as in *fero**c**ious/fero**c**ity.* 4. Vowel sounds can change from **/t/ to /sh/** in related word pairs, as in *permi**t**/ permi**ss**ion.* 5. Vowel sounds can change from **/t/ to /s/** in related word pairs, as *silent/ silence.* 6. Vowel sounds can change from **/d/ to /zh/** in related word pairs, as in *explode/explosion.*
Greek and Latin Roots Word or word parts, often of Greek or Latin origin, that are often combined with other roots to form words, such as *telephone* (*tele* and *phone*).	**Meaning and Position** ✓ Greek roots such as *photo* and *graph* may combine in different places in words—at the beginning, middle, or end (***telephoto***, ***graph****ic*, ***photograph***). ✓ Latin roots tend to stay in one place with prefixes and suffixes attached (***cred****ible,* ***cred****ence, in****cred****ible*). **Related Words** ✓ Words are related in both spelling and meaning. For example, the root ***photo,*** meaning light, connects the following words: *photograph, photographs, photographing, photography, photographer, photosynthesis, photocell, photogenic, photocopier, telephoto, photon.*

Sort Support for Derivational Relations Stage of Spelling	
FEATURE	Big Ideas and Underlying Generalizations
Advanced Suffix Study	**Sound and Pattern** ✓ If the accent in the base word falls on the final syllable, then double the final consonant before adding the suffix. If the accent does not fall on the last syllable, do not double it. For example, *omitted* doubles the final *t* because the accent is on the first syllable, whereas *piloting* does not double the final *t* because the stress is on the second syllable. **Meaning** ✓ If you know how to spell one word that ends in *–ent* and *–ence* or *–ant* and *–ance*, it provides insight into how to spell the unknown word. ✓ Words that end with *–ent* and *–ant* create adjectives. ✓ Words that end with*–ence* and *–ance* create nouns.
Suffixes *–ible, –able*	**Sound** ✓ Words that end in *e* that are preceded by a soft *c* or *g* (soft *c* as in *circle* and soft *g* as in *gymnast*) may retain the *e* to keep the soft sound, as in *noticeable* and *manageable*. **Pattern** ✓ The suffix *–able* is usually added to words with a *base word,* a word that stands alone, such as *depend* in *dependable.* ✓ The suffix *–ible* is usually added to words that have a word part, such as *vis-* in *visible*. ✓ Words that end in a final *e* often drop the *e* and add *–able,* as in *desire* to *desirable*. ✓ Words that end in *y* as in *vary* change the *y* to *i* and add *–able,* as in *vary/variable, justify/justifiable*, and *envy/enviable.* ✓ Words that end in *–ate,* such as *irritate,* drop the *–ate* and add *–able,* as in *irritate/irritable* and *tolerate/tolerable*. **Meaning** ✓ The suffixes *–ible* and *–able* both mean "having the power or skill of something." **Frequency** ✓ The suffix *–able* is more common than *–ible.* ✓ The suffix *–ible* is rarely affixed to words that end in *e*, but there are exceptions, such as *digestible*, *resistible*, and *combustible*.
Assimilated Prefixes Prefixes in which the spelling and sound of the consonant has been absorbed into the spelling and sound at the beginning of the base or root to which the prefix is affixed (e.g., *ad* + *tract* = *attract*).	**Meaning** ✓ An *assimilated prefix* is one in which the sound and spelling of the final consonant in the prefix is *absorbed* into the initial consonant of the base word to which the prefix is attached, often leading to a double consonant, as in *accompany, accommodate,* and *accelerate* (*ad-* meaning to or toward). ✓ Assimilated prefixes may pose a significant spelling challenge for our children and to us because they depend on considerable prior knowledge about other basic spelling–meaning patterns, processes of adding prefixes to base words, and simple roots. ✓ Assimilated prefixes maintain the meaning of the original prefix despite the change in spelling.

APPENDIX B

Sound Board for Beginning Consonants and Digraphs

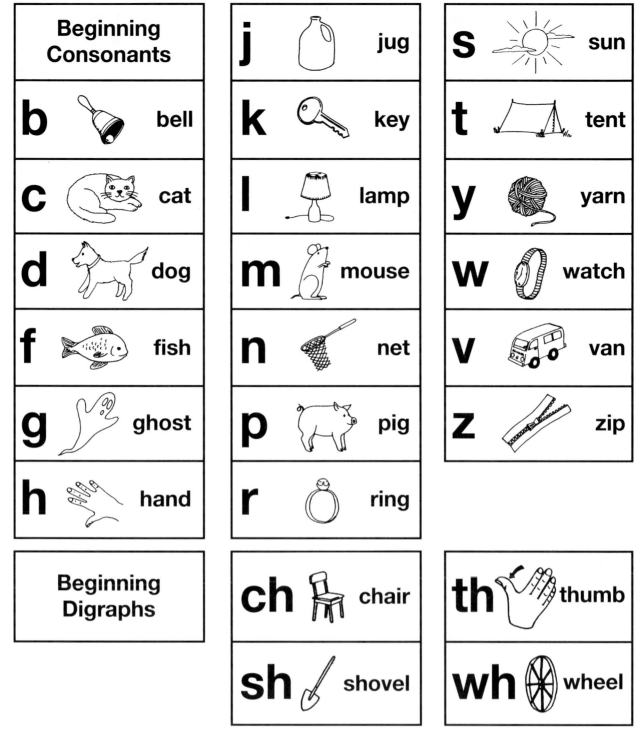

Beginning Consonants

b		bell
c		cat
d		dog
f		fish
g		ghost
h		hand
j		jug
k		key
l		lamp
m		mouse
n		net
p		pig
r		ring
s		sun
t	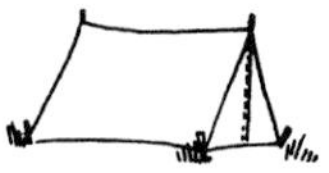	tent
y		yarn
w		watch
v		van
z		zip

Beginning Digraphs

ch		chair
sh		shovel
th	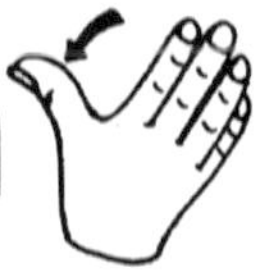	thumb
wh		wheel

Source: Bear, Donald R.; Invernizzi, Marcia R.; Templeton, Shane R.; Johnston, Francine, *Words Their Way: Word Study for Phonics, Vocabulary, and Spelling Instruction*, 5th Ed., ©2012. Reprinted and Electronically reproduced by permission of Pearson Education, Inc., New York, NY.

Sound Board for Beginning Blends

Beginning Blends			**br**		**broom**	**sc**		**scooter**
bl		**block**	**cr**		**crab**	**sk**		**skate**
cl		**cloud**	**dr**		**drum**	**sm**		**smile**
fl		**flag**	**fr**		**frog**	**sn**		**snail**
gl		**glasses**	**gr**		**grapes**	**sp**		**spider**
sl		**slide**	**pr**		**present**	**st**		**star**
pl	2+1=3	**plus**	**tr**		**tree**	**sw**		**swing**
tw		**twins**	**qu**		**quilt**			

Source: Bear, Donald R.; Invernizzi, Marcia R.; Templeton, Shane R.; Johnston, Francine, *Words Their Way: Word Study for Phonics, Vocabulary, and Spelling Instruction*, 5th Ed., ©2012. Reprinted and Electronically reproduced by permission of Pearson Education, Inc., New York, NY.

APPENDIX C Games and Templates for Sorts

Game Boards

Figures C.1 through C.8 are game board templates that can be used to create some of the games described throughout the book. Note that there are two sides for each game board. When the two sides are placed together, they form a continuous track or path. These games can be adapted for many different features and for many different levels. Here are some general tips on creating the games.

1. The game boards can be photocopied (enlarge slightly) and mounted on manila file folders (colored ones are nice), making them easy to create and store. All the materials needed for the game, such as spinners, word cards, or game markers, can be put in plastic bags or envelopes labeled with the name of the game and stored in the folder. You might mark the flip side of word cards in some way so that lost cards can be returned to the correct game. Rubber stamp figures work well.
2. When mounting a game board in a folder, be sure to leave a slight gap (about an eighth of an inch) between the two sides so that the folder will still fold. If you do not leave this gap, the paper will buckle. Trim the sheets of paper so the two new sides line up neatly, or cut around the path shape and line up the two pieces of the pathway.
3. A variety of objects (buttons, plastic discs, coins, and bottle caps) can be used for game markers or pawns that the children will move around the board. Flat objects store best in the folders or you may just want to put a collection of game markers, dice, and spinners in a box. This box can be stored near the games, and students can take what they need.
4. Add pizazz to games with pictures cut from magazines or old workbooks, stickers, comic characters, clip art, and so on. Rubber stamps, your drawings, or children's drawings can be used to add interest and color. Create catchy themes such as Rabbit Race, Lost in Space, Through the Woods, Mouse Maze, Rainforest Adventure, and so forth.
5. Include directions and correct answers (when appropriate) with the game. They might be stored inside along with playing pieces or glued to the game itself.
6. Label the spaces around the path or track according to the feature you want to reinforce, and laminate for durability. If you want to create open-ended games that can be adapted to a variety of features, laminate the path before you label the spaces. Then you can write in letters or words with a washable overhead marker and change them as needed. Permanent marker can also be used and removed with hairspray or fingernail polish remover.
7. Add interest to the game by labeling some spaces with special directions (if you are using a numbered die or spinner) or add cards with special directions to the deck of words. Directions might offer the students a bonus in the form of an extra turn or there might be a penalty such as lose a turn. These bonus or penalty directions can tie in with your themes. For example, in the Rainforest Adventure the player might forget a lunch and be asked to go back to the starting space. Keep the reading ability of your children in mind as you create these special directions.

Spinners

Many of the word study games described in this book use a game spinner. Figure C.8 provides simple directions for making a spinner.

FIGURE C.1 Racetrack and Game Board (left and right)

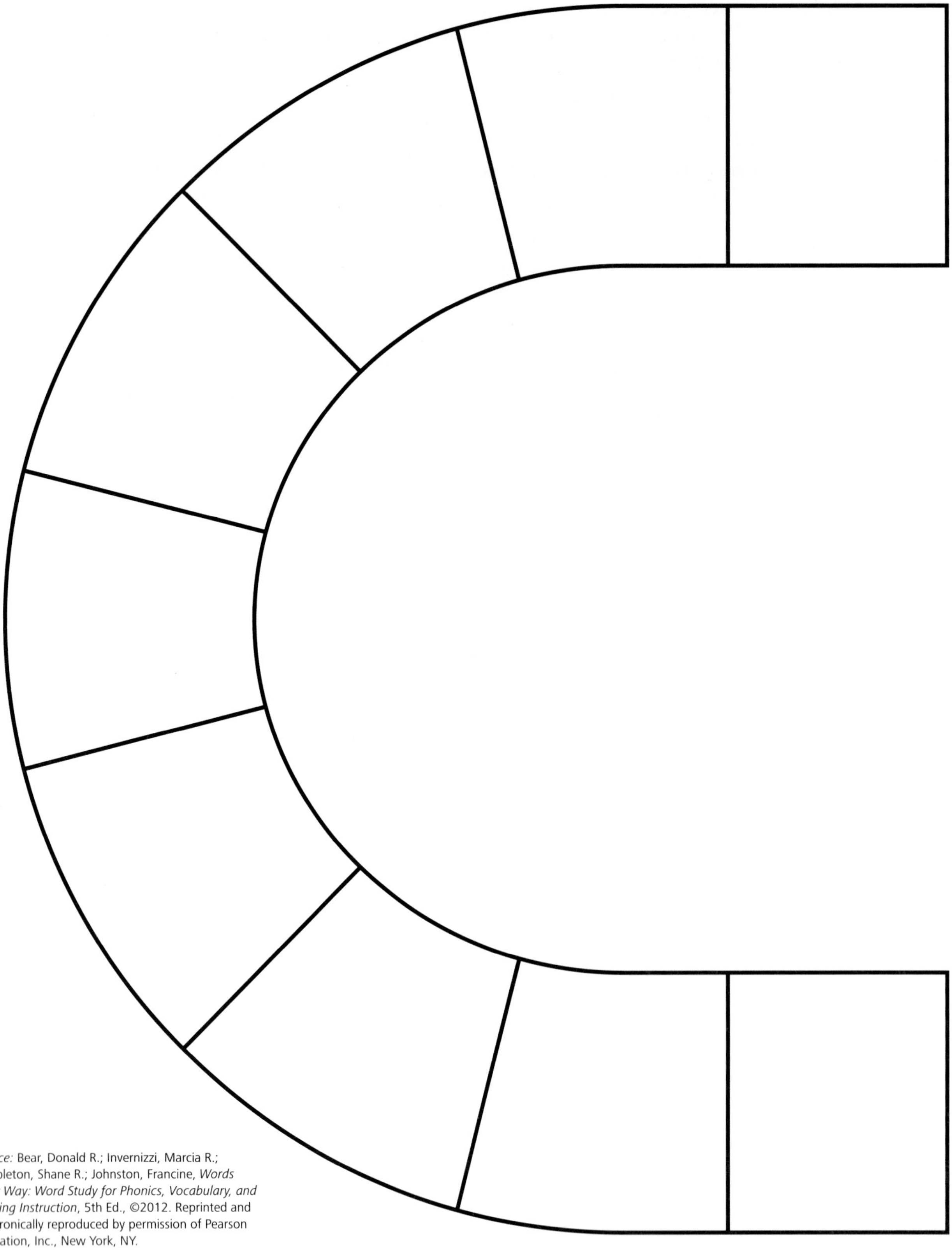

Source: Bear, Donald R.; Invernizzi, Marcia R.; Templeton, Shane R.; Johnston, Francine, *Words Their Way: Word Study for Phonics, Vocabulary, and Spelling Instruction*, 5th Ed., ©2012. Reprinted and Electronically reproduced by permission of Pearson Education, Inc., New York, NY.

FIGURE C.2 U Game Board (left)

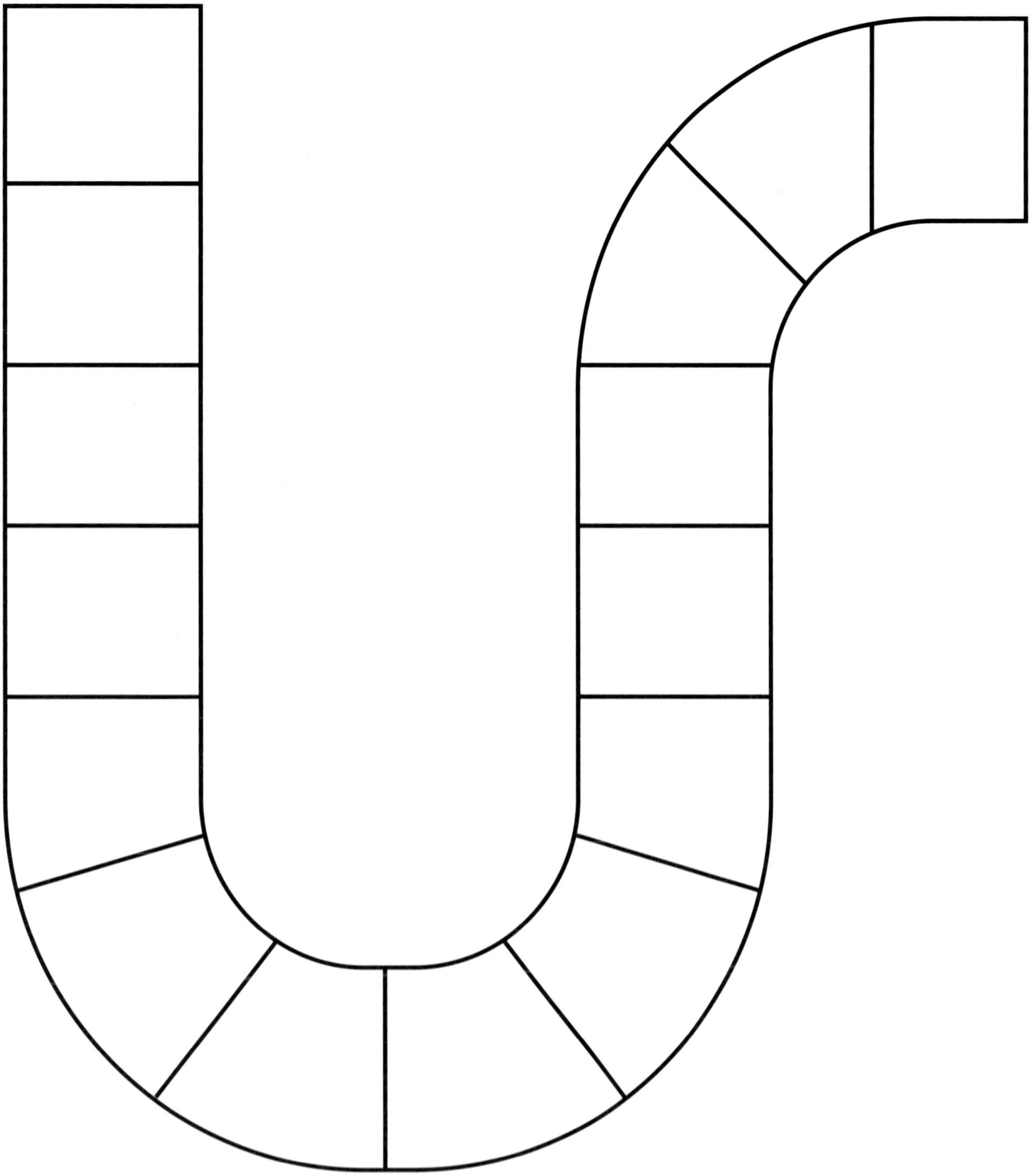

Source: Bear, Donald R.; Invernizzi, Marcia R.; Templeton, Shane R.; Johnston, Francine, *Words Their Way: Word Study for Phonics, Vocabulary, and Spelling Instruction*, 5th Ed., ©2012. Reprinted and Electronically reproduced by permission of Pearson Education, Inc., New York, NY.

FIGURE C.3 U Game Board (right)

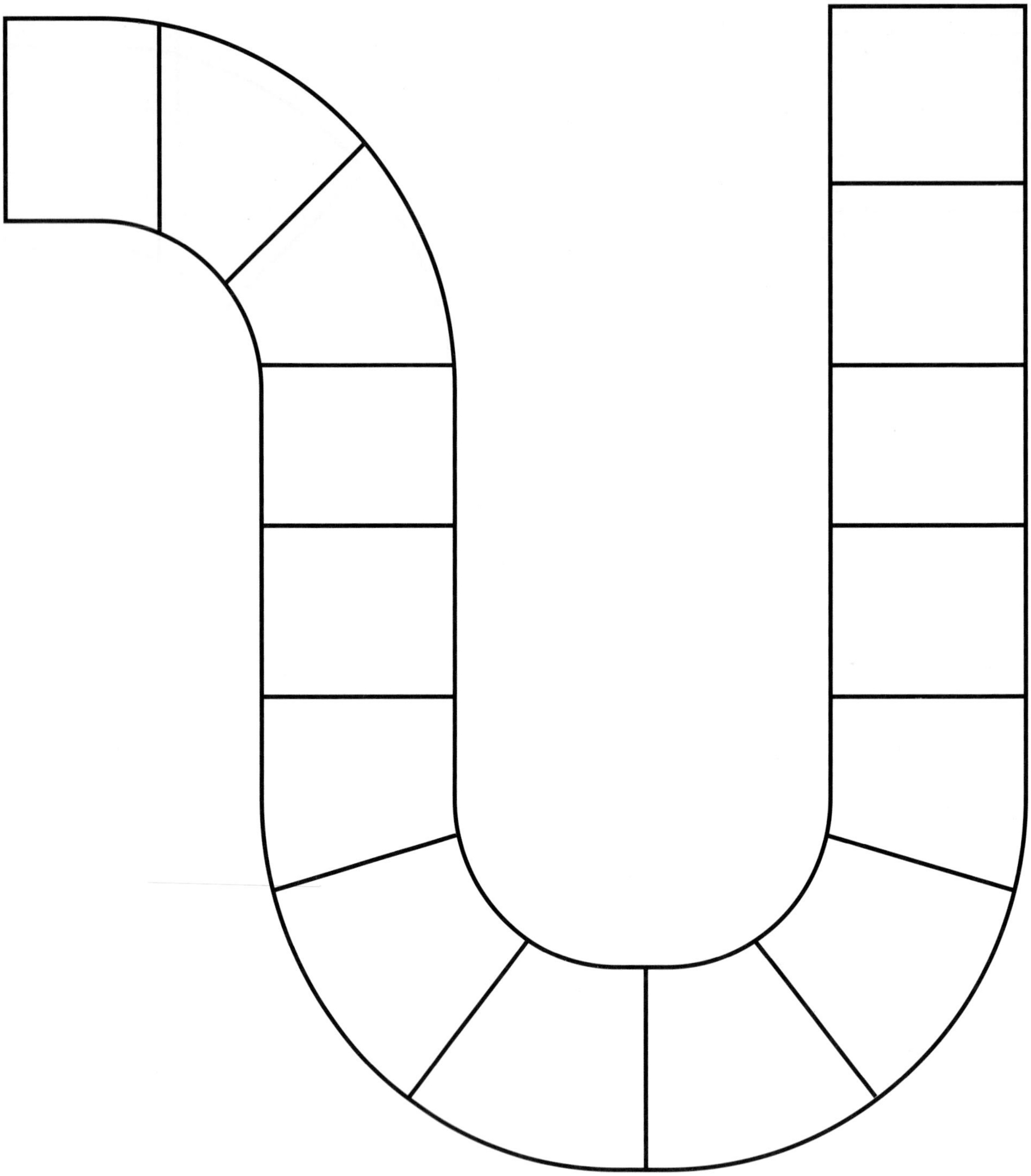

Source: Bear, Donald R.; Invernizzi, Marcia R.; Templeton, Shane R.; Johnston, Francine, *Words Their Way: Word Study for Phonics, Vocabulary, and Spelling Instruction*, 5th Ed., ©2012. Reprinted and Electronically reproduced by permission of Pearson Education, Inc., New York, NY

FIGURE C.4 S Game Board (left)

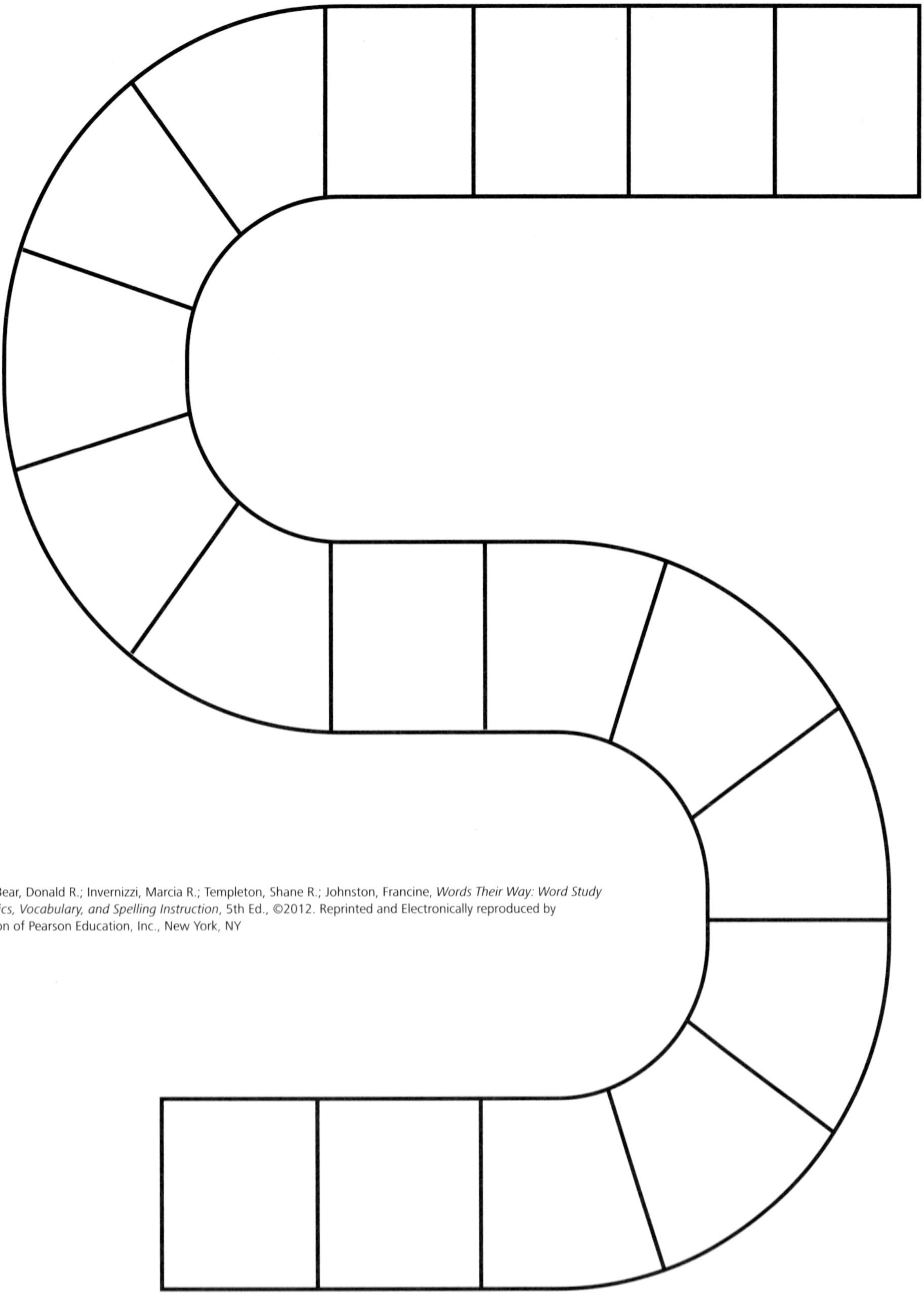

Source: Bear, Donald R.; Invernizzi, Marcia R.; Templeton, Shane R.; Johnston, Francine, *Words Their Way: Word Study for Phonics, Vocabulary, and Spelling Instruction*, 5th Ed., ©2012. Reprinted and Electronically reproduced by permission of Pearson Education, Inc., New York, NY

FIGURE C.5 S Game Board (right)

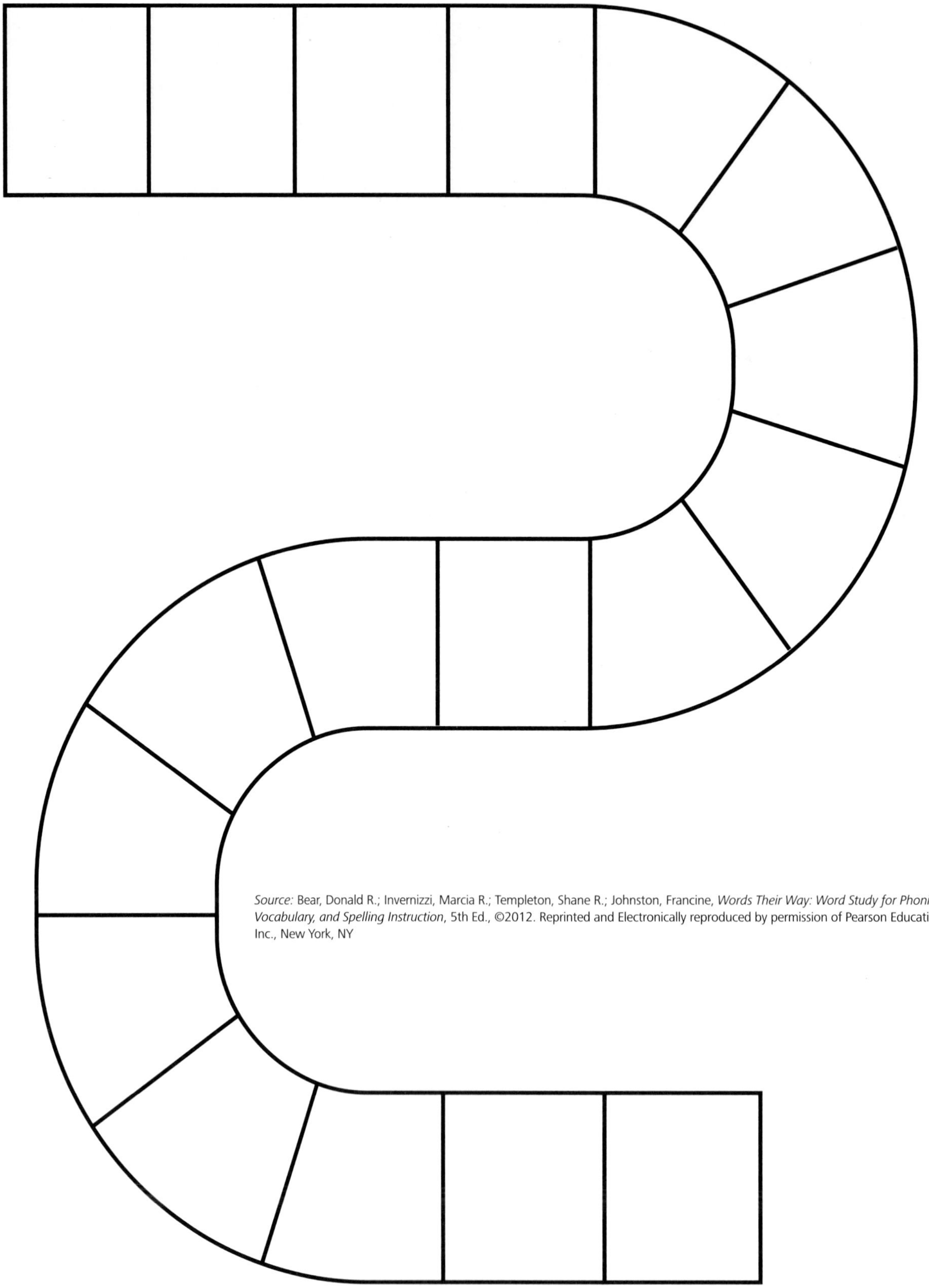

Source: Bear, Donald R.; Invernizzi, Marcia R.; Templeton, Shane R.; Johnston, Francine, *Words Their Way: Word Study for Phonics, Vocabulary, and Spelling Instruction*, 5th Ed., ©2012. Reprinted and Electronically reproduced by permission of Pearson Education, Inc., New York, NY

FIGURE C.6 Rectangle Game Board (right)

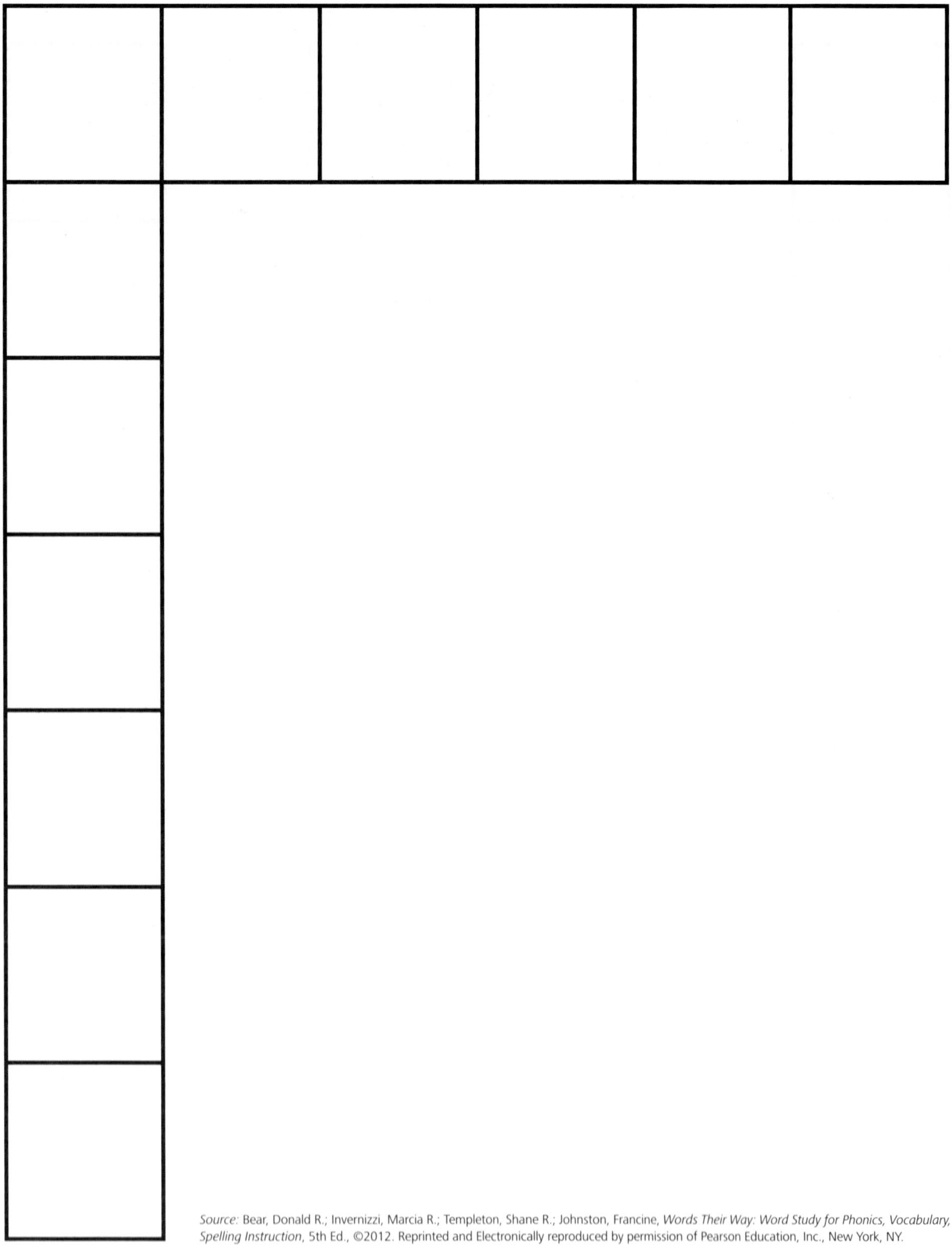

Source: Bear, Donald R.; Invernizzi, Marcia R.; Templeton, Shane R.; Johnston, Francine, *Words Their Way: Word Study for Phonics, Vocabulary, and Spelling Instruction*, 5th Ed., ©2012. Reprinted and Electronically reproduced by permission of Pearson Education, Inc., New York, NY.

FIGURE C.7 U Rectangle Board (right)

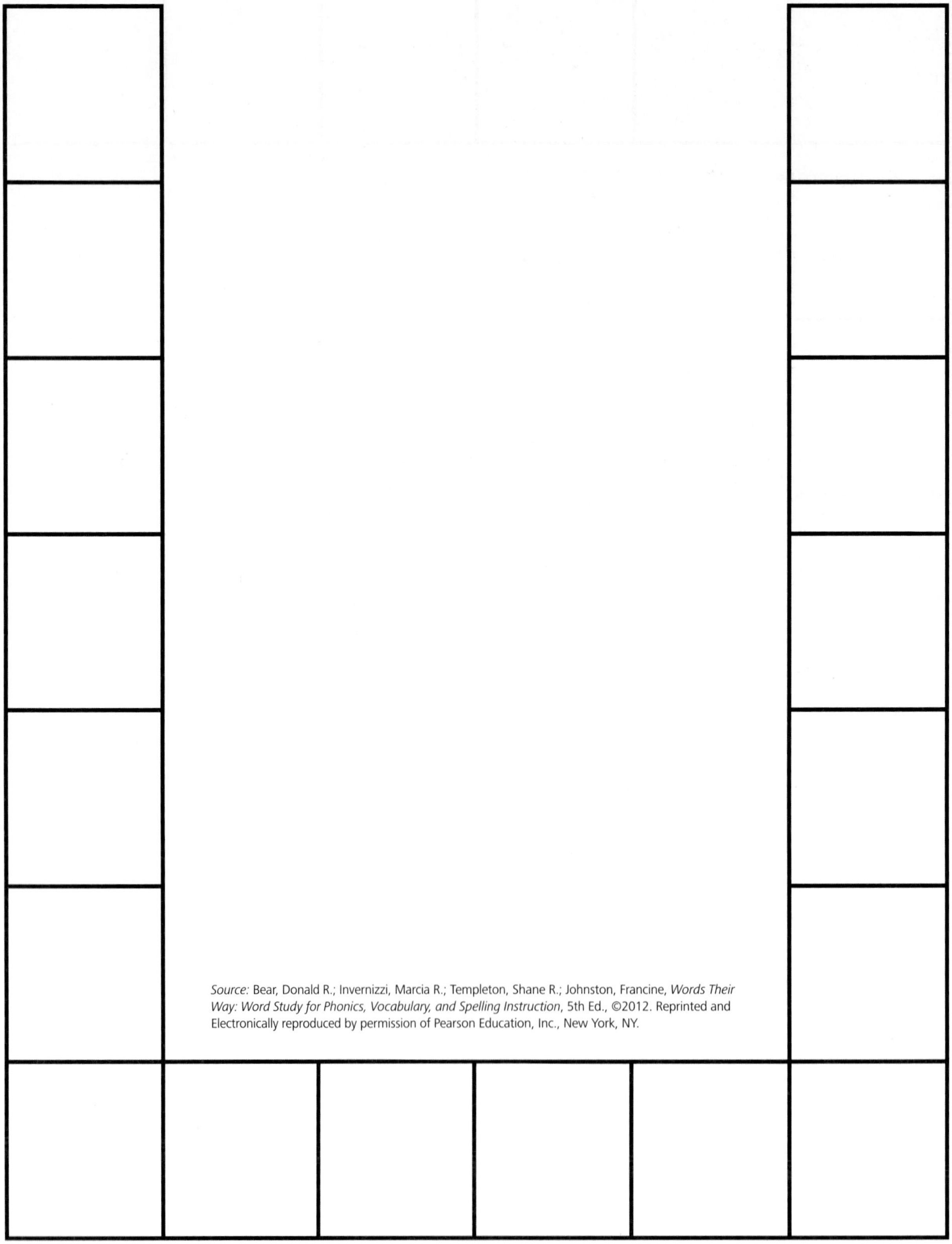

Source: Bear, Donald R.; Invernizzi, Marcia R.; Templeton, Shane R.; Johnston, Francine, *Words Their Way: Word Study for Phonics, Vocabulary, and Spelling Instruction*, 5th Ed., ©2012. Reprinted and Electronically reproduced by permission of Pearson Education, Inc., New York, NY.

FIGURE C.8 Directions for Making a Game Spinner

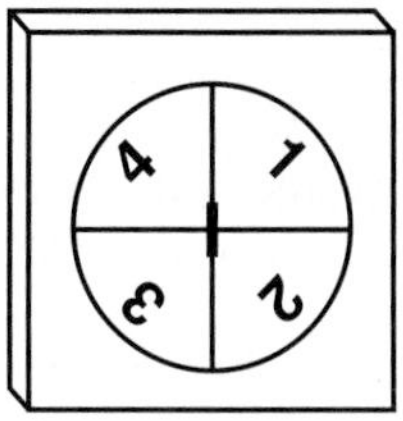

1. Glue a circle (patterns or cutouts to the right) onto a square of heavy cardboard that is no smaller than 4" × 4". Square spinner bases are easier to hold than round bases.

2. Cut a narrow slot in the center with the point of a sharp pair of scissors or a razor blade.

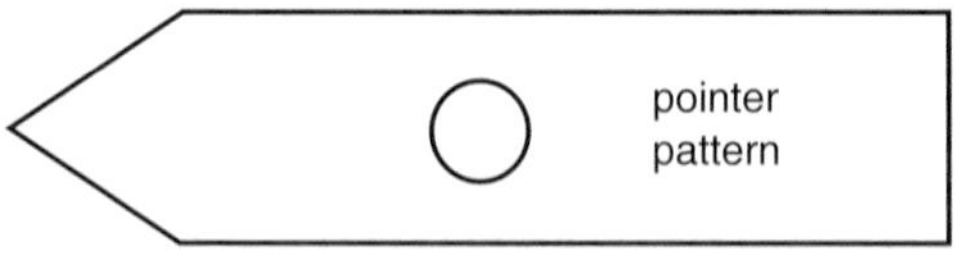

3. Cut the pointer from soft plastic (such as a milk jug) and make a clean round hole with a hole punch.

4. A washer, either a metal one from the hardware store or one cut from cardboard, helps the pointer move freely.

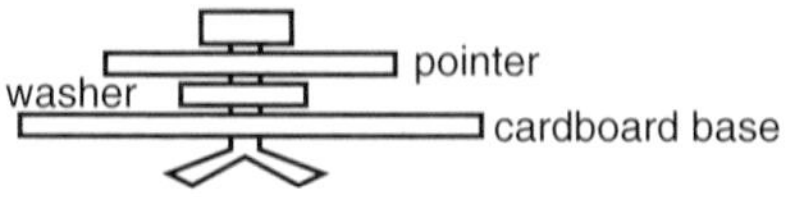

5. Push a paper fastener through the pointer hole, the washer, and the slot in the spinner base. Flatten the legs, leaving space for the pointer to spin easily.

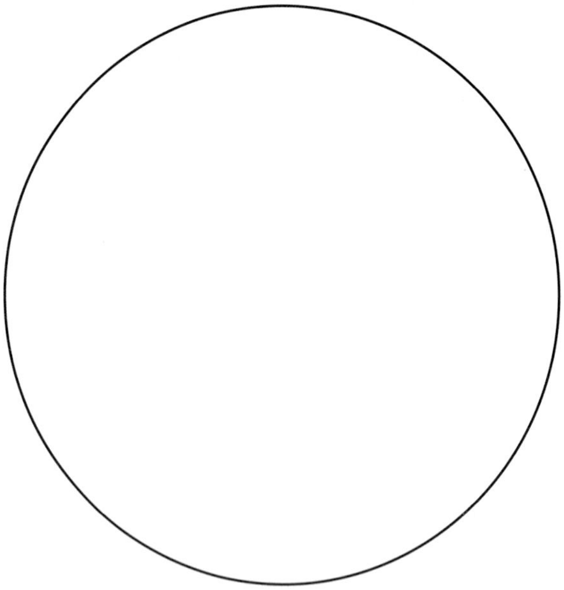

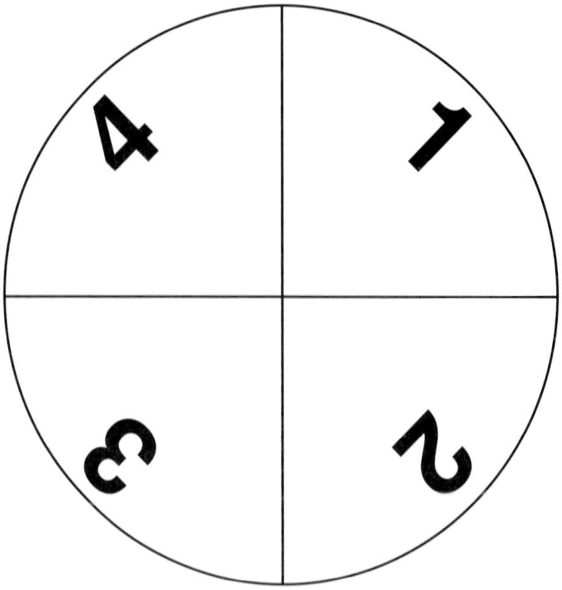

Source: Bear, Donald R.; Invernizzi, Marcia R.; Templeton, Shane R.; Johnston, Francine, *Words Their Way: Word Study for Phonics, Vocabulary, and Spelling Instruction*, 5th Ed., ©2012. Reprinted and Electronically reproduced by permission of Pearson Education, Inc., New York, NY.

Glossary

absorbed (assimilated) prefixes Prefixes in which the spelling and sound of the consonant has been absorbed into the spelling and sound at the beginning of the base or root to which the prefix is affixed (e.g., *ad* + *tract* = *attract*).

accented/stressed syllable The syllable in a word that receives more emphasis when spoken and usually has a clearly pronounced vowel sound. Compare to *unaccented syllable.*

affix Most commonly a suffix or prefix attached to a base word, stem, or root.

affricate A speech sound produced when the breath stream is stopped and released at the point of articulation, usually where the tip of the tongue rubs against the roof of the mouth just behind the teeth, such as when pronouncing the final sound in the word *clutch* or the beginning sound in the word *trip.*

alphabetic A writing system containing characters or symbols representing individual speech sounds.

alphabetic layer The first layer of word study instruction, focusing on letter–sound correspondences. Old English was phonetically regular to a great extent.

alphabetic principle The concept that letters and letter combinations, are used to represent phonemes in orthography. See also *orthography; phoneme.*

ambiguous vowels A vowel sound represented by a variety of different spelling patterns, or vowel patterns that represent a wide range of sounds (e.g., the *ou* in *cough*, *through*, and *could*).

assimilated prefixes See *absorbed (assimilated) prefixes.*

automaticity Refers to the speed and accuracy of word recognition and spelling. Automaticity is the goal of word study instruction and frees cognitive resources for comprehension.

base word A word to which prefixes and/or suffixes are added. For example, the base word of *unwholesome* is *whole.*

blends A phonics term for an orthographic unit of two or three letters at the beginning or end of words that are blended together. There are *l*-blends such as *bl, cl* and *fl; r*-blends such as *gr, tr,* and *pr; s*-blends such as *pc, scr,* and *squ;* and final blends such as *ft, rd,* and *st.* Every sound represented in a blend is pronounced, if only briefly.

blind sort A picture or word sort done with a partner in which students who are responsible for sorting cannot see the word. They must instead attend to the sounds and sometimes visualize the spelling pattern to determine the category.

blind writing sort A variant of a blind sort in which one student (or teacher) names a word without showing it to another student, who must write it in the correct category under a key word.

choral reading Oral reading done in unison with another person or persons.

closed sorts Word sorts based on predetermined categories.

closed syllable A syllable that ends with or is "closed" by a consonant sound. In polysyllabic words, a closed syllable contains a short vowel sound that is closed by two consonants (e.g., *rabbit, racket*). Compare to *open syllable.*

cognates Words in different languages derived from the same root.

complex consonant patterns Consonant units occurring at the end of words determined by the preceding vowel sound. For example, a final *tch* follows the short vowel sound in *fetch* and *scotch*, while a final *ch* follows the long vowel sound in *peach* and *coach.* Other complex consonant patterns include final *ck* (*pack* vs. *peak*) and final *dge* (*badge* vs. *cage*).

compound words Words made up of two smaller words. A compound word may or may not be hyphenated, depending on its part of speech.

concept of word The ability to match spoken words to printed words, as demonstrated by the ability to point to the words of a memorized text while reading.

concepts about print (CAP) Understandings about how books are organized (front to back page turning, titles, illustrations), how print is oriented on the page (top to bottom, left to right), and features of print such as punctuation and capitalization.

concept sorts A categorization task in which pictures, objects, or words are grouped by shared attributes or meanings to develop concepts and vocabulary.

consonant alternation The process in which the pronunciation of consonants changes in the base or root of derivationally related words while the spelling does not change (e.g., the silent-to-sounded *g* in the words *sign* and *signal;* the /k/ to /sh/ pattern in the words *music* and *musician*).

consonant blend See *blends.*

consonant digraph See *digraph.*

consonants Letters that are not vowels (*a, e, i, o,* and *u*). Whereas vowel sounds are thought of as musical, consonant sounds are known for their noise and the way in which air is constricted as it is stopped and released or forced through the vocal tract, mouth, teeth, and lips.

derivational affixes Affixes added to base words that affect the meaning (sign, **re**sign; break, break**able**) and/or part of speech (beauty, beauti**ful**). Compare to *inflectional endings.*

derivational relations spelling stage The last stage of spelling development, in which spellers learn about derivational relationships preserved in the spelling of words. *Derivational* refers to the process by which new words are created from existing words, chiefly through affixation; and the development of a word from its historical origin. *Derivational constancy* refers to spelling patterns that remain the same despite changes in pronunciation across derived forms. For example, *bomb* retains the *b* from *bombard* because of its historical evolution.

developmental level An individual's stage of spelling development: emergent, letter name–alphabetic, within word pattern, syllables and affixes, or derivational relations.

digraph Two letters that represent one sound. There are consonant digraphs and vowel digraphs, though the term most commonly refers to consonant digraphs. Common consonant digraphs include *sh, ch, th,* and *wh.* Consonant digraphs at the beginning of words are *onsets.*

directionality The left-to-right direction used for reading and writing English.

echo reading Oral reading in which the student echoes or imitates the reading of the teacher or partner. Echo reading is used with very beginning readers as a form of support. Echo reading can also be used to model fluent reading.

emergent A period of literacy development ranging from birth to beginning reading. This period precedes the letter name–alphabetic stage of spelling development.

eponyms Places, things, and actions that are named after an individual.

etymology The study of the origin and historical development of words.

frustration level A dysfunctional level of instruction where there is a mismatch between instruction and what an individual is able to grasp. This mismatch precludes learning and often results in frustration.

generative An approach to word study that emphasizes processes that apply to many words, as opposed to an approach that focuses on one word at a time.

headers Words, pictures, or other labels used to designate categories for sorting.

high-frequency words Words that make up roughly 50 percent of any text—those that occur most often (e.g., *the, was, were, is*).

homographs Words that are spelled alike, but have different pronunciations and different meanings (e.g., "*tear* a piece of paper" and "to shed a *tear*"; "*lead* someone along" and "the element *lead*").

homonyms Words that share the same spelling but have different meanings (tell a *yarn*, knit with *yarn*). See *homographs; homophones*.

homophones Words that sound alike, are spelled differently, and have different meanings (e.g., *bear* and *bare*, *pane* and *pain*, and *forth* and *fourth*).

independent level That level of academic engagement in which an individual works independently, without need of instructional support. Independent level behaviors demonstrate a high degree of accuracy, speed, ease, and fluency.

inflected/inflectional endings Suffixes that change the verb tense (walk**s**, walk**ed**, walk**ing**) or number (dog**s**, box**es**) of a word.

instructional level A level of academic engagement in which instruction is comfortably matched to what an individual is able to grasp. See also *zone of proximal development (ZPD)*.

key pictures Pictures placed at the top of each category in a picture sort. Key pictures act as headers for each column and can be used for analogy.

key words Words placed at the top of each category in a word sort. Key words act as headers for each column and can be used for analogy.

letter name–alphabetic spelling stage The second stage of spelling development, in which students represent beginning, middle, and ending sounds of words with phonetically accurate letter choices. Often the selections are based on the sound of the letter name itself, rather than abstract letter–sound associations. The letter name *h* (aitch), for example, produces the /ch/ sound, and is often selected to represent that sound (HEP for *chip*).

long vowels Every vowel (*a, e, i, o,* and *u*) has two sounds, commonly referred to as "long" and "short." The long vowel sound "says its letter name." The vocal cords are tense when producing the long vowel sound. Because of this, the linguistic term for the long vowel sound is *tense*.

meaning layer The third layer of English orthography, including meaning units such as prefixes, suffixes, and word roots. These word elements were acquired primarily during the Renaissance, when English was overlaid with many words of Greek and Latin derivation.

meaning sorts A type of word sort in which the categories are determined by semantic categories or by spelling–meaning connections.

memory reading An accurate recitation of text accompanied by fingerpoint reading.

morphology The study of word parts related to syntax and meaning.

nasals A sound such as /m/, /n/, or /ng/ produced when the air is blocked in the oral cavity but escapes through the nose. The first consonants in the words *mom* and *no* represent nasal sounds.

oddballs Words that do not fit the targeted feature in a sort.

open sorts A type of picture or word sort in which the categories for sorting are left open. Students sort pictures or words into groups according to the students' own judgment.

open syllable Syllables that end with a long vowel sound (e.g., *la-bor, sea-son*). Compare to *closed syllable*.

orthography The writing system of a language—specifically, the correct sequence of letters, characters, or symbols.

pattern A letter sequence that functions as a unit to represent a sound (such as *ai* in *rain, pain* and *train*) or a sequence of vowels and consonants, such as the consonant-vowel-consonant (CVC) pattern in a word such as *rag* or at a syllable juncture such as the VCCV pattern in *button*.

pattern layer The second layer or tier of English orthography, in which patterns of letter sequences, rather than individual letters themselves, represent vowel sounds. This layer of information was acquired during the period of English history following the Norman invasion. Many of the vowel patterns of English are of French derivation.

pattern sort A word sort in which students categorize words according to similar spelling patterns.

personal readers Individual books of reading materials for beginning readers. Group experience charts, dictations, rhymes, and short excerpts from books comprise the majority of the reading material.

phoneme The smallest unit of speech that distinguishes one word from another. For example, the *t* of *tug* and the *r* of *rug* are two phonemes.

phoneme segmentation The process of dividing a spoken word into the smallest units of sound within that word. The word *bat* can be divided or segmented into three phonemes: /b/, /a/, /t/.

phonemic awareness The ability to consciously manipulate individual phonemes in a spoken language. Phonemic awareness is often assessed by the ability to tap, count, or push a penny forward for every sound heard in a word like *cat:* /c/, /a/, /t/.

phonetic Representing the sounds of speech with a set of distinct symbols (letters), each denoting a single sound. See also *alphabetic principle.*

phonics The systematic relationship between letters and sounds.

phonics readers Beginning reading books written with controlled vocabulary that contain recurring phonics elements.

phonological awareness An awareness of various speech sounds such as syllables, rhyme, and individual phonemes.

picture sort A categorization task in which pictures are sorted into categories of similarity and difference. Pictures may be sorted by sound or by meaning. Pictures cannot be sorted by pattern.

preconsonantal nasals Nasals that occur before consonants, as in the words *bump* or *sink.* The vowel is nasalized as part of the air escapes through the nose during pronunciation. See also *nasals.*

predictable Text for beginning readers with repetitive language patterns, rhythm and rhyme, and illustrations that make it easy to read and remember.

prefix An affix attached at the beginning of a base word or word root that changes the meaning of the word.

pretend reading A paraphrase or spontaneous retelling told by children as they turn the pages of a familiar story book.

print referencing The practice of referring to features of print such as punctuation, capital letters, directionality, and so forth as a way to teach children concepts about print. See also *concepts about print (CAP).*

***r*-influenced (*r*-controlled) vowels** In English, *r* colors the way the preceding vowel is pronounced. For example, compare the pronunciation of the vowels in *bar* and *bad.* The vowel in *bar* is influenced by the *r.*

root word/roots Words or word parts, often of Latin or Greek origin, they are often combined with other roots to form words such as *telephone* (*tele* and *phone*). See also *stems.*

salient sounds A prominent sound in a word or syllable that stands out because of the way it is made or felt in the mouth, or because of idiosyncratic reasons such as being similar to a sound in one's name.

schwa A vowel sound in English that often occurs in an unstressed syllable, such as the /uh/ sound in the first syllable of the word *above.*

shared reading An activity in which the teacher prereads a text and then invites students to join in on subsequent readings.

short vowels Every vowel (*a, e, i, o,* and *u*) has two sounds, commonly referred to as "long" and "short." The vocal cords are more relaxed when producing the short vowel sound than the long vowel sound. Because of this, short vowel sounds are often referred to as *lax.* The five short vowels can be heard at the beginning of these words: *apple, Ed, igloo, octopus,* and *umbrella.* Compare to *long vowels.*

sight words/vocabulary Printed words stored in memory by the reader that can be read immediately, "at first sight," without having to use decoding strategies.

sound board Charts used by letter name–alphabetic spellers that contain pictures and letters for the basic sound–symbol correspondences (e.g., the letter *b,* a picture of a bell, and the word *bell*).

sound sort Sorts that ask students to categorize pictures or words by sound as opposed to visual patterns.

speed sorts Pictures or words that are sorted under a timed condition. Students try to beat their own time.

spelling inventories Assessments that ask students to spell a series of increasingly difficult words used to determine what features students know or use but confuse, as well as a specific developmental stage of spelling.

spelling–meaning connections Words that are related in meaning often share the same spelling despite changes in pronunciation from one form of the word to the next. The word *sign,* for example, retains the *g* from *signal* even though it is not pronounced, thus "signaling" the meaning connection through the spelling.

suffix An affix attached at the end of a base word or word root.

syllable juncture The transition from one syllable to the next. Sometimes this transition involves a spelling change such as consonant doubling or dropping the final *e* before adding *ing.*

syllable juncture patterns The alternating patterns of consonants (C) and vowels (V) at the point where syllables meet. For example, the word *rabbit* follows a VCCV syllable pattern at the point where the syllables meet.

syllables Units of spoken language that consist of a vowel that may be preceded and/or followed by several consonants. Syllables are units of sound and can often be detected by paying attention to movements of the mouth. Syllabic divisions indicated in the dictionary are not always correct because the dictionary will always separate meaning units regardless of how the word is pronounced. For example, the proper syllable division for the word *naming* is *na-ming;* however, the dictionary divides this word as *nam-ing* to preserve the *ing.*

syllables and affixes stage The fourth stage of spelling development, which coincides with intermediate reading. Syllables and affixes spellers learn about the spelling changes that often take place at the point of transition from one syllable to the next. Frequently this transition involves consonant doubling or dropping the final *e* before adding a suffix.

tracking The ability to fingerpoint read a text, demonstrating concept of a word.

unaccented/unstressed syllable The syllable in a word that gets little emphasis and may have an indistinct vowel sound such as the first syllable in *about,* the second syllable in *definition,* or the final syllables in *doctor* or *table.* See also *schwa.*

vowel A speech sound produced by the easy passage of air through a relatively open vocal tract. Vowels form the most central sound of a syllable. In English, vowel sounds are represented by the following letters: *a, e, i, o, u,* and sometimes *y.* Compare to *consonants.*

vowel alternation The process in which the pronunciation of vowels changes in the base or root of derivationally related words, while the spelling does not change (e.g., the long-to-short vowel change in the related words *crime* and *criminal;* the long-to-schwa vowel change in the related words *impose* and *imposition*).

vowel digraphs A phonics term for pairs of vowels that represent a single vowel sound (such as *ai* in *rain, oa* in *boat, ue* in *blue*). Compare to *digraph.*

vowel marker A silent letter used to indicate the sound of the vowel. In English, silent letters are used to form patterns associated with specific vowel sounds. Vowel markers are usually vowels, as the *i* in *drain* or the *a* in *treat,* but they can also be consonants, as the *l* in *told.*

within word pattern spelling stage The third stage of spelling development, which coincides with the transitional period of literacy development. Within word pattern spellers have mastered the basic letter–sound correspondences of written English and they grapple with letter sequences that function as a unit, especially long vowel patterns. Some of the letters in the unit may have no sound themselves. These silent letters, such as the silent *e* in *snake* or the silent *i* in *drain,* serve as important markers in the pattern.

word A unit of meaning. A word may be a single syllable or a combination of syllables. A word may contain smaller units of meaning within it. In print, a word is separated by white space. In speech, several words may be strung together in a breath group. For this reason, it takes a while for young children to develop a clear concept of word. See also *concept of word.*

word bank A collection of known words harvested from frequently read texts such as little leveled books, dictated stories, basal preprimers, and primers. Word bank words are written on small cards. These words, which students can recognize with ease, are used in word study games and word sorts.

word cards Words written on 2-by-1-inch pieces of cardstock or paper.

word consciousness An attitude of curiosity and attention to words critical for vocabulary development.

word families Phonograms or words that share the same rime. (For example, *fast, past, last,* and *blast* all share the *ast* rime.) In the derivational relations stage, *word families* refers to words that share the same root or origin, as in *spectator, spectacle, inspect,* and *inspector.* See *phonograms; rimes.*

word hunts A word study activity in which students go back to texts they have previously read to hunt for other words that follow the same spelling features examined during the word or picture sort.

word root See *root word/roots.*

word sort A basic word study routine in which students group words into categories. Word sorting involves comparing and contrasting within and across categories. Word sorts are often cued by key words placed at the top of each category.

word study A learner-centered, conceptual approach to instruction in phonics, spelling, word recognition, and vocabulary, based on a developmental model.

word study notebooks Notebooks in which students write their word sorts into columns and add other words that follow similar spelling patterns throughout the week. Word study notebooks may also contain lists of words generated over time, such as new vocabulary, homophones, cognates, and so on.

writing sorts An extension activity in which students write the words they have sorted into categories.

Index

A

-able sorting example, 30–32
-able suffix, 165
Academic reading, 154, 176
Academic writing, 177
Accented syllables, 145–146
Advanced readers and writers. *See also* Derivational relations stage of spelling
  affixes, 165–167
  characteristics, 21, 160
  games and activities, 174–175
  instructional focus, 160
  middle-/high-school reading selections, 161
  online resources for word study, 173–174
  polysyllabic word sorts, 164–171
  Qualitative Literacy Checklist, 11
  reading, 159–161
  reading support, 175–176
  sort support, 165–171
  spelling, 163–164
  spelling characteristics and common errors, 22
  spelling strategies, 171
  stage overview, 159–164
  vocabulary, 163
  vocabulary and spelling development strategies, 172–175
  vocabulary note cards, 175
  word collection routine, 172
  word origins, 172–173
  word study notebooks, 171–172
  word trees, 174
  writing, 162–163
  writing support, 176–177
Advanced suffixes, 170
Affixes, 147–148, 165–167
Affricates, 94–95
Alphabet books, 70–71
Alphabet games, 69, 71, 72
Alphabet song, 70
Alphabetic recognition
  defined, 51, 54
  emergent learners, 54–55, 57
  learning, 55
  support, 70–72
Ambiguous vowels, 121–122, 146
Analogy, 96, 123, 188
Assessment, 4, 5, 27
Assimilated prefixes, 170–171
Audiobooks, 154, 175–176
Automaticity, 33

B

Beginning reader texts, 102–104
Beginning readers, 103
Beginning readers and writers. *See also* Letter name-alphabetic stage of spelling
  affricates, 94–95
  blends and digraphs, 92, 93
  characteristics, 21, 84
  consonant sounds, 91–92
  early literacy development skills, 84
  games and activities, 97–100
  guided reading, 104–107
  instructional focus, 84
  mixed vowel word families, 93–94
  oddballs, 94
  picture and word sorts, 89–96
  preconsonantal nasals, 95
  Qualitative Literacy Checklist, 10
  reading, 83–86
  reading support, 101–107
  same vowel word families, 92–93
  short vowels, 94
  sight words, 13
  sort support, 91–95
  spelling, 87–89
  spelling characteristics and common errors, 22, 84
  spelling strategies, 95–96
  stage overview, 83–89
  word study, 96–100
  writing, 86–87
  writing support, 107–108
"Best bet" strategy, 124, 148, 188
Big ideas or underlying generalizations
  for beginning learners, 90–91
  for emergent learners, 58
  for intermediate learners, 142
  for transitional learners, 119
Bingo, 97–98
Blends, 92, 93
Blind or no peeking sort, 43
Board games, 152–153
Books
  alphabet, 70–71
  for beginning readers, 101
  for children to handle, 73–74
  concept, 65
  homophones and homographs in, 127–128
  predictable pattern, 75
  reading and talking about, 62–63
  rereading, 63–64
  with rhyme and language play, 66–67
  with rhymes, jingles, and songs, 67
  selecting with child, 129–130
  tips for reading aloud, 63
  for transitional readers, 113
  wordless, 64
Brainburst, 174–175
Build, Blend, and Extend, 98

C

CAP. *See* Concepts about print
Card games, 151
Child's name, 70
Choral reading, 104
Chunk known word parts, 96, 188
Closed syllables, 145
Commercial games, 43–44, 100
Comparatives, 144
Complex consonants, 122–123
Compound words, 143
Comprehension, 131
Concept books, 65
Concept of word (COW)
  beginning readers and writers, 85
  defined, 49, 51, 55
  development of, 56
  emergent learners, 55–56
  game, 75
  support, 74–76
  tips for prompting, 74
  trying to match voice to print, 55
Concept sorts
  defined, 56
  with hot-/cold-weather items, 66
  play with, 65–66
  for vehicles, 56
Concepts about print (CAP)
  beginning readers and writers, 85
  defined, 51, 55
  emergent learners, 55
  print referencing examples and, 73
  support, 72–74
Consonant alterations, 167–168
Consonants
  beginning sounds, 91
  complex, 122–123
  hard, 146
  patterns, 146–147
  predictable spelling changes in, 168–169
  silent, 146–147
  soft, 146
Contrasts, beginning with, 33
COW. *See* Concept of word
Cut-up sentences, 75–76

D

Daily student sorting, 35, 37
Declare Your Category!, 126
Decodable readers, 103
Dedicated captions, 77
Derivational relations stage of spelling. *See also* Advanced readers and writers
 characteristics of, 22, 160, 163
 common errors, 22, 160
 correct spelling, 163
 polysyllabic word sorts, 164–171
 sorts for, 27
 stage overview, 159–164
 strategies, 171
 strategies and activities to develop, 172–175
 use but confuse, 164
Developmental Reading Assessment (DRA), 193
Developmental spelling. *See also* Spelling
 assessment, 4, 5
 grading and monitoring process, 5, 7
 instructional methods and routines, 4–7
 purpose and principles, 4, 5
 school not practicing, 190
 traditional spelling versus, 4–7
Dictations, 107–108
Digital devices, 176
Digraphs, 92, 93
Diphthongs, 121–122
Dyslexia, 193–194

E

Early literacy skills
 alphabetic recognition, 51, 54–55, 57, 70–72
 beginning readers and writers, 85
 concept of word (COW), 51, 55–56, 74–76
 concepts about print (CAP), 51, 55, 72–74
 development, 85
 emergent learners, 51–56
 oral language, concepts, and vocabulary, 51, 52, 56, 60–66
 with parents, tutors, and school volunteers, 60–77
 phonemic awareness, 53–54
 phonics, 51, 54, 57, 69
 phonological awareness, 51, 52–53, 66–68
Echo reading, 104
Educational television, 60–62
Emergent learners
 alphabetic recognition, 51, 54–55, 57, 70
 characteristics of, 21–22, 48
 concept of word (COW), 51, 55–56, 74–76
 concept sorts, 56
 concepts about print (CAP), 51, 55, 72–74
 defined, 9
 early literacy skills, 51–56
 instructional focus, 48
 letter sounds, 57
 oral language, concepts, vocabulary, 51, 52, 60–66
 phonemic awareness, 51, 53–54
 phonics, 51, 54, 69
 phonological awareness, 51, 52–53, 56, 66–68
 picture sorts, 56–60
 in pre-alphabetic stage, 49
 as pretend writers, 50
 reading, 12, 13, 47–49
 reading characteristics, 21
 stage overview, 43
 vocabulary, 51, 52
 writing, 12–13, 49–50, 76–77
 writing characteristics, 21
 writing evolution, 49
Emergent spellers
 characteristics of, 22, 48
 common spelling errors, 22, 48
 pretend spelling, 12
 sorts for, 27
English language layers, 7–8
English learners, word study for, 186
Essential techniques
 daily student sorting, 35, 37
 overview, 34
 reflection, 35, 40
 sort introduction, 35–37
 table of, 35
 word hunt, 35, 38–40
 word study notebooks, 35, 41, 42
 writing sort, 35, 37–38
Etymologies, 171, 173
Everyday experiences, 62

F

Fiction, intermediate readers, 137
Fingerpoint reading, 74–75
Follow-the-path games, 97, 128–129
Font sorts, 58, 72
Frayer model, 151
Frequently asked questions, 181–194

G

Games and activities
 alphabet, 71, 72
 Bingo, 97–98
 board, 152–153
 Brainburst, 174–175
 Build, Blend, and Extend, 98
 card, 151
 concepts about print (CAP), 74
 COW, 75
 Declare Your Category!, 126
 dictations, 107–108
 follow-the-path, 97, 128–129
 Go Fish!, 100
 Guess My Category, 125
 Guess My Word, 100
 Homophone Rummy, 127
 Homophone Win, Lose, or Draw, 127
 Match!, 98
 Memory, 98
 phonics, 69
 Prefix Spin, 153
 rhyming, 68
 Roll the Dice, 100
 Shades of Meaning, 175
 Show Me, 99
 sound boards, 107
 Spelling Game, 129
 for transitional readers and writers, 125–129
 Vowel Concentration, 126
 Vowel Rummy, 126
 word bank, 106
 word family wheels and flip books, 98–99
 Word Part Shuffle, 175
 word study, 41, 43–44
 Word Study Uno, 125
 words with cubes, 99–100
Generative vocabulary approach, 140
Gifted students, 186
Go Fish!, 100
Goldilocks Rule, 130
Grade level
 not reading at, 193
 retaining children not reading/writing at, 193
 spelling expectations, 185
Grading and monitoring process, 5, 7
Greek roots, 169
Guess My Category, 125
Guess My Word, 100
Guided reading, 104–107

H

Hard consonants, 146
"Have-a-go" strategy, 124, 148–149, 188–189
High-achieving students, 186
Homographs
 books that feature, 127–128
 defined, 127
 polysyllabic, 143
Homophone dictionaries, 127
Homophone pairs, 122
Homophone Rummy, 127

Homophone Win, Lose, or Draw, 127
Homophones
  books that feature, 127–128
  defined, 123, 143
  polysyllabic, 143

I
-ible sorting example, 30–32
Idiomatic phrases, 124
Inflected endings, 143–144
Informational text, intermediate readers and writers, 137
Instructional focus
  advanced readers and writers, 160
  emergent learners, 48
  intermediate readers and writers, 136
  transitional readers and writers, 112
Instructional level, 4
Instructional methods and routines, 4–7
Intermediate readers and writers. *See also* Syllables and affixes stage of spelling
  academic vocabulary development strategies, 149–151
  board games, 152–153
  card games, 151
  characteristics of, 21, 136
  fiction examples, 137
  informational text, 137
  instructional focus, 136
  polysyllabic word sorts, 140–149
  Prefix Spin, 153
  Qualitative Literacy Checklist, 11
  reading, 135
  reading support, 153–154
  sort support, 142–148
  spelling, 138–139
  spelling characteristics and common errors, 22, 136
  spelling development strategies and activities, 151–153
  spelling strategies, 148–149
  stage overview, 135–140
  vocabulary, 139–140
  word study notebooks, 149
  word study with parents, tutors, and volunteers, 149–153
  writing, 137–138
  writing support, 154–155
Invented spelling, 96, 188
-ion suffix, patterns for adding, 167

K
Know it in a snap, 96, 188

L
Language, referring to literacy vocabulary, 74
Latin roots, 31, 168, 169
Learning disabled students, 186
Let's Talk About It
  advanced readers and writers, 164–165
  beginning readers and writers, 89–91
  emergent learners, 57–60
  intermediate readers and writers, 141–142
  transitional readers and writers, 116–119
Letter hunt, 72
Letter name-alphabetic stage of spelling. *See also* Beginning readers and writers
  characteristics, 22, 84, 88
  common errors, 22, 84
  correct spelling, 88
  deliberate effort, 87
  sort support, 91–95
  sorts for, 27
  stage overview, 83–89
  strategies, 95–96
  use but confuse, 88–89
  what is absent, 89
  writing sample, 87
Letter names. *See also* Alphabetic recognition
  not teaching, 182
  order to teach, 182
  table of, 87
List-Group-Label, 151, 152
Literacy development. *See also specific stages*
  parent determination of stage, 8–9
  Qualitative Literacy Checklist, 9, 10–11
  stages of, 8–22
  stages table, 9
Long *e* patterns, 118
Long vowel patterns, 120, 146

M
Magnetic alphabet letters, 71–72
Match!, 98
Meaning, influence on spelling, 119
Meaning layer, 8
Meaning sorts
  defined, 29
  with Latin roots, 31
  with objects, 30
  with reading vocabulary, 30
Meaningful texts, returning to, 34
Memorization, 185
Memory game, 98
Memory reading, 49, 75
Middle-/high-school reading selections, 161
Mispronunciation, 190
Mixed-vowel family sort, 90

N
The name game, 69

O
Object sorts, 69
Oddballs, 94, 117–118
Online resources for word study, 173–174
Open syllables, 144–145
Oral language, concepts, and vocabulary
  emergent learners, 51, 52
  support, 60–66

P
Parents
  beginning readers and writers support, 96–100
  child literacy development stage determination, 8–9
  early literacy skills support, 60–77
  intermediate readers and writers support, 149–153
  transitional readers and writers support, 124–129
Partner (buddy) reading, 103
Pattern layer, 8
Pattern sorts
  defined, 29
  examples, 29, 33
  within word pattern, 118
Patterns
  consonant, 146–147
  -ion suffix, 167
  long vowel, 120
  within word, frequency, 118
  within word, location, 118–119
Personal readers, 103–104
Phonemic awareness, 51, 53–54
Phonics
  defined, 54
  emergent learners, 51, 54
  support, 69
Phonological awareness
  defined, 51, 56
  elements of, 66
  emergent learners, 52–53, 56
  prompts to develop, 66
  support, 66–69
Picture sorts, 56–60, 69, 89–96
Pig Latin, 54
Plurals, 143–144
Poetry, 131
Polysyllabic word sorts, 141–149, 164–171
Polysyllabic words, 143
Practical writing, 76–77, 108
Pre-alphabetic stage, 49
Preconsonantal nasals, 95
Predictable pattern books, 75
Predictable readers, 103
Prefix Spin, 153
Prefixes
  assimilated, 170–171
  common, 147–148

studied at derivational relations stage, 166
using as spelling strategy, 189
Pretend writers, 50
Print, drawing attention to, 72–73

Q
Qualitative Literacy Checklist, 9, 10–11
Qualitative spelling inventory, 4

R
Readers. *See also specific literacy development stages*
advanced, 19–20, 159–177
beginning, 13–15, 83–108
emergent, 13, 47–77
intermediate, 17–19, 135–155
transitional, 15–17, 111–132
Reading
academic, 154, 176
advanced readers and writers, 159–161
beginning readers and writers, 83–86
characteristics, 21
choral, 104
COW, 74–75
echo, 104
emergent learners, 12, 47–49
fingerpoint, 74–75
with fluency, 17
grade level assessment, 190–191
guided, 104–107
intermediate readers and writers, 135, 153–154
memory, 49, 75
middle-/high-school selections, 161
not at grade level, 193
partner (buddy), 104
sharing, 176
silent, 15
as social, 154
talking about, 104, 131
time, monitoring, 130
transitional readers and writers, 111–114
with your child, tips for, 63
Reading aloud, 101–102, 130, 153–154, 175–176
Reading levels
description of, 191–192
factors affecting, 192
Reading support
advanced readers, 175–176
beginning readers, 101–107
intermediate readers, 153–154
transitional readers, 129–131
Reflection. *See also* Essential techniques
on big ideas or underlying generalizations, 35, 40
in daily student sorting, 37
in sort instruction, 36
in word hunt, 39–40
in writing sort, 38
written, 40
Repeated readings, 131
Revisions, 138, 155
Rhymes, jingles and songs, 67
Rhyming games, 68
Rhyming sorts, 57, 68
Rhyming story extensions, 68
R-influenced vowels, 120–121, 146
Roll the Dice, 100
Roots
Greek, 168
Latin, 31, 168, 169
using as spelling strategy, 189
Rules, avoiding, 33

S
Scholastic Reading Inventory (SRI), 193
Semantic maps, 150
Shades of Meaning, 175
Short vowels, 94
Show Me, 99
Sight vocabulary, 105–107
Sight words, 13, 85
Silent consonants, 146–147
Silent sound consonant alterations, 168
Soft consonants, 146
Sort instruction. *See also* Essential techniques
defined, 35
steps in, 35–37
Sort support
advanced readers and writers, 165–171
beginning readers and writers, 91–95
emergent learners, 56–57
intermediate readers and writers, 142–148
transitional readers and writers, 119–123
Sorting
correct, and misspelling in daily use, 183
defined, 28
role of, 28–30
by sound and sight, 32–33
student continued interest in, 186
suffix, 30–32
by word families, 29
Sorts. *See also* Meaning sorts; Pattern sorts; Sound sorts
blind or no peeking game, 43
concept, 56, 65–66
font, 58, 72
as key to word study, 34
object, 69
picture, 56–60, 69
polysyllabic, 140–149, 164–171
rhyming, 57, 68
speed game, 43
for spellers, 27
types of, 28
writing, 37–38
Sound bags, 69
Sound boards, 107
Sound I spy game, 69
Sound layer, 7–8
Sound sorts
defined, 28–29
for emergent learners, 58, 59
examples, 28, 33
within word pattern, 117
Sound-It-Out, 96, 188
Sounds
consonant, 91
letter, 57
writing for, 38, 77
Specific vocabulary approach, 140
Speed sort, 43
Spell check, 149, 189
Spelling. *See also specific stages of spelling*
advanced readers and writers, 20, 163–164
beginning readers and writers, 14–15, 87–89
emergent learners, 12, 13–15, 48, 51
features by stage of development, 184
grade level expectations and, 185
intermediate readers and writers, 18–19, 138–139
invented, 96, 182–183, 188
misspelling corrections and, 187
predictable changes in consonant and vowels, 168–169
pretend, 12
progress assessment, 183–185
rules of, not teaching, 185
stage progression, 185
by syllable, 189
theme-based list, 6
transitional readers and writers, 16–17
within word pattern stage of, 16–17
Spelling dictionaries, 149, 189
Spelling features, 89
Spelling Game, 129
Spelling strategies
advanced readers and writers, 171
beginning readers and writers, 95–96
intermediate readers and writers, 148–149
transitional readers and writers, 123–124
types of, 188–189
use of, 187

Spelling-meaning connection, 148, 189
Stories, telling, 64–65
Suffix sort, 30–32
Suffixes
advanced, 170
common, 147–148
studied at derivational relations stage, 166
using as spelling strategy, 189
Superlatives, 144
Syllables
accented, 145–146
closed, 144–145
open, 144–145
spelling by, 189
unaccented, 146
Syllables and affixes stage of spelling. *See also* Intermediate readers and writers
"best bet" strategy, 148
characteristics of, 22, 136, 139
common errors, 22, 136
correct spelling, 138
"have-a-go" strategy, 148–149
overview, 135–140
sorts for, 27
spell by syllable, 148
spell check, 149
spelling dictionaries, 149
spelling-meaning connection, 148
strategies, 148–149
use but confuse, 138–139
what is absent, 139
word parts, 148

T

Taboo, 47
Talk, 60
Teachers, questions to ask, 27
Theme-based spelling list, 6
Traditional spelling. *See also* Developmental spelling
assessment, 4, 5
grading and monitoring process, 5, 7
instructional methods and routines, 4–7
purpose and principles, 4, 5
Transitional readers and writers. *See also* Within word pattern stage of spelling
characteristics of, 21, 112
characteristics of books for, 113
Declare Your Category! for, 126
follow-the-path games for, 128–129
games for, 125–129
Guess My Category for, 125
homophone dictionaries for, 127
Homophone Rummy for, 127
Homophone Win, Lose, or Draw for, 127
instructional focus, 112
picture and word sorts, 116–124
Qualitative Literacy Checklist, 20
reading, 111–114
reading support, 129–131
sort support, 119–123
spelling, 115–116
spelling characteristics and common errors, 22, 112
Spelling Game for, 129
spelling strategies, 123–124
stage overview, 111–114
vocabulary, 114
Vowel Concentration for, 126
Vowel Rummy for, 126
word operations, 125–126
word study, 124–129
word study notebooks, 124–125
Word Study Uno for, 125
writing, 114
writing support, 131–132

U

Unaccented syllables, vowel patterns in, 146
Use but confuse
derivational relations stage of spelling, 164
letter name-alphabetic stage of spelling, 88–89
syllables and affixes stage of spelling, 138–139
within word pattern stage of spelling, 115–116

V

Visual Thesaurus, 173
Vocabulary
academic, development strategies, 149–151
advanced readers and writers, 163
discussing, 154
emergent learners, 51, 52
generative approach, 140
intermediate readers and writers, 139–140
literacy, language referring to, 74
sight, 105–107
specific approach, 140
tips for developing, 61
transitional readers and writers, 114
Vocabulary note cards, 175
Vocabulary notebooks, 41, 42, 43
Vowel alterations, 168
Vowel Concentration, 126
Vowel Rummy, 126
Vowels
ambiguous, 121–122, 146
long, patterns, 120, 146
predictable spelling changes in, 168–169
R-influenced, 120–121, 146
short, 94

W

Web resources about words, 173
Within word pattern stage of spelling. *See also* Transitional readers and writers
characteristics, 22, 112, 115
common errors, 22, 112, 115
meaning and, 119
pattern frequency, 118
pattern location, 118–119
pattern sorts, 118
picture and word sorts, 116–124
sorts for, 27
sound sorts, 117
strategies, 123–124
use but confuse, 115–116
what is absent, 115, 116
word study and, 124–129
Word banks, 106–107
Word boundaries, 50
Word collection routine, 172
Word families
mixed vowel, 93–94
same vowel, 92–93
wheels and flip books, 97
Word hunt
completion illustration, 39
defined, 6, 35, 37
overview, 38–39
steps in, 39–40
Word operations, 125–126
Word origins, 172–173
Word Part Shuffle, 175
Word parts, 148, 150, 188, 189
Word sorting. *See* Sorting
Word study. *See also* Developmental spelling
benefits of, 4
in the classroom, 27–34
defined, 3
for English learners, 186
gifted and high-achieving students and, 186
group instruction, 6
importance of, 181
learning disabilities and, 186
online resources for, 173–174
overview, 3–8
practices in, 34–44
principles of instruction, 32–34
sort as key, 34
traditional spelling versus, 4–7
transitional readers and writers, 124–129

Word study games
  blind or no peeking sort, 43
  commercial, 43–44
  memory, 41
  speed sort, 43
  taboo, 41
Word study notebooks. *See also* Essential techniques
  advanced readers and writers, 171–172
  defined, 35
  examples, 42
  intermediate readers and writers, 149
  purposes of, 41
  transitional readers and writers, 124–125
  use of, 41
  vocabulary, 41, 43
Word Study Uno, 125
Word trees, 174
Wordless books, 64
Words
  compound, 143
  different and alike, 141
  "do" and "don't" comparisons, 32
  mispronunciation of, 190
  not fitting, 142
  pointing to, 75
  polysyllabic, 143
  prompts to help figure out, 105
  sight, 13, 85
  unknown, prompts to read, 191
  Web resources about, 173
Words with cubes, 99–100
Writers. *See also specific literacy development stages*
  advanced, 19–20, 159–177
  beginning, 10, 13–15, 83–108
  emergent, 12–13, 47–77
  intermediate, 17–19, 135–155
  pretend, 50
  transitional, 15–17, 111–132
Writing
  academic, across disciplines, 177
  advanced readers and writers, 162–163
  for authentic audiences, 177
  beginning readers and writers, 86–87
  characteristics, 21
  emergent learners, 49–50, 76–77
  encouragement, 77
  with fluency, 17
  intermediate readers and writers, 137–138, 153–154
  materials, 131–132
  practical, 76–77, 108
  revisions, 138, 155
  sharing, 155, 176
  for sounds, 77
  transitional readers and writers, 114
  without word boundaries, 50
Writing assignments, 132
Writing for sounds, 38
Writing sort. *See also* Essential techniques
  completion illustration, 38
  defined, 35, 37
  steps in, 37–38
Writing support
  advanced writers, 176–177
  beginning writers, 107–108
  emergent learners, 76–77
  intermediate writers, 154–155
  transitional writers, 131–132
Written reflection, 40